Microfinance and Sustainable Development in Africa

Yahaya Alhassan
University of Sunderland in London, UK

Uzoechi Nwagbara
University of the West of Scotland, UK & Cardiff Metropolitan University, UK

A volume in the Advances in Finance, Accounting, and Economics (AFAE) Book Series

Published in the United States of America by
IGI Global
Business Science Reference (an imprint of IGI Global)
701 E. Chocolate Avenue
Hershey PA, USA 17033
Tel: 717-533-8845
Fax: 717-533-8661
E-mail: cust@igi-global.com
Web site: http://www.igi-global.com

Copyright © 2022 by IGI Global. All rights reserved. No part of this publication may be reproduced, stored or distributed in any form or by any means, electronic or mechanical, including photocopying, without written permission from the publisher.
Product or company names used in this set are for identification purposes only. Inclusion of the names of the products or companies does not indicate a claim of ownership by IGI Global of the trademark or registered trademark.

Library of Congress Cataloging-in-Publication Data

Names: Alhassan, Yahaya, 1971- editor. | Nwagbara, Uzoechi, editor, author.
Title: Microfinance and sustainable development in Africa / Yahaya
   Alhassan, and Uzoechi Nwagbara, editors.
Description: Hershey : Business Science Reference, 2021. | Includes
   bibliographical references and index. | Summary: "This book offers great
   insight into theoretical, policy-oriented and practical ways to address
   some of the challenges of using microfinance for sustainable development
   in Africa"-- Provided by publisher.
Identifiers: LCCN 2021040439 (print) | LCCN 2021040440 (ebook) | ISBN
   9781799874997 (hardcover) | ISBN 9781799875000 (paperback) | ISBN
   9781799875017 (ebook)
Subjects: LCSH: Sustainable development--Africa, Sub-Saharan. |
   Microfinance--Africa, Sub-Saharan. | Poverty--Africa, Sub-Saharan. |
   Africa, Sub-Saharan--Economic conditions--21st century.
Classification: LCC HC800.Z9 E5483 2021 (print) | LCC HC800.Z9 (ebook) |
   DDC 338.967--dc23
LC record available at https://lccn.loc.gov/2021040439
LC ebook record available at https://lccn.loc.gov/2021040440

This book is published in the IGI Global book series Advances in Finance, Accounting, and Economics (AFAE) (ISSN: 2327-5677; eISSN: 2327-5685)

British Cataloguing in Publication Data
A Cataloguing in Publication record for this book is available from the British Library.

All work contributed to this book is new, previously-unpublished material.
The views expressed in this book are those of the authors, but not necessarily of the publisher.

For electronic access to this publication, please contact: eresources@igi-global.com.

Advances in Finance, Accounting, and Economics (AFAE) Book Series

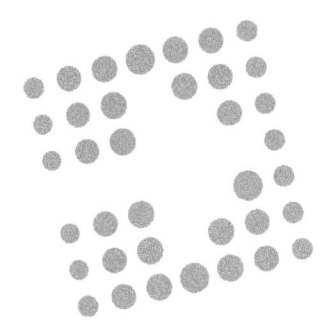

ISSN:2327-5677
EISSN:2327-5685

Editor-in-Chief: Ahmed Driouchi, Al Akhawayn University, Morocco

MISSION

In our changing economic and business environment, it is important to consider the financial changes occurring internationally as well as within individual organizations and business environments. Understanding these changes as well as the factors that influence them is crucial in preparing for our financial future and ensuring economic sustainability and growth.

The **Advances in Finance, Accounting, and Economics (AFAE)** book series aims to publish comprehensive and informative titles in all areas of economics and economic theory, finance, and accounting to assist in advancing the available knowledge and providing for further research development in these dynamic fields.

COVERAGE

- Development Economics
- International Trade
- E-finance
- Microeconomics
- Field Research
- Finance
- Auditing
- Evidence-Based Studies
- Banking
- Economics of Risks, Uncertainty, Ambiguity, and Insurance

IGI Global is currently accepting manuscripts for publication within this series. To submit a proposal for a volume in this series, please contact our Acquisition Editors at Acquisitions@igi-global.com or visit: http://www.igi-global.com/publish/.

The Advances in Finance, Accounting, and Economics (AFAE) Book Series (ISSN 2327-5677) is published by IGI Global, 701 E. Chocolate Avenue, Hershey, PA 17033-1240, USA, www.igi-global.com. This series is composed of titles available for purchase individually; each title is edited to be contextually exclusive from any other title within the series. For pricing and ordering information please visit http://www.igi-global.com/book-series/advances-finance-accounting-economics/73685. Postmaster: Send all address changes to above address. © © 2022 IGI Global. All rights, including translation in other languages reserved by the publisher. No part of this series may be reproduced or used in any form or by any means – graphics, electronic, or mechanical, including photocopying, recording, taping, or information and retrieval systems – without written permission from the publisher, except for non commercial, educational use, including classroom teaching purposes. The views expressed in this series are those of the authors, but not necessarily of IGI Global.

Titles in this Series

For a list of additional titles in this series, please visit:
http://www.igi-global.com/book-series/advances-finance-accounting-economics/73685

Handbook of Research on Developing Circular, Digital, and Green Economies in Asia
Patricia Ordóñez de Pablos (The University of Oviedo, Spain)
Business Science Reference • © 2022 • 521pp • H/C (ISBN: 9781799886785) • US $225.00

Handbook of Research on Climate Change and the Sustainable Financial Sector
Odunayo Magret Olarewaju (Durban University of Technology, South Africa) and Idris Olayiwola Ganiyu (University of KwaZulu-Natal, South Africa)
Business Science Reference • © 2021 • 573pp • H/C (ISBN: 9781799879671) • US $295.00

CSR and Management Accounting Challenges in a Time of Global Crises
Ionica Oncioiu (Titu Maiorescu University, Romania)
Business Science Reference • © 2021 • 278pp • H/C (ISBN: 9781799880691) • US $215.00

Impact of Global Issues on International Trade
Ahu Coşkun Özer (Marmara University, Turkey)
Business Science Reference • © 2021 • 291pp • H/C (ISBN: 9781799883142) • US $215.00

Handbook of Research on the Empirical Aspects of Strategic Trade Negotiations and Management
Nuno Crespo (ISCTE – Instituto Universitário de Lisboa, Portugal) and Nadia Simoes (ISCTE – Instituto Universitário de Lisboa, Portugal)
Business Science Reference • © 2021 • 446pp • H/C (ISBN: 9781799875680) • US $265.00

Handbook of Research on Financial Management During Economic Downturn and Recovery
Nuno Miguel Teixeira (Center for Research in Business and Administration, School of Business Sciences, Polytechnic Institute of Setúbal, Portugal) and Inês Lisboa (CARME, School of Management and Technology, Polytechnic of Leiria, Portugal)

For an entire list of titles in this series, please visit:
http://www.igi-global.com/book-series/advances-finance-accounting-economics/73685

IGI Global
PUBLISHER of TIMELY KNOWLEDGE

701 East Chocolate Avenue, Hershey, PA 17033, USA
Tel: 717-533-8845 x100 • Fax: 717-533-8661
E-Mail: cust@igi-global.com • www.igi-global.com

Editorial Advisory Board

Samuel Idowu, *London Metropolitan University, UK*
Valentine Udoh James, *Department of Biology and Environmental Sciences, Clarion University of Pennsylvania, USA*

Table of Contents

Foreword xv

Preface xvii

Acknowledgment xxvii

Introduction xxviii

Chapter 1
Microfinance Impact on Microbusiness Development in Africa: Evidence From a Control Group Experiment in Ghana 1
    Yahaya Alhassan, University of Sunderland in London, UK
    Samuel Salia, De Montfort University, UK
    Uzoechi Nwagbara, University of Sunderland in London, UK

Chapter 2
Role of Microfinance in Entrepreneurship Development 27
    Neeta Baporikar, Namibia University of Science and Technology, Namibia & University of Pune, India

Chapter 3
The Role of Microfinance in Africa: A Review of Outcomes From Ghana and Nigeria 54
    Yahaya Alhassan, University of Sunderland in London, UK
    Francis Kuagbela, University of Sunderland in London, UK
    Caesar D. Nurokina, University of Sunderland in London, UK
    Bernard Appiah, University of Sunderland in London, UK

Chapter 4
Microfinance for achieving Sustainable Development Goals: Pondering Over Indian Experiences for the Preservation of Magnificent African Natural Resources 82

    Manpreet Arora, School of Commerce and Management Studies, Central University of Himachal Pradesh, Dharamshala, India
    Swati Singh, Maharaja Agrasen University, India

Chapter 5
Analysis of Factors That Affect the Use of Microfinance for Microbusiness Development in Ghana..103

    Yahaya Alhassan, University of Sunderland in London, UK
    Uzoechi Nwagbara, University of Sunderland in London, UK
    Samuel Salia, De Montfort University, UK

Chapter 6
Islamic Social Finance: Integrating Zakah Funds in Microfinance and Microenterprise Support Programs: Selected Case Studies..............................127

    Omar Ahmad Kachkar, Ibn Haldun University, Turkey
    Marwa Alfares, İstanbul Sabahattin Zaim University, Turkey

Chapter 7
Investigating Entrepreneurial Success Factors of Businesses Owned by Nigerian Women in the UK 160

    Victoria Temitope, University of Sunderland in London, UK
    Seema Sharma, University of the West of Scotland, UK

Chapter 8
Analysis of the Performance of Microfinance Institutions in Sub-Saharan Africa: Observations and Perspectives 188

    Lawrence Jide Jones-Esan, University of Sunderland in London, UK

Chapter 9
SME Financing: Understanding the Barriers and Potentials for Entrepreneurs – Developing and Under-Developed World Perspectives 207

    Emmanuel E. Oghosanine, University of Sunderland, London, UK

Chapter 10
Service Failure, Recovery, and Sustainable Development: Towards Justice in the Extractive Industry of Nigeria...234

    Anthony Nduwe Kalagbor, University of Cumbria, London, UK

Chapter 11
The Shortfalls of the Nigerian Oil and Gas Industry Content Act 2010 in
Achieving Sustainable Development 264
    Manuchim Lawrence Adele, Canterbury Christ Church University, UK

Chapter 12
The Relationship Between Developmental Social Work, Poverty Alleviation,
and Sustainable Development in Nigeria: Issues, Challenges, and
Opportunities 279
    Chigozie Ugwoji, Canterbury Christ Church University, UK

Compilation of References 306

About the Contributors 361

Index 364

Detailed Table of Contents

Foreword xv

Preface xvii

Acknowledgment xxvii

Introduction xxviii

Chapter 1
Microfinance Impact on Microbusiness Development in Africa: Evidence
From a Control Group Experiment in Ghana 1
    Yahaya Alhassan, University of Sunderland in London, UK
    Samuel Salia, De Montfort University, UK
    Uzoechi Nwagbara, University of Sunderland in London, UK

This chapter applies the control group experiment to study whether microfinance improved microbusiness growth in Ghana. According to this approach, statistically significant difference in the outcome between treatment and control groups is an indication of impact of the microcredit on microbusiness development. Thus, this chapter compares the mean monthly sales, number of employees, business assets, and capital stock of microbusinesses that received microfinance (the treatment group) and the mean monthly sales, number of employees, business assets, and capital stock of microbusinesses that did not receive microfinance (the non-treatment group) in seven municipalities identified by various non-governmental organisations as areas of financial exclusion in the Northern Region of Ghana using survey data. Results indicate that microfinance impacted positively on microbusiness development. These findings have policy implications for the government of Ghana and agencies that are interested in using microfinance as a catalyst for economic growth in deprived communities in other countries.

Chapter 2
Role of Microfinance in Entrepreneurship Development 27
    Neeta Baporikar, Namibia University of Science and Technology,
      Namibia & University of Pune, India

Entrepreneurship and entrepreneurship development are crucial for social and economic development. Various studies highlight and reckon this aspect of entrepreneurship development both in developed and developing economies. However, entrepreneurship development though the aim of many developing economies, the growth rate of entrepreneurs is not satisfactory. One of the prominent reasons for this is attributable to financing or lack of financing. Hence, adopting a systematic literature review method the aim of this chapter is to review critically the role of microfinance for entrepreneurship development. Further, the chapter provides solutions and recommendations for proper microfinancing to boost entrepreneurship development.

Chapter 3
The Role of Microfinance in Africa: A Review of Outcomes From Ghana and Nigeria..54
    Yahaya Alhassan, University of Sunderland in London, UK
    Francis Kuagbela, University of Sunderland in London, UK
    Caesar D. Nurokina, University of Sunderland in London, UK
    Bernard Appiah, University of Sunderland in London, UK

This chapter examines the role of microfinance in developing countries, particularly Ghana and Nigeria. The chapter begins with an overview of the link between microfinance, poverty, and women empowerment in the chapter introduction. The background to the chapter sets out the main difference between microfinance and microcredit. The role of microfinance in contemporary development finance is then discussed. In this context, existing literature on the role of microfinance in reducing poverty, women empowerment, and microenterprise growth is extensively reviewed. Key solutions and recommendations are then presented next, followed by future research direction and the chapter conclusion.

Chapter 4
Microfinance for achieving Sustainable Development Goals: Pondering Over Indian Experiences for the Preservation of Magnificent African Natural Resources 82
    Manpreet Arora, School of Commerce and Management Studies, Central
      University of Himachal Pradesh, Dharamshala, India
    Swati Singh, Maharaja Agrasen University, India

This chapter focuses on the possibilities of exploring the areas where credit intervention can be done by the government in the form of schemes which are dependent on sustainable business practices. Nature has provided us abundance of raw material which if used wisely can help to remove poverty across the globe; on the same hand we can preserve the natural resources also if we use sustainable practices. In the current scenario where the world is facing pandemic and natural calamities, the time has to come to focus on sustainable rural micro financing activities which can not only solve the problem of linking the deprived sections of society with the mainstream, but it can also help them to improve their standard of living, and simultaneously, it can take care of various environmental issues too.

Chapter 5
Analysis of Factors That Affect the Use of Microfinance for Microbusiness Development in Ghana..103
    Yahaya Alhassan, University of Sunderland in London, UK
    Uzoechi Nwagbara, University of Sunderland in London, UK
    Samuel Salia, De Montfort University, UK

This chapter examined the factors that affect the use of microfinance for microbusiness development in Ghana. The study employed semi-structured survey questionnaire to determine whether an entrepreneur's personal attributes impede or facilitate microbusiness development in Ghana. Multiple linear regression analysis was conducted to determine the effects of entrepreneur's personal attributes on the monthly sales, number of employees, business assets, and capital stock of microbusinesses that received credit from a microfinance provider in the northern region of Ghana. The findings of the study suggest that micro-entrepreneur prior work experience, occupation, and prior income facilitate the use of microfinance for microbusiness development. These findings have policy implications for the government of Ghana and other agencies that are interested in using microfinance as a catalyst for economic growth in deprived communities in the country.

Chapter 6
Islamic Social Finance: Integrating Zakah Funds in Microfinance and Microenterprise Support Programs: Selected Case Studies..............................127
    Omar Ahmad Kachkar, Ibn Haldun University, Turkey
    Marwa Alfares, İstanbul Sabahattin Zaim University, Turkey

Alleviating poverty and inequality are among the central objectives of zakah in the Islamic economic system. These objectives are also on top of the 17 SDGs of the UN 2030 Agenda. This research argues that microenterprise support programs (MSPs) have been proven as effective tools in combating poverty. However, lack of funds has always been a major challenge for the sustainability of those programs. Channeling zakah funds to MSPs will directly contribute to empowering deprived populations and helping them to lift themselves out of the poverty cycle. Two zakah-based MSPs have been analyzed in this chapter. The first one is the Asnaf Entrepreneurship Program of Lembaga Zakah, Malaysia and the second one is Baitul Maal Muamalat Indonesia (BMMI). According to literature, using zakah in (MSPs) requires a strict implementation of best practices including screening program beneficiaries, providing professional training and monitoring to businesses, and finally applying a graduation scheme.

Chapter 7
Investigating Entrepreneurial Success Factors of Businesses Owned by
Nigerian Women in the UK 160
    Victoria Temitope, University of Sunderland in London, UK
    Seema Sharma, University of the West of Scotland, UK

The aim of this study is to investigate the entrepreneurial success factors of Nigerian women entrepreneurs based in the UK. An exploratory case study approach was used to gather the primary data from 15 small businesses run by Nigerian women entrepreneurs in the UK. The data collection was conducted through face-to-face semi-structured interviews, observations, and published sources. The data was thematically analysed using NVivo. The main findings indicated that Nigerian women entrepreneurs in the UK primarily depend on personal traits, self-funding, work experience, personal satisfaction, physical networking, and family support for business success. The most significant entrepreneurial success factor was the personal success factor. The study provided feasible recommendations for Nigerian women entrepreneurs based in the UK to put emphasis on environmental success factors and online networking, taking advantage of social media platforms for easy and quicker reach of more customers and business partners.

Chapter 8
Analysis of the Performance of Microfinance Institutions in Sub-Saharan
Africa: Observations and Perspectives 188
    Lawrence Jide Jones-Esan, University of Sunderland in London, UK

This chapter examines the performance of microfinance institutions in Sub-Saharan Africa through observations from different perspectives. It examined the effects of microfinance institutions in Sub-Saharan Africa. Relevant literature on the sustainability and outreach of microfinance institutions are also analysed in this chapter. Sub-Saharan Africa's future achievement of necessary economic growth is very likely to depend partly on its ability to develop its economic and financial sectors to be more inclusive of small and medium enterprises in a more comprehensive way. Currently, microfinance directly promotes the development of the intermediate financial sector in Africa, which is positively correlated with economic growth. Despite the worsening of the current industrial crisis, microfinance is seen as an essential developmental tool and continues to grow in Sub-Saharan Africa.

Chapter 9
SME Financing: Understanding the Barriers and Potentials for Entrepreneurs
– Developing and Under-Developed World Perspectives 207
> *Emmanuel E. Oghosanine, University of Sunderland, London, UK*

Small and medium-scale enterprises around the world go through several challenges in a bid to achieve success. Many studies argue SMEs face challenges in different areas; some are critical for success whilst other are not. One of the critical challenges put forward by several studies is finding appropriate funding. Academics have described funds as the blood of every business and a key element that prescribes the supply of entrepreneurship. The challenge of funding remains a problem around the world both in developing and underdeveloped environments. The chapter provides insight into the funding issues faced by SMEs and provides practiced ways in which businesses in developing and underdeveloped environments can address the issue of funding.

Chapter 10
Service Failure, Recovery, and Sustainable Development: Towards Justice in
the Extractive Industry of Nigeria... 234
> *Anthony Nduwe Kalagbor, University of Cumbria, London, UK*

Extant literature on corporate social responsibility (CSR) and marketing shows that CSR plays an important role when a service fails; thus, application of recovery strategy becomes crucial for sustainable development. CSR creates greater performance expectations amongst stakeholders as well as helps to legitimise organisational activities when a service fails. This study maintains that CSR is crucially important not only in legitimising organisational actions, but in ensuring that stakeholders' loyalty, trust, and justice are assured. This CSR, service failure, and recovery nexus is more needed in the controversial extractive industry in Nigeria, which has a history of illegitimacy, irresponsible corporate responsibility, lack of accountability, and failure of justice, which have triggered and sustained corporate-stakeholder conflict. This landscape has negative impact on sustainable development, peace, and justice in the Niger Delta region of Nigeria, where oil is extracted.

Chapter 11
The Shortfalls of the Nigerian Oil and Gas Industry Content Act 2010 in
Achieving Sustainable Development 264
> *Manuchim Lawrence Adele, Canterbury Christ Church University, UK*

This chapter examines the impact that the concept of "sustainable development" in the Nigerian oil and gas industry has had and is likely to have upon the development of energy, resources, and economic growth in the future of Nigeria upon the focus and scope of energy, resource, and environmental law practice associated with that development. The chapter will adopt the definition of sustainable development as articulated in the Brundtland Report by the World Commission on Environment and

Development. It will examine the legal status of Sections 10 and 12 of the Nigerian Oil Industry Content Development Act 2010 and its implication on international trade and sustainable development. The chapter argues that Sections 10 and 12 of the Nigerian Oil and Gas Industry Content Act 2010 do not reflect the meaning and intention of the Brundtland's definition of sustainable development, which evinces normative values, values of equity, and justice for all.

Chapter 12
The Relationship Between Developmental Social Work, Poverty Alleviation, and Sustainable Development in Nigeria: Issues, Challenges, and Opportunities 279
    Chigozie Ugwoji, Canterbury Christ Church University, UK

This chapter explores the nexus between developmental social work (DSW) and sustainable development in Nigeria with the specific aim of outlining the issues, challenges, and opportunities involved therein as they affect Nigeria's social development and social work. Social work, which promotes the advancement of social wellbeing, social change, empowerment, and liberation of the vulnerable groups, is an integral concept of DSW. DSW maps out a new direction for social work practice, offering processes to address the causes of societal dysfunction and socioeconomic challenges faced by the people. This approach could be used to tackle Nigeria's social issues and poverty. This chapter argues that there is overlap for DSW to promote and contribute to the realisation of sustainable development, the literary and documentary sources, and the review thereof shows that there is a relationship between DSW and sustainable development as both are geared towards promoting the welfare of the people.

Compilation of References 306

About the Contributors 361

Index 364

Foreword

This book explores the theoretical underpinnings surrounding microfinance and how the application in the real world through the operationalization of the concepts/paradigms of sustainable development can be beneficial to the economic development of Africa. Microfinance has been around since 1976 in exploring how small savings and loans can build the capacities of the poor to succeed in their small businesses. In recent times, microfinance is making financial assistance available to poor people who cannot get traditional loans from banks.

Sustainable development puts emphasis on intergenerational equity while sustainability focuses more specifically on the sustainability of policies, programs, and projects. Thus, this book is quite a timely one in that it endeavors to link microfinance to the sustainability of the programs meant to alleviate poverty. African countries are plagued by poverty particularly in the rural as well as urban centers with high concentration of populations that have relocated from the rural areas. The microfinance loans and service will certainly usher in a new era when linked with local, regional, and national economic development programs.

The search for a sustainable recipe for economic development and economic growth may be through microfinance supported by some government and private sector policies. This book's approach to examining the crux of the matter dealing with the link between microfinance and sustainable development is by including contribution from the following areas: developmental social work, entrepreneurship development, microbusiness, small business, social finance, success factors of business, poverty alleviations, sustainable development and sustainable microfinance. These areas certainly do justice to the attempt to explain the connection between microfinance and sustainable development.

There is no doubt that this work is a significant contribution to knowledge because it is filling a gap in the literature that has not been seriously addressed or adequately covered. In assessing the significance of this book, the reader must contemplate these levels of its importance.

1. At the local level, it is imperative to empower the poor to achieve the goals of economic development and growth. The majority of the poor are women and children and as such every effort to build the capacity of women to succeed

in the informal economy as well as the formal economy improves the lives of families. This effort would also reduce the migration of the rural poor to the cities. The burgeoning populations of the urban centers in Africa is a clear indication that the rural poor are migrating to the cities in order to seek employment. Nine out of ten of these new arrivals do not achieve their dreams and hopes in the cities. Empowering them in their communities is certainly a great economic strategy. Microfinance has an added population distribution/management advantage.

2. At the regional level, microfinance has a cumulative sustainable development impact that links its possible success to the Millenium Development Goals (MDGs) that began in 2000 and ended in 2015. It also enables African communities to accomplish some of the objectives of Sustainable Development Goals (SDGs) which began in the year 2016 and projected to continue till the year 2030. Lifting people from poverty and enabling them to develop themselves through entrepreneurship provides growth on a regional basis which is the corner stone of regional planning.

3. The third and final level to which this book makes significant contributions is the national level. Economic development at the national level must take into consideration what happens at the local government level and the importance of leveraging the resources to reach the poor in the country. The mechanism for such endeavor is quite vivid in areas addressed in the book. The social work, small business, sustainable microfinance are pivotal issues that can be addressed at the national level which would assist the economic development of the countries of Africa.

Overall, this book enables its readers and users to envision the process of creating sustainable and successful communities throughout Africa by embarking upon microfinance approaches which lay the groundwork or foundation for economic development at the grassroots, regional, and national levels. Its fundamental premise is that microfinance is an imperative for alleviating poverty and helping to attain some of the United Nations' Sustainable Development Goals (SDGs) such as: Goal 1: No Poverty; Goal 2: Zero Hunger; Goal 5: Gender Equality; Goal 6: Decent Work and Economic Growth; Goal 10: Reduced Inequality; and Goal 11: Sustainable Cities and Communities. The book offers important context for sustainable design for African neighborhood economic development particularly for local self-sufficiency. This reference book offers theoretical and practical ideas of how microfinance can aid in achieving some of the sustainable development goals across Africa.

Valentine Udoh James
Department of Biology and Environmental Sciences, Clarion University of Pennsylvania, USA

Preface

Microfinance system offers financial services globally, particularly in emerging economies, to a population that suffers from limited access to the conventional financial market system and/or at risk of financial exclusion (García-Pérez, Fernández-Izquierdo & Muñoz-Torres, 2020; García-Pérez, Muñoz-Torres & Fernández-Izquierdo, 2018). The sector concentrates on low-money products and services, which enable easy access to financial instruments, regulated return guarantees and simple opening processes, amongst others (García-Pérez et al., 2018; Spiegel, 2012; Van Rooyen, Stewart & de Wet, 2012). Low-income clients or entrepreneurs seek microfinance to deal with basic needs, expansion of their small businesses or personal emergencies (García-Pérez et al., 2020; World Bank, 2018). This lending approach and financing entrepreneurial effort is on the rise (Alhassan & Nwagbara, 2021; Marini, Andrew, Van der Laan, 2017; Ferdousi, 2015). In 2018 about 916 Microfinance Institutions (MFIs), with an estimated $124 billion gross loan portfolio, where 80% of borrowers are women and 65% rural borrowers resulting in 140 million active borrowers globally (García-Pérez et al., 2010).

The key objective of the microfinance system as well as its MFIs is to empower the poorest members of society financially and to support Sustainable Development (Ferdousi, 2015; Mazumder, 2015; World Commission of Environment and Development, WCED, 1997). Sustainable development is the kind of developmental effort that meets the needs of the present "without compromising the ability of future generations to meet their own needs" (Nwagbara, 2014; United Nations Development Programme, UNDP, 2006). It takes into cognisance the commitment of societal evolution toward a more equitable society for future generations (Kolk, Kourula, & Pisani, 2017).

According to Aras & Crowther (2016) from a micro-level approach, sustainable development is fostered through corporate sustainability practices and policies that entail an equilibrium among the social, financial, governance and environmental performance dimensions both in the short and long haul (James, 2018; Bebbington & Unerman, 2018; Bateman, 2011). All over the world, poverty is distributed unevenly (Aras & Crowther, 2008). According to prior literature that is supported by the data from the World Bank (2018) 736 million people globally live below the international poverty line and; and sadly about 41% these people are located mostly in Sub-Saharan Africa.

Guided by the above contention, microfinance is persuaded to alleviate poverty in developing countries like Africa, and grassroots development mediated by microfinance practices and systems that have long been considered as a way of not only empowering small businesses but a method of involving stakeholders to actualise sustainable rural development (Ferdousi, 2015). Rural employment generation is a top priority for developing countries and microfinance emphasises economic liberalisation and macroeconomic stability (Mazumder, 2015). Since its inception, microfinance in Africa has spread quite rapidly but how much this helps the poor is a contested. African countries have made tremendous effort in this regard; however, there is need to further explore the impact of microfinance on rural development and in achieving the broader agenda of sustainable development as declared by the United Nations (Ferdousi, 2015).

Although microfinance is being considered as a crucial instrument for poverty alleviation, which is fundamental to realising the ideals of Millennium Development Goals (MDGs) and now Sustainable Development Goals (SDGs) (James, 2018; Kolk et al., 2017; Aras & Crowther, 2016). Nevertheless, evidence on the impacts of microfinance is mixed (García-Pérez et al., 2020). For example, some of the essential findings of Nawaz (2010) was that microfinance resulted in a moderate alleviation in poverty but did not reach many of the poorest potential recipients; however, other works in this regard have concluded the opposite (Bateman, 2011). Similarly, Focusing on the Bangladeshi context, Bateman (2011) reported that up to 5% of participants in three key microfinance institutions lifted their families out of poverty; whereas Roodman & Morduch (2009) reported that there was almost no evidence confirming that microfinance has any tangible role in poverty alleviation and contributing to sustainable development.

Sustainable development, which stems from corporate global effort towards sustainability started with the publication of the Brundtland Report in 1987 – *Our Common Future* (Aras & Crowther, 2016; World Commission on Environment and Development, WCED, 1987). At the core of sustainable development are multilateralism and interdependence amongst nations in the search for a fairer, equitable and more inclusive arrangement around the globe that would not diminish the prospects of future generations (United Nations, UN, 2017; Elkington, 1997). Although sustainable development (and to add sustainability) originated in natural resource economics, it has gained attention and influence as well as wider currency regarding social equality, justice, fairness, accountability and development (James, 2018).

Preface

Microfinance is touted as having important positive relationship with reducing inequality, reducing socio-economic disequilibrium, addressing injustice, mitigating risks associated with weak institutions, and developing microbusiness, which form the logic of the ideals of sustainable development goals (SDGs) (United Nations, 2017) given the limitations of the Millennium Development Goals (MDGs). These SDGs are a collection of 17 interlinked goals established as a roadmap to realising a better, more sustainable future for all and more just world (James, 2018) by 2030. In the main, the logic of the present is moored to the ideals of SDGs particularly Goal, 1 (No poverty), Goal 2 (Zero hunger), Goal 10 (reduced inequalities) and Goal 16 (peace, justice and strong institutions).

1. THE CHALLENGES

Arising from the preceding sections, the nexus between microfinance and sustainable development cannot be over-emphasised. And any efforts towards bettering the prospects of humanity through the intervention of microfinance for sustainable development is undeniably crucial for realising the ideals and principles enshrined in the United Nation's SDGs (UNDP, 2006).

The problems that microfinance addresses are more complex in developing countries, specifically, Africa as has been highlighted earlier, where there is high incidence of weak institutions (Alhassan & Nwagbara, 2021), poor governance regime (Mazumder, 2015) leadership problems (Nwagbara, 2014), and in some instance what development economists refer to "resource curse" (Karl, 1997) phenomenon, which negatively impact sustainable development (Marini et al., 2017). Accordingly, Nwagbara (2014) avers that unless these development, institutional and governance issues are addressed, the African continent would seemingly lag behind in the comity of nations thus negatively impacting the actualisation and manifestation of sustainable development. Such challenges can be classified into five categories as seen below:

- The challenge of establishing effective institutions and financial bodies that world regulate lending and business financing;
- The challenge of institutionalising effective corporate governance frameworks and financial policies and procedures that adequately support the ideals of sustainable development through empowering entrepreneurs and small business
- The challenge of establishing effective structures and institutions for responsibility, accountability and transparency given the spate of institutional voids (weak institutions) in Africa

- The challenge of ensuring that microfinance institutions, systems and governance regimes are fir for purpose as well as advance the principles of poverty alleviation, socio-economic development and mutual co-existence

Despite huge human and natural endowments, the African continent is still plagued by developmental dilemma (Marini et al., 2017) militating against achieving the principles of SDGs. Thus, the present book study maintains that examining the interface between microfinance and sustainable development could be one of the most effective means of not only shedding a new light on Africa's rise but a way to depend the realisation of SDGs. In extending the confines of this proposition, on the one hand, prior research on microfinance has considered different areas of performance and effectiveness, but they were essentially done from the prism of economic and socio-economic perspective with results and findings that shy away from reaching a consensus (Aras & Crowther, 2016;). Nevertheless, to the authors' best knowledge, the relationship between microfinance and sustainable development is still an area of scholarship that is under-researched and under-theorised from a holistic approach, which is the intention here.

2. SEARCHING FOR A SOLUTION

Solutions to the complex issue of microfinance are lodged in following through to the tenets and core ideals of sustainable development, which is the mainstay of this book (WCED, 1987). The concept of sustainable development is drawn from a plethora of issues and aspirations aimed at peace, justice, development, freedom, capacity building as well as socio-economic emancipation and environmentalism (Mazumder, 2015). It is now taking a centre stage in movements, strategies, policies, practices and beliefs that advance corporate, institutional, business, national and global goals about development (WCED, 1987). Within the spirit of this volume, sustainable development resonates with searching for solutions through socio-economic development on a global level that cannot be separated from issues bordering on ecological stability, equity and social justice and pursuing a community vision that respects human prosperity for co-existence and conflict-free relationship (Desjardins 2000). This process parallels what has been identified as 'microfinancing for sustainability' (Marini et al., 2017).

3. ORGANISATION OF THE BOOK

The book is organised into 12 chapters. A brief description of each of the chapters is outlined below:

In 'The Role of Microfinance in Africa: A Critical Review of Existing Literature', Yahaya Alhassan, Bernard Appiah, Caesar Nurokina, and Francis Kuagbela examine the role of microfinance in developing countries, particularly Africa. The chapter is steeped in shedding light on the link between microfinance, poverty, and women empowerment. It also unearths the main difference between microfinance and microcredit as well as the role of microfinance in contemporary development finance. Key solutions and recommendations are also highlighted critically in the chapter. Similarly, using the lens of phenomenological approach, Emmanuel Oghosanine's 'SME financing: Understanding the barriers and potentials for entrepreneurs' advances the idea that entrepreneurship can solve unemployment issues. However, whether entrepreneurship can achieve the same result across different environments is a pertinent question.

In continuing this debate, Yahaya Alhassan, Uzoechi Nwagbara, and Samuel Salia in their 'Analysis of Factors that Impede or Facilitate the Use of Microfinance for Microbusiness Development in Ghana' lucidly present the factors that impede or facilitate the use of microfinance for microbusiness development in Ghana. The study employed semi-structured survey questionnaire combined with multiple linear regression analysis to determine whether an entrepreneur's personal attributes impede or facilitate microbusiness development. The findings suggest that the micro-entrepreneurs prior work experience, occupation and prior income facilitate the use of microfinance for microbusiness development. The study further signposts policy implications for the Ghanaian government and other agencies using microfinance as a catalyst for economic growth. Along analogous axis, same authors examined 'Microfinance Impact on Microbusiness Development in Africa: Evidence From a Control Group Experiment in Ghana'. The chapter applies the control group experiment approach to study whether microfinance improved microbusiness growth in Ghana. According to this approach, statistically significant difference in the outcome between treatment and control groups is an indication of impact of microfinance on microbusiness development. This chapter compares the mean monthly sales, number of employees, business assets and capital stock of microbusinesses that received microfinance (the treatment group) and the mean monthly sales, number of employees, business assets and capital stock of microbusinesses that did not receive microfinance (the non-treatment group). Results indicate that microfinance impacted positively on microbusiness development.

Also in this volume, Omar Kachkar and Marwa Alfares interrogate 'Islamic Social Finance Integrating Zakah Funds in Microfinance and Microenterprises Programs:

Selected Case Studies'. The chapter argues that instead of giving zakah as cash assistance to the poor and needy only, zakah funds can be used to provide microcredit to finance microenterprises of potential entrepreneurs from poor household and low-income poor. Two Zakah-based microenterprise support programmes were used as case studies to contextualise the argument presented. However, using Zakah in such programmes does not make them different from other traditional microenterprise support programmes (MSPs). In other words, best practices of MSPs must be fully observed. Such practices include screening potential beneficiaries, providing training, monitoring, follow up mechanism and applying a graduation scheme. In a comparable context, Neeta Baporikar's 'Role of Microfinance in Entrepreneurship Development' maintains that entrepreneurship and entrepreneurship development is widely regarded as one of the critical issues to ensure social and economic development and thereby overall national development by all countries and more specifically by emerging countries. Nonetheless, the influence of microfinance on entrepreneurial development has gained traction recently. Thus, it is generally accepted that both developed and developing countries are embracing entrepreneurship as the key driver of socio-economic development. Furthermore, it is worth mentioning that this discourse is making waves in the emerging trend towards the adoption of entrepreneurship worldwide especially in developing countries.

The relevance of microfinance in sustainable development is further taken to a new horizon with the chapter by Manpreet Arora and Swati Singh titled 'Microfinance for Achieving Sustainable Development Goals: Pondering Over the Indian Experiences for the Preservation of Magnificent African Natural Resources'. The central thesis of this chapter is that the concept of microfinance, poverty alleviation and rural credit are interlinked with each other advancing the philosophy of sustainable development. This chapter further argues the possibilities of exploring the areas where the credit intervention can be done by the government in the form of schemes which can propel sustainable business practices. In Africa the poor are severally experiencing the incidence of poverty, which microfinance intervention could address positively as the chapter avers. The chapter also takes into consideration the fact that the time has to come to focus on sustainable rural micro financing initiatives that can not only solve the problem of linking the deprived sections of society with the mainstream but on the same hand it can help them to improve their standard of living and environmental issues.

Using the context of Nigeria, Anthony Kalagbor investigated insightfully 'Service Failure, Recovery, and Sustainable Development: Towards Justice in the Extractive Industry in Nigeria'. The preoccupation of this chapter is that corporate social responsibility (CSR) research and marketing shows that CSR plays important role when a service fails, thus, application of recovery strategy becomes crucial for sustainable development. The chapter argues that CSR is crucially important in not only in legitimising organisational actions, but in ensuring that stakeholders' loyalty, trust and justice are assured for the purpose of building sustainable development. Thus, framing CSR practice in this way would impact stakeholders trust, loyalty, and satisfaction within the context of service recovery for sustainable development. Essentially, the study uses the lens of justice theory to tease out how responsible CSR practice could be instrumental in rising above service failure when a service fails. The chapter further notes that perceived CSR will have a positive outcome on customer loyalty after service failure and subsequent recovery.

Following in the footsteps of the Nigerian realities, Manuchim Adele critically focuses the searchlight on 'The Shortfalls of the Nigeria Oil and Gas Act 2010 in Achieving Sustainable Development'. From a legal cum regulatory standpoint, he examines the mechanisms that are put in place to ensure that prior to and during the development process of the resources, the environment is reasonably spared of the consequences of the harmful exploitation activities. This makes it necessary for states to put in place laws and regulations that would guarantee the achievement of sustainable development in the natural resources section of its economy such as Nigeria. Specifically, the Nigerian Oil and Gas Industry is the focus in the chapter, which has a history of regulatory malfeasance and corporate social irresponsibility militating against business responsibility and sustainable development. In sum, the Oil and Gas Act of 2010 and its associated shortfall in addressing the ideals of sustainable development were central to the objective of this chapter. Additionally, the paper argues that sections 10 and 12 of the Nigerian Oil and Gas Industry Content Act 2010 do not reflect the meaning and intention of the Brundtland's definition of sustainable development which evinces normative values, values of equity and justice for all.

From a related but disparate context, Chigozie Agatha Ugwoji has presented with candour 'The Relationship Between Developmental Social Work, Poverty Alleviation, and Sustainable Development in Nigeria: Issues, Challenges, and Opportunities'. In sum, the chapter explores the nexus between developmental social work, poverty alleviation, and sustainable development with the specific aim of outlining the issues, challenges, and opportunities involved therein as they affect Nigeria's social development and social work. As argued here, developmental social work maps out a new direction for social work practice, strategy, and approach, offering processes and mechanisms that address the causes of societal dysfunction and the structural, political, and socioeconomic challenges faced by the people including sustainable development challenges. This approach could be used to tackle Nigeria's social issues, specifically social exclusion, discrimination, and alleviation of poverty, which are central to the tenet of sustainable development, which aims to meet the present needs of the people without compromising future needs, particularly in respect to poverty alleviation. In moving the debate, Victoria Temitope and Seema Sharma's

'Investigating Entrepreneurial Success Factors of Businesses Owned by Nigerian Women in the UK' zeroes in on the entrepreneurial success factors of Nigerian women entrepreneurs based in the UK using an exploratory case study approach with data from 15 face-to-face semi-structured interviews with small businesses by Nigerian women entrepreneurs in the UK as well as observations and published sources. The main findings indicated that Nigerian women entrepreneurs in the UK primarily depend on personal traits, self-funding, work experience, personal satisfaction, physical networking, and family support for business success. The study provided feasible recommendations for Nigerian women entrepreneurs based in the UK, to put emphasis on environmental success factors: online networking; taking advantage of social media platforms for easy and quicker reach of more customers and business partners. These findings have parallel with the principles of sustainable development as outlined by the United Nations. Finally, Lawrence Jide Jones-Esan interrogate the performance of microfinance institutions in Sub-Saharan Africa through observations from different perspectives. The outcomes showed that MFIs provide necessary financial services to poor and low-income families, entrepreneurs, and early-stage businesses who cannot otherwise access these services.

Yahaya Alhassan
University of Sunderland in London, UK

Uzoechi Nwagbara
University of the West of Scotland, UK & Cardiff Metropolitan University, UK

REFERENCES

Alhassan, Y., & Nwagbara, U. (2021). Institutions, Corruption and Microfinance Viability in Developing Countries: The Case of Ghana and Nigeria. *Economic Insights - Trends and Challenges*, *10*(73), 61–70. doi:10.51865/EITC.2021.02.06

Aras, G., & Crowther, D. (2016). *A Handbook of Corporate Governance and Social Responsibility*. Routledge. doi:10.4324/9781315564791

Aras, G., & Crowther, D. (2008). Governance and sustainability: An investigation into the relationship between corporate governance and corporate sustainability. *Management Decision*, *46*(3), 433–448. doi:10.1108/00251740810863870

Bateman, M. (Ed.). (2011). Confronting Microfinance: Undermining Sustainable Development. Kumarian Press.

Bebbington, J., & Unerman, J. (2018). Achieving the United Nations Sustainable Development Goals: An enabling role for accounting research. *Accounting, Auditing & Accountability Journal, 31*(1), 2–24. doi:10.1108/AAAJ-05-2017-2929

Ferdousi, F. (2015). Impact of microfinance on sustainable entrepreneurship development. *Development Studies Research, 2*(1), 51–63. doi:10.1080/21665095.2015.1058718

García-Pérez, I., Fernández-Izquierdo, M. A., & Muñoz-Torres, M. J. (2020). Microfinance Institutions Fostering Sustainable Development by Region. *Sustainability, 12*(7), 1–23. doi:10.3390u12072682

García-Pérez, I., Muñoz-Torres, M. J., & Fernández-Izquierdo, M. A. (2018). Microfinance institutions fostering sustainable development. *Sustainable Development, 26*(6), 606–619. doi:10.1002d.1731

James, V. (Ed.). (2018). Capacity Building for Sustainable Development. Boston: CABI.

Kolk, A., Kourula, A., & Pisani, N. (2017). Multinational enterprises and the sustainable development goals: What do we know and how to proceed? *Transnational Corporations, 24*(3), 9–32. doi:10.18356/6f5fab5e-en

Marini, L., Andrew, J., & Van der Laan, S. (2017). Tools of accountability: Protecting microfinance clients in South Africa? *Accounting, Auditing & Accountability Journal, 30*(6), 1344–1369. doi:10.1108/AAAJ-04-2016-2548

Mazumder, M. S. U. (2015). Role of Microfinance in Sustainable Development in Rural Bangladesh. *Sustainable Development, 23*(6), 396–413. doi:10.1002d.1599

Nwagbara, U. (2014). *Leading Sustainability in Nigeria: Problems, Processes and Prospects*. Lambert Academic Press.

Roodman, D., & Morduch, J. (2009). *The Impact of Microcredit on the Poor in Bangladesh: Revisiting the Evidence*. Working Paper Number 174. Centre for Global Development.

Spiegel, S. J. (2012). Microfinance services, poverty and artisanal mineworkers in Africa: In search of measures for empowering vulnerable groups. *Journal of International Development, 24*(4), 485–517. doi:10.1002/jid.1781

United Nations (UN). (2017). *Sustainable development goals report 2017*. http.www.un.org

United Nations Development Programme (UNDP). (2006). *Beyond scarcity: power, poverty and the global water crisis*. United Nations Development Programme.

Van Rooyen, C., Stewart, R., & de Wet, T. (2012). The Impact of Microfinance in Sub-Saharan Africa: A Systematic Review of the Evidence. *World Development*, *40*(11), 2249–2262. doi:10.1016/j.worlddev.2012.03.012

World Bank. (2018). *Poverty and Shared Prosperity 2018: Piecing Together the Poverty Puzzle*. World Bank.

World Commission of Environment and Development. (1997). *Our Common Future*. Oxford University Press.

Acknowledgment

We wish to offer this rider: without the various effort made by all and sundry, this book would not have been possible, although, Yahaya and Uzoechi ''fathered'' the concept of the volume!

Having said that, we wish to heartily thank and congratulate those who have been instrumental to the writing and production of this book.

First, without God the writing of this book would have been possible. We thank Him for giving us the strength, knowledge and sound mind to execute this book project!

Second, we would also like to thank the members of the editorial and acquisition team of IGI for their professionalism, dedication, prop and hard work during the production of this volume. We want to say a big 'thank-you' to them, for the opportunity to co-edit this book. Particularly, we we're indebted to Gianna Walker, Assistant Development Editor (Book Development); Jan Travers, Director of Intellectual Property & Contracts IGI Global.

Third, we're sincerely grateful to all the contributors – Bernard Appiah, Caesar Nurokina, Francis Kuagbela, Anthony Kalagbor, Chigozie Ugwoji, Manuchim Adele, Omar Kachkar, Samuel Salia, Marwa Alfares, Swati Singh, Neeta Baporikar, Manpreet Arora, Victoria Temitope, Seema Sharma and Lawrence Jide Jones-Esan – for the kindred spirit and sense of commitment shown.

Finally, our profound gratitude goes to our families for the time granted us to do this book!

Yahaya & Uzoechi

October 2021

Introduction

Following the positive contribution of microfinance to economic development in some parts of South East Asia and Africa, a huge amount of time has been devoted by researchers, consultants and policymakers to understand this concept for sustainable development, particularly in Sub-Saharan Africa.

Microfinance is the provision of financial and non-financial services to individuals or groups who have no access to such services from traditional financial institutions such as banks. Microfinance entails the provision of financial products to low-income earners and financially disadvantaged individuals such as women particularly in rural households. It is inextricably linked to poverty reduction and therefore a viable strategy for reducing poverty in poor communities. Access to microfinance has been shown to have helped low-income earners build their assets and improved their earning capacity leading to an improvement in their quality of life and business development. Evidence of positive impact of microfinance on women empowerment in the developing world has also been reported by various authors. Furthermore, microfinance has also been shown to provide opportunities for employment generation in poor communities.

Microfinance also has significant positive relationship with developing microbusiness, reducing inequalities, tackling poverty, fighting socio-economic imbalance and addressing injustice and weak institutions, which are central to the ideals of sustainable development goals (SDGs) as declared by the United Nations. These SDGs are an assemblage of 17 interlinked global goals, which are developed as a "blueprint to achieve a better and more sustainable future for all" as well as propelling a fairer and more just world. The SDGs were designed by the United Nations General Assembly in 2015 and are aimed at being achieved by the year 2030. It was birthed at the backdrop of the limitations of Millennium Development Goals (MDGs).

The General Assembly of the United Nations has urged governments around the globe to commit to definite, time-bound goals, strategies and actions to promote peace, justice, equality, healthy living, environmental sustainability, empowerment and global partnership as well as reduction of poverty among others. This rationality

Introduction

underscores the MDGs. The MDGs have been supplanted by the SDGs on the heels of the adoption of the 2030 Agenda for sustainable development by United Nations General Assembly in 2015. SDGs are a collection of 17 goals, which have 169 associated targets specifying both qualitative and quantitative core objectives across environmental, economic and social aspects of sustainable development. These goals (SDGs) are the most comprehensive and widely supported development goals the world has ever had. Specifically, the persuasion of this book is linked to some of the cardinal SDGs including Goal, 1 (No poverty), Goal 2 (Zero hunger), Goal 10 (reduced inequalities) and Goal 16 (peace, justice and strong institutions). Furthermore, this volume advocates the objectives and values incorporated in the adoption of the 2030 Agenda for Sustainable Development.

However, from relevant, prior literature examined, there is no specific book that explores the relationship between microfinance and sustainable development in Africa. Although there exist few books on the relationship between microfinance and sustainable development globally, scholarship that addresses this interface is sparse at best and at embryonic stage at worst, despite the universal clarion call to widen the purview of sustainable development discourse on the African continent, which would aid transcend the gory state of poverty, inequalities and developmental challenges. In this regard, this book hopes to examine the complex relationship between microfinance, poverty reduction, economic growth and microbusiness development, focusing on the provision of small credit facilities as a driver for sustainable development in Africa.

This book thus follows in the footsteps of debate and effort premised on safeguarding and sustaining Africa's future, rise and development that have contemporarily taken a centre stage following the publication of *Our Common Interest: An Argument* in 2005 by The Commission for Africa (Blair Commission for Africa). It also parallels the debate enshrined in the second part of this Report in 2010 called *Still Our Common Interest*, which was launched to precipitate effort by African leaders to concertedly expedite actions to convert incomparable economic opportunities on the African continent into protecting the environment, advancing national development, healing social wounds, and for the foremost part advancing the logic of sustainable development on the continent.

In sum, *Microfinance and Sustainable Development in Africa: Problems, Processes and Prospects* is predicated on envisioning "a world with less poverty, hunger and disease, greater survival prospects for mothers and infants, better educated children, equal opportunities for women, and a healthier environment" (United Nations, 2006, p. 3). This vision chimes with galvanising actions towards a socio-economic, political and cultural practice that can help people at the bottom of the pyramid as presaged by cerebral Harvard professor, Prahalad, in his path-breaking book, *The Fortune at the Bottom of the Pyramid*, as well as echoes in Elkington's "triple bottom line" approach for sustainable development as declared in his seminal treatise *Cannibals with Forks: the Triple Bottom Line of 21st Century Business*, amongst comparable texts.

Certainly, the use of microfinance for poverty reduction and economic development in the developing world is growing. However, this concept needs broadening to ensure its application with the view to achieving sustainable development in developing countries, particularly in Africa. This book aims to examine and bring on board the various views and perspectives on the relationship between microfinance and sustainable economic development in Africa through industry experts, experienced researchers and policymakers. The concept of microfinance and its relationship with sustainable development in Africa will be explored by these experts and contributors from different perspectives with the view to forming an opinion on the problems, processes and prospects of microfinance in Africa.

The focus here is Sub-Saharan Africa, which has witnessed growing activities of microfinance institutions on the continent. Africa has a history of low standard of living, high incidence of poverty, political violence, social inequality, poor corporate governance, war, corruption and a plethora of reverses that characterise a sadly rich continent. This continent is arguably at the crossroads of underdevelopment, unsustainable political experimentation and 'institutional voids' and incidence of poverty that constitute a roadblock to its rise. Given the incidence of poverty and weak regulatory institutions, and corruption, the various perspectives shared in this book support the thesis that microfinance could aid in lifting the continent from the shambles for a blissful continent. With a population of about 1.4 trillion, Africa has been described as a continent with one of the worst forms of deprivations, inequalities, social dissonance and political upheaval, and whose people perennially live below the poverty line.

Theoretical and empirical insight to be provided in this book will be a priceless resource to microfinance institutions, policymakers, state institutions, managers and non-governmental organisations working in developing countries particularly in Africa. This book is envisaged to also benefit financial institutions that are looking to expand their product portfolio and outreach. The book will offer great insight into theoretical, policy-oriented and practical ways to address some of the challenges of using microfinance for sustainable development. Given the focus of this book there will be a broadening of ideas on how the provision of microfinance can aid sustainable development in Africa. Target Audience include academics, researchers, universities, the civil society (NGOs), governments, policymakers, mangers, organisations and financial institutions. Recommended topics include, but are not limited to the concept of microfinance, evolution of microfinance, models of microfinance, microfinance outreach, sustainable development, employment

Introduction

creation, economic development, poverty reduction, micro enterprise development, women empowerment, and microfinance relationship, etc.

Yahaya Alhassan
University of Sunderland in London, UK

Uzoechi Nwagbara
University of the West of Scotland, UK & Cardiff Metropolitan University, UK

Chapter 1
Microfinance Impact on Microbusiness Development in Africa:
Evidence From a Control Group Experiment in Ghana

Yahaya Alhassan
https://orcid.org/0000-0001-6700-635X
University of Sunderland in London, UK

Samuel Salia
De Montfort University, UK

Uzoechi Nwagbara
University of Sunderland in London, UK

ABSTRACT

This chapter applies the control group experiment to study whether microfinance improved microbusiness growth in Ghana. According to this approach, statistically significant difference in the outcome between treatment and control groups is an indication of impact of the microcredit on microbusiness development. Thus, this chapter compares the mean monthly sales, number of employees, business assets, and capital stock of microbusinesses that received microfinance (the treatment group) and the mean monthly sales, number of employees, business assets, and capital stock of microbusinesses that did not receive microfinance (the non-treatment group) in seven municipalities identified by various non-governmental organisations as areas of financial exclusion in the Northern Region of Ghana using survey data. Results indicate that microfinance impacted positively on microbusiness development. These findings have policy implications for the government of Ghana and agencies that are interested in using microfinance as a catalyst for economic growth in deprived communities in other countries.

DOI: 10.4018/978-1-7998-7499-7.ch001

INTRODUCTION

Recent control group studies in developing countries have shown that microfinance presents benefits to the unbanked in society (Sultana, et al., 2017; Agbola and Mahmood, 2017). In the area of funds mobilisation, microfinance has contributed significantly towards financial sector deepening by including the unbanked (Ranjani and Bapat, 2015; Ibrahim, 2018). In driving growth, microfinance has empowered a significant portion of the workforce in poor countries and contributed to economic development (Hilson and Ackah-Baidoo, 2010; Gretta, 2017; Bateman, 2017; Sethi and Acharya, 2018; Amin and Uddin, 2018). In the campaign for gender development, microfinance is commonly used as a strategy for women empowerment (Ganle, Afriyie and Segbefia, 2015; Salia et al., 2018). The implications of these findings from the literature are far reaching. Therefore, the low supply of microfinance in Africa; particularly Ghana, where a huge number of unbanked microbusinesses exist, despite its acknowledged contribution to poverty alleviation and financial deepening raises a significant puzzle.

Generally, supply of credit in developing countries is very low. Policy makers in these poor countries have shied away from launching appropriate credit programs for unbanked microbusinesses, frustrated by the disappointing absence of credit within the lending space, the unbanked in developing countries may slip into the traps of "loan sharks" or "pay-day loans" providers. Therefore, there are negative repercussions for developing nations that lack an appropriate lending space for unbanked micro-businesses. Recent efforts to provide microfinance services in Ghana however, illustrates how with a renewed level of commitment and a developmental blueprint the microfinance model may be successfully replicated in Ghana.

Developing nations are increasingly looking towards access to finance for microenterprises as a means to further financial deepening and decreasing poverty rates. This chapter contributes to this ongoing search and addresses aspects of the puzzle referred to above. In this chapter, a control group experiment is implemented to investigate the impact of microfinance on some selected microbusinesses ignored by banks in Ghana. The chapter present the results from a treatment and a non-treatment group where the debriefing from a microfinance provider is used to design the experiment for the treatment and non-treatment groups.

BACKGROUND

Several scholars (Chowdhury, 2009; Hermes, et al., 2011; Van Rooyen, et al., 2012) regard microfinance, as a significant intervention for reducing poverty and achieving financial inclusion in both developed and developing countries. Nonetheless, what precisely is microfinance? Luo & Rahman (2010) define microfinance as the provision of finance and related services to financially disadvantaged individuals who are unable to access such services from banks and other orthodox financial institutions. Similarly, Mayoux and Hartl (2009) define microfinance as all financial products that are available to low-income earners and financially disadvantaged individuals and rural households. In addition to the above definitions, Babajide (2011) added microbusinesses to the clients of microfinance institutions. He defines microfinance as a variety of monetary services provided exclusively to microbusinesses, financially disadvantaged individuals and low-income families.

Analysis of the three definitions above, suggests that microfinance is mainly about providing financial services to the underprivileged (Ledgerwood and White, 2006; Karmani, 2009; Hermes, et al., 2011). However, Wright and Rippey (2003) criticised these definitions and argued for a broader view of microfinance. They reasoned that microfinance should not be limited to the provision of financial services by microfinance institutions but should also include informal supply of finance such as financial support from family members of micro-entrepreneurs and low-income earners. Even though informal lending arrangements are essentially part of microfinance, the word is largely known to mean the provision of credit to the poor by recognised micro-lending institutions. In this context, some researchers have used the term institutional microfinance to describe microfinance excluding informal lending such as financial support from relatives and friends. For example, Robinson (2001) argues for microfinance to be designed on a commercial basis instead of the subsidised schemes in both developed and developing countries. It is obvious that he was advocating for micro-loan provided by formal micro-lending institutions.

Microfinance has also been defined from the perspective of beneficiaries. For instance, Copestake (2007) described microfinance as a potential source of income to the needy and an effective tool that can assist low-income earners to improve on their living standards. However, Rutherford (2000) regards microfinance as the method through which the financially disadvantaged convert small amount of money into lump sums. While these two definitions added some new twist to the formal definition of microfinance, Rutherford and Copestake failed to identify the kind of facilities, which low-income earners could access from microfinance. Furthermore, Rutherford's notion of microfinance also failed to clarify how the financially disadvantaged could convert small amount of money into lump sum.

A more comprehensive definition of microfinance is provided by Ledgerwood (1999) who refers to microfinance as the provision of both financial (loans, savings and insurance) and non-financial (financial literacy training, management skills development, group formation and self-confidence building) services to low-income earners and the self-employed. It is significant to note that Ledgerwood's concept of microfinance highlighted non-financial services, which are crucial component of microfinance but consistently ignored in other definitions. From the analysis of the various definitions of microfinance, one can conclude that microfinance is the provision of financial and non-financial services to individuals or groups for the purpose of setting up their own businesses to help reduce poverty.

MICROFINANCE IMPACT ON MICROBUSINESS DEVELOPMENT

Issues, Controversies, Problems

Analysis of existing literature suggests that the provision of microfinance has produced positive outcomes on microbusiness growth in several countries, particularly in Sub-Saharan Africa and the Asian continent. Rotich, et al. (2015) for example found that the provision of microfinance increased the performance of microbusinesses in Sub-Saharan Africa. Analysis of Masanga and Jera, (2017) also suggests that microbusinesses that received from microfinance institutions in Zimbabwe may have improved their level of income from the use of microfinance. Cooper (2012) support this view as he also argues that microfinance services have helped businesses in Kenya to grow their turnover from micro to small and from small to medium. A recent study that also provides evidence of positive outcomes of microfinance experiments is Hameed, et al. (2017) who found that microfinance services have a positive impact on the success of microbusinesses in Africa. Indeed, most studies conducted on the outcomes of microfinance on microbusiness development have focused on the impact of microfinance on monthly sales, capital stock, total assets and the number of people employed by microenterprises. This section, therefore, explores issues, controversies and problems relating to the impact of microfinance on microbusiness monthly sales, business assets, capital stock and employment creation.

1. Microfinance Impact on Microbusiness Sales

Microfinance has been reported to have made a significant positive contribution to the monthly sales of microenterprises in poor communities across Africa, Asia and South America. Evidence of positive outcomes of microfinance on microbusiness total sales has also been reported in some Eastern European countries. For example, Cooper (2012) examined the impact of microfinance services on the growth of small and medium enterprises in Kenya and found that microfinance has a positive impact on microbusiness sales. Similarly, using a survey research design Naeem, et al., (2015) analysed the impact of microfinance on women microenterprises in the Quetta District of Pakistan and found that microfinance is helpful in enhancing microenterprise average sales revenue and net income. This is consistent with Taiwo, et al., (2016) who also found that microenterprises in Nigeria experienced a positive percentage change as well as positive annual sales growth as a result of microfinancing. The question therefore is, will the provision of microfinance to microbusinesses in the Ghana yield similar results?

The results of Al Mamun, et al., (2011) also reveal that the provision of microfinance increase microenterprise sales. This conclusion was reached through a cross-sectional study conducted in Malaysia. Another evidence that supports the view that microfinance has a positive impact on microbusiness sales is the outcomes of Isaia (2005) who found that the sales and profits of microbusinesses that received credit were 58 and 43 per cent respectively higher than the businesses that did not receive any credit. However, Atmadja, et al. (2016) found a negative impact of microfinance on the performance of women-owned microenterprises in Indonesia. This is inconsistent with Hameed, et al. (2017) who found that the provision of microfinance has a positive impact on the performance of microenterprises in Africa. Analysis of the above literature on the impact of microfinance on microbusiness growth is not clear and therefore require further research.

2. Microfinance Impact on Microbusiness Assets

Microfinance has also been reported to have made a positive contribution to the total assets of microbusinesses in a number of countries across the world. In particular, a study conducted in Malaysia found that microfinance impacted positively on total assets of microbusinesses (Al Mamun, et al., 2012). Similarly, Haile et al (2012) found that access to microfinance helped microbusinesses owned by women increase their income base and acquired more business assets in Ethiopia. More so, the outcome of Khandker and Samad (2013) also support the view that the provision of microfinance impacts positively on microbusiness assets. In this context, will the provision of microfinance to microbusinesses in Ghana yield similar positive outcomes?

Other studies that examined the impact of only microfinance on microbusiness growth have also produced positive outcomes on microbusiness assets. For instance, Al Mamun, et al., (2010) found that microenterprises that participated in a microfinance programme in Malaysia increased their total assets significantly compared to businesses that did not participate in the programme. Similarly, Salia (2014) found that participants of a finance programme in Tanzania improved their long term-assets by investing the credit received in microbusiness activity. In respect of the impact of microfinance on microbusiness assets, the outcomes of Atmadja, et al., (2018) suggests that non-financial factors such as human capital development including financial management training are important factors for improving microbusiness assets. Similarly, Kessy and Temu (2010) found that microfinance client enterprises owned by recipients of financial training have higher-level of assets compared to enterprises owned by non-recipients of financial advice.

3. Microfinance Impact on Microbusiness Employment Creation

Prior research suggests that the provision of microfinance has produced positive outcomes on microbusiness employment creation. For example, in a quasi-experiment conducted on the impact of microfinance on rural households in the Philippines, Kondo, et al., 2008 concluded that generally, microfinance increases microbusiness productivity and creates jobs for the poor. Similarly, a mixed methods study on the role of microfinance in employment generation in Nepal found that microfinance provides opportunities for employment generation by microbusinesses in rural communities (Pathak and Gyawali, 2012). Furthermore, evidence from Kumar (2017) suggests that SKDRDP's microfinance innovations through group enterprises with an 'integrated approach' have contributed to improving the employment and income of female entrepreneurs in rural areas in India.

A case study conducted by Dunn and Arbuckle (2012) also found that microbusinesses that received services from a microfinance provider performed better in terms of employment creation than businesses that did not receive credit. Similarly, the outcomes of Crépon, et al., (2011) in Morocco support the above findings as they also concluded that the provision of microfinance increased the number of people employed by the microbusiness that received the credit. It may, therefore, be the case that the provision of microfinance to microbusinesses in Ghana could yield similar results.

4. Microfinance Impact on Microbusiness Capital Stock

Analysis of microfinance literature suggests that microfinance impacts positively on microbusiness working capital. For instance, a mixed methods study conducted in Uganda by Mbabazi, (2018) has shown that the provision of microfinance to women-owned microbusinesses in Uganda has helped increased their earnings and capital stock. Similarly, a survey conducted by Mbugua (2010) found that the provision of microfinance services increased the working capital of microenterprises in Kenya. The outcomes of Ngugi and Kerongo (2014) also support the above findings as they too found that receipt of microfinance services have a positive impact on microbusiness growth profile including capital stock. Furthermore, Naeem, et al., (2015) also found that microfinance had a positive impact on the networking capital of microenterprises in Pakistan. The work of Salia and Mbwambo (2014) is major literature that appears to support the view that the provision of microfinance has a positive impact on microbusiness capital as they found that businesses of borrowers in three cities in Tanzania performed significantly better than non-borrowers on capital stock. Furthermore, using participatory programme evaluation methods Arnold (2012) have shown that microfinance institutions are providing capital for microbusiness development in Bolivia. This is consistent with Mbugua (2010) who found that the provision of microfinance increased the working capital of microenterprises in Kenya. The question therefore is, will the provision of microfinance to microbusinesses in Ghana yield similar results?

Hypotheses Tested

To determine whether access to microfinance made any significant difference in the growth of the microbusinesses studied, the following hypotheses are proposed:

H_1. There is a difference between the monthly sales of the treatment group and the non-treatment group.

H_2. There is a difference between the number of employees of the treatment group and the non-treatment group.

H_3. There is a difference between the business assets of the treatment group and the non-treatment group.

H_4. There is a difference between the capital stock of the treatment group and the non-treatment group.

Conceptual Framework

The resources-based entrepreneurship theory of Alvarez and Busenitz (2001) is used as the underpinning theory for this chapter. The theory suggests that access to resources can contribute to the relative advantage of a microbusiness and therefore its growth (Davidson and Honing, 2003). Such resources according to Aldrich (1999) include; financial resources, social and human resources. With regards to financial resources, Clausen (2006) argues that entrepreeneurs who possess financial resources are in a better position to acquire the necessary resources needed to exploit business opportunities. In this regard, Hurst and Lusardi (2004) concludes that access to financial resources such microfinance could enhance microbusiness development. Access to a larger social network is also viewed as necessary for exploiting business opportunities and therefore the possession of such resources in the context of the resource-based theory could foster a firm's development (Shane and Eckhardt, 2003). A microbusiness ability to identify and exploit business opportunities which could enhance its growth is also viewed in the context of the resource-based theory to depend on the entrepreneur's level of education and experience (Becker, 1975).

A firm's development in most entrepreneurship theories including the resource-based theory is conceived to be in three stages. That is; discovering an opportunity, evaluating the opportunity and making a decision to exploit this opportunity. For instance, in the context of the resource-based theory of entrepreneurship, the external environment provides opportunities for a microbusiness to take advantage of or to improve upon their own development. However, the ability to take advantage of these opportunities is dependent on the micro entrepreneur's ability to access resources to exploit such opportunities. In other words, the possession of the necessary resources such as financial resources by the microbusiness is important to its development (Aldrich, 1999). However, other factors such as; personal traits of the entrepreneur, prior experience, level of education, industry and location of the microbusiness and so on; which are considered as attributes affect the decisions of microbusinesses to access and use such resources to enhance their development (Arenius and Minniti, 2005).

The decision to utilise the entrepreneurial opportunity is what usually motivates the microbusiness search for resources (microfinance); that is acquisition of resources (Ekpe, et al., 2010). Once the resources are acquired there is the urge to apply it to an entrepreneurial activity; that is new business or business expansion. The deserved use of the acquired resources in terms of business strategy and organisational design could lead to microbusiness development (Ekpe, et al., 2010). This is the grounds on which this chapter proposes to investigate the manner in which microfinance have impacted microbusiness development in Ghana. Consistent with the conceptualisation of microbusiness development above, this chapter is guided by the framework given in figure 1 below, focusing on the relationship between the provision of microfinance and microbusiness development.

Figure 1. Framework for examining microfinance impact on microbusiness development (Authors, 2021)
Source: Authors, 2021

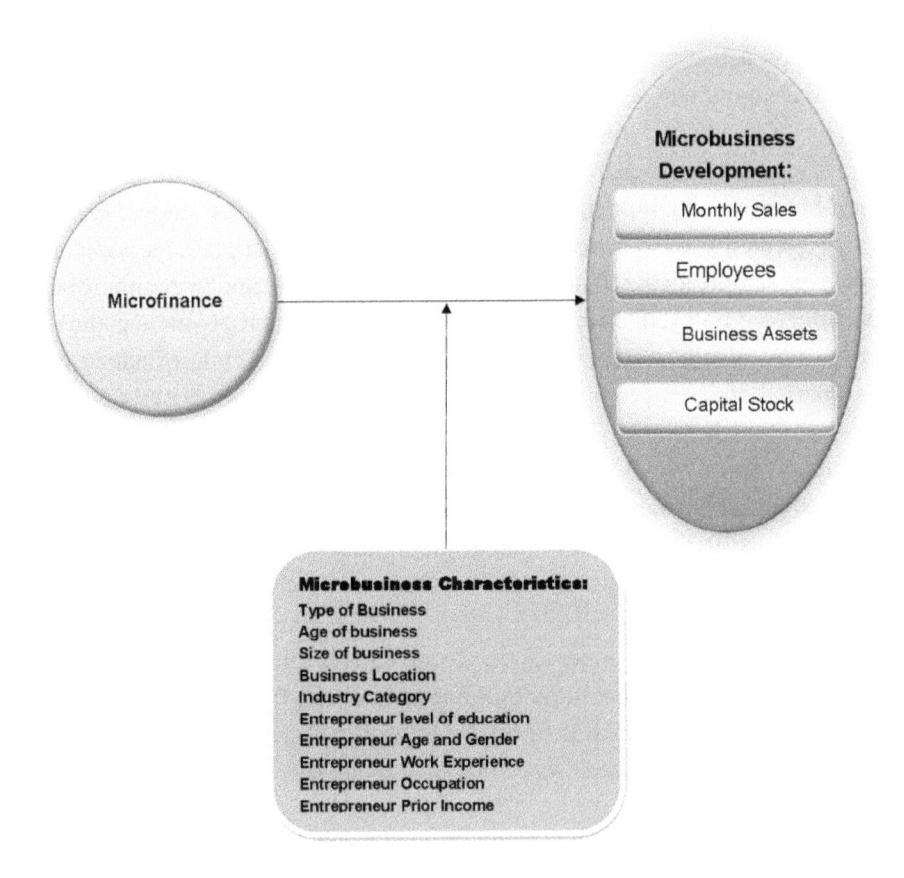

Microbusiness Development:
- Monthly Sales
- Employees
- Business Assets
- Capital Stock

Microfinance

Microbusiness Characteristics:
Type of Business
Age of business
Size of business
Business Location
Industry Category
Entrepreneur level of education
Entrepreneur Age and Gender
Entrepreneur Work Experience
Entrepreneur Occupation
Entrepreneur Prior Income

METHODOLOGY

The determination of which variables to measure the results from improved access to credit is usually the first step in most microfinance impact studies. Poverty, empowerment, microenterprise growth, employment and income are usually the main variables of interest. The second step is to determine a suitable control group that best resembles the client group of a microcredit provider whose impact is being studied. Statistically significant difference in the outcome between treatment and control groups is an indication of impact of the microcredit provider (Hartarska & Nadolnyak, 2008; Attanasio, et al., 2015; Garcia, et al., 2020).

The approach employed in this chapter is different in three ways. First, since the only microfinance impact studies in Ghana used multiple microfinance institutions, the focus of this chapter is not on multiple microcredit providers but a single microfinance institution. A second difference in the approach adopted in this chapter is that the focus is not on the general impact of microfinance intervention. Instead we measure the impact of access to microcredit on microbusiness growth. The third difference of the approach employed here is that a debriefing from a microfinance provider is used to design the experiment for the treatment and non-treatment groups.

The experimental research design is employed to examine the impact of microfinance on microbusiness development in Ghana. In deciding which microbusiness to include in the treatment group, the number of employees' criteria which is widely used by European Union was adopted. Therefore, the population from which the sample for the treatment group was drawn from included; microbusinesses that directly employed fewer than 10 employees. The microbusiness in the treatment group must also have received financial support from a microfinance institution for a period of at least two years. The number of employees' criteria was also used to decide which microbusiness to include in the non-treatment group. Thus, the population from which the sample for the non-treatment group was drawn from included; microbusinesses that directly employed a maximum of 9 employees. The microbusiness in the non-treatment group must also not received financial support from a formal bank or microfinance institution in the last two years preceding the date of this study.

Overall, 125 microbusinesses that received credit from a microfinance provider and another 125 microbusiness that did not benefit from any microfinance were studied to obtain empirical data on the impact of the microfinance received. This sample size for both groups was calculated using the following formula proposed by Yamane (1967):

$$n = \frac{N}{1 + N(e)^2}. \tag{1}$$

Where n denotes sample size required, N is size of the population and e is the e is the level of precision. Consistent with the above formula, the sample size for the treatment group based on eligible population of 182 microbusinesses drawn from the database of a microfinance provider in Ghana and confirmed with the debriefing from the microfinance provider was calculated as follows:

$$n = \frac{182}{1 + 182(0.05)^2}. = 125 \tag{2}$$

Similarly, the sample size for the non-treatment group based on eligible population of 182 microbusinesses drawn from a list of microbusinesses recommended by entrepreneurs in the treatment group and confirmed with the debriefing from the microcredit provider was also calculated as follows:

$$n = \frac{182}{1 + 182(0.05)^2} . = 125 \tag{3}$$

The use of the experimental or control group design helped to determine the impact of microfinance on the selected microbusineses by comparing the profile of beneficiaries of microfinance (treatment group) and non beneficiaries (non-treatment group) using independent samples t-test. Microfinance was the independent variable for this investigation. Therefore, from the literature reviewed and the conceptual framework, it is envisaged that the use of microfinance could foster microbusiness development. The dependent variable was microbusiness development. Thus, capital stock, sales, number of employees and assets are identified to represent the dependent variable. The moderating variable is the personal characteristics of the entrepreneur. Hence, gender, age, level of education, occupation, work experience, income and ethnic origin of the micro entrepreneur, type of business, industry, location of business, source of capital and duration of operation are recognised as the moderating variable.

The proof of microbusiness development in this study is measured by any improvement in the capital stock, increase in sales/turnover, increase in number of employees and assets after a sustained use of microcredit for a minimum period of two years. Rotich, et al. (2015) measured microbusiness development in Sub-Saharan Africa using similar variables. This is consistent with Cooper (2012) who also measured small and medium size enterprise development in Kenya using total turnover. Overall, the use of the above variables to measure enterprise development is very common in microfinance literature and therefore provides justification for their use in this study.

In view of the objective of finding the relationship between microfinance and microbusiness development in Ghana, the mean of the treatment group is compared with the mean of the non-treatment group on the four (4) depended variables studied using two independent samples t-tests at 5% significant level. This test was carried out to estimate how the development of the microbusinesses studied depended on receipt of microfinance. This is consistent with Kapila, et al., (2017) who have shown that independent samples t-tests is most appropriate for analysing the effects of an independent variable involving two group.

SOLUTIONS AND RECOMMENDATIONS

1. Microcredit Impact on Microbusiness Development

Independent samples t-test was employed to analyse the effects of microfinance on the microbusinesses studied. The use of the independent samples t-test is to determine if the mean differences between the two groups of the microbusinesses studied were statistically significant. The summary of the results of the independent samples t-tests and descriptive statistics are shown in table 1 below.

Table 1. Results of t-tests and descriptive statistics for monthly sales, business assets, capital stock and number of employees

Variable	Group						95% CI for Mean Difference			
	Treatment			Non-Treatment						
	M	SD	n	M	SD	n			t	df
Sales	3720.00	866.58	125	2464.00	330.54	125	1092.16	1419.84	15.14	159.33
Assets	8033.60	1272.72	125	4912.80	675.49	125	2866.58	3375.02	24.22	188.72
Capital	9028.80	1425.73	125	5608.80	544.18	125	3150.43	3689.57	25.06	159.38
Employees	2.98	.678	125	1.36	.545	125	1.46	1.77	20.78	237.07

Source: (Authors, 2021)

As shown in table 1 the treatment group with a sample of 125 ($N = 125$) was associated with a mean monthly sales of 3720.00 ($M = 3720.00$) and a standard deviation of 866.58 ($SD = 866.58$). By comparison, the non-treatment group, also with a sample size of 125 ($N = 125$) was associated with a numerically smaller sales mean of 2464.00 ($M = 2464.00$), and a standard deviation of 330.54 ($SD = 330.54$). With regards to the number of employees, the treatment group with a sample of 125 ($N = 125$) was associated with a mean number of employees of 2.98 ($M = 2.98$) and a standard deviation of .678 ($SD = .678$), with the non-treatment group, as well, with a sample size of 125 ($N = 125$), associated with a numerically smaller mean number of employees of 1.36 ($M = 1.36$), and a standard deviation of .545 ($SD = .545$).

As with the monthly sales, and the number of employees, the respective samples of the business assets of the treatment group and the non-treatment group are 125 ($N = 125$). The sample for the treatment group was associated with a mean business asset of 8033.60 ($M = 8033.60$) and a standard deviation of 1272.725 (SD

= 1272.725), and that of the non-treatment group, associated with a numerically smaller mean business assets of 4912.80 ($M = 4912.80$), and a standard deviation of 675.490 ($SD = 675.490$). As with the foregoing variables, the respective samples of the capital stock of the treatment group and the non-treatment group are 125 ($N = 125$). While the sample for the treatment group was associated with a mean capital stock of 9028.80 ($M = 9028.80$) and a standard deviation of 1425.732 ($SD = 1425.732$), and that of the non-treatment group, associated with a numerically smaller mean capital stock of 5608.80 ($M = 5608.80$), and a standard deviation of 544.180 ($SD = 544.180$).

2. Microfinance Impact on Monthly Sales

To test the hypothesis that the treatment group was associated with statistically significant different mean sales from the non-treatment group, an independent samples *t*-test was performed. Before then however the assumption of equality of variances, that is, whether the shapes of distributions of the monthly sales of both the treatment group and the non-treatment group were similar was tested and validated through the Levene's *F* test. In this case the *F* statistic was 98.48, with a p-value of = 0.00, which means the null hypothesis of equal variances is rejected at 1%, and it is concluded that there is a difference between the variances in the populations from which the two samples were drawn which confirms our hypothesis $\boldsymbol{H}_1$. This practically means the distribution of the monthly sales for the two groups are not of similar shapes, and that the assumption of equality of variances, is rejected at 1%. Proceeding with the test of equality of means between the treatment and the non-treatment groups, the results show that the null hypothesis which says there is no difference between the means of monthly sales of the two groups in a two-tailed test is also rejected at 1% with a t-statistic of 15.140 and 248 degrees of freedom ($t = 15.140$, $p = 0.00$). Thus, the treatment group was associated with a statistically significantly larger mean monthly sales volume than that of the non-treatment group.

The outcome above suggest that the provision of microfinance improved microbusiness monthly sales. These results have very strong link to existing literature (Kondo, et al., 2008; Cooper, 2012; Naeem, et al., 2015). For instance, in a quasi-experiment conducted on the impact of microcredit on rural households in the Philippines, Kondo, et al., 2008 concluded that generally, microfinance increases microbusiness sales. Similarly, Cooper (2012) prediction of positive relationships between the use of microfinance and microbusiness sales in Kenya has also been confirmed in this study in the United Kingdom. The study found a significant improvement in the monthly sales of the microbusinesses that received microfinance from the microfinance company studied. This is consistent with Naeem, et al., (2015) who have shown that microfinance is helpful in enhancing microenterprise average sales revenue and net income. The policy implication arising out of the above findings of this study is that the provision of financial support to microfinance organisations to strengthen their ability to provide adequate credit for microbusiness development may have positive impact on economic development.

3. Microfinance Impact on Number of Employees

Again, to test the hypothesis that the treatment group was associated with statistically significant different mean number of employees from the non-treatment group, an independent samples *t*-test was performed. Before then, however, the assumption of equality of variances, that is, whether the shapes of the distributions of the number of employees of both the customer group and the control group were similar was tested and validated through the Levene's F test. In this case the F statistic was. 1.136, with a p-value of = .288. This means the null hypothesis of equal variances cannot be rejected at 10% level of statistical significance, and it is concluded that there is no difference between the variances in the populations from which the two samples were drawn. This practically means the distribution of the number of employees for the two groups are of similar shapes, and that, again, the assumption of equality of variances, cannot be rejected at 10%. Proceeding with the test of equality of means between the treatment and the non-treatment groups the results show that the null hypothesis which says there is no difference between the means of the number of employees of the two groups in a two-tailed test is rejected at 1% with a t-statistic of 20.781 and 248 degrees of freedom ($t = 20.781, p = 0.00$). Thus, the treatment group was associated with a statistically significantly larger mean number of employees than that of the non-treatment group. Therefore, our hypothesis H_2. which assumes there is a difference between the number of employees of the treatment group and the non-treatment group is accepted.

The result of the *t*-test reveals that the provision of microfinance improved microbusiness employment creation. This outcome has very strong link to existing literature (Kondo, et al., 2008; Pathak and Gyawali, 2012; Masanga and Jera, 2017). For example, Kondo, et al., 2008 have shown that generally, microfinance increases microbusiness productivity and creates jobs for the poor in the Philippines. Similarly, a mixed methods study on the role of microfinance in employment generation in Nepal found that microfinance provides opportunities for employment generation by microbusinesses in rural communities (Pathak and Gyawali, 2012). The Philippines and Nepal evidence therefore supports the findings of this study that the microbusinesses that received microfinance created more jobs than those that did not benefit from any microfinance intervention. This finding has policy implications for the government of Ghana and other agencies that are interested in using microbusiness development as a catalyst for economic growth in deprived communities in the country.

4. Microfinance Impact on Business Assets

Testing the hypothesis that the treatment group was associated with statistically significant different mean business assets from the non-treatment group, an independent samples t-test was again employed. We however before then tested the assumption of equality of variances, that is, whether the shape of distributions of the business assets of both the treatment group and the non-treatment group were similar and validated through the Levene's F test. In this case the F statistic was 23.659, at 1% statistical significance (p-value = 0.00). This means the null hypothesis of equal variances is rejected at 1% level of statistical significance, and it is concluded that there is a difference between the variances in the populations from which the two samples were drawn. This practically means the distribution of the business assets for the two groups are not of similar shapes, and that the assumption of equality of variances is rejected at 1%. Proceeding with the test of equality of means between the treatment and the non-treatment groups, the results show that the null hypothesis which says there is no difference between the means of the business assets of the two groups in a two-tailed test is rejected at 1% with a t-statistic of 24.216 and 248 degrees of freedom ($t = 24.216, p = 0.00$). Thus, the treatment group was associated with a statistically significantly larger mean business assets than that of the non-treatment group which confirms our hypothesis $\boldsymbol{H_3}$.

The positive relationships also found between microfinance and the assets owned by the microbusinesses in this chapter have also been previously acknowledged by Al Mamun, et al., (2012); Haile, et al. (2012) and Khandker and Samad (2013). A study conducted by Al Mamun, et al., (2012) in Malaysia found evidence that support the conclusions of this chapter that microfinance impacts positively on total assets of microbusinesses. Similarly, Haile et al (2012) found that access to microfinance helped microbusinesses owned by women increase their income base and acquired more business assets in Ethiopia. More so, outcome of Khandker and Samad (2013) also support the findings of this chapter that the provision of microfinance impacts positively on microbusiness assets. The significance of the similarity of the outcomes of this chapter and the previous research referred to above, is that the provision of microfinance can be used as a viable strategy for promoting microbusiness development in poor communities in Ghana and beyond.

5. Microfinance Impact on Capital Stock

Testing the hypothesis that the treatment group was associated with statistically significant different mean capital stock from the non-treatment group, we again employ an independent samples t-test. Before then, however, we tested the assumption of equality of variances that is, whether the shape of distributions of the capital stock of both the treatment group and the non-treatment group were similar and validated through the Levene's F test. In this case the F statistic was 64.359, at 1% statistical significance (p-value = 0.00). This means the null hypothesis of equal variances is rejected at 1% level of statistical significance, and it is concluded that there is a difference between the variances in the populations from which the two samples were drawn. This practically means the distribution of the business assets for the two groups are not of similar shapes, and that the assumption of equality of variances is rejected at 1%. Proceeding with the test of equality of the capital stock means between the treatment and the non-treatment groups the results show that the null hypothesis which says there is no difference between the means of the business assets of the two groups in a two-tailed test is rejected at 1% with a t-statistic of 25.056 and 248 degrees of freedom ($t = 25.056$, $p = 0.00$). Thus, the customer group was associated with a statistically significantly larger mean capital stock than that of the control group. Therefore, our hypothesis H_4 .which assumes that there is a difference between the capital stock of the treatment group and the non-treatment group is confirmed.

The result of the t-test reveals that a positive relationship exists between use of microfinance and capital stock of the microbusinesses studied. This result is significant but not surprising as substantial evidence in the existing literature support this outcome. For instance, a mixed methods study conducted in Uganda by Mbabazi, (2018) have shown that the provision of microfinance to women owned microbusinesses in Uganda has helped increased their earnings and capital stock. Similarly, a survey conducted by Mbugua (2010) found that the provision of microfinance increased the working capital of microenterprises in Kenya. The outcomes of Ngugi and Kerongo (2014) also support the findings of this study as they too found a positive relationship between receipt of microfinance and microbusiness growth profile including capital stock. Furthermore, Naeem, et al., (2015) also found that microfinance had a positive impact on the net working capital of microenterprises in Pakistan. There is therefore sufficient basis to state that the findings of this chapter that positive relationships between microfinance and capital stock of microbusinesses in the Ghana is verifiable and reliable. These findings and the supporting evidence have implication for policy makers as it provides the basis to use microfinance as a developmental instrument for improving microbusiness working capital in Ghana and elswhere. Thus, governments and their developmental partners could use microfinance as a catalyst to solving the working capital difficulties experienced by microbusiness set ups.

FUTURE RESEARCH DIRECTIONS

This research was conducted in Tamale Municipality, Savelugu, Walewale, Salaga, Yendi, Tolon and Bimbila.. However, since the provision of microfinance to microbusinesses is not limited to the above locations, conducting similar research at other locations in Ghana to determine microfinance impact could enhance our knowledge of the impact of microfinance in different contexts.

Also, this study focused on the automobile, catering, construction, food and grocery, health and beauty and the transportation industry. Thus, the data used in this research was collected from seven industries which suggest that the outcomes may be overly general. In this regard, future research on the impact of microfinance experiments on microbusiness growth in specific industries in Ghana is important for our understanding of the use and impact of microfinance in a specific industry context. Besides, going forward, conducting research on microfinance impact on microbusiness growth in Ghana using a collaborative approach between industry experts and academic institutions could yield more robust and in-depth research outcomes.

Furthermore, future comparative studies on the impact of microfinance experiment on microbusiness development in Ghana, other counties in Africa and developed countries could provide wide and comprehensive outcomes that could be explained in the context of both developed and developing countries. Besides, the current study was conducted using one microfinance provider. However, evidence from existing literature suggests that often microenterprises often borrow from multiple providers. In this regard, future investigations on the impact of multiple sources of microfinance on microbusiness development in Ghana and elsewhere is required.

Future research on the impact of microfinance on sustainable development in Ghana is required as the current study focused on microbusiness development. Some studies have also examined the impact of microfinance on poverty reduction in other developing countries, there is however no evidence of any investigation in Ghana that has investigated the impact of microfinance on poverty reduction. Hence, future studies should consider measuring the impact of microfinance on poverty reduction in poorer communities in Ghana which could help policymakers formulate strategies for improving the standard of living in financially excluded communities in the country.

CONCLUSION

In view of the chapter aim of establishing the impact of microfinance on microbusiness development in Ghana, quantitative data was collected and analysed by comparing the mean monthly sales, number of employees, business assets and capital stock of microbusinesses that received credit from a microfinance provider in Ghana and the mean monthly sales, number of employees, business assets and capital stock of microbusinesses that did not receive any services from a microfinance provider using independent samples t-test. Accordingly, the following conclusions consistent with the chapter objectives were reached:

Findings from the independent samples t-test analysis found a significant improvement in the monthly sales of the microbusinesses that received microfinance. Thus, the microbusinesses that received microfinance services were found to be associated with a statistically significantly larger mean monthly sales than the microbusinesses that did not benefit from any microfinance intervention. This chapter therefore concludes that a positive relationship exist between microfinance and microbusiness monthly sales.

With regard to the relationship between microfinance and microbusiness employment creation, it was found that the provision of microfinance improved microbusiness employment creation. The t-test analysis revealed that the microbusinesses that received microfinance were associated with a statistically significantly larger mean number of employees than the microbusinesses that did not benefit from microfinance. This chapter therefore concludes that there is a positive relationship between receipt of microcredit and the number of people employed by microbusinesses.

In the case of the relationship between the provision of microfinance and microbusiness assets, it was found that the microbusinesses that received microfinance improved their assets significantly. The independent samples t-tests used to examine the impact of microfinance on microbusiness assets produced significantly positive outcomes. Therefore, this chapter concludes that where microbusinesses are provided with microfinance their business assets improves.

In respect of the possible impact of microfinance on microbusiness capital stock, it is found that the provision microfinance had a positive impact on capital stock of the microbusinesses that received the microfinance. Besides, the results of the independent samples t-test suggests that the microbusinesses that used microfinance to finance their business were associated with a statistically significantly larger mean capital stock than microbusinesses that did not benefit from microfinance intervention. Thus, this chapter concludes that a positive relationship exist between use of microfinance and capital stock of microbusinesses in Ghana.

ACKNOWLEDGMENT

This research received no specific grant from any funding agency in the public, commercial, or not-for-profit sectors.

REFERENCES

Abe, M., Troilo, M. & Batsaikhan, O. (2015). Financing small and medium enterprises in Asia and the Pacific. *Journal of Entrepreneurship and Public Policy, 4*(1), 2-32.

Agbola, F. W., Acupan, A., & Mahmood, A. (2017). Does microfinance reduce poverty? New evidence from Northeastern Mindanao, the Philippines. *Journal of Rural Studies, 50*, 159–171. doi:10.1016/j.jrurstud.2016.11.005

Al Mamun, A., Abdul Wahab, S., & Malarvizhi, C. (2010). Impact of Amanah Ikhtiar Malaysia's microcredit schemes on microenterprise assets in Malaysia. *International Research Journal of Finance and Economics, 60*, 144–154. doi:10.2139srn.1946089

Al Mamun, A., Adaikalam, J., & Mazumder, M. N. H. (2012). Examining the effect of Amanah Ikhtiar Malaysia's microcredit program on microenterprise assets in rural Malaysia. *Asian Social Science, 8*(4), 272–280. doi:10.5539/ass.v8n4p272

Al Mamun, A., Malarvizhi, C. A., Abdul Wahab, S. & Mazumder, M. N. H. (2011). Investigating the effect of microcredit on microenterprise income in Peninsular Malaysia. *European Journal of Economics, Finance and Administrative Sciences,* 122-132.

Aldrich, H. (1999). *Organisations Evolving*. Sage Publications.

Ali, M., Saeed, G., Zeb, A., & Jan, F. (2016). Microcredit & its Significance in Sustainable Development and Poverty Alleviation: Evidence from Asia, Africa, Latin America and Europe. Dialogue, 11(3).

Alimukhamedova, N. & Hanousek, J. (2015). *What Do We Know about Microfinance at Macro Glance?* Academic Press.

Alvarez, S. & Busenitz, L. (2001). The entrepreneurship of resource based theory. *Journal of Management, 27*, 755-775.

Alvi, E., & Senbeta, A. (2012). Does foreign aid reduce poverty? *Journal of International Development, 24*(8), 955–976. doi:10.1002/jid.1790

Amin, M. F. B., & Uddin, S. J. (2018). Microfinance-economic growth nexus: A case study on Grameen bank in Bangladesh. *International Journal of Islamic Economics and Finance, 1*(1). Advance online publication. doi:10.18196/ijief.112

Anane, G. K., Cobbinah, P. B., & Manu, J. K. (2013). Sustainability of Small and Medium Scale Enterprises in Rural Ghana: The Role of Microfinance Institutions. *Asian Economic and Financial Review, 3*(8), 1003–1017.

Arenius, P., & Minniti, M. (2005). Perceptual variables and nascent entrepreneurship. *Small Business Economics, 24*(3), 233–247. doi:10.100711187-005-1984-x

Arnold, K. J. (2012). *Microfinance for microenterprises? Investigating the usefulness of microfinance services for microenterprises in Bolivia.* Simon Fraser University.

Atmadja, A. S., Sharma, P., & Su, J. J. (2018). Microfinance and microenterprise performance in Indonesia: An extended and updated survey. *International Journal of Social Economics, 45*(6), 957–972. doi:10.1108/IJSE-02-2017-0031

Atmadja, A. S., Su, J. J., & Sharma, P. (2016). Examining the impact of microfinance on microenterprise performance (implications for women-owned microenterprises in Indonesia. *International Journal of Social Economics, 43*(10), 962–981. doi:10.1108/IJSE-08-2014-0158

Attanasio, O., Augsburg, B., De Haas, R., Fitzsimons, E., & Harmgart, H. (2015). The impacts of microfinance: Evidence from joint-liability lending in Mongolia. *American Economic Journal. Applied Economics, 7*(1), 90–122. doi:10.1257/app.20130489

Augsburg, B., De Haas, R., Harmgart, H. & Meghir, C. (2013). Microfinance and Poverty Alleviation. *American Economic Journal: Applied Economics.*

Ayodele, A. E., & Arogundade, K. (2014). The impact of microfinance on economic growth in Nigeria. *Journal of Emerging Trends in Economics and Management Science, 5*(5), 397–405.

Babajide, A. (2011). Impact analysis of microfinance in Nigeria. *International Journal of Economics and Finance, 3*(4).

Bateman, M. (2017). Local economic development and microcredit. In *The Essential Guide to Critical Development Studies* (pp. 235–248). Routledge. doi:10.4324/9781315612867-19

Becker, G. S. 1975. Human Capital. Chicago, IL: Chicago University Press.

Bruhn, M., & Love, I. (2014). The real impact of improved access to finance: Evidence from Mexico. *The Journal of Finance, 69*(3), 1347–1376. doi:10.1111/jofi.12091

Chen, J., Chang, A. Y., & Bruton, G. D. (2017). Microfinance: Where are we today and where should the research go in the future? *International Small Business Journal, 35*(7), 793–802. doi:10.1177/0266242617717380

Chliova, M., Brinckmann, J., & Rosenbusch, N. (2015). Is microcredit a blessing for the poor? A meta-analysis examining development outcomes and contextual considerations. *Journal of Business Venturing, 30*(3), 467–487. doi:10.1016/j.jbusvent.2014.10.003

Chowdhury, A. (2009). *Microfinance as a poverty reduction tool-a critical assessment.* United Nations, Department of Economic and Social Affairs (DESA) working paper.

Churchill, S. A. (2020). Impact of Microfinance on Poverty and Microenterprises. In *Moving from the Millennium to the Sustainable Development Goals.* Palgrave Macmillan. doi:10.1007/978-981-15-1556-9_14

Clausen, T. H. (2006). Who identifies and exploits entrepreneurial opportunities? Centre for Technology, Innovation, and Culture, University of Oslo.

Cooper, J. N. (2012). *The impact of microfinance services on the growth of small and medium enterprises in Kenya* (Doctoral dissertation). University of Nairobi.

Copestake, J. (2007). Mainstreaming microfinance: Social performance management or mission drift? *World Development, 35*(10), 1721–1738. doi:10.1016/j.worlddev.2007.06.004

Crépon, B., Devoto, F., Duflo, E., & Parienté, W. (2011). *Impact of microcredit in rural areas of Morocco: Evidence from a Randomized Evaluation.* MIT Working Paper.

Crépon, B., Devoto, F., Duflo, E., & Pariente, W. (2014). Estimating the impact of microcredit on those who take it up: Evidence from a randomized experiment in Morocco. National Bureau of Economic Research. doi:10.3386/w20144

Crisp, R. (2016). *Community-led approaches to reducing poverty in neighbourhoods: A review of evidence and practice.* Sheffield University: Centre for Regional Economic and Social Research.

Dunn, E., & Arbuckle, J. G. (2012). *Microcredit and microenterprise performance: impact evidence from Peru.* Small Enterprise Development.

Ganle, J. K., Afriyie, K., & Segbefia, A. Y. (2015). Microcredit: Empowerment and disempowerment of rural women in Ghana. *World Development, 66,* 335–345. doi:10.1016/j.worlddev.2014.08.027

Garcia, A., Lensink, R., & Voors, M. (2020). Does microcredit increase aspirational hope? Evidence from a group lending scheme in Sierra Leone. *World Development, 128,* 108861. doi:10.1016/j.worlddev.2019.104861

Gloukoviezoff, G. (2016). *Evaluating the impact of European microfinance.* The Foundations. (No. 2016/33). EIF Working Paper.

Gretta, S. A. A. B. (2017). Financial inclusion and growth. *The Business & Management Review, 8*(4), 434.

Gueyie, J. P., Manos, R. & Yaron, J. (2013). *Microfinance in developing countries: issues, policies and performance evaluation.* Palgrave Macmillan.

Haile, H. B., Bock, B., & Folmer, H. (2012, August). Microfinance and female empowerment: Do institutions matter? *Women's Studies International Forum, 35*(4), 256–265. doi:10.1016/j.wsif.2012.04.001

Hameed, W. U., Hussin, T., Azeem, M., Arif, M., & Basheer, M. F. (2017). Combination of microcredit and micro-training with mediating role of formal education: A micro-enterprise success formula. *Journal of Business and Social Review in Emerging Economies, 3*(2), 285–291. doi:10.26710/jbsee.v3i2.191

Hartarska, V., & Nadolnyak, D. (2008). An impact analysis of microfinance in Bosnia and Herzegovina. *World Development, 36*(12), 2605–2619. doi:10.1016/j.worlddev.2008.01.015

Hermes, N., & Hudon, M. (2018). Determinants of the performance of microfinance institutions: A systematic review. *Journal of Economic Surveys, 32*(5), 1483–1513. doi:10.1111/joes.12290

Hermes, N., Lensink, R., & Meesters, A. (2011). Outreach and efficiency of microfinance institutions. *World Development, 39*(6), 938–948. doi:10.1016/j.worlddev.2009.10.018

Hilson, G., & Ackah-Baidoo, A. (2010). Can microcredit services alleviate hardship in African Samll-scale mining communities? *World Development, 39*(7), 1191–1203. doi:10.1016/j.worlddev.2010.10.004

Ibrahim, S. A. (2018). *Effect of Microfinance Banks Activities on Financial Inclusion in Nigeria* (Doctoral dissertation). Kwara State University, Nigeria.

Isaia, E. (2005). *Microcredit in Morocco: The Zakoura Foundation's Experience.* University of Turin.

Kessy, S., & Temu, S.S. (2010). *The impact of training on performance of micro and small enterprises served by microfinance institutions in Tanzania.* Academic Press.

Khandker, S. R. & Samad, H. (2013). *Microfinance growth and poverty reduction in Bangladesh: what does the longitudinal data say?* World Bank Working Paper.

Kondo, T., Orbeta, A. Jr, Dingcong, C., & Infantado, C. (2008). Impact of microfinance on rural households in the Philippines. *IDS Bulletin, 39*(1), 51–70. doi:10.1111/j.1759-5436.2008.tb00432.x

Kumar, K. N. (2017). Microfinance for entrepreneurial development: Study of women's group enterprise development in India. In *Microfinance for Entrepreneurial Development* (pp. 53–71). Palgrave Macmillan. doi:10.1007/978-3-319-62111-1_3

Ledgerwood, J. (1999). *Microfinance handbook: an institutional and financial perspective.* World Bank.

Ledgerwood, J., & White, V. (2006). Transforming microfinance institutions: providing full financial services to the poor. World Bank Publications. doi:10.1596/978-0-8213-6615-8

Luo, J., & Rahman, M. W. (2010). The development perspective of finance and microfinance sector in China: How far Is microfinance regulations? *International Journal of Economics and Finance, 3*(1).

Mann, G. (2019). *Does Consumer Microfinance Expand Financial Inclusion in the UK?* Academic Press.

Masanga, G. G., & Jera, M. (2017). The Significance of Microfinance to Urban Informal Traders in Zimbabwe. *Development and Resources Research Institute Journal, Ghana, 26*(3), 4.

Mayoux, L., & Hartl, M. (2009). *Gender and rural microfinance: Reaching and empowering women. International Fund for Agricultural Development.* IFAD.

Mbabazi, N. M. (2018). *The contribution of microfinance institutions to the economic development of women: A case of Uganda Cooperative Savings and Credit Union Limited (UCSCU) in Katabi Town Council* (Doctoral dissertation). Nkumba University.

Mbugua, M. (2010). *Impact of microfinance services on financial performance of small and micro enterprises in Kenya. Unpublished MBA project.* University of Nairobi.

McHugh, N., Baker, R., & Donaldson, C. (2019). Microcredit for enterprise in the UK as an 'alternative' economic space. *Geoforum, 100,* 80–88. doi:10.1016/j.geoforum.2019.02.004

Naeem, A., Khan, S., Ali, M., & Hassan, F. S. (2015). The Impact of Microfinance on Women Micro-Enterprises "A Case Study of District Quetta, Pakistan. *American International Journal of Social Science, 4*(4), 19–27.

Nair, T. S. (2018). Microfinance in India: Approaches, Outcomes, Challenges. Taylor & Francis. doi:10.4324/9781315656250

Ngugi, V. W., & Kerongo, F. (2014). Effects of Micro-Financing on Growth of Small and Micro Enterprises in Mombasa County. *International Journal of Scientific and Engineering Research, 2*(4), 2347–3878.

Pathak, H. P., & Gyawali, M. (2012). Role of microfinance in employment generation: A case study of Microfinance Program of Paschimanchal Grameen Bikash Bank. *Journal of Nepalese Business Studies, 7*(1), 31–38. doi:10.3126/jnbs.v7i1.6401

Ranjani, K. S., & Bapat, V. (2015). Deepening Financial Inclusion beyond account opening: Road ahead for banks. *Business Perspectives and Research, 3*(1), 52–65. doi:10.1177/2278533714551864

Robinson, M. S. (2001). *The microfinance revolution: sustainable finance for the poor* (Vol. 1). World Bank Publications.

Rotich, I., Lagat, C., & Kogei, J. (2015). Effects of microfinance services on the performance of small and medium enterprises in Kenya. *African Journal of Business Management, 9*(5), 206–211. doi:10.5897/AJBM2014.7519

Rowe-Haynes, M. D. (2017). *Micro-finance and small and medium-sized enterprises: the social, economic and environmental impacts of community development finance institutions in the UK* (Doctoral dissertation). University of Birmingham.

Rutherford, S. (2000). The poor and their money. Oxford: Oxford University Press.

Salia, P. J. (2014). The effect of microcredit on the household welfare (empirical evidences from women micro-entrepreneurs in Tanzania). *International Journal of Academic Research in Business & Social Sciences, 4*(5), 259. doi:10.6007/IJARBSS/v4-i5/853

Salia, P. J., & Mbwambo, J. S. (2014). Does microcredit make any difference on borrowers' businesses? Evidences from a survey of women owned microenterprises in Tanzania. *International Journal of Social Sciences and Entrepreneurship*, *1*(9), 431–444.

Salia, S., Hussain, J., Tingbani, I., & Kolade, O. (2018). Is women empowerment a zero sum game? Unintended consequences of microfinance for women's empowerment in Ghana. *International Journal of Entrepreneurial Behaviour & Research*, *24*(1), 273–289. doi:10.1108/IJEBR-04-2017-0114

Sethi, D., & Acharya, D. (2018). Financial inclusion and economic growth linkage: Some cross country evidence. *Journal of Financial Economic Policy*, *10*(3), 369–385. doi:10.1108/JFEP-11-2016-0073

Sheremenko, G., Escalante, C. L. & Florkowski, W. J. (2017). Financial sustainability and poverty outreach: The case of microfinance institutions in Eastern Europe and Central Asia. *The European Journal of Development Research*, *29*(1), 230-245.

Sultana, H. Y., Jamal, M. A., & Najaf, D. E. (2017). Impact of Microfinance on Women Empowerment Through Poverty Alleviation: An Assessment of Socio-Economic Conditions in Chennai City of Tamil Nadu. *Asian Journal for Poverty Studies*, *3*(2).

Taiwo, J. N., Agwu, M. E., Adetiloye, K. A., & Afolabi, G. T. (2016). Financing women entrepreneurs and employment generation–a case study of microfinance banks. *European Journal of Soil Science*, *52*(1), 112–141.

Van Rooyen, C., Stewart, R., & de Wet, T. (2012). The impact of microfinance in sub-Saharan Africa: A systematic review of the evidence. *World Development*, *40*(11), 2249–2262. doi:10.1016/j.worlddev.2012.03.012

Wright, G. A. N., & Rippey, P. (2003). *The competitive environment in Uganda: implications for microfinance institutions and their clients*. MicroSave Africa.

KEY TERMS AND DEFINITIONS

Assets: Resource owned by a business that have significant financial value.

Capital: Any resources both tangible and intangible that confers value or benefit to a business organisation.

Development: Improvement in the performance of microbusiness such as increased amount of capital, sales, assets, and number of people employed.

Experiment: A procedure designed to test the effect of microfinance services received by the microbusiness studies.

Impact: The effects of the provision of microfinance.

Microbusiness: Any business organisation that directly employs fewer than ten employees.

Microcredit: The provision of small loans to low-income earners to set up or develop their existing businesses.

Microfinance: The provision of small loans and training exclusively to microbusinesses, financially disadvantaged individuals, and low-income families.

Chapter 2
Role of Microfinance in Entrepreneurship Development

Neeta Baporikar

https://orcid.org/0000-0003-0676-9913

Namibia University of Science and Technology, Namibia & University of Pune, India

ABSTRACT

Entrepreneurship and entrepreneurship development are crucial for social and economic development. Various studies highlight and reckon this aspect of entrepreneurship development both in developed and developing economies. However, entrepreneurship development though the aim of many developing economies, the growth rate of entrepreneurs is not satisfactory. One of the prominent reasons for this is attributable to financing or lack of financing. Hence, adopting a systematic literature review method the aim of this chapter is to review critically the role of microfinance for entrepreneurship development. Further, the chapter provides solutions and recommendations for proper microfinancing to boost entrepreneurship development.

INTRODUCTION

Entrepreneurship and entrepreneurship development is widely regarded as a one of the critical issues to ensure social and economic development and thereby overall national development by all countries and more specifically by emerging countries (Baporikar, 2020a; 2018). With this in mind, the potency of entrepreneurship has not escaped the attention of both scholars and policymakers. Nonetheless, the influence of microfinance on entrepreneurial development has generated a heated scholarly debate. It is generally accepted that both developed and developing countries across the globe are embracing entrepreneurship as the key driver of socio-economic development (Baporikar, 2020a; Baumol & Strom, 2007; Omri & Ayadi-Frikha, 2014; Rahman, Amran, Ahmad, & Taghizadeh, 2015). Furthermore, according to Sussan & Obamuyi (2018), Global Entrepreneurship Monitor (GEM) revealed that countries associated with higher levels of entrepreneurial activity tend to enjoy higher levels of economic growth. In fact, the relentless pursuit for fostering an entrepreneurial spirit among members of the society is the need of the hour when it comes to acceleration of economic growth. More strikingly, it is worth mentioning that the positive contributions of entrepreneurship towards economic growth are well-documented (Baporikar, 2018b). It is in this context that there has been an emerging trend towards the adoption of entrepreneurship worldwide especially in developing countries (Fierro, Noble, Hatem, & Balunywa, 2018; Park, 2017; Rudhumbu, Svotwa, Munyanyiwa, & Mutsau, 2016).

Accordingly, the importance of the concept of entrepreneurship has attracted much attention of researchers, practitioners, and policymakers. With the importance of microfinance in mind, it is deemed appropriate to mention that Muhammad Yunus is widely recognized as the Father of Modern Microfinance because he managed to come up with Grameen Bank aimed at financing the poor (Hinrichsen, 2019). It is salient to observe that the Latin American model of microfinance is not the same as Asian or African models in the sense that microfinance organizations in Latin America are more inclined to operate as private businesses. In the context of Latin American countries, Peru has witnessed an exponential growth of the microfinance sector owing to its favorable conditions for microfinance (Burneo & Lizarzaburu, 2018).

In the case of India, the concept of microfinance was introduced by the National Bank of Agriculture and Rural Development (NABARD) after borrowing the idea from Bangladesh (Grameen Bank) (Kannan & Panneerselvan, 2013). Going forward, many microfinance programs were launched in India such as Group Lending program, SHG-Bank Linkage program and Joint Liability Group (JLG) model. Following the effective implementation of microfinance programs, India witnessed a rapid growth of clients as evidenced by the fact that microfinance institutions served about 35.1 million customers from 2017 to 2018 (Sa-Dhan, 2018). It is imperative to note that there is an increase in the provision of microfinance services to the poor and SMEs in India through alternative approaches (Mohammed & Waheed, 2019). Further, this emerged trend towards entrepreneurship has heightened the strong need for the advancement of our understanding of entrepreneurship in post pandemic in the face of twin problems of an economies becoming fragile and increase in unemployment rate. While there is a noticeable growing knowledge base on the subject of entrepreneurship, it is salient to observe that the contexts in which entrepreneurship takes place in terms of historical, sectoral, national and socio-economic contexts should be taken into account seriously in order to enrich future research work in entrepreneurship (Baporikar, 2018; Stam, 2016; Watson, 2013; Welter & Gartener, 2016). As such, it appears that there is a dire need for more empirical evidence on entrepreneurship as a field from the perspective of developing countries (Baporikar, 2017). It is salient to observe that entrepreneurs ensure value creation through the commercialization of innovative products and services that stimulate new business ventures. This has led to an increase in the number of Small and Medium Enterprises (SMEs) globally. Undoubtedly, the SMEs are playing a crucial role when it comes to the economic development in many countries as they are the seed-bed of innovation and the key pillar of youth employment creation (Baporikar, 2020a; 2019).

There is no doubt that microfinance institutions are providing financial resources as a way to support entrepreneurial activities (Sussan & Obamuyi, 2018). Despite the significance of the concept of microfinance, there is a controversy surrounding its effect on entrepreneurial success (Sultakeev, Karymshakov, & Sulaimanova, 2018). With thorough cross-examination of the available literature on microfinance and entrepreneurship, the authors noticed that several quantitative studies predominately focused on the impact of microfinance on entrepreneurship development (El-Hadidi, 2018; Gedion, Maizs, & Toroitich, 2016; Osunde & Agboola, 2012; Sussan & Obamuyi, 2018). However, the nexus and qualitative aspects between microfinance and entrepreneurship development and entrepreneurial success have received scant attention in the extant literature up to now. So globally many governments have implemented many microfinance support schemes to stimulate and support entrepreneurship as a strategic response to the calls for a need to address the financial challenges of entrepreneurs especially the small and micro entrepreneurs. This raises the question: do microfinance services influence the entrepreneurship development? Surprisingly, the influence of microfinance intermediation and microfinance services on entrepreneurship development remains unexplored. Hence, the current chapter aims to cover this knowledge gap by examining the influence of microfinance on entrepreneurship development.

The remainder of the chapter is structured as follows: After providing an introduction and background, critical review of microfinance and entrepreneurship development is presented. Then a detailed discussion of the role of microfinance in entrepreneurship development and its significance is discussed. Following that is recommendations and solutions, future areas of research and the chapter ends with conclusion.

BACKGROUND

Few recent ideas have generated as much hope for alleviating poverty in low-income countries as the idea of microfinance. Microfinance promises both to combat poverty and to develop the institutional capacity of financial systems through finding ways to lend cost-effectively money to poor households (Morduch, 1999). Confronting the schism between rhetoric and action and between financially minded donors and socially minded programs will first require that both donors and practitioners pay greater attention to who is being served (Woller, Dunford & Woodworth, 1999; Rhyne, 1998).

Government economic and social policies, as well as the development level of the financial sector, influence microfinance organizations in the delivery of financial services to the poor. Understanding these factors and their effect on microfinance is called assessing the country context. This process asks the following questions:

- Who are the suppliers of financial services? What products and services do they supply? What role do governments and donors play in providing financial services to the poor?
- How do existing financial sector policies affect the provision of financial services, including interest rate policies, government mandates for sectored credit allocation, and legal enforcement policies?
- What forms of financial sector regulation exist, and are MFIs subject to these regulations?
- What economic and social policies affect the provision of financial services and the ability of micro entrepreneurs to operate?

As can be seen in figure 1, contextual factors affect how suppliers of financial intermediation reach their clients. This chapter uses a macroeconomic approach to place microfinance in the overall context of entrepreneurship development and so make clear how important macro-level policy and regulation are for developing microfinance providers and micro enterprises. Practitioners and donors need to examine the financial system to locate needs and opportunities for providing microfinance services. Analyzing the country context reveals whether changes in policy or in the legal framework are needed to allow more efficient markets to emerge.

Figure 1. Country Context

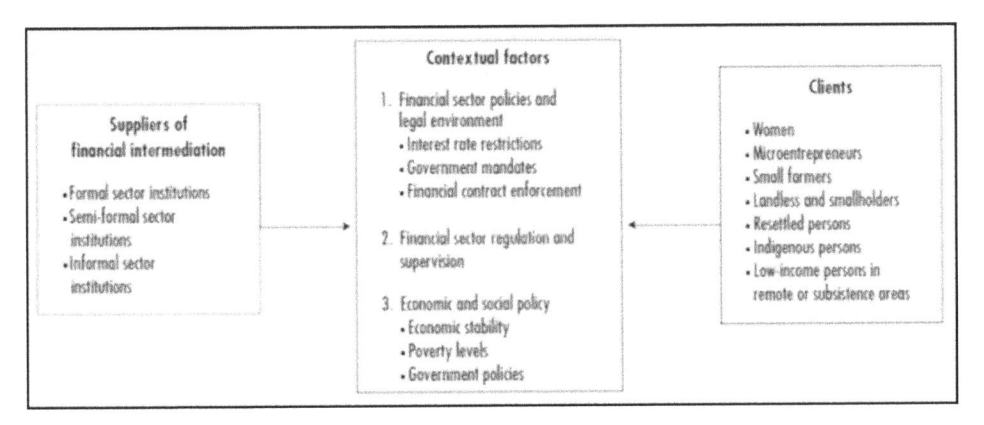

Methodology and Approach

The chapter reviewed literature on different approaches used by researchers in the struggle to understand the role of microfinance for entrepreneurship development and also define micro fiancé in the context of entrepreneurship development. It critically examines the concept of microfinance and explains what is micro finance, risk in microfinance, role of micro finance on entrepreneurship and entrepreneurship development. It also attempts provide solutions and recommendations as to how microfinance can optimize in entrepreneurship development and provides future research questions that will do justice to the development and simplification of the complexity of entrepreneurship development.

MICROFINANCE THEORY

Microfinance arose in the 1980s as a response to doubts and research findings about state delivery of subsidized credit to poor farmers. In the 1970s government agencies were the predominant methods of providing productive credit to those with no previous access to credit facilities. In addition to providing subsidized agricultural credit, donors set up credit unions inspired by the Raiffeisen model developed in Germany in 1864. The focus of these cooperative financial institutions was mostly on savings mobilization in rural areas in an attempt to "teach poor farmers how to save." Beginning in the mid-1980s, the subsidized, targeted credit model supported by many donors was the object of steady criticism, because most programs accumulated large loan losses and required frequent recapitalization to continue operating. It became more and more evident that market-based solutions were required. This led to a new approach that considered microfinance as an integral part of the overall financial system.

Thus, microfinance as a concept has been defined in various ways in the extant literature and there is no universally accepted definition of microfinance. The major reason for such various definitions is that microfinance is a broad concept that is multi-dimensional and dynamic. Bernard, Kevinb, & Khinc, (2017) defined microfinance as the small-scale financial services given to low income clients so that they can provide services and produce goods. It is important to mention that credit and savings are common small-scale financial services that can be given to the poor. Micro insurance and micro money transfer can also be provided to low-income clients by microfinance institutions (Akinbola, Ogunnaike, & Tijani, 2013). As per the definition of Consultative Group to Assist the Poor (CGAP) (2012), microfinance refers to the provision of small-scale financial services to the poor especially those who are excluded from the conventional financial organizations. These people include owners of SMEs (Karlan & Goldberg, 2011; Zingoni, 2010). Moreover, Bangoura, (2012) defined microfinance as the provision of financial services to low-income earners, poor and self-employed people so that they can meet their normal financial needs and also seize economic opportunities. Based on the above different definitions of microfinance, it is salient to observe that micro finance is a complex, multifaceted, and relative concept.

Rationale for Microfinance Growth

Microfinance is growing for several reasons:

1. *The promise of reaching the poor.* Microfinance activities can support income generation for enterprises operated by low-income households.
2. *The promise of financial sustainability.* Microfinance activities can help to build financially self-sufficient, subsidy-free, often locally managed institutions.
3. *The potential to build on traditional systems.* Microfinance activities sometimes mimic traditional systems (such as rotating savings and credit associations). They provide the same services in similar ways, but with greater flexibility, at a more affordable price to microenterprises and on a more sustainable basis. This can make microfinance services very attractive to a large number of low-income clients.
4. *The contribution of microfinance to strengthening and expanding existing formal financial systems.* Microfinance activities can strengthen existing formal financial institutions, such as savings and loan cooperatives, credit union networks, commercial banks, and even state-run financial institutions,

by expanding their markets for both savings and credit—and, potentially, their profitability.

5. *The growing number of success stories.* There are an increasing number of well-documented, innovative success stories in settings as diverse as rural Bangladesh, urban Bolivia, and rural Mali. This is in stark contrast to the records of state-run specialized financial institutions, which have received large amounts of funding over the past few decades but have failed in terms of both financial sustainability and outreach to the poor.

6. *The availability of better financial products because of experimentation and innovation.* The innovations that have shown the most promise are solving the problem of lack of collateral by using group-based and character-based approaches; solving problems of repayment discipline through high frequency of repayment collection, the use of social and peer pressure, and the promise of higher repeat loans; solving problems of transaction costs by moving some of these costs down to the group level and by increasing outreach; designing staff incentives to achieve greater outreach and high loan repayment; and providing savings services that meet the needs of small savers.

Risks of Microfinance

Microfinance faces market and other systemic risks. These risks need to be managed to ensure a portfolio meets its objectives. However, risk can also be managed if this risk is first quantified. There are many types of investment risks, both at the portfolio level and the individual security level. Figure 2 gives the types of investments risks.

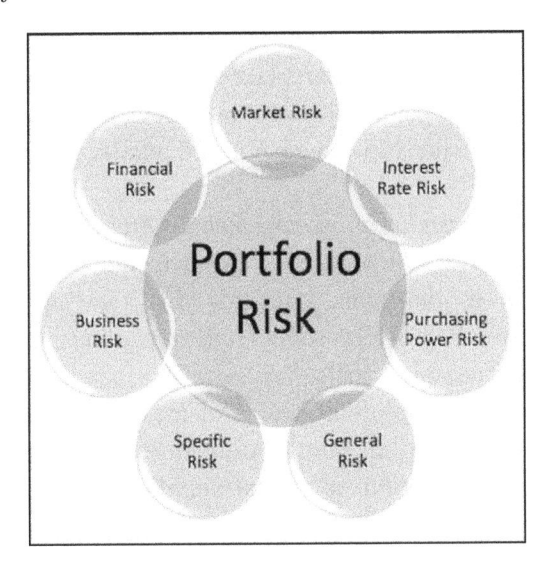

Figure 2. Types of Risks

Following are examples of risks that are specific to individual securities like, liquidity, default, regulatory, political, duration, style risks and these risks can easily be managed through diversification. These broader portfolio risks can affect the entire portfolio. Hence, managing these risks requires more creative diversification and other strategies. However, the four main areas of risk that are specific to MFIs are portfolio risk, ownership and governance, management, and "new industry." A brief discussion of each risk follows.

Portfolio risk: Portfolio risk reflects the overall risk for a portfolio of investments. It is the combined risk of each individual investment within a portfolio. The different components of a portfolio and their weightings contribute to the extent to which the portfolio is exposed to various risks. The greatest risk facing any portfolio is market risk. This is also known as systematic risk. Most assets correlate to some extent. The result is that a stock market crash will result in most stocks falling. In fact, most financial assets will lose value during a bear market. At the other end of the risk spectrum is inflation risk. A portfolio's buying power will not keep up with inflation this risk. Thus, the reason a portfolio needs to include *"risky assets"* and risk needs to be managed. Over the long term, owning risky assets allows you to outperform inflation. portfolio risks include: external business risks (industry disruption, mergers and acquisitions, economic conditions, political environments, regulatory changes, new legal requirements, natural events such as COVID-19), internal business risks (such as operational challenges, leadership and organizational changes, weak portfolio governance, and company financial health), and execution related risks (major project risks that impact two or more other projects, project dependencies, limited resource capacity, and weak project management standards).

Ownership and Governance: Although effective external regulation and supervision by regulatory bodies are important to the health of the financial system, no amount of external oversight can replace accountability that stems from proper governance and supervision performed by the owners of financial institutions. Critical issues of ownership and governance relative to adequate supervision of MFIs are:

- *Adequate oversight of management.* Often, investors in MFIs are motivated by social objectives. As a result, they may not hold this investment to the same standards that they apply to commercial investments. Regulators should encourage meaningful participation of private investors, particularly local business leaders. These private investors are an important source of local governance and a valuable resource if the MFI encounters difficulties. Furthermore, MFIs benefit from the participation of several significant shareholders who bring

- *Organizational and ownership structures.* If a social organization, which is funded with public resources and does not have owners, oversees the management and determines the policies of the regulated financial intermediary, social objectives may take priority over financial objectives. This may make it difficult to determine the true performance of the regulated financial intermediary, hindering bank regulators from gaining an accurate financial profile of the regulated entity. Successful arrangements between the social organization (the nongovernmental organization) and the regulated MFI can be attained if the structure adheres to certain basic principles, including transparency, arm's-length transactions, honest transfer pricing, and operational independence. The regulated MFI must maintain independent management and oversight of its financial services. Regulators can require that the composition of the MFI's board of directors include professional individuals who are prepared to define sound policies and to oversee management. All directors should be held legally liable for the performance of the MFI, as is the case for directors of private sector companies.
- *Sufficient financial depth.* MFIs may be capable of raising the initial capital requirements from their founding shareholders. However, these owners may lack the financial depth or the motivation to respond to additional calls for capital as required. Development institutions may require a lengthy approval process to secure disbursement of funds. Regulators can introduce measures to compensate for the owners' limited capacity to provide additional capital. This can be addressed by the following options: establishing additional reserve funds, limiting dividend distribution until capital benchmarks are reached, and requiring standby financing commitments by MFI owners.

Management Risks: The management risks that apply to MFIs are generated by the specific methods of providing financial services.
- *Decentralized operational systems.* A decentralized organizational structure that permits the provision of financial services directly at the borrower's or savers location is central to microfinance. Consequently, senior management must train and supervise midlevel management, introduce appropriate reporting systems, and maintain adequate communication systems so that uniform policies and procedures are adopted. Furthermore, decentralized operating methods create

an environment that can easily be subject to fraudulent practices. Regulators should require MFIs to maintain strong internal auditing capabilities and aggressive internal auditing procedures. Guidelines should be established for the performance of external audits for MFIs. Finally, adequate measures of internal communications and financial controls are essential.
- *Management efficiency.* MFIs offer a high-volume, repetitive service that operates on very tight margins. If funds are not relenting promptly, earnings will suffer. Regulators should ensure a high quality of management to ensure that brisk and timely services are provided.
- *Management information.* Decentralized operating methods, high volume of short-term loans, rapid portfolio turnover, and the requirement for efficient service delivery make accurate and current portfolio information essential for effective MFI management. In general, MFIs have not focused on providing adequate and appropriate financial information for making judgments about their financial viability. Reporting requirements for regulated institutions make it necessary for MFIs to be able to produce accurate, useful, and timely management information.

New Industry: A number of the risks that face MFIs stem from the fact that microfinance is a relatively new field. Formal financial services may also be new to the micro market.
- *Growth management.* MFIs that expand into new markets often face little competition. These institutions can experience dramatic growth in their initial years of operation. Regulators should closely monitor MFIs that dramatically surpass the growth projections presented in the license application.
- *New products and services.* Although this industry has made considerable advances in the design of appropriate microfinance products and services, the field remains relatively young and untested. It is difficult to assess when a new product or service is an ill-conceived deviation from an existing model or a breakthrough in new services for the market. New products and services must be well tested before being implemented on a broad scale. It may be appropriate to limit the number of new products or services that are introduced at any one time. The challenge facing MFIs is to conduct a large volume of very small transactions and to do so sustainably. Given this challenge, it is most appropriate to limit MFIs to relatively simple products and services that can be easily mastered.

Sound microfinance activities based on best practices play a decisive role in providing the poor with access to financial services through sustainable institutions. However, there have been many more failures than successes:

- Some MFIs target a segment of the population that has no access to business opportunities because of lack of markets, inputs, and demand. Productive credit is of no use to such people without other inputs.
- Many MFIs never reach either the minimal scale or the efficiency necessary to cover costs.
- Many MFIs face non-supportive policy frameworks and daunting physical, social, and economic challenges.
- Some MFIs fail to manage their funds adequately enough to meet future cash needs and, as a result, they confront a liquidity problem. Others develop neither the financial management systems nor the skills required to run a successful operation.
- Replication of successful models has at times proved difficult, due to differences in social contexts and lack of local adaptation.

Ultimately, most of the dilemmas and problems encountered in microfinance have to do with how clear the organization is about its principal goals. Does an MFI provide microfinance to lighten the heavy burdens of poverty or to encourage economic growth? Or to help poor women develop confidence and become empowered within their families? And so on. In a sense, goals are a matter of choice; and in development, an organization can choose one or many goals -provided its constituents, governance structure, and funding are all in line with those goals.

Generic View of the Microenterprise Sector

Some governments recognize the positive contribution of microenterprises to the economy and may actively include informal sector development in the national plan. However, in many countries informal sector issues and their relationship to government policy receive little attention. Most policy frameworks favor large manufacturing sectors and have bias against the informal sector and small enterprises. Most governments want to encourage the development of businesses in their countries. Some governments supplement general policy goals that apply to business with specific policies and programs aimed at micro and small enterprises. It is helpful if policies are in place that establishes a favorable climate for the start-up of new businesses and the growth of existing businesses. Examples are policies that minimize the costs of licensing and registering a business, provide easy access to information about laws and regulations, and facilitate commercial codes, which establish rules to minimize the cost of doing business by defining the rights and responsibilities of all parties to a transaction (USAID 1995).

The decision of governments to become actively involved in microenterprise development through credit programs or other enterprise development services can affect the environment for private microfinance providers, either by negatively distorting the market or by positively contributing to the supply of services. Alternatively, governments can choose to support the informal sector through macro policies, the allocation of resources that affect micro production, or work with NGOs that provide services and training. "Active collaboration in this sense involves the establishment of a favorable climate to enable these institutions to continue and expand their work with support but no interference from government entities. This can include national recognition of the microenterprise sector, support to discuss the issue, funding research, and scaling up pilot programs." (Stearns & Otero 1990. p. 27)

Microenterprises and small businesses may be affected by government policies, including excessive regulation, prohibitive levels of taxation, inadequate government protection against cheap imported products, laxity about black markets (which results in unfair competition for the micro business sector), and harassment by government officials for operating businesses on the streets, and inadequate services and high user fees in public market structures. Many of these regulations work effectively to encourage microenterprises to remain outside the legal or formal mainstream.

ENTREPRENERUSHIP

Entrepreneurship has been recognized as an important aspect and functioning of organization and economies (Dickson et al, 2008). It contributes in an immeasurable ways toward creating new job, wealth creation, poverty reduction, and income generating for both government and individuals (Baporikar, 2016). Schumpeter in 1934 argued that entrepreneurship is very significant to the growth and development of economies (Keister, 2005). Entrepreneurship is one of the most important economic growth and development factors of countries. The mechanism of entrepreneurship and its effects on the performance of countries are less known (Thurik and Wennekers, 2004). Entrepreneurship creates new opportunities for entrepreneurs to increase their income and assets. In addition, by creation of new institutions and small and medium businesses, it improves living standards (Henley, 2005).

In recent years, entrepreneurship has become a term that has primarily focus by politicians and they refer to its importance, while the entrepreneurship quality and policies have been less focused (Ahmad & Hoffmann, 2008). Sometimes self-employed person by criterion of non-payment of wages by individuals or organizations is also an entrepreneur and the entry rate of these companies as entrepreneurship (Gartner & Shane, 1995). Bird (1988) considers entrepreneurship process by focus on the opportunity of a strategic process with the ability to make quick decisions in a changing or flexible environment (Bird, 1988). Ireland et al. (2003) argue entrepreneurship process is linear and sequential that includes mind of the entrepreneur, management of resources to deal with the situation, creativity, innovation and competitive advantage. People may choose a business different from the one they socialized into (Chakraborty et al., 2016). Coduras et al. (2016) argue the main variables of entrepreneurial profiles have been grouped into three categories including sociological, psychological and managerial-entrepreneurial. The concept of entrepreneurship initiated from economic schools and it was extended to psychology, sociology and management schools. There are differences in the definitions of entrepreneurship among researchers of a particular school, a difference seen in ideas of Kirzner & Schumpeter (Metcalfe, 2004). Kirzner discuss that some people identify existing information in the market (Shane, 2000). Schumpeter contends that entrepreneurs (Hayton et al., 2011) create opportunities. An opportunity is seen because of creative ability of an individual who introduces innovations to the market (Scheiner, 2014).

Measurement of entrepreneurship is difficult, because it is a multi-dimensional concept (Wang et al., 2015). Due to the various definitions and measurements, entrepreneurship is a multifaceted concept (Iversen et al., 2008), while specifying entrepreneurs' share of economic prosperity dependents on the perception of entrepreneurship actions within the specified time framework (Gartner and Shane, 1995). Thus, creating entrepreneurship quality index leads to identification a wide range of effective economic, social, political and organizational factors that have impact on entrepreneurship with high quality. Measurement of entrepreneurship quality would be enabled researchers to explore the critical role of high quality entrepreneurship in economic growth in general and rural development in particular (Cheng et al., 2009).

Many studies have been conducted on entrepreneurship of small businesses, whereas some issues have remained unknown. Previous studies have provided evidences for distinguishing between self-employment, business ownership, new business creation and entrepreneurship (Urbano & Aparicio, 2016). Hjorth & Holt (2016) focus on social side of entrepreneurship and argue that entrepreneurship is different from enterprise, as the management is not leadership. Although there is an overlapping among definitions of entrepreneurship and creation of small businesses; small businesses are not always entrepreneurship companies and their owners are not always entrepreneurs (Carland et al., 1984). Small firms are more frequent incubators of entrepreneurs due to less hierarchical. Hierarchy is less prevalent in small businesses and is associated with frequent transitions of employees into self-employment and entrepreneurship (Tåg et al., 2016). In any definition, entrepreneurship is a behavior and a dynamic phenomenon requires the provision of necessary conditions (Cheraghali, 2011). There is wide literature on small units providing different definitions on this concept worldwide. These definitions vary given the age, demographic, and cultural structures and level of development (Institute for Business Studies and Research, 2005). Since recognizing the importance of small businesses in the 1920s, no comprehensive and single definition until date exists (Talebi, 2007).

ENTREPRENEURSHIP DEVELOPMENT

Entrepreneurship development is an evolving process. It requires entrepreneurs taking advantage of the opportunities and is affected by various components. This requires the structure and following the planed supportive functions and providing appropriate areas. Entrepreneurship development in quick-impact enterprises is a process seeking for profitability, employment, innovation, adaptability, flexibility, customer and staff satisfaction, regional welfare development, challenging opportunities, environmental protection, the commercialization of ideas and localization to develop the region. According to the results, the effective factors in the quick-impact enterprises include management skills, knowledge management use, business environment, self-managed trainings, and policies of government. Regarding entrepreneurship process, the components of entrepreneurship development are affected by three elements of individual, environment, and enterprise-related factors hence, entrepreneurship development should be viewed as a process. It should be noted that none of these three elements individually can lead to entrepreneurship development. Moreover, entrepreneurship should not be viewed only through an economic lens but also through social and environmental.

According to entrepreneurship characteristics, there is a range of factors rooted on different variables to deter entrepreneurship development. Figure 3 gives the range of factors that determine entrepreneurship development.

Figure 3. Range of Factors in Entrepreneurship Development

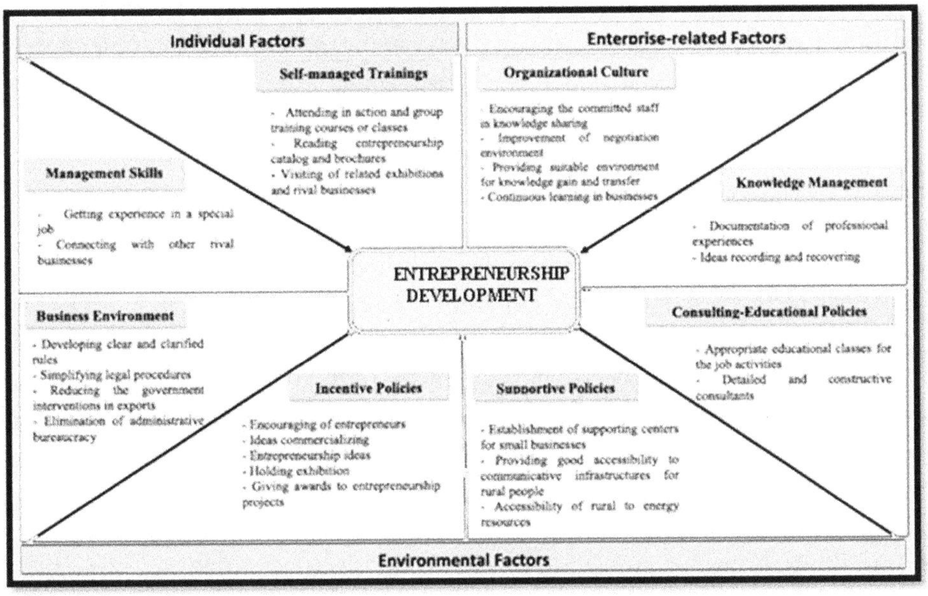

Entrepreneurship Development and SMEs Concept

Entrepreneurship development and SMEs concept though very crucial is yet of great importance to note that there no one-size-fits-all definition in the extant literature. The heterogeneity of entrepreneurship development SMEs definitions can be attributed to different sources of such definitions, which include definitions of SMEs by scholars, definitions of SME by industry, definitions of SMEs by national laws, and definitions of SMEs by international institutions (Berisha & Pula, 2015; Muriithi, 2017; Nyathi, Nyoni, Nyoni & Bonga, 2018). Undoubtedly, the most used SME definition criteria in the available literature are quantitative criteria such as total annual revenue and number of employees at the expense of qualitative criteria such as the unity of leadership and capital, and personal principle (Baporikar, 2018; Berisha & Pula 2015; Tinarwo, 2016). According to Muriithi (2017), SMEs refer to enterprises with the number of employees, which is less than 250. However, SMEs in Canadians and United States refer to enterprises with the number of employees, which is less than 500 while small enterprises are businesses with less than 100 employees (Muriithi, 2017). According to Katua (2014), SMEs in Belgium refers to businesses with not more than 100 employees whereas SMEs in Germany have an upper limit of 250 employees. Based on the above definitions, it is salient to observe that SME is a relative concept since the number of people employed by the enterprises varies from one sector to another and in turn, this complicates the comparisons of SMEs across sectors (Baporikar, 2018b). Thus, entrepreneurship development and SMEs as a concept is defined in various ways in the existing stream of literature.

The next section deals with microenterprises which is the where the microfinance has a vital role to play.

Types of Microenterprises

In addition to determining the characteristics of the population group to be served by the Micro Finance Intermediation (MFI), it is also important to consider the types of activities in which the target market is active and the level of development of the enterprise being financed. This will further define the types of products and services suitable for the MFI's market. Enterprises vary by whether they are existent or start-up businesses; unstable, stable, or growing; and involved in production, commercial, or service activities as given in figure four.

Figure 4. Types of Enterprises
Source: Goldberg & Ramanathan, (2008).

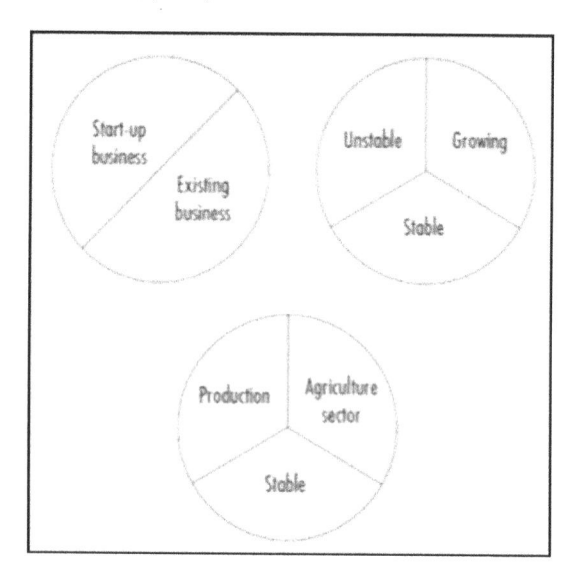

Existing or Start-Up Microenterprises

When identifying a target market, an MFI needs to consider whether it will focus on entrepreneurs already operating a microenterprise or on entrepreneurs (or potential entrepreneurs) who need financial services to start a business and possibly some form of business training. Working capital is the most common constraint identified by entrepreneurs of *existing microenterprises*. To access working capital, micro entrepreneurs often borrow from informal financial sources, such as family or friends, suppliers, or a local moneylender. Usually moneylenders charge relatively high interest rates and may not offer loan products or terms suited to the borrower. The ability to both borrow and save with an MFI may increase micro entrepreneurs' profits (through lower interest rates and access to appropriately designed loan products) and improve their ability to manage working capital needs (through borrowing and saving at different times as required).

Profits can also be increased through the acquisition of capital assets, such as sewing machines or rickshaws. Access to continued financial services, including loans for capital purchases and savings services to build up reserves, allows micro entrepreneurs to increase their asset base and improve their ability to generate revenue. There are many advantages to working with existing micro entrepreneurs. Active businesses have a history of success, which greatly reduces the risk to the MFI. Furthermore, existing micro entrepreneurs have the potential to grow and create employment opportunities. However, some may have other debts (to moneylenders, suppliers, family, or other MFIs), which they may pay off with the proceeds of new loans, thereby increasing the risk of default to the new lender. MFIs that target potential entrepreneurs often have poverty alleviation as an objective. The belief is that by aiding potential entrepreneurs to *start up* their own businesses, they will increase their incomes and consequently reduce their level of poverty. However, potential entrepreneurs often need more than financial services. Many need skills training or other inputs to make their enterprises a success. When there are significant barriers to entry into certain fields (due to minimum investment requirements, technology levels, and market contacts), an integrated approach can prepare potential entrepreneurs prior to taking on debt. However, the impact of training courses and technical assistance does not have a clear link to increased production, profitability, job creation, and reinvestment (Baporikar, & Akino, 2020).

If services are subsidized, it can be difficult to remove these subsidies and put the enterprise on an equal footing with local competitors. In addition, training programs often assume that anyone can become an entrepreneur, which is not the case, because not everyone is willing to take the risks inherent in owning and operating a business (Baporikar, 2018b; 2017). Furthermore, training courses linked to credit access sometimes assume that entrepreneurs cannot contribute their own equity and that credit should be arranged for 100 percent of the investment. Most MFIs prefer to focus on existing businesses, with perhaps a small portion of their portfolio invested in start-up businesses, thereby reducing their risk. This is again dependent on their objectives and the trade-off between increased costs (and lower loan sizes) for startup businesses, on the one hand, and sustainability, on the other.

Level of Business Development

The level of business development is another consideration when identifying tends to share some characteristics and face similar problems. Most have both production and risk-taking experience, keep minimal accounting records, and usually do not pay taxes. In addition, they often have little or no formal management experience. Other similarities include:

- *Product line and labor.* Firms that produce a single product or line of products serving a narrow range of market outlets and clients tend to use labor-intensive production techniques and rely on family and apprentice labor.
- *Working capital and fixed asset management.* These firms build their asset base slowly, in an ad hoc manner. They depend largely on family credit for initial investment capital and on informal sector loans for working capital. Cash flow is a constant concern, and they are very sensitive to output and raw material price changes. They often use second-hand equipment. Growth-oriented microenterprises may be an attractive target group, because they offer potential for job creation and vocational training within the community. They can resemble formal sector enterprises in terms of fixed assets, permanence, and planning, which offers the potential for physical collateral and more thorough business analysis. All these offset risk for the MFI. However, selecting growth-oriented microenterprises can require a more involved approach on the part of the MFI. Growth-oriented businesses may need some or all of the following services:
- Assistance in choosing new product lines and value added services
- Working capital and sometimes longer-term investment credit
- Accounting systems to track costs
- Marketing advice to help find new markets.

Type of Business Activity

While the level of business development is an important consideration when identifying a target market, the economic sector of activities is also important. Enterprises can generally be divided among three primary sectors: production, services, and agriculture. Each sector has its own specific risks and financing needs, which directly influence the choices made by the MFI and the products and services provided. Depending on the MFI's objectives, selecting a target market based on the business sector allows it to clearly differentiate its products and influence the type of activities in a given area. Once a target market has been identified, the MFI needs to design its products and services to meet the types of microenterprise to

Role of Microfinance in Entrepreneurship Development

which an MFI wishes to provide financial services. This is closely linked with the level of poverty existing in a potential target market. There are typically three levels of business development of microenterprises that benefit from access to financial services:

- *Unstable survivors,* with operators who have not found other employment and tend to have very unstable enterprises for a limited time. Unstable survivors comprise the group most difficult to provide financial services to in a sustainable fashion; because loan sizes tend to remain small and the risk of business, failure is high. Focusing on unstable survivors as a target market can result in a great deal of time spent with the clients just to ensure that their businesses will survive and that they will continue to be able to make loan payments. Some technical assistance may also be required, resulting in further time and cost increases. In addition, unstable survivors often need credit for consumption-smoothing rather than income-generating activities. Depending on the objectives of the MFI, these stopgap loans may or may not be appropriate. Generally, the debt capacity of unstable survivors does not increase. Accordingly, the MFI is limited in its attempts to reduce costs or increase revenue, because loan sizes remain small. While not all MFIs have the immediate goal of reaching financial self-sufficiency, over the long term the choice to focus on unstable survivors will likely be a time-bound strategy, because access to donor funding may be limited.
- *Stable survivors,* with operators for whom the microenterprise provides a modest but decent living while rarely growing. Stable survivors comprise the group that many MFIs focus on and for which access to a permanent credit supply is vital. This is the group that benefits from access to financial services to meet both production and consumption needs, while not necessarily requiring other inputs from the MFI. Stable survivors are targeted by microfinance providers with poverty reduction objectives. For these businesses, returns on labor are relatively low and market imperfections and near monophony conditions may result in uneven bargaining positions. Stable survivors are often women who simultaneously maintain family-related activities (providing food, water, cooking, medicine, and child care) while engaging in income-generating activities. Seasonal changes and household life cycles often force such people to consume rather than invest in the business. Generally, profits are low, leading to low reinvestment, low output, and a high level of vulnerability. Profits remain low due to:
- The unspecialized nature of the product
- The lack of timely and complete market information (beyond the local market)
- Underdeveloped infrastructure facilities

- The lack of value-added services (such as packaging)
- The number of producers with similar products.

Experiences with this target group have demonstrated both advantages and disadvantages. Advantages may include:

- The high poverty impact of a financial services project, since these enterprises are run by poor households
- High repayment, due to limited access to alternative sources of credit and the economic, social, and financial costs of those alternatives
- Effective savings services, since there are rarely secure, liquid alternative forms of savings that offer a return for the operators of these enterprises (they also help to smooth consumption for poor households)
- A general willingness to work with new credit technologies (such as groups) as an alternative to tangible collateral.

Disadvantages may include:

- Little or no new job creation resulting from support to these enterprises
- Limited growth potential or high covariance risk, because many entrepreneurs are active in the same businesses (financing them may create excess competition,
- meaning that the loan portfolio has to grow by increasing the number of clients rather than increasing loan amounts to good clients)
- Difficulty in mobilizing long-term savings, since households are accustomed to seasonal savings buildup and liquidation cycles.

Having understood the vital role of entrepreneurship in economic development, it become apparent that careful attention is needed to invest and promote entrepreneurship.

IMPLICATIONS

Based on findings, any government would be able to enhance and strengthen the implementation of microfinance policies by holding formal and informal training sessions such as seminars and panels, establishment of various centers in line with consulting of entrepreneurship businesses and forming entrepreneurship sites. Broadcasting related programs in public media, giving annual awards to micro entrepreneurs' businesses and entrepreneurship projects, adopting special terms and privileges for organizations supporting of entrepreneurship development projects, holding exhibitions and creating the conditions for small businesses, and holding small businesses achievement exhibitions are some suggestions to encourage entrepreneurs as well as their knowledge improvement. Improving the business environment, it is recommended that clear rules to be developed to monitor issues such as licensing and receiving facilities, simplifying procedures, reducing the time and costs of the implementation of the components of the business environment, especially the efficiency of the judicial system and reduced government intervention in export and elimination of administrative bureaucracies.

SOLUTIONS AND RECOMMENDATIONS

For quick-impact and enterprises development and maintain business cycle in initial years of their activity, micro financing needs to have clear policies and procedures. Adopting fintech approach would also aid time, cost effectiveness to financing for both the lender, and borrow (Baporikar, 2021). According to these cases, capital is seen as a very important in order to keep the business cycle and the improving other components, especially at the beginning of enterprises. Therefore, obtaining loans and financing are suggested to be in the priority, followed by commercialization of ideas and innovation. The impact of knowledge management and management skills on entrepreneurship development confirms that development of entrepreneurship in quick-impact enterprises is based on management and using of knowledge (Baporikar, 2020a; 2020c; 2018). In other words, these enterprises are knowledge-based. According to the analysis, knowledge management explains part of the changes in business entrepreneurship development quick-impact enterprises. So small businesses should be leading in obtaining correct information in various fields and they should seize the information more quickly and effective than their rivals so that they can provide a base for development of entrepreneurship sustainable competitive advantage. Information technology as a tool of information distribution by the businesses is essential as these tools enable managers to transfer data into information and then into knowledge, and start to planning and budgeting based on scientific principles (Baporikar, & Shikokola, 2020). Encouraging staff that have great role in knowledge development is highly recommended in order to share implicit and internal knowledge, a negotiation atmosphere would shape informal chats in the form of discussions, and debate since it paves for acquisition and transfer of knowledge (Baporikar, 2018a; 2020b). Creating a culture of continuous learning in the business improves capabilities and abilities in the business and overall enhances the societal cognitive abilities, and this can lead into obtaining information and knowledge in various fields of business such as market conditions, the purchase and advertising (Baporikar, 2015).

In the extant empirical literature, research on the relationship between the business owner's age and entrepreneurial success has yielded conflicting results. Lucas (2017) carried out quantitative research in Kenya on the influence of demographic and social factors on performance of Micro, Small and Medium Enterprises (MSMEs). The results of the study revealed that the age of the business owner has a positive influence on performance of MSMEs. Akinyemi, Alarape, & Erinfolani, (2017) conducted another study in Kenya on the association between socio-demographic factors on performance of SMEs using a sample size of 500 business owners. The study found that there is a positive link between the age of business owners and performance of SMEs. Nonethelesss, Gielnik, Zacher, & Frese (2012) carried out a study in Germany using a sample size of 84 small business owners and they found that the age of business owners has a negative influence on venture growth. Another critical issue is the education level and entrepreneurial success and that leads to real entrepreneurship development. Education level has been widely recognized within the current entrepreneurship literature as an important demographic variable that can predict entrepreneurial success. Level of education refers to the highest level of formal education an individual has completed. Radipere & Dhliwayo (2014) conducted a study in South Africa on the role of education level and gender on business performance using a sample size of 500 SMEs from the retail industry. The results showed that education level has a positive impact on performance of SMEs. On the contrary, Isaga (2015) carried out a study in Tanzania and found that the level of education of owners of SMEs does not influence business growth.

Based on the above discussion, some of the recommendations applicable for policymakers, management of microfinance institutions and owners of SMEs include:

- The government should provide adequate financial resources to MFI to support the growth of SMEs. Moreover, the government should also embark on mainstream impact assessment programs to measure the impact of microfinance on entrepreneurship.
- The management of microfinance entities should conduct awareness programs that focus on proper orientation on their unique and innovative products and services designed for entrepreneurs and how such products and services could augment the business performance of entrepreneurs.
- The management of microfinance organizations should provide the pre-requisite financial and management skills in a manner that supports the growth of SMEs.
- The SME owner-managers should attend seminars and workshops on financial literacy to acquire and augment their financial management skills.

FUTURE RESEARCH DIRECTIONS

It is imperative to mention that the current study opens new research opportunities. The current study is to understand the role of microfinance for entrepreneurship development in general and the generalization to various kinds or specific sector of entrepreneurship development is limited. Accordingly, there is need to undertake country based studies to assess and compare the impact of microfinance on entrepreneurial development. Moreover, a comparative study among different countries especially countries in the Southern African Development Community (SADC) is required to effectively capture the regional context factors that influence entrepreneurial success and development. Reviewing previous studies, it is required to improve and develop the measurement methods of entrepreneurship and small businesses (Wang et al., 2015), because there is no comprehensive framework regarding the entrepreneurship process components. Thus, more entrepreneurship studies require theory development (Davidsson et al., 2001). Some other areas, which need exploration include:

- Assessment and monitoring of entrepreneurship activities in order to ensure optimization of returns for micro financing institutions;
- Evaluation of entrepreneurship activities based on the developed index of financing norms;
- Development of the microfinance index for evaluating of entrepreneurship activities globally.

CONCLUSION

The aim of the current study was to establish the influence of microfinance on entrepreneurial development. The discussion reveals that there is a strong positive relationship between microfinance and entrepreneurial development and success. Notably, this study adds value to the limited but growing literature on entrepreneurial development. More precisely, this research provides a critical debate on the role of microfinance for entrepreneurial development success. To conclude, microfinance and services thereto play a crucial role in promoting the entrepreneurs, enterprises development and entrepreneurial success apart from ensuring equitable social and economic development.

REFERENCES

Ahmad, N., & Hoffmann, A. N. (2008). A framework for addressing and measuring entrepreneurship. *OECD Statistics Working Paper, 2*, 2–36.

Akinyemi, F. O., Alarape, A. A., & Erinfolami, T. P. (2017). The impact of socio-demographic factors on performance of small and medium enterprises in Lagos State, Nigeria. *IFE Research Publications in Geography, 15*, 107–115.

Baporikar, N. (2015). Societal Influence on the Cognitive Aspects of Entrepreneurship. *International Journal of Civic Engagement and Social Change, 2*(4), 1–15. doi:10.4018/ijcesc.2015100101

Baporikar, N. (2016). *Handbook of Research on Entrepreneurship in the Contemporary Knowledge-Based Global Economy*. IGI Global. doi:10.4018/978-1-4666-8798-1

Baporikar, N. (2017). Cluster Approach for Entrepreneurship Development in India. *International Journal of Asian Business and Information Management, 8*(2), 46–61. doi:10.4018/IJABIM.2017040104

Baporikar, N. (2018a). *Knowledge Integration Strategies for Entrepreneurship and Sustainability*. IGI Global. doi:10.4018/978-1-5225-5115-7

Baporikar, N. (2018b). Entrepreneurship Development and Project Management (Text & Cases). Himalaya Publishing House.

Baporikar, N. (2019). Influence of Business Competitiveness on SMEs Performance. *International Journal of Productivity Management and Assessment Technologies, 7*(2), 1–25. doi:10.4018/IJPMAT.2019070101

Baporikar, N. (2020a). *Handbook of Research on Entrepreneurship Development and Opportunities in Circular Economy*. IGI Global. doi:10.4018/978-1-7998-5116-5

Baporikar, N. (2020b). Learning Link in Organizational Tacit Knowledge Creation and Dissemination. *International Journal of Sociotechnology and Knowledge Development, 12*(4), 70–88. doi:10.4018/IJSKD.2020100105

Baporikar, N. (2021). Fintech Challenges and Outlook in India. In Y. A. Albastaki, A. Razzaque, & A. M. Sarea (Eds.), *Innovative Strategies for Implementing FinTech in Banking* (pp. 136–153). IGI Global. doi:10.4018/978-1-7998-3257-7.ch008

Baporikar, N., & Akino, S. (2020). Financial Literacy Imperative for Success of Women Entrepreneurship. *International Journal of Innovation in the Digital Economy, 11*(3), 1–21. doi:10.4018/IJIDE.2020070101

Baporikar, N., & Shikokola, S. (2020). Information Technology Adoption Dynamics for SMEs in the Manufacturing Sector of Namibia. *International Journal of ICT Research in Africa and the Middle East, 9*(2), 60–77. doi:10.4018/IJICTRAME.2020070104

Chakraborty, S., Thompson, J. C., & Yehoue, E. B. (2016). The culture of entrepreneurship. *Journal of Economic Theory, 163*, 288–317.

Cheraghali, A. R. (2011). *Factors affecting the development of entrepreneurship in agricultural cooperatives* (Master's thesis). Entrepreneurship Department, Tehran University.

Coduras, A., Saiz-Alvarez, J. M., & Ruiz, J. (2016). Measuring readiness for entrepreneurship: An information tool proposal. *J Inn Knowledge, 1*(2), 99–108. doi:10.1016/j.jik.2016.02.003

Davidsson, P., Low, M., & Wright, M. (2001). Editors' introduction: Low and Macmillan ten years on–achievements and future directions for entrepreneurship research. *Entrepreneurship Theory and Practice, 25*(4), 5–16. doi:10.1177/104225870102500401

Gartner, W. B., & Shane, S. A. (1995). Measuring entrepreneurship over time. *Journal of Business Venturing, 10*(4), 283–301. doi:10.1016/0883-9026(94)00037-U

Gielnik, M. M., Zacher, H., & Frese, M. (2012). Focus on opportunities as a mediator of the relationship between business owners' age and venture growth. *Journal of Business Venturing, 27*(1), 127–142. doi:10.1016/j.jbusvent.2010.05.002

Goldberg, M., & Ramanathan, C. S. (2008). *Micro insurance matters in Latin America*. Academic Press.

Hansen, D. J., Lumpkin, G. T., & Hills, G. E. (2011). A multidimensional examination of a creativity-based opportunity recognition model. *International Journal of Entrepreneurial Behaviour & Research, 17*(5), 515–533. doi:10.1108/13552551111158835

Hayton, J., Chandler, G. N., & DeTienne, D. R. (2011). Entrepreneurial opportunity identification and new firm development processes: A comparison of family and non-family new ventures. *International Journal of Entrepreneurship and Innovation Management, 13*(1), 12–31. doi:10.1504/IJEIM.2011.038445

Institute for Business Studies and Research. (2005). *The role of clustering in increasing the competitiveness of small and medium-sized enterprises with a focus on marketing development*. Author.

Ireland, D. R., Hitt, M. A., & Sirmon, D. G. (2003). A model of strategic entrepreneurship: The construct and its dimensions. *Journal of Management, 29*(6), 963–989. doi:10.1016/S0149-2063(03)00086-2

Isaga, N. (2015). Owner-managers' demographic characteristics and the growth of Tanzanian small and medium enterprises. *International Journal of Business and Management, 10*(5), 168–181. doi:10.5539/ijbm.v10n5p168

Iversen, J., Jorgensen, R., & Malchow-Moller, N. (2008). Defining and measuring entrepreneurship. *Foundations Trends Entrepreneur, 4*(1), 1–63. doi:10.1561/0300000020

Lucas, S. (2017). The impact of demographic and social factors on firm performance in Kenya. *Journal of Business and Economic Development, 2*(4), 255–261.

Metcalfe, J. S. (2004). The entrepreneur and the style of modern economics. *Journal of Evolutionary Economics, 14*(2), 157–175. doi:10.100700191-004-0210-3

Morduch, J. (1999). The microfinance promise. *Journal of Economic Literature, 37*(4), 1569–1614. doi:10.1257/jel.37.4.1569

Radipere, S., & Dhliwayo, S. (2014). The role of gender and education on small business performance in the South African small enterprise sector. *Mediterranean Journal of Social Sciences, 5*(9), 104–110.

Rhyne, E. (1998). *The yin and yang of microfinance: reaching the poor and sustainability.* Micro Banking Bulletin.

Shane, S. (2000). Prior knowledge and the discovery of entrepreneurial opportunities. *Organization Science, 11*(4), 448–469. doi:10.1287/orsc.11.4.448.14602

Stearns, K., & Otero, M. (1990). *The Critical Connection: Governments.* Private Institutions, and the Informal Sector in Latin America.

Tåg, J., Åstebro, T., & Thompson, P. (2016). Hierarchies and entrepreneurship. *European Economic Review, 89*, 129–147. doi:10.1016/j.euroecorev.2016.06.007

Talebi, K. (2007). *Strategic role of small and medium enterprises in national development. Tehran.* University Press.

Thurik, R., & Wennekers, S. (2004). Entrepreneurship, small business and economic growth. *Journal of Small Business and Enterprise Development, 11*(1), 140–149. doi:10.1108/14626000410519173

Wang, M. C., & Fang, S. C. (2012). The moderating effect of environmental uncertainty on the relationship between network structures and the innovative performance of a new venture. *Journal of Business and Industrial Marketing, 27*(4), 311–323. doi:10.1108/08858621211221689

Woller, G., Dunford, C., & Woodworth, W. (1999). Where to microfinance? *International Journal of Economic Development.*

KEY TERMS AND DEFINITIONS

Business: Pertains broadly to commercial, financial, and industrial activities.

Challenges: Something that by its nature or character serves as a call to make a special effort, a demand to explain, justify, or difficulty in an undertaking that is stimulating to one engaged in it.

Competence: Refers to the capacity of individuals/employees to act in a wide variety of situations. It is their education, skills, experience, energy, and attitudes.

Development: Means 'steady progress' and stresses effective assisting in hastening a process or bringing about the desired end, a significant consequence or event, the act or process of growing, progressing, or developing.

Impact: To affect, the effect of coming into contact with a thing or person; the force exerted by a new idea, concept, technology, or ideology, the impression made by an idea, cultural movement, social group, it is to drive or press (an object) firmly into (another object, thing, etc.) to have an impact or strong effect (on).

Knowledge Development: The development of knowledge includes not only processes of external knowledge procurement (i.e., through cooperative efforts, consultants, new contacts, etc.) or the creation of specific knowledge resources like research and development departments.

Sustainability: Sustainability is the ability or capacity of something to maintain or to sustain itself.

Chapter 3
The Role of Microfinance in Africa:
A Review of Outcomes From Ghana and Nigeria

Yahaya Alhassan
https://orcid.org/0000-0001-6700-635X
University of Sunderland in London, UK

Francis Kuagbela
University of Sunderland in London, UK

Caesar D. Nurokina
University of Sunderland in London, UK

Bernard Appiah
University of Sunderland in London, UK

ABSTRACT

This chapter examines the role of microfinance in developing countries, particularly Ghana and Nigeria. The chapter begins with an overview of the link between microfinance, poverty, and women empowerment in the chapter introduction. The background to the chapter sets out the main difference between microfinance and microcredit. The role of microfinance in contemporary development finance is then discussed. In this context, existing literature on the role of microfinance in reducing poverty, women empowerment, and microenterprise growth is extensively reviewed. Key solutions and recommendations are then presented next, followed by future research direction and the chapter conclusion.

DOI: 10.4018/978-1-7998-7499-7.ch003

INTRODUCTION

Microfinance is intricately linked to poverty reduction in developing countries (Bakhtiari, 2011; Imai, et al., 2010; Nawaz, 2010; Chowdhury, 2009). For example, Kristof (2009) argue that microfinance is the most visible innovative policy for poverty reduction and financial inclusion in developing countries. Similarly, Bakhtiari (2011) has shown that access to microfinance can help low-income earners build their assets and improve their income earning capacity leading to an improvement in their quality of life. Likewise, using a cross country data in Bangladesh, Imai, et al. (2012) found that the provision of microfinance does not merely reduce the occurrence of poverty but also the intensity and severity of it. This view is consistent with Khandker and Samad (2013) who also discovered that the provision of microfinance could perhaps help users earn more income, thus helping them out of the cycle of poverty. Furthermore, microfinance has been reported to have alleviated poverty of women, considered marginalised in some societies in both developed and developing countries (Islam, 2012). However, according to Ebomuche, et al. (2014) the role of microfinance on poverty reduction is still unclear. In this context, Van Rooyen, et al. (2012) have found that microfinance has both positive and negative impact on poverty alleviation as their findings suggest that microfinance increases both capital and loan stocks of beneficiaries. Similarly, Bateman (2012) established that microfinance has rather left several rural communities with more debts, making them more impoverished than before. In fact, the author argues that even prominent advocates of microfinance now accept that microfinance has failed to impact poverty positively. The analysis and evaluation of the above studies suggest the role of microfinance on poverty alleviation is inconclusive and therefore requires rigorous evaluation to determine the exact impact of microfinance on poverty reduction.

The role of microfinance in women empowerment has also been reported by several studies (Islam, 2012; Rehman, et al., 2015; Sarumathi and Mohan, 2011). For instance, Sanyal (2009) suggests that microfinance plays a pivotal role in fostering women's social capital and influence in society. Similarly, Aruna and Jyothirmayi (2011) have shown that microfinance has a significant impact on the economic and social status of women. This is because microfinance creates employment opportunities for unemployed women thus increasing the level of their income and productive capacity. On the contrary, Khan and Noreen (2012) argue that microfinance has a positive impact on women empowerment only if the support provided by the microfinance institution is utilised by the beneficiary women and complemented by the provision of education. The implication of this is that microfinance can only empower women if it is provided together with training and the opportunity to use the support for productive purposes. This view is supported by Taimur and Hamid (2013) who also argue that the provision of microfinance in conjunction with education fosters women empowerment by improving the economic conditions and wellbeing of women. However, Kabeer (2005) argue that although microfinance has been found to have a positive impact on the economic productivity and wellbeing of women, it does not foster women empowerment automatically. The question then is how can the positive outcomes of microfinance such as improved social wellbeing and economic productivity be translated into women empowerment? Evidence of a positive relationship between microfinance and economic development in developing countries has also been reported by various studies (Sultan and Masih, 2016; Donou-Adonsou and Sylwester, 2017). The objective of this chapter therefore is to determine the role that microfinance play in reducing poverty, empowering women and fostering microbusiness and economic growth in Africa particularly Ghana and Nigeria.

Background

Is microfinance the same as microcredit? According to Bayulgen (2008), the terms microfinance and microcredit have often been wrongly used interchangeably. Using these terms interchangeably is not only wrong but also misleading as the terms refer to products and services provided to low-income earners but not credit and finance (Dowla and Alamgir, 2003). Microcredit, according to Islam (2012) comprises the provision of only credit. Accordingly, while microcredit is generally concerned with the provision of small loans to low-income earners to set up or develop their existing businesses, microfinance entails a far larger scope (Fant, 2011). Nasir (2012) suggest that microfinance involves the provision of financial services including small loans. The other financial services provided by microfinance institutions include savings, insurance, financial and business management training, payment services and deposits. In this context, Asher (2014) argue that microcredit is a component of microfinance. The implications of the close relationship between microcredit and microfinance are that selection of variables for any analysis of the impact of microfinance and microcredit may create confusion. For instance, any attempt to examine the impact of microcredit must be based only on the evaluation of credit. On the other hand, any microfinance impact study must examine credit, capacity building training, savings, deposits, insurance and payment service. Therefore, any attempt to use the same variables to evaluate the impact of microcredit and microfinance may be a grave methodological error.

Certainly, researchers who have tried to describe microfinance rather explained the services microfinance institutions provide which in actual sense differ depending on the provider and the context within which such services are provided. Microfinance according to Ledgerwood, et al. (2013) is a combination of financial services made up of loans and savings designed purposely to alleviate poverty. Equally, Ebomuche, et al. (2014) define microfinance as the provision of credit at higher interest rates to individuals who have no access to traditional banks. Moreover, microfinance has been described by Martin, et al. (2002) as the provision of credit, deposits and insurance to financially disadvantaged households and microbusinesses. Perhaps the differences that emerged from the various explanation of microfinance are due to the fairly new nature of the concept of microfinance. Therefore, it is reasonable to suggest that microfinance institutions are still trying different services in order to ascertain the right mix of services for reducing poverty, empowering women and promoting microbusiness and economic growth. Nevertheless, outcomes of analysis and evaluation of the various definitions offer a common basis for understanding microfinance. Overall, the outcomes of the review of the above definitions suggest that microfinance is designed to deliver credit and other financial services to people who have no access to traditional formal banks. In this regard, this chapter seeks to explore the role that microfinance has played in Africa particularly Ghana and Nigeria.

THE ROLE OF MICROFINANCE

Issues, Controversies, Problems

What is the role of microfinance in contemporary development finance? Is microfinance merely designed to reduce poverty as suggested by some researchers? (Quinones and Remenyi, 2014; Berhane and Gardebroek, 2011; Duong and Nghiem, 2014). Surely not, as several other studies (Khandke and Samad, 2013; Sanyal, 2009; Odebiyi and Olaoye, 2012; Rehman et al., 2015) have identified different roles of microfinance. For instance, Sarumathi and Mohan (2011) suggest that microfinance plays a vital role in women empowerment. However, Aggarwal, et al., (2012) discovered a crucial role for microfinance in small business financing. Moreso, Pathak and Gyawali (2012) found that microfinance provides opportunities for employment generation in rural communities.

Microfinance Outcomes on Poverty Reduction

Poverty has often been defined based on inequality factors in society. For instance, Lloyds-Jones and Rakodi (2014) described poverty as a situation where an individual's or a household's income is not sufficient to enable them to acquire goods and services required for a decent living. Similarly, Hagenaars (2014) defines poverty as a condition where households' needs are not adequately satisfied. Besides, Elhadary and Samat (2012) found that often the magnitude of poverty in a community is due to the failure of policymakers to address inequality factors in the community over a period of time. Perhaps, this is what prompted Hatta and Ali (2013) to suggest that poverty alleviation strategies are designed to provide resources to disadvantaged communities for the purpose of satisfying their basic needs adequately. Accordingly, Townsend (2014) argues that the IMF, the World Bank and other international organisations are known to have made concerted efforts to reduce poverty in several countries through financial grants and food aid. However, Alvi and Senbeta (2012) found that such handouts provide short term relief with very limited impact on poverty reduction in low-income households, particularly in developing countries.

Khan (2011) has shown that achieving greater financial inclusion is perhaps very important if the gap in poverty levels between the rich and poor is to be reduced. This view is supported by Ledgerwood (2013) as the author argues that providing credit to financially disadvantaged individuals could improve their income level and achieve food security. Similarly, Hermes and Lensink (2011) have found that increasing access to microcredit by low-income earners engenders greater economic and social benefits (increased income, assets accumulation, and better education) to such borrowers. Likewise, Milana and Ashta (2012) have demonstrated that the provision of microfinance can help create a workable project for poverty reduction. In this regard, Ayodele and Arogundade (2014) conclude that microfinance is perhaps the most potent strategy for promoting microbusinesses for low-income earners to move them out of poverty. Indeed, most microfinance schemes designed for microenterprise development are often aimed at reducing poverty (Arnold, 2012).

According to Quibria (2012) outcomes of microfinance projects have often been measured by their contribution to poverty reduction. Similarly, Bruhn and Love (2014) argue that microfinance positive outcomes are frequently determined by assessing the microfinance institution's ability to help low-income households and "unbanked individuals" out of poverty. For instance, the provision of microfinance in Eastern Europe has been found to have helped low-income earners increased their assets, level of income and standard of living (Hartarska, et al., 2013). Equally, other studies have also found that access to microfinance loans has led to increases in savings and per capita income of beneficiaries in both developed and developing countries (Imai, et al., 2012; Attanasio, et al., 2013; Iqbal, et al., 2015). More so, Khanker and Samad (2013) have demonstrated that the provision of microfinance in East Asia is helping financially disadvantaged people out of poverty annually. Perhaps, it is in this context that Quinones and Remenyi (2014) concludes that access to microfinance enables low-income earners to acquire goods and services required for a decent living.

Other studies, however, do not support the notion that the provision of microfinance always reduce poverty. For example, analysis of Duong and Nghiem (2014) suggest the provision of microfinance alone is unlikely to move people out of poverty. They argue that other factors such as the creation of jobs and good infrastructure are required together with microfinance in order to reduce poverty. Similarly, Van Rooyen, et al. (2012) have found that in some cases, access to microfinance can increase poverty due to the high-interest rates charged by microfinance institutions. Besides, Odell (2010) demonstrates that the expansion of microfinance to rural households in Bangladesh only increased household consumption but no significant impact on poverty alleviation. Furthermore, Crepon, et al. (2014) examined microfinance outcomes and found that in the short to medium term, microfinance positively impacted on the capital stock of micro entrepreneurs but showed no influence on poverty reduction. Perhaps, the negative outcomes of microfinance on poverty alleviation reported by various studies suggest that the use of microcredit as a poverty reduction strategy is increasingly diminishing. Besides, the implication of the negative experiences of microfinance experiments on poverty alleviation indicates that microfinance institutions are gradually becoming weak. Therefore, should microfinance be remodelled in line with Mersland and Strom (2014) sustainability paradigm to promote growth for microfinance institutions? May be, providing microfinance using the new sustainability model could yield positive results on poverty reduction and achieve greater financial inclusion in disadvantaged communities.

Outcomes of Microfinance Experiments Based on Sustainability

Microfinance institutions all over the world are spending huge sums of money, time and efforts to alleviate poverty by providing loans mainly to disadvantaged individuals and need to be continued (Islam, 2012). For instance, the International Finance Corporation alone have invested a cumulative amount of over $3.5 billion in microfinance as at 31st December 2014 (IFC, 2014). Besides, Tchuigoua (2014) suggest other international institutions provide over $1 billion every year to microfinance institutions around the world. Analysis and evaluation of existing literature on microfinance experiments suggest sustainable microfinance projects often demonstrate a high degree of quality loan stock and realistic interest rates that ensures a reasonable return on investment (Harper, 2012). In this context, Kinde (2012) found that the sustainability of a microfinance project solely depends on the operational cost, economic conditions of the clients and the capital stock of the microfinance institution. According to Etzensperger (2014), a very small number (3%) out of the total of about 10,000 microfinance institutions all over the world are viable and sustainable. These institutions are often the well-known and well-managed organisations such as the Grameen Bank in Bangladesh, Bandhan (Society and NBFC) in India, Banco do Nordeste in Brazil, Consumer Credit Union 'Economic Partnership' in Russia and EKI in Bosnia (Swibel, 2007). It is important to note that although the sole aim of microfinance providers is to alleviate poverty, they are also required to be profitable to remain viable. Consequently, Jang (2013) argue that microfinance institutions should be managed with a clear aim of making a profit to ensure a continuous flow of financial resources from investors. Perhaps, this is what prompted microfinance institutions such as Equity Group in Kenya, Brac Bank in Bangladesh and Banco in Mexico to start trading in stock markets (Monroy and Huerga, 2012).

According to Milana and Ashta (2012), the high loan repayment rates reported by various microcredit organisations demonstrate that microfinance is a sustainable project. In particular, the Grameen Bank alone has been reported to have a yearly loan repayment rate of about 99% (Khandker, 2012). Similarly, Jachimowicz (2013) have shown that Banco in Mexico has also consistently reported over 95% loan repayment rates in the last five years.

Analysis of existing literature on microfinance practices also suggests that there is a positive relationship between the depth of microfinance outreach and financial sustainability. For instance, Hermes, et al. (2011) found that highly leveraged microfinance institutions have greater outreach and often achieve better economies of scale, making such institutions more sustainable. Similarly, Abate, et al. (2014) have shown that the sustainability of a microfinance project largely depends on the growth of its outreach and the ability to cover all operational costs. Perhaps, it is in this context that Battilana and Dorado (2010) concludes that under founded microfinance institutions should adopt conventional commercial banking practices to ensure financial sustainability. However, Holth (2011) argue that any attempt to commercialise microfinance could defeat the main aim of providing credit to the poor. Besides, evidence from Manos, et al. (2013) suggests that the recent drive for microfinance institutions to adopt financially sustainable practices may rather increase the gap between the rich and the poor in both developed and developing countries. Furthermore, other studies have found no relationship between microfinance outreach and financial sustainability (Quayes, 2012). Moreover, Louis, et al. (2013) found a negative link between operational efficiency of microfinance projects and their outreach to the poor. This conflicting evidence about the relationship between microfinance experiments and the microfinance institution's sustainability provide further perspectives about microfinance experiments.

Microfinance Outcomes on Female Empowerment

Various researchers have long argued that efforts aimed at improving the living standards of individuals in deprived communities have often benefited men rather than women (Nelson, 2013). Consequently, during the 1970s tools such as the "assessment of basic needs" have been designed to assess the outcomes of schemes that purport to build the economic capacity of women (Soriano, 2012). Subsequent studies on the impact of microfinance experiments on gender adopted the "basic need analysis approach".

Evidence from Arora (2012) suggests inequalities between men and women often emanates from disparities in household decision-making. The low contribution to household income by women appears to justify their low influence in the family unit. Hence, according to Khan and Noreen (2012), one major aim of microfinance as a financial inclusion strategy is to empower women. In this regard, Kato and Kratzer (2013) suggest that providing credit to women could empower them socially and economically to actively participate in household decision making. Therefore, it is reasonable to conclude as Dineen and Le (2015) did that the provision of small loans to female entrepreneurs could improve their earnings capacity and increase their influence in society. Perhaps, it is in this context that Blumberg (2005) found that over 75% of most microfinance clients in Asia and Sub Saharan Africa are women. This view is consistent with Radhakrishnan (2015) he also suggests women form the majority of microfinance beneficiaries in most countries in Eastern Europe.

It is significant to note that inequality between male and female often inhibits women development and their contribution to economic growth (Branisa, et al., 2013). Analysis of Siddiqui (2012) suggests women entrepreneurs often encounter several obstacles from members of their community. Besides, Rehman and Azam (2012) argue that the household duties of female entrepreneurs and managing an enterprise often constraints their work-life balance. Moreover, Mutaleb, et al. (2015) suggest a lack of credit and other resources are perhaps among the factors inhibiting entrepreneurship growth in poor communities in America. However, these constraints have been found to be even greater for women than male entrepreneurs (Poon, et al., 2012). Despite these constraints, it appears that the contribution of female entrepreneurs to global economic growth has increased significantly. For instance, Dankelman and Davidson (2013) suggest that about 85% of the food produced in most parts of Africa is produced by women entrepreneurs. Also, about 60% and approximately 35% of the food in Asia and the Middles East respectively are produced by female entrepreneurs. Besides, in Bangladesh microfinance has been found to be fostering female entrepreneurship in rural communities (Ronoh, et al., 2014). This is consistent with Churchill (2015) who suggests the provision of microfinance to women in India improved their decision-making ability. In this context, Mahmood, et al. (2014) argue that microfinance is influencing and increasing the number of female entrepreneurs. Hence, there is substantial evidence that microfinance has the potential to empower women (Vikas and Vijayalakshmi, 2017).

However, in some cases microfinance experiments have impacted negatively on women empowerment. For example, microfinance has been found to have prevented female beneficiaries from taking collective action in Africa (Howson, 2013). Similarly, Ghosh (2013) found that the high level of transaction cost of microfinance in both developed and developing countries often prevents women from moving out of poverty. Besides, Milana and Ashta (2012) have shown that female beneficiaries of small loans from microfinance institutions achieved negative profits from their businesses than their male counterparts who experienced higher profits. Furthermore, there are other narratives that suggest targeting women borrowers is perhaps not a deliberate strategy to empower women but a well-designed scheme by microfinance institutions to minimise the risk of loan default (Griffin, 2012).

According to Hoff (2013), female borrowers have been found to be associated with fewer loan defaults and lower credit write-offs. Similarly, analysis of evidence from Van Den Berg, et al. (2015) suggests microfinance institutions appear to target women because female borrowers are often associated with better repayment of loans. Likewise, Brana (2013) found that microfinance institutions in developing countries favoured women groups because they are often good at loan repayment. For instance, D'espallier, et al. (2011) argue that female borrowers are more reliable at making loan repayments than their male counterparts. Perhaps, this is what prompted Kondongo and Kendi (2013) to conclude that targeting women often enhances the capacity of a microfinance institution to reduce the risk of loan defaults. Overall, it is significant to note that while several studies have found a negative relationship between microfinance and women empowerment, there is overwhelming evidence that female borrowers are better clients for microfinance institutions than men. Accordingly, it will be exciting to further explore the relationship between female empowerment and microfinance.

Microfinance Outcomes on Microbusiness Development

Analysis of existing literature suggests that the provision of microfinance has produced positive outcomes on microbusiness growth in several countries, particularly in Sub-Saharan Africa and the Asian continent. Rotich, et al. (2015) for example found that the provision of microfinance increased the performance of microbusinesses in Sub-Saharan Africa. Analysis of Masanga and Jera, (2017) also suggests that microbusinesses that received credit from microfinance institutions in Zimbabwe may have improved their level of income from the use of microfinance. Cooper (2012) support this view as he also argues that microfinance services have helped businesses in Kenya to grow their turnover from micro to small and from small to medium. A recent study that also provides evidence of positive outcomes of microfinance experiments is Hameed, et al. (2017) who found that microfinance services have a positive impact on the success of microbusinesses in Africa. Indeed, most studies conducted on the outcomes of microfinance on microbusiness development have focused on the impact of microfinance on monthly sales, capital stock, total assets and the number of people employed by microenterprises.

Microfinance Outcomes on Economic Development

The contribution of microfinance to economic development in developing countries has also been reported by various studies. For instance, using a time series technique 'Auto-Regressive Distributive Lag (ARDL) Sultan and Masih (2016) found that there is significant impact of microfinance on domestic growth (GDP) in Bangladesh. The study also suggest that economic growth has strong relationship with microfinance. This implies that there is bi-directional relationship between microfinance and growth and that microfinance is an important "ingredient" in promoting growth through various channels. Similarly, a study in India by Sharma and Puri (2013) found a strong relationship between microfinance and economic development. The India experiment also shows a high level of positive coefficient of correlation between microloans and the GDP of India. Equally, using a panel of 85 developing countries over the period 2002–2013, Donou-Adonsou and Sylwester (2017) found that microfinance loans promote economic growth in developing countries. Evidence from Suleiman (2014) further suggest that microfinance institutions have a positive impact on SMEs, which led to economic growth through business expansion and employment creation.

Other narratives in existing literature suggest that microfinance has no any significant impact on economic growth. For instance, using panel data model for six Arab countries over the period 1999-2016, Khalaf and Saqfalhait (2019) found that microfinance institutions have no effect on improving economic growth in Arab countries. This unusual outcome could be attributed to financial strength of these countries which makes the makes the contribution of small loans insignificant to economic activities and therefore economic growth. However, Khalily (2020) has demonstrated that microfinance contributed to GDP growth and even largely to real rural GDP growth in Bangladesh. Such macroeconomic impacts are results of the penetration of microfinance, increase in loans for micro enterprises, productive use of microcredit and increase in total factor productivity. Similarly, annual time-series data, Amin and Uddin (2018) have shown that both financing and depositing aspects of Grameen Bank have positive effect on economic growth of Bangladesh in the long run. Despite the negative relationship found between microfinance and economic growth in some Arab countries, analysis of the above literature overall suggest that microfinance promotes economic growth in developing countries.

CONCEPTUAL FRAMEWORK

Consistent with the outcomes of microfinance from the literature reviewed above, this chapter is guided by the framework given in figure 1 below. The focus of this chapter is to investigate the relationship between the provision of microfinance, poverty reduction, microbusiness growth, female empowerment and economic development in Ghana and Nigeria. Figure 1, the conceptual framework, illustrates the causal relationship between microfinance, poverty reduction, microbusiness growth, female empowerment and economic development. This gives rise to whether the provision of microfinance empowers women and reduces poverty as observed in Dineen and Le (2015) and Milana and Ashta (2012). Besides, financial theory suggests that economic growth and microbusiness development have strong relationship with microfinance, as illustrated in figure 1 below. This, therefore, raises important questions. Firstly, will the provision of microfinance reduce poverty in Ghana and Nigeria or not. Secondly, does microfinance play a role in women empowerment in Ghana and Nigeria? Thirdly, will the provision of microfinance improve microbusiness and economic growth in Ghana and Nigeria?

Figure 1.

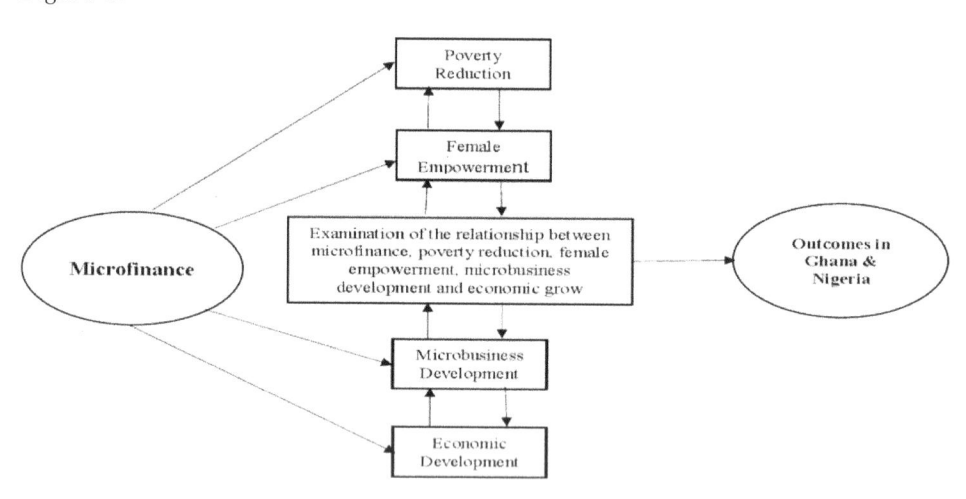

Microfinance Outcomes in Ghana

A study conducted by Quaye, et al (2014) suggest that the operations of microfinance institutions (MFIs) are having positive impact on SMEs by helping to bridge the financing gap faced by SMEs in Ghana. Similarly, using a case study approach, Anane, et al (2013) found that recipients of microfinance products and services are better off in terms of enhancing the activities of their SMEs, improving outputs and ensuring prudent financial management than those without microfinance services in rural Ghana. Furthermore, Akanfewon and Kere (2016) have shown that micro-credit and other services extended to SMEs by microfinance institutions has positively impacted on the lives of owners and employees of SMEs, in terms of better and higher incomes, food security, ability to send and retain their children in school, generation of employment and economic and social empowerment. The evidence above suggests that overall microfinance has played a major role in promoting small and medium size enterprises in Ghana.

The role of microfinance in reducing poverty in Ghana has also been reported by various studies. For instance, Adjei, et al. (2009) have shown that Sinapi Aba Trust, a microfinance institution in Ghana has contributed positively to poverty reduction among rural and urban poor especially women in Ghana. Equally, Sulemana, et al. (2019) found that microfinance contributed to poverty reduction in the Ashaiman Municipality of Ghana. The work of Adu, et al. (2014) in the Ashanti Region of Ghana, proved that microfinance activities bring improvement in the standard of living of the participant not only in economic terms but also in social terms. The significant role of microfinance in reducing poverty in poor communities in Ghana has therefore been extensively documented in existing literature.

Addai (2017) has also reported a statistically significant positive relationship between microfinance and women empowerment, for both economic and social in Ghana. Similarly, Addae-Korankye and Abada (2017) found that microfinance indeed has a direct correlation with Profit and hence socio-economic well-being of women (women empowerment) in Madina a suburb of Accra in Ghana. Awudjah (2019) has also shown that microfinance has demonstrated to be a critical instrument in empowering women from poor households by providing of financial services rather than just credit in Ghana. Other financial products such as savings, investments and insurance aid in the empowerment of women; women can have some capital to rely on when faced with financial challenges. Thus, the role of microfinance in women empowerment in Ghana has also been proven.

Recent studies have also examined the effects of microfinance on economic development in Ghana. For instance, Aidoo, et al (2012) argues that microfinance institutions have contributed immensely to the development of Ghana through provision of monetary services in the form of loans, promoting small scale businesses and reduction of unemployment rate. However, Egyir (2014) suggests that the real problems for women's effective contribution in local economic development are more profound and cannot be tackled solely by capital injections by the micro financial sector but require fundamental structural changes of the socioeconomic conditions that define local economic development activity and a fuller support of all stakeholders at the local level. On the positive side, Odoom, et al (2019) have demonstrated that MFIs in Takoradi contribute variously to the local economy including provision of financial capital to the people; income generation; employment creation; engaging the non-formal economy and providing support for SMEs to grow. Perhaps, the above evidence is a proof that microfinance contributes positively to economic development in Ghana and elsewhere in the African continent.

Microfinance Outcomes in Nigeria

Evidence from Odebiyi and Olaoye (2012) suggest that both financial and non-financial services provided by microfinance banks and institutions have greatly assisted small businesses in Nigeria and have enhanced the distribution of business skills and the sharing of innovative ideas. The implication of this outcome is that micro-financing significantly promotes businesses by reducing the resource gap for small businesses. This further implies that microfinancing has a huge potential for increasing the performance of small businesses through the frequent contributions in microfinancing and provision of non-financial services. Duru, et al (2017) also found that Microfinance Banks credits have impact on the expansion capacity of Small and Medium Enterprises in Lokoja, Nigeria. Microfinance Banks have also mobilized savings for intermediation and Small and Medium Enterprises development in Lokoja. The evidence above proves that microfinance plays a major role in small and medium size enterprise development in Nigeria.

The role of microfinance in poverty reduction in Nigeria has also been reported by various studies. For example. Kasali, et al. (2015) revealed that microfinance loan made significant impact on the loan beneficiaries which lead to poverty reduction in South-West Nigeria. However, Nwigwe, et al. (2012) argues that while microfinance has developed some innovative management and business strategies, its impact on poverty reduction remains in doubt in Nigeria but certainly plays an important role in providing safety-net and consumption smoothening. Similarly, Appah, et al. (2012) suggest that microfinance alone cannot reduce poverty in a society where basic infrastructure such as good roads steady power supply, good transportation system are nearly not available for people to benefit from the introduction of microfinance in Nigeria. Analysis of the above studies suggest that the role of microfinance in poverty reduction in Nigeria requires further investigation to determine the relationship between microfinance and poverty reduction in the country.

Microfinance role in women empowerment in Nigeria has also been documented in existing literature. For instance, evidence from Ukwueze, et al. (2019) suggest that age of women, education, belonging to saving association, and operating an account are the determinants of women empowerment and welfare as they access finance from microfinance banks. A study conducted by Awojobi (2014) found a significant improvement in the household well-being, income and employment, and women's empowerment, as a result of participating in micro-finance programmes. However, all the respondents bemoaned the high interest rates being charged by the microfinance banks. The outcomes of Ilavbarhe and Izekor (2015) also suggest that micro credit is a tool that could be used to improve the income and savings level of women and thus empower them for better living. It is therefore plausible to suggest that microfinance plays a significant role in women empowerment in Nigeria.

Outcomes from several investigations in Nigeria also provide evidence that microfinance contributes to economic development in the country. For examples, using secondary data and applying ordinary least square of multiple regressions, Ayodele and Arogundade (2014) found that microfinance loans to the public has a significant impact on economic growth in Nigeria. Thus, the overall significance of the activities of microfinance banks cannot be overemphasized in the pursuance of a sustained economic growth in Nigeria. However, Oluyombo (2011) found a weak positive relationship between microfinance banks' finance and long run economic growth in Nigeria. This view is supported by Murad and Idewele (2017) who found that microfinance loans enhanced consumption per capita in the short run with an impressive coefficient, although these banks' loans do not have a significant impact on economic growth in the long run. Analysis of the above literature therefore suggest that outcomes of microfinance on economic development in Nigeria is inconclusive and requires further investigation.

SOLUTIONS AND RECOMMENDATIONS

Evidence from the literature reviewed suggest that the provision of microfinance play a major role in reducing poverty in developing countries, particularly Ghana and Nigeria. This finding has policy implications for governments across Africa and other agencies that are interested in using microfinance as a catalyst for reducing poverty and fostering economic growth in deprived communities in developing countries. A further policy implication arising out of the above outcome from the literature reviewed is the provision of financial support to microfinance organisations to strengthen their ability to provide adequate credit to individuals and microenterprises which may have a positive impact on economic development.

The positive role of microfinance in fostering microbusiness growth also found from the literature review has implications for policymakers as it provides the basis to use microfinance as a developmental instrument for improving small and medium size enterprises working capital in Africa and elsewhere. Thus, governments and their developmental partners could use microfinance as a catalyst to solving the working capital difficulties experienced by microbusiness setups in developing countries such as Ghana and Nigeria.

Further evidence from the literature reviewed suggest that the provision of microfinance to women contributed positively to women empowerment in Ghana and Nigeria. The implications of this positive role and outcome of microfinance on women empowerment is that microfinance providers and other policymakers particularly in Ghana and Nigeria should find more innovative ways of providing credit to businesses owned by women to enhance their economic value and yield benefit for women entrepreneurs and society in general. It is further recommended that policymakers including government agencies should provide financial and technical support to providers of microfinance to enable them to increase their outreach particularly to women in deprived and financially excluded communities.

Furthermore, evidence from the literature reviewed in this chapter suggest that the provision of some type of microfinance services yield positive outcomes whilst others produce negative outcomes on poverty, women empowerment and microbusiness development. In this regard, it is recommended that policymakers and microfinance providers should focus their attention on providing credit and training to the poor instead of the current attempt of providing only loans which have proved to yield very minimal results. Moreover, policymakers and microfinance institutions are encouraged to formulate strategies that will enable providers of microfinance to poorer communities to offer loans together with appropriate financial management training. Thus, providers of microfinance services should be encouraged to consider a good mix of credit and non-financial services for the purpose of helping the poor to make good use of the credit received. The timely and regular provision of business advisory services to users of microfinance will ensure they invest the loans prudently to yield the right returns to facilitate a perpetual improvement in their living conditions.

Further recommendations on how microfinance outreach programmes could be enriched especially among the rural women since enhanced microfinance accessibility has been shown to be a perfect tool to accelerate economic and social empowerment of women in Ghana and Nigeria. Besides, the governments of these countries are advised to provide more enabling environment to make Microfinance operations more effective particularly in the rural areas. Furthermore, microfinance institutions in Nigeria and Ghana are implored to create more awareness on their operations and make less stringent conditions for loan accessibility. In addition to the above, it is recommended that microfinance Banks at all levels should be mandated by the Central Bank of Ghana and Nigeria to support and promote Small and Medium Enterprises as part of the object of their establishment with proper enforcement measures to ensure compliance. Finally, it is recommended that the government should create an enabling environment capable of supporting microfinance banks in microcredit delivery in Ghana and Nigeria.

FUTURE RESEARCH DIRECTIONS

This chapter used evidence from existing literature to examine the role of microfinance in Ghana and Nigeria, conducting similar research using primary data could enhance our knowledge of the role of microfinance in developing countries, particularly Africa.

Also, this chapter focused on the relationship between microfinance, poverty, female empowerment, economic development and microenterprise growth. Thus, the data used in this chapter related to the influence of microfinance on poverty, women empowerment, economic growth and microbusiness development. In this regard, future research on the role of microfinance experiments in poverty reduction only in Africa is important for our understanding of the role of microfinance in reducing poverty in developing countries. Besides, going forward, conducting primary research on microfinance role in enhancing only female empowerment instead of the general role of microfinance could further enhance our knowledge of the influence of microfinance on women. Furthermore, future comparative studies on the role of microfinance experiment in reducing poverty or female empowerment in different continents could provide wide and comprehensive outcomes that could be explained in the context of different economies.

Future research on the role of microfinance in developed countries is required as this chapter focused on the role of microfinance in developing countries. Some studies have also examined the role of microfinance in poverty reduction in developing countries, there is however limited evidence of empirical investigations in the developed world that have investigated the role of microfinance in poverty reduction. Hence, future studies should consider examining the role of microfinance in poverty reduction in poor communities in the developed world which could help policymakers formulate strategies for improving the standard of living in financially excluded communities in developed countries.

In addition to the above, future research on models used to deliver microfinance services is also required as microfinance model replication difficulties have not been sufficiently researched. Besides, the rural household model of microfinance has been under researched. It will, therefore, be fascinating to carry out a further investigation on the rural household model to determine if it can be adopted as the best microfinance model for poverty reduction, female empowerment and microbusinesses development.

CONCLUSION

Analysis of the evidence provided in this chapter suggest that microfinance has produced positive outcomes on poverty, women empowerment, microbusiness development and economic growth in Ghana and Nigeria. However, the evidence presented also suggest that microfinance has no impact on economic growth in some Arab countries.

A major conclusion drawn from the evidence presented in this chapters is that microfinance has played a significant role in reducing poverty in poor communities in Ghana. Besides, the chapter concludes that overall microfinance has played a major role in promoting small and medium size enterprises in Ghana. Moreso, microfinance has demonstrated to be a critical instrument in empowering women from poor households by providing of financial services rather than just credit in Ghana. In respect of the relationship between microfinance and economic development, the evidence presented in this chapter suggest that microfinance contributes positively to economic development in Ghana and elsewhere in the African continent.

The outcomes of the investigation of the relationship between microfinance and microbusiness development in Nigeria suggest that microfinance plays a major role in small and medium size enterprise development in Nigeria. However, analysis of the evidence presented in this chapter suggest that the role of microfinance in poverty reduction in Nigeria requires further investigation to determine the relationship between microfinance and poverty reduction in the country as the outcomes reported a mixed and therefore inconclusive. With regards to the relationship between microfinance women empowerment, the evidence presented suggest that microfinance pays a significant role in women empowerment in Nigeria. This conclusion was reached in view of the fact that microfinance has been reported to be a tool that could be used to improve the income and savings level of women and thus empower them for better living. The final conclusion drawn from analysis of the evidence presented in this chapter is that outcomes of microfinance on economic development in Nigeria is inconclusive and requires further investigation as most studies found a weak positive relationship between microfinance banks' finance and long run economic growth in Nigeria.

ACKNOWLEDGMENT

This research received no specific grant from any funding agency in the public, commercial, or not-for-profit sectors.

REFERENCES

Abate, G. T., Borzaga, C., & Getnet, K. (2014). Financial Sustainability and Outreach of MFIs in Ethiopia: Does Ownership Form Matter? In Microfinance Institutions (pp. 244-270). Palgrave Macmillan.

Addae-Korankye, A., & Abada, A. (2017). Microfinance and women empowerment in Madina in Accra, Ghana. *Asian Economic and Financial Review*, 7(3), 222–230. doi:10.18488/journal.aefr/2017.7.3/102.3.222.231

Addai, B. (2017). Women empowerment through microfinance: Empirical evidence from Ghana. *Journal of Finance and Accounting,* 5(1), 1-11.

Adjei, J. K., Arun, T., & Hossain, F. (2009). *The role of microfinance in asset-building and poverty reduction: The case of Sinapi Aba Trust of Ghana*. Brooks World Poverty Institute, University of Manchester.

Adu, J. K., Anarfi, B. O., & Poku, K. (2014). The Role of Microfinance on Poverty Reduction: A Case Study of Adansi Rural Bank in Ashanti Region, Ghana. *Social and Basic Sciences Research Review*, 2(3), 96–109.

Aggarwal, S., Klapper, L. F., & Singer, D. (2012). *Financing businesses in Africa: The role of microfinance*. World Bank Policy Research Working Paper, (5975).

Aidoo, F., Adjei, D. M., Akoto, B., Attakora, M., & Carl, C. (2012). *The Role of Microfinance Institutions on the Economic Development of Ghana* (Doctoral dissertation).

Akanfewon, P. A., & Kere, O. D. (2016). The Role of Microfinance in the Growth and Development of Small and Medium Scale Businesses in the Builsa Districts of Upper East Region, Ghana. *ADRRI Journal (Multidisciplinary)*, 25(10), 1–24.

Alvi, E., & Senbeta, A. (2012). Does foreign aid reduce poverty? *Journal of International Development*, 24(8), 955–976. doi:10.1002/jid.1790

Amin, M. F. B., & Uddin, S. J. (2018). Microfinance-economic growth nexus: A case study on Grameen bank in Bangladesh. *International Journal of Islamic Economics and Finance*, 1(1), 25–38. doi:10.18196/ijief.112

Anane, G. K., Cobbinah, P. B., & Manu, J. K. (2013). Sustainability of small and medium scale enterprises in rural Ghana: The role of microfinance institutions. *Asian Economic and Financial Review*, 3(8), 1003–1017.

Appah, E., John, M. S., & Wisdom, S. (2012). An analysis of microfinance and poverty reduction in Bayelsa State of Nigeria. *Kuwait Chapter of the Arabian Journal of Business and Management Review, 1*(7), 38–58.

Arnold, K. J. (2012). *Microfinance for microenterprises? Investigating the usefulness of microfinance services for microenterprises in Bolivia.* Simon Fraser University.

Arora, R. U. (2012). Gender inequality, economic development, and globalization: A state level analysis of India. *Journal of Developing Areas, 46*(1), 147–164. doi:10.1353/jda.2012.0019

Aruna, M., & Jyothirmayi, M. R. (2011). The role of microfinance in women empowerment: A study on the SHG bank linkage program in Hyderabad (Andhra Pradesh). *Indian Journal of Commerce & Management Studies ISSN, 2229,* 5674.

Asher, S. N. (2014). Improving the well-being of the women through microfinance: Evidence from Swabi District. *Putaj Humanities & Social Sciences, 21*(1), 57–65.

Attanasio, O., Augsburg, B., De Haas, R., Fitzsimons, E., & Harmgart, H. (2013). Group lending or individual lending? Evidence from a randomized field experiment in rural Mongolia. *American Economic Journal: Applied Economics.*

Awojobi, O. N. (2014). Empowering women through micro-finance: Evidence from Nigeria. *Australian Journal of Business and Management Research, 4*(1), 17–26. doi:10.52283/NSWRCA.AJBMR.20140401A03

Awudjah, I. E. (2019). *Microfinance and Women Empowerment in Ghana* (Doctoral dissertation). University of Ghana.

Ayodele, A. E., & Arogundade, K. (2014). The impact of microfinance on economic growth in Nigeria. *Journal of Emerging Trends in Economics and Management Science, 5*(5), 397–405.

Bakhtiari, S. (2011). Microfinance and poverty reduction: some international evidence. International Business and Economics Research Journal, 5(12).

Bateman, M. (2012). The role of microfinance in contemporary rural development finance policy and practice: Imposing neoliberalism as best practice. *Journal of Agrarian Change, 12*(4), 587–600.

Battilana, J., & Dorado, S. (2010). Building sustainable hybrid organizations: The case of commercial microfinance organizations. *Academy of Management Journal, 53*(6), 1419–1440. doi:10.5465/amj.2010.57318391

Bayulgen, O. (2008). Muhammad Yunus, Grameen Bank and the Nobel Peace Prize: What political science can contribute to and learn from the study of microcredit. *International Studies Review, 10*(3), 525–547. doi:10.1111/j.1468-2486.2008.00803.x

Berhane, G., & Gardebroek, C. (2011). Does microfinance reduce rural poverty? Evidence based on household panel data from northern Ethiopia. *American Journal of Agricultural Economics, 93*(1), 43–55. doi:10.1093/ajae/aaq126

Blumberg, R. L. (2005). Women's Economic Empowerment as the Magic Potion of Development? *100th Annual Meeting of the American Sociological Association*, Philadelphia, PA.

Brana, S. (2013). Microcredit: An answer to the gender problem in funding? *Small Business Economics, 40*(1), 87–100. doi:10.100711187-011-9346-3

Branisa, B., Klasen, S., & Ziegler, M. (2013). Gender inequality in social institutions and gendered development outcomes. *World Development, 45*, 252–268. doi:10.1016/j.worlddev.2012.12.003

Bruhn, M., & Love, I. (2014). The real impact of improved access to finance: Evidence from Mexico. *The Journal of Finance, 69*(3), 1347–1376. doi:10.1111/jofi.12091

Chowdhury, A. (2009). *Microfinance as a poverty reduction tool-a critical assessment*. United Nations, Department of Economic and Social Affairs (DESA) working paper.

Cooper, J. N. (2012). *The impact of microfinance services on the growth of small and medium enterprises in Kenya* (Doctoral dissertation). University of Nairobi.

Crépon, B., Devoto, F., Duflo, E., & Parienté, W. (2015). Estimating the impact of microcredit on those who take it up: Evidence from a randomized experiment in Morocco. *American Economic Journal. Applied Economics, 7*(1), 123–150. doi:10.1257/app.20130535

D'espallier, B., Guérin, I., & Mersland, R. (2011). Women and repayment in microfinance: A global analysis. *World Development, 39*(5), 758–772. doi:10.1016/j.worlddev.2010.10.008

Dankelman, I., & Davidson, J. (2013). *Women and the environment in the third world: alliance for the future*. Routledge. doi:10.4324/9781315066219

Dineen, K., & Le, Q. V. (2015). The impact of an integrated microcredit program on the empowerment of women and gender equality in rural Vietnam. *Journal of Developing Areas, 49*(1), 23–38. doi:10.1353/jda.2015.0028

Donou-Adonsou, F., & Sylwester, K. (2017). Growth effect of banks and microfinance: Evidence from developing countries. *The Quarterly Review of Economics and Finance, 64*, 44–56. doi:10.1016/j.qref.2016.11.001

Dowla, A., & Alamgir, D. (2003). From microcredit to microfinance: Evolution of savings products by MFIs in Bangladesh. *Journal of International Development, 15*(8), 969–988. doi:10.1002/jid.1032

Duong, H. A., & Nghiem, H. S. (2014). Effects of microfinance on poverty reduction in Vietnam: A pseudo-panel data analysis. *Journal of Accounting, Finance and Economics, 4*(2), 58–67.

Duru, I.U., Yusuf, A., & Kwazu, V.C. (2017). Role of microfinance banks credit in the development of small and medium enterprises in Lokoja, Kogi State, Nigeria. *Asian Journal of Economics, Business and Accounting*, 1-9.

Ebomuche, N. C., Ihugba, O. A., & Bankong, B. (2014). The impact of Nigeria microfinance banks on poverty reduction: Imo State experience. *International Letters of Social and Humanistic Sciences*, (05), 92–113.

Egyir, I. S. (2014). *Microfinance, Women and Local Economic Development in Ghana*. University of Ghana Readers.

Elhadary, Y. A. E. & Samat, N. (2012). Political economy and urban poverty in the developing countries: Lessons learned from Sudan and Malaysia. *Journal of Geography and Geology, 4*(1), 212-223.

Etzensperger, C. (2014). *Microfinance market outlook 2014: no "sudden stop": demand for microfinance soars*. ResponsAbility.

Fant, E. K. (2011). *Fighting poverty with micro-credit. Experiences from Micro-Finance and Small-Loan Center (MASLOC) in Savelugu/Nanton District of Northern Ghana*. Academic Press.

Ghosh, J. (2013). Microfinance and the challenge of financial inclusion for development. *Cambridge Journal of Economics, 37*(6), 1203–1219. doi:10.1093/cje/bet042

Griffin, D. J. (2012). *Loan methodology, gender, environment and the formation of capital by Mexican microfinance institutions* (Doctoral dissertation). Instituto Technologico De Estudios Superiores De Monterrey.

Hagenaars, A. J. (2014). *The perception of poverty*. Elsevier.

Hameed, W. U., Hussin, T., Azeem, M., Arif, M., & Basheer, M. F. (2017). Combination of microcredit and micro-training with mediating role of formal education: A micro-enterprise success formula. *Journal of Business and Social Review in Emerging Economies*, *3*(2), 285–291. doi:10.26710/jbsee.v3i2.191

Harper, M. (2012). Microfinance interest rates and client returns. *Journal of Agrarian Change*, *12*(4), 564–574. doi:10.1111/j.1471-0366.2012.00374.x

Hartarska, V., Nadolnyak, D., & McAdams, T. (2013). Microfinance and microenterprises' financing constraints in Eastern Europe and Central Asia. In *Microfinance in Developing Countries* (pp. 22–35). Palgrave Macmillan. doi:10.1057/9781137301925_2

Hatta, Z. A., & Ali, I. (2013). Poverty reduction policies in Malaysia: Trends, strategies and challenges. *Asian Culture and History*, *5*(2), 48–56. doi:10.5539/ach.v5n2p48

Hermes, N., & Lensink, R. (2011). Microfinance: Its impact, outreach, and sustainability. *World Development*, *39*(6), 875–881. doi:10.1016/j.worlddev.2009.10.021

Hermes, N., Lensink, R., & Meesters, A. (2011). Outreach and efficiency of microfinance institutions. *World Development*, *39*(6), 938–948. doi:10.1016/j.worlddev.2009.10.018

Hoff, T. S. (2013). *Female loan clients-a safer bet?: A study of default rates in a microfinance institution* (Master's thesis).

Holth, L. C. R. (2011). *Commercialization of Microfinance*. Oslo University College: Faculty of Social Science.

Howson, C. (2013). Adverse Incorporation and Microfinance among Cross-Border Traders in Senegal. *World Development*, *42*, 199–208. doi:10.1016/j.worlddev.2012.06.002

IFC. (2014). *IFC and Microfinance*. The World Bank Group.

Ilavbarhe, K. O., & Izekor, O. B. (2015). The role of microcredit in women empowerment and poverty alleviation in Edo State, Nigeria. *Journal of Agricultural and Crop Research*, *3*(6), 80–84.

Imai, K. S., Arun, T., & Annim, S. K. (2010). Microfinance and household poverty reduction: New evidence from India. *World Development*, *38*(12), 1760–1774. doi:10.1016/j.worlddev.2010.04.006

Imai, K. S., Gaiha, R., Thapa, G., & Annim, S. K. (2012). Microfinance and poverty—A macro perspective. *World Development*, *40*(8), 1675–1689. doi:10.1016/j.worlddev.2012.04.013

Iqbal, Z., Iqbal, S., & Mushtaq, M. A. (2015). Impact of Microfinance on Poverty Alleviation: The Study of District Bahawal Nagar, Punjab, Pakistan. *Management and Administrative Sciences Review*, *4*(3), 487–503.

Islam, T. (2012). *Microcredit and poverty alleviation*. Ashgate Publishing, Ltd.

Jachimowicz, J. (2013). Microfinance: Fortune at or also for the bottom of the pyramid? *Journal of Sustainability*, *1*(1), 13–13.

Jang, R. (2013). *Microfinance business models: comparing and contrasting Grameen Bank and Compartamos Banco* (Doctoral dissertation). Massachusetts Institute of Technology.

Kabeer, N. (2005). Is microfinance a 'magic bullet' for women's empowerment? Analysis of findings from South Asia. *Economic and Political Weekly*, 4709–4718.

Kasali, T. A., Ahmad, S. A., & Lim, H. E. (2015). The role of microfinance in poverty alleviation: Empirical evidence from South-West Nigeria. *Asian Social Science*, *11*(21), 183–192. doi:10.5539/ass.v11n21p183

Kato, M. P., & Kratzer, J. (2013). Empowering women through microfinance: Evidence from Tanzania. *ACRN Journal of Entrepreneurship Perspectives*, *2*(1), 31–59.

Khalaf, L. S., & Saqfalhait, N. I. (2019). The effect of microfinance institutions activities on economic growth in Arab countries. *Academy of Accounting and Financial Studies Journal*, *23*(1), 1–8.

Khalily, B. (2020). Microfinance in Sustainable Development and Economic Growth in Bangladesh. In Bangladesh's Macroeconomic Policy (pp. 419-448). Palgrave Macmillan.

Khan, H. R. (2011). *Financial Inclusion and Financial stability: are they two sides of the same coin*. Speech at BANCON.

Khan, R. E. A., & Norèen, S. (2012). Microfinance and women empowerment: A case study of District Bahawalpur (Pakistan). *African Journal of Business Management*, *6*(12), 4514–4521.

Khandker, S. R. (2012). *Grameen bank lending: does group liability matter?* World Bank Policy Research Working Paper, (6204).

Khandker, S. R., & Samad, H. (2013). *Microfinance growth and poverty reduction in Bangladesh: what does the longitudinal data say?* World Bank Working Paper.

Kinde, B. A. (2012). Financial sustainability of microfinance institutions (MFIs) in Ethiopia. *European Journal of Business and Management, 4*(15), 1–10.

Kodongo, O., & Kendi, L. G. (2013). Individual lending versus group lending: An evaluation with Kenya's microfinance data. *Review of Development Finance, 3*(2), 99–108. doi:10.1016/j.rdf.2013.05.001

Kristof, N. D. (2009). The role of microfinance. *New York Times.*

Ledgerwood, J., Earne, J., & Nelson, C. (2013). The new microfinance handbook: A financial market system perspective. World Bank Publications. doi:10.1596/978-0-8213-8927-0

Lloyd-Jones, T., & Rakodi, C. (2014). *Urban livelihoods: A people-centred approach to reducing poverty.* Routledge. doi:10.4324/9781849773805

Louis, P., Seret, A., & Baesens, B. (2013). Financial efficiency and social impact of microfinance institutions using self-organizing maps. *World Development, 46*, 197–210. doi:10.1016/j.worlddev.2013.02.006

Mahmood, S., Hussain, J. Z., & Matlay, H. (2014). Optimal microfinance loan size and poverty reduction amongst female entrepreneurs in Pakistan. *Journal of Small Business and Enterprise Development, 21*(2), 231–249. doi:10.1108/JSBED-03-2014-0043

Manos, R., Gueyie, J. P. & Yaron, J. (2013). Dilemmas and Directions in Microfinance Research. *Microfinance in Developing Countries: Issues, Policies and Performance Evaluation.*

Masanga, G. G., & Jera, M. (2017). The Significance of Microfinance to Urban Informal Traders in Zimbabwe. *ADRRI Journal (Multidisciplinary), 26*(3), 44–61.

Matin, I., Hulme, D., & Rutherford, S. (2002). Finance for the poor: From microcredit to microfinancial services. *Journal of International Development, 14*(2), 273–294. doi:10.1002/jid.874

Mersland, R., & Strøm, Ø. (Eds.). (2014). *Microfinance institutions: Financial and social performance.* Springer. doi:10.1057/9781137399663

Milana, C., & Ashta, A. (2012). Developing microfinance: A survey of the literature. *Strategic Change, 21*(7-8), 299–330. doi:10.1002/jsc.1911

Monroy, R., & Huerga, A. (2012). A Study of Four Listed Micro Finance Institutions. *6th International Conference on Industrial Engineering and Industrial Management*, 44-51.

Murad, A. B., & Idewele, I. E. O. (2017). The impact of microfinance institution in economic growth of a country: Nigeria in focus. *International Journal of Development and Management Review*, *12*(1), 1–17.

Mutaleb, M. Z., Baharanyi, N. R., Tackie, N. O., & Zabawa, R. (2015). An assessment of microlending programs in the Alabama black belt region. *Professional Agricultural Workers Journal*, *2*(2), 1–10.

Nasir, S. (2013). Microfinance in India: Contemporary issues and challenges. *Middle East Journal of Scientific Research*, *15*(2), 191–199.

Nawaz, S. (2010). Microfinance and poverty reduction: Evidence from a village study in Bangladesh. *Journal of Asian and African Studies*, *45*(6), 670–683. doi:10.1177/0021909610383812 PMID:21174878

Nelson, N. (2013). Why has development neglected rural women? A review of the South Asian literature. Elsevier.

Nwigwe, C. A., Omonona, B. T., & Okoruwa, V. O. (2012). Microfinance and poverty reduction in Nigeria: A critical assessment. *Australian Journal of Business and Management Research*, *2*(4), 33–40. doi:10.52283/NSWRCA.AJBMR.20120204A05

Odebiyi, O. C., & Olaoye, O. J. (2012). Small and medium scale aquaculture enterprises (SMES) development in Ogun State, Nigeria: The role of microfinance banks. *Development*, *2*(3), 1–6.

Odell, K. (2010). *Measuring the impact of microfinance*. Grameen Foundation.

Odoom, D., Fosu, K. O., Ankomah, K., & Amofa, M. B. (2019). Exploring the Contributions of Microfinance Institutions to the Ghanaian Economy: A Study at Takoradi. *Journal of Economics and Sustainable Development*, *10*(1), 77–90.

Oluyombo, O. O. (2011). The impact of microfinance bank credit on economic development of Nigeria (1992–2006). *International Journal of Development and Management Review*, *6*(1), 139–150.

Pathak, H. P., & Gyawali, M. (2012). Role of microfinance in employment generation: A case study of Microfinance Program of Paschimanchal Grameen Bikash Bank. *Journal of Nepalese Business Studies*, *7*(1), 31–38. doi:10.3126/jnbs.v7i1.6401

Poon, J. P., Thai, D. T., & Naybor, D. (2012). Social capital and female entrepreneurship in rural regions: Evidence from Vietnam. *Applied Geography (Sevenoaks, England)*, *35*(1), 308–315. doi:10.1016/j.apgeog.2012.08.002

Quaye, I., Abrokwah, E., Sarbah, A., & Osei, J. Y. (2014). Bridging the SME financing gap in Ghana: The role of microfinance institutions. *Open Journal of Business and Management*, *2*(04), 339–413. doi:10.4236/ojbm.2014.24040

Quayes, S. (2012). Depth of outreach and financial sustainability of microfinance institutions. *Applied Economics*, *44*(26), 3421–3433. doi:10.1080/00036846.2011.577016

Quibria, M. G. (2012). *Microcredit and Poverty Alleviation: Can microcredit close the deal?* WIDER Working Paper.

Quinones, B., & Remenyi, J. (2014). *Microfinance and poverty alleviation: Case studies from Asia and the Pacific.* Routledge. doi:10.4324/9781315800455

Radhakrishnan, S. (2015). "Low Profile" or Entrepreneurial? Gender, Class, and Cultural Adaptation in the Global Microfinance Industry. *World Development*, *74*, 264–274. doi:10.1016/j.worlddev.2015.05.017

Rehman, H., Moazzam, A., & Ansari, N. (2015). Role of Microfinance Institutions in Women Empowerment: A Case Study of Akhuwat, Pakistan. *South Asian Studies*, *30*(1), 107.

Rehman, S., & Azam, R. M. (2012). Gender and work-life balance: A phenomenological study of women entrepreneurs in Pakistan. *Journal of Small Business and Enterprise Development*, *19*(2), 209–228. doi:10.1108/14626001211223865

Ronoh, E. K., Korir, S., Rotich, J. C., & Onguso, B. (2014). Constraints to the Success of Women Small Scale Entrepreneurs in Kenya. A Case of Microfinance Institution Borrowers in Rongai District of Nakuru County, Kenya. *European Journal of Business and Management*, *6*(21), 124–136.

Rotich, I., Lagat, C., & Kogei, J. (2015). Effects of microfinance services on the performance of small and medium enterprises in Kenya. *African Journal of Business Management*, *9*(5), 206–211. doi:10.5897/AJBM2014.7519

Sanyal, P. (2009). From credit to collective action: The role of microfinance in promoting women's social capital and normative influence. *American Sociological Review*, *74*(4), 529–550. doi:10.1177/000312240907400402

Sarumathi, S., & Mohan, K. (2011). Role of Microfinance in women's empowerment; an empirical study in Pondicherry region rural SHG's. *Journal of Management and Science*, *1*(1), 1–10.

Sharma, G. L., & Puri, H. (2013). An empirical testing of relationship between microfinance and economic growth in india. *Journal of Indian Research*, *1*(2), 87–94.

Siddiqui, A. B. (2012). Problems encountered by women entrepreneurs in India. *International Journal of Applied Research & Studies*, *1*(2), 1–11.

Soriano, F. I. (2012). Conducting needs assessments: A multidisciplinary approach (Vol. 68). Sage.

Suleiman, M. S. (2014). Microfinance banks and their impact on small and medium scale industries for economic growth. In *Green technology applications for enterprise and academic innovation* (pp. 48–64). IGI Global. doi:10.4018/978-1-4666-5166-1.ch004

Sulemana, M., Naiim, F. M., & Adjanyo, C. (2019). Role of microfinance in poverty reduction in the Ashaiman Municipality, Ghana. *African Research Review*, *13*(3), 1–14. doi:10.4314/afrrev.v13i3.1

Sultan, Y., & Masih, M. (2016). Does microfinance affect economic growth? Evidence from Bangladesh based on ARDL approach (No. 72123). University Library of Munich, Germany.

Swibel, M. (2007). *The 50 top microfinance institutions*. Forbes.com.

Taimur, I., & Hamid, S. (2013). Determinants of women empowerment: The role of microfinance in the devastated areas of Pakistan. *The Journal of Business Strategy*, *7*(2), 39–52.

Tchuigoua, H. T. (2014). Institutional framework and capital structure of microfinance institutions. *Journal of Business Research*, *67*(10), 2185–2197. doi:10.1016/j.jbusres.2014.01.008

Townsend, P. (2014). *International Analysis Poverty*. Routledge. doi:10.4324/9781315835099

Ukwueze, E. R., Asogwa, H. T., David-Wayas, O. M., Emecheta, C., & Nchege, J. E. (2019). How Does Microfinance Empower Women in Nigeria? A Study. In Handbook of Research on Microfinancial Impacts on Women Empowerment, Poverty, and Inequality (pp. 1-22). IGI Global.

Van Den Berg, M., Lensink, R., & Servin, R. (2015). Loan Officers' Gender and Microfinance Repayment Rates. *The Journal of Development Studies*, *51*(9), 1–14. doi:10.1080/00220388.2014.997218

Van Rooyen, C., Stewart, R., & de Wet, T. (2012). The impact of microfinance in sub-Saharan Africa: A systematic review of the evidence. *World Development*, *40*(11), 2249–2262. doi:10.1016/j.worlddev.2012.03.012

Vikas, B., & Vijayalakshmi, B. (2017). Microfinance and Women's Empowerment: An Exploratory Demographic Study in Karnataka, India. *South Asian Journal of Management*, *24*(3), 46–61.

KEY TERMS AND DEFINITIONS

Empowerment: The degree of autonomy and self-determination in women and in communities.

Lending: Money given by a microfinance institution to individuals or businesses, with the expectation that the borrower will repay the money to the microfinance institution.

Microbusiness: Any business organisation that directly employs fewer than ten employees.

Microcredit: The provision of small loans to low-income earners to set up or develop their existing businesses.

Microfinance: The provision of small loans and training exclusively to microbusinesses, financially disadvantaged individuals, and low-income families.

Outcomes: The result of using microfinance services or the consequence of using it.

Poverty: A state or condition in which a person or community lacks the financial resources and essentials for a minimum standard of living.

Chapter 4
Microfinance for achieving Sustainable Development Goals:
Pondering Over Indian Experiences for the Preservation of Magnificent African Natural Resources

Manpreet Arora
School of Commerce and Management Studies, Central University of Himachal Pradesh, Dharamshala, India

Swati Singh
Maharaja Agrasen University, India

ABSTRACT

This chapter focuses on the possibilities of exploring the areas where credit intervention can be done by the government in the form of schemes which are dependent on sustainable business practices. Nature has provided us abundance of raw material which if used wisely can help to remove poverty across the globe; on the same hand we can preserve the natural resources also if we use sustainable practices. In the current scenario where the world is facing pandemic and natural calamities, the time has to come to focus on sustainable rural micro financing activities which can not only solve the problem of linking the deprived sections of society with the mainstream, but it can also help them to improve their standard of living, and simultaneously, it can take care of various environmental issues too.

DOI: 10.4018/978-1-7998-7499-7.ch004

INTRODUCTION

The concept of microfinance, poverty alleviation and rural credit are interlinked with each other (Kamal Vatta, 2003). In many countries till now the outreach of the banking network and the substantial flow of resources is not in equity to various areas that is why they have to choose for going into priority lending. A majority of population in various nations still do not avail the benefit of various institutions which are the credit providers. That is why there is always inequality in credit distribution across the world. The needs of the poor clients are somewhat different and the products which banking structure offers they are something different because they are pursuing the objective of profit making. Many studies provide evidence that poor need different, better and unique ways of access to various financial services in order to be linked with the mainstream (Basu & Srivastava, 2005; Leyshon, & Thrift, 1995). In countries like India it's been 25 years that a pilot program called as Self Help Group Bank linkage programme is working and the program has grown exponentially and has proven to be a success in providing access to large number of loans under this scheme. The Indian financial landscape has benefited a lot with micro financing activities in various states.

BACKGROUND

Various studies and researches provide evidence that the formal financial institutions used to fail to reach to the poorer sections of the society (Ledgerwood, 1998; Ananth & Öncü, 2013) especially to the rural people because there is information asymmetry and there are certain issues relating to enforcement of various programmes initiated by the governments in order to reach to the poorest of the poor residing in the rural areas therefore there is a dire need of having certain alternatives for the rural credit systems which can help us to solve the various problems relating with the rural credits which can serve the marginalized and vulnerable sections of the society. Financial institutions are regarded as the saviors who can help to solve various problems relating to the issues which generally the formal financial institutions or banking structures face while reaching to the deprived sections of the society. The concept of group lending phenomenon, joint liability system and mentored credit help us to solve various problems relating with the issues which generally are pertaining to the formal banking structure (Bangoura, 2012).

Microfinance is regarded as a powerful tool/instrument for or giving the basic financial facilities to rural poor especially women (Javid & Abrar, 2015). There are certain sections of the society which are working as small and marginal farmers; there are certain rural artisans and economically weaker sections of the society where the needs of the borrowers are somewhat different because they do not have any collateral to provide to the formal financial banking structure credit providers. So that is why microfinance is regarded as a best tool to solve the problems of such people who do not have credit collateral to offer. It is defined as the provision of thrift and credit where the financial services and products of very small amounts can be given to the poor in rural and semi rural areas where they can help them to raise their standard of living by producing certain small articles. There are so many underdeveloped regions across the worlds which are still fighting with the higher pressures of population, extreme poverty and there are various kinds of social economic disparities which play a crucial role in making their life tougher. Economies like Africa are also constrained with low basic socio-economic infra. They are not having proper facilities of production, transportation, energy and education. That is why the information level or the rural outreach in terms of the financial sector is relatively poor. That is why it is necessary that certain different ways of reaching to the poorest sections of the society can be devised so that they can be financially included into the mainstream. Challenges of the formal banking structure are high as operational costs and the low value of large volume transactions do not hold a proper balance. That is why giving credit to the poorer sections of society is a very non beneficial activity for them. In many countries microfinance has been used as an anti poverty tool(Ledgerwood, 1998; Addae-Korankye, 2012; Leikem, 2012; Bakhtiari, 2006; Khandker, 1998; Devaraja, 2011; Rahman, 2004; Boateng, Boateng, & Bampoe, 2015; Midgley, 2008). Eradication of poverty, solving various socio economic disparities and uplifting the poorest of the poor especially women are the evidences available in countries like India, Bangladesh where microfinance interventions proved successful (Adjei, Arun & Hossain, 2009). When we talk about providing access to the financial services especially about giving credit to the vulnerable sections of society, the main target of every government is to focus on the all round development of a economy therefore in various nations cooperative sector gained momentum and they basically focus on a continued and a steady flow of institutional credit to the grass root level. Characteristics which make the rural credit different from the other facilities of credit is that it is very difficult to analyze the impact of such credit programs and the flow of credit to the borrowers need special interventions because they are more vulnerable and the excluded sectors of the society. Absence of mutual confidence between the borrower as well as lenders is another pertinent area because the demand for credit is somewhat low and the level of transactions can be extremely less also. The disadvantaged are also prone to failures, as there are so many disparities across the sections of the society. There is huge income inequality and growth oriented strategies are not properly established. Effective training and a proper communication between the borrower and lender plays an important role. Therefore the safest way of improving the rural economic prosperity is only to improve the agricultural productivity without harming the environment and adopting the sustainable practices which can help them to flourish and it on the same hand preserves our natural environment also. Micro finance activities those are focused on sustainability projects and that can help preserve our natural resources can prove to be a wonderful tool for the upliftment of the society as well as preservation of the natural environment.

MAIN FOCUS OF THE CHAPTER

This chapter focuses on the possibilities of exploring the areas where the credit intervention can be done by the government in the form of schemes which are dependent on sustainable business practices. In Africa the downtrodden tribals and the poor can get access to financial services with the help of microfinance intervention and by this simultaneously their traditions are also taken care of. Nature has provided us the humans abundance of raw material which if used wisely can help to remove poverty across the globe; on the same hand we can preserve the nature also if we use sustainable business practices. In the current scenario where the world is facing pandemic and natural calamities, the time has to come to focus on sustainable rural micro financing activities which can not only solve the problem of linking the deprived sections of society with the mainstream but on the same hand it can help them to improve their standard of living and simultaneously it can take care of various environmental issues too.

The Concept of Microfinance

Provision of credit is monetary but the benefits of the microfinance are far more than the monetary benefits. It often targets the underprivileged and the disadvantaged sections of the society that are unable to get credit from commercial banks and thus remain deprived from the basic amenities of life. Due to lack of financial resources, many women are subject to domestic violence; their psychological and mental health is badly affected; they are deprived of education; they are not socially and economically empowered; and many commit suicides and are vulnerable to heinous crimes such as rapes. In developing countries like India, microfinance has been acknowledged as a pro-poor growth intervention as it may focus on various special programs/ models which can fulfill the needs of the poor and vulnerable sections of the society such as women in particular. Many studies done all across the countries exploring the contributions of microfinance programmes reveal that it is an effective tool of poverty reduction and empowerment of women (Cheston & Kuhn, 2002; Morduch & Haley, 2002). In addition to this, it also helps achieve the developmental goals. It has emerged as an alternative to the failure of the mainstream financial sector in order to make financial services available to the poor. Various microfinance schemes are spread widely across the world because they are considered as one of the effective and flexible strategies to fight against global poverty. This chapter also focuses on the qualitative dimensions of the microfinance with the help of evidences available in literature, along with secondary data available on the govt. portals, International Agencies like UN, World Bank etc.

Microfinance is related with providing financial services to poor and unprivileged. The term micro signifies providing small amounts may it be in the form of credit or thrift. It is also related with savings, insurance and various other services related with small amounts. When we look at the developing nations where a significant percentage of population lives below poverty line and have no access to any mainstream credit facilities, then microfinance appears to be an important as well as an effective tool to uplift the weaker, vulnerable and deprived sections of the society. We can find significant demand of short term credit especially in rural and backward areas. A lot of innovation and experimentation had been done in this area which was initially started by Mohd. Yunus in Bangladesh. His Grameen model of banking based on thrift and credit was replicated in many nations and achieved significant success in the various parts of the world. In many nations various practices are followed to reach to the poorer sections of the society. Low rate of interest, welfare programmes, subsidies and formal banking structures could not fill the gap between the haves and haves not. The simple reason is that the prime motive of a commercial bank is to earn profits. They demand collateral for access to credit which is not available with the poor borrowers who belong to the deprived and weaker sections of the society. There are so many constraints which are faced by the weaker sections of the society therefore they require special types of programmes or more specifically interventions. Talking specifically about the rural poor their needs are different as they are not most of the times socially included in the mainstream. In India typically the nature of microfinance is basically rural and semi-urban (Kaladhar, 1997).

The Underlying Concept of Sustainability

Whenever we think about Africa the gifts of nature in terms of wildlife comes into one's mind. It becomes our utmost duty to indulge into sustainable practices which do not harm the resources of nature and the future generations are also able to see what nature has offered to Africa. Focusing on sustainable development becomes indispensable agenda in this scenario where nations are facing pandemic and the human race is facing the consequences of natural equilibriums. United Nations has adopted the agenda for sustainable development 2030 which gives a blueprint for focusing on peace and prosperity of the people as well as the whole planet, taking care of the future. They have adopted 17 Sustainable Development Goals which require urgent actions by the countries in global partnership whether they are developed or under developing. One of the main focus of the sustainable development goals is removal of poverty, climate control, preserving land, forest and oceans which can be achieved only by investing in sustainable projects and such projects can be financed through microfinace.

The sustainable development goals were adopted in Earth summit where more than 178 countries adopted the agenda Number 21 which provides a comprehensive plan of action in order to build a global partnership for focusing on sustainable development which can lead to improvement of human rights and protection of the environment. The sustainable development goals adopted by United Nations provide substantial help and support as well as capacity building for the sustainable goals and their related thematic issues which include preservation of water, energy, climate, oceans, science and technology etc.

The concept of Sustainable Development is focused on fulfilling the Human Development Goals with simultaneous focus on sustaining the ability of the natural systems in order to preserve the natural resources and ecosystems on which the entire globe depends. When we talk about sustainable development it focuses on taking care of the natural systems in such a way that human demands are met without undermining the importance of the natural systems. There is a dire need to meet the present day scenario without compromising the ability of future generations to meet their needs. There are so many global challenges which require attention as well as intervention in various parts of the globe that include environmental degradation, inequality, poverty, justice, climate change etc. It is evident that when economic structures grow they affect the natural systems negatively. While focusing on economic and social development generally environment protection and climate control are taken to be granted. In order to follow the sustainability concept we need to follow the environmental friendly practices because without nature we cannot sustain. It includes preservation of forests, wildlife ecosystems, water and everything which nature has offered us. The natural biotic systems degrade with excessive use for human needs they have got their own carrying capacity and should be taken care of while developing for rapid industrialization. An additional focus is required by the current generation to take care of the environmental and ecological issues as it is our responsibility towards the future generations to maintain and improve the planetary resources. The concept of Sustainable Development is very wide it is not just taking care of the sustainability of natural resources but it also imbibes activities towards achieving the goals of having a peaceful global society. In which information integration and participation of various countries equally play an important role. Therefore the economies all over the world are now focusing on preserving the economic, environmental and social factors in order to achieve the sustainable development goals. The ecological stability is equally important for achieving the economic as well as social goals of a country. The way towards achieving sustainability goals is to fund projects relating to agriculture and rural development especially in countries like Africa. The research efforts should be directed towards development of the country focusing on sustainable goals. The planning and implementation of these goals will lay a sound foundation for the future development of the country. Over the period of time many international agencies have supported rural development process which lead to the achievement of sustainable goals but the country now needs to focus on its resources, which can not only be source of earnings but will also lead a way towards sustainability, as, the rural tribes had always remain dependent on sustainable ways of living.

The need is to redefine the priority areas and make sustainable strategies for such areas. The possible areas which this chapter would try to peep into are discussed in the later half which can not only help in eradication of social issues but can also lead to environment preservation if microcredit for these areas is provided in the current scenario especially in countries like Africa.

1. Sustainable Development Goals

In 2025 when UN member states adopted the agenda of sustainable development by 2030 a global sustainable development report was agreed to be published by United Nations. The High Level Political Forum has been also established for leading the goals of sustainable development and poverty eradication across the world. This high level political forum will be informed by Global Development report. This report is global in its coverage (sustainabledevelopment.un.org). The report of 2021 has outlined the impacts of COVID-19 on the sustainable development goals. It also suggests measures to recover. A sustainable development index has been prepared in this report on the basis of which countries are ranked in the report. The report highlights the fact that due to COVID-19 rate of poverty and unemployment has increased in 2020-2021. The economic, social as well as environmental sectors of the globe in terms of sustainable goals have been negatively affected by COVID-19. Thereby all the nations across the world are facing challenges to achieve the sustainable goals. The top twenty countries in terms of achieving SDG and the SDI are shown below in Table 1:

Table 1. SDI 2021 Rankings published at sdgindex.org

Rank	Country	Score
1	Finland	85.9
2	Sweden	85.6
3	Denmark	84.9
4	Germany	82.5
5	Belgium	82.2
6	Austria	82.1
7	Norway	82.0
8	France	81.7
9	Slovenia	81.6
10	Estonia	81.6
11	Netherlands	81.6
12	Czech Republic	81.4
13	Ireland	81.0
14	Croatia	80.4
15	Poland	80.2
16	Switzerland	80.1
17	United Kingdom	80.0
18	Japan	79.8
19	Slovak Republic	79.6
20	Spain	79.5
107	**South Africa**	**63.7**
120	**India**	**60.1**

Source: https://sdgs.un.org/

Finland has topped in following the SDG's with Sweden at second number. Countries like India and Africa are still at very low rank to achieve the sustainable development goals. There is long way to go to make these countries following highly sustainability driven practices. The SDG report highlights the status of 52 African countries also in regard to achieving the sustainable development goals (The 2020 edition of the Africa SDG Index and dashboards report). According to the report SDG 13 i.e Climate action is the area on which most of the African countries are positively responding. Responsible consumption and production is another area where the African countries are doing well overall. The greatest challenge which African nations are facing is that of achieving the sustainable goals of good health, wellbeing, industry, innovation, infrastructure, peace, justice and strong institutions.

Tunisia and North Africa are the African nations which have performed well in overall and Central Africa performed the worst. Overall the report highlights the fact that there are wide, diverse and immense inequalities which are being found in African nations in terms of achievement of sustainable development goals. To get a better picture the Sustainable development goals propounded by UN are listed below in Table 2:

Table 2. Sustainable Development Goals adopted by United Nations

Goal Number	Goal theme
Sustainable Development Goal 1	No poverty
Sustainable Development Goal 2	Zero Hunger
Sustainable Development Goal 3	Good Health and Well-Being
Sustainable Development Goal 4	Quality Education
Sustainable Development Goal 5	Gender Equality
Sustainable Development Goal 6	Clean Water and Sanitation
Sustainable Development Goal 7	Affordable and Clean Energy
Sustainable Development Goal 8	Decent Work and Economic Growth
Sustainable Development Goal 9	Industry, Innovation and Infrastructure
Sustainable Development Goal 10	Reduced Inequalities
Sustainable Development Goal 11	Sustainable Cities and Communities
Sustainable Development Goal 12	Responsible Consumption and Production
Sustainable Development Goal 13	Climate Action
Sustainable Development Goal 14	Life below water
Sustainable Development Goal 15	Life on Land
Sustainable Development Goal 16	Peace, Justice and Strong Institutions
Sustainable Development Goal 17	Partnerships for the Goals

Source: https://sdgs.un.org/

2. Microfinance as a Successful Intervention Tool to Uplift Poor and Vulnerable: Certain Empirical Evidences

In India poor still have very less access to formal finance. Microfinance has been used as an intervention tool to reach to the rural public in India and proved to be an effective tool (Basu & Srivastva, 2005). In rural areas where the micro financing activities are promoted women are largely the benefiters. The SHG Bank linkage programe has proved to be a successful tool in the state of Himachal Pradesh where the women felt empowered after microfinance interventions were made (Arora & Singh, 2018). In the state it was found by the authors that microfinance programmes have been contributing to the economic and social development of the women in the areas. They feel empowered and motivated. Many reported freedom of taking household decisions and they have also reported inculcation of leadership qualities in them as they feel socially empowered. In India under SHG Bank linkage model the financial resources are linked with formal banking structure and is in a way controlled by the apex banks. Therefore the legal and formal hassles of reaching to the poor and vulnerable are taken care off to a great extent (Basu & Srivastava, 2005). Microfinance is considered as one of the effective tools to make people self sufficient and help them walk towards the path of self development. Those people, who are extremely poor, are not self sufficient, lack skill, training and knowledge; they can be targeted well by mixed methods of welfare oriented activities as well as microfinance interventions. Microfinance has been effective in promoting micro-entrepreneurial activities in countries like India (Khandelwal, 2007). The Indian microfinance activities are pursued by not only by government, but there are so many NGO's, commercial banks, regional rural banks, volunteers who are indulged in promoting activities catering to the poor in rural and semi urban areas at a very vast level (Kaladhar, 1997). Cooperative sector has played an important role in providing micro credit in India. It has proved to be a successful tool to increase the outreach of finance. The progress of providing microcredit through SHG Bank linkage programme in India can be shown with the help of following table:

Table 3. Progress of SHG-Bank Linkage Programme

Particulars	2018-19 No. of SHG's	2018-19 Amount (Rs. Crore)	2019-20 No. of SHG's	2019-20 Amount (Rs. Crore)	%change No. of SHG's	%change Amount
Loans Disbursed	26,98,400	58,317	31,46,002	77,659.35	16.59	33.17
Loans Outstanding	50,77,332	87,098	56,77,071	1,08,075.07	11.81	24.08
Savings with Banks	1,00,14,243	23,324	1,02,43,323	26,152.05	2.29	12.12
NPA level (%)	5.19		4.92			
Average Loan disbursed per SHG	Rs 2.16 Lakh		Rs 2.7 Lakh			

Source: NABARD.com

3. Thrust Areas where Sustainable Microfinance Interventions in Africa can Help

In the African continent where there is abundance of resources there is a huge possibility of exploring the natural resources in a sustainable manner. The nature has given immense to this continent and it becomes the duty of mankind to preserve and use its natural resources in the best manner so as to preserve the resources for the future generations. On the same hand the excluded communities of African continent which have not yet been connected with the mainstream, can get opportunities to grow and gain immensely if the sustainable development goals are pursued wisely. Some of the areas where the sustainable development goals can be pursued with the microfinance interventions are listed below:

Possibilities of Using the Animal Waste and Other Wastes as a Substitute of Fuel or Energy

In this age of modernization each country is producing tons of animal and other wastes, which are not only hazardous but are threat to sustainability also. But it is a known fact that various waste materials can be successfully converted into fuels such as gases which become substitute of energy (Al-Hamamre, Saidan, Hararah, Rawajfeh, Alkhasawneh & Al-Shannag, 2017). Converting animal, plant or other wastes into energy can be an area where developing nations like India and Africa can benefit people as well as environment. It will not only help in reducing wastages which later on can become a big trouble by contaminating water, land and other natural resources, but can be an effective way of saving energy and national money in many ways (Afazeli, Jafari, Rafiee & Nosrati, 2014). Africa is rich in animals, and various kinds of natural flora and fauna. If the microfinance is allocated for the projects related to conservation of energy and effectively using animal and other wastes as substitute of fuel or energy it can also help in rural upliftment as various sections of the society will get involved in various activities and many can be environment preservers as well as employment providers. Many incidents are available in Asia where cow dung is used to prepare methane which is an excellent source of energy and the waste is used as manures for vegetation (Bhattacharya, Thomas & Salam, 1997). Countries like China and India have been working on various kinds of small and efficient digesters which are cost effective. Digesters have proved successful in conservation of energy and recycle of waste. Biogas has got a great potential to serve as a sustainable source of energy (Surendra, Takara, Hashimoto & Khana, 2014). In India it has been used as a clean fuel for cooking and transportation needs (Vijay, Kapoor, Trivedi & Vijay, 2015; (Kumar, Kumar, Baredar & Shukla, 2015; Minde, Magdum & Kalyanraman, 2013; Rao, Baral, Dey & Mutnuri, 2010; Mottaleb,2019;

Lewis, Hollingsworth, Chartier, Cooper, Foster, Gomes,... & Pattanayak, 2017). Still the potential of this renewable source of energy is much high in India (Mittal, Ahlgren & Shukla, 2019). Such projects through microfinance intervention can help the African communities to uplift their standard of living, pursue sustainable development goals and save environment. Moreover solid waste which is generated from various industries can also be used as a source of energy as well as a building material which in turn has the potential to lower down the pressure on the natural resources of energy Pappu, Saxena & Asolekar, 2007).

Use of Solar as Well as Wind Energy for Various Small and Micro Sector Enterprises

Africa is known as a sun continent that is why there are tremendous ways and possibilities to harness the solar energy in the country. Solar electricity has a potential to change many sectors as we all understand that in various segments of industry/projects/plants consumption of fuel is one of the major component. To electrify the various rural areas of Africa no doubt there are certain unique challenges but by using various innovative alternatives and by harnessing solar as the well as wind energy we can give rural families efficient means to light up their homes. As we all know sun is free and that is why solar energy along with wind energy has the capacity to connect the rural areas of Africa with the mainstream, therefore a strong need is there for the African nations to think out of the box and explore the possibilities of financing the projects relating to wind energy and solar energy in the nation. Solar panels have the capacity to generate electricity to run cooking gas stoves, water pumps (Mekhilef, Saidur, & Safari, 2011) and can be an important source in production of various small items which are generally the traditions of the rural tribal communities of Africa ultimately helping them to connect with the outer world. With the help of innovative financing schemes like microfinance various service arrangements can be made to overcome the cost of installation of such plants which after a point of time can be covered with proper planning and they can act as a right way towards sustainable future. It requires government intervention as well as a regional cooperation in order to set up such plants. Besides the domestic use, energy can be harnessed to run small businesses and it can trigger the entrepreneurial activities in the nation especially in the rural areas where there are rich natural resources and sustainability should be of prime importance but they are not connected with the rest of world. Priority in relation to the generation and distribution of solar and wind energy needs to be identified and require special attention as well as action. It would require a proper training and consultancy so that the rural communities understand about its importance as well as its advantages. It can pave their way towards having access to information and communication technology which is a distant dream of many of the tribal communities of the nation. With proper usage of energy a focus on health, education and skill development is also expected. It can also promote agricultural activities of varied nature which ultimately can provide boost to businesses. In India government agencies like Rural Electrification Corporation, Power finance Corporation, Indian Renewable Energy Development Agency are the major fund providers for the renewable energy sector in India. "The government of India has set a target of 175 GW renewable electricity (RE) capacity by 2022 & 450 GW RE capacity by 2030" (Kapur, 2021). India has pledged to increase the renewable energy capacity by 2030. The directions to become "a renewable energy powerhouse" has been set. Many states of India have already grown rich in terms of production of RE, amongst them are Andhra Pradesh, Telengana, Gujrat, Karnataka, Madhaya Pradesh, Maharashtra and Rajasthan.

Use of Bamboo and Similar Kind of raw Materials Which Take Less Time to Grow and Mature and to be Able to Use as Raw Material

Asia, Africa and Latin America are rich in various species of bamboo (Kusters, Achdiawan, Belcher & Pérez, 2006). Rural communities can be seen to use mostly bamboo for fuel, fencing and their local furniture needs. Some of the species of bamboo are also used as food as well as animal fodder. But bamboo has got much more many uses. It is used in various parts of the world to produce fabric, cloth, paper, charcoal, ornamental plantations etc (Farrelly, 1996). The demand of bamboo in various parts of the world is tremendous and it can be tapped perfectly by the nation by financing certain sustainable bamboo processing units in the country which can later enter into export of the process form of bamboo Africa has got huge reserves of various species of indigenous bamboo and it has also got excellent conditions for growing certain cultivated species also which are demanded in various parts of the world. The strength and the weight are the two main characteristics of the bamboo which makes them one of the most used building materials in various areas of the world and Africa can be a leading provider of this raw material. Not only bamboo as a raw material of various things but it is also regarded as a crucial element in maintaining the balance of oxygen and carbon dioxide in the atmosphere. Use of bamboo is also very important for the sustainable development of the country. It can also be used to reduce the carbon footprints and to help fight global warming etc. It's very viable replacement of the wood. Another aspect of growing bamboo is the use of bamboo in various medicines too. Not only human beings but various kinds of livestock are also given medicines which generally are prepared from the extracts of bamboo. The tribal communities of Africa have a great knowledge about the medicinal plants. The knowledge can be shared with the world where bamboo as well as other sustainable products along with natural resources of Africa can become a source of livelihood as well as a way of achieving sustainable development goals. A proper Micro Finance intervention for setting up the units related with use of bamboo for furniture, raw material, for paper industry, ornamental plants etc can do wonders. The rural communities should be educated to grow bamboo on commercial basis to make it as a source of livelihood which not only will save the environment but is also going to help them increase their standard of living. Over 40 indigenous species of bamboo are found in Africa, there is a great need for special focus and action on use of bamboo and its export from the nation in its pure as well as processed form to make it a source of livelihood and development for the rural communities of the nation. Bamboos have the potential of offering a wide range of solutions to the problems caused by climate change (Thokchom & Yadava,2015). Bamboo is a great wood substitute and is widely available in the regions of southeast Asia, Africa as well as Latin America (Song, Zhou, Jiang,Yu, Fu, Li, Ma & Peng, 2011). Countries like China which have vast forests covered with bamboo have paid a great degree of attention to the management of bamboo forests in order to encash ecological benefits associated with it. The plant has got immense features which distinguishes it from other plants. It's in fact a species of grass. Bamboo has got immense capacity of controlling soil erosion, it helps to protect soil thus helps to conserve water. The degraded vast lands can be quickly rehabilitated with the growth of bamboo. The economic as well as social benefits of bamboo are also immense. Not only it can be used in building infrastructure but it acts as a wonderful food item too. It can also be used to produce home utilities, clothing, and instruments and can be used to make paper. Thus giving training and focusing on, micro financing activities related with bamboo and related products can promote small ventures thereby provide sustainable solutions to the economic development. Bamboo is also regarded as one of the fastest "carbon- sequestering plant" (Kirchhof,2021).

Sustainable Food Production and Micro Financing for Food Processing Units Like Juices, Pickles etc

One of the major problems across the world is food security (Udmale, Pal, Szabo, Pramanik, & Large, 2020). In developing nations like India as well as Africa the problem of food security remains an issue. It is still to be tackled fully as there is a big chunk of section which is below poverty line. The possible and one of the feasible solutions to tackle the problem can be encouragement to sustainable food production activities. In the sustainable food production orientation processes and systems which can help conservation of natural resources are used. A focus on non-polluting activities and the conservation of non-renewable energy sources is also done. The sustainable food productions as well as food processing activities are already used by the indigenous communities and tribes in different parts of Africa as well as India (Amoa-Awua, Ngunjiri, Anlobe, Kpodo, Halm, Hayford & Jakobsen, 2007; Hudson, Krogman & Beckie, 2016) The traditions which are especially used by indigenous communities need to be carried forward and their survival should be ensured by appropriate practices.

Such practices should be aligned with sustainable business practices related with not only to boost food production in African continent but also to start new start ups and sustain the food processing units . Many food products need to be identified which can have international market and bamboo is one of them (Lobovikov, Paudel, Ball, Piazza, Guardia, Ren, ... & Wu, 2007). Many indigenous societies and tribes have immense knowledge of medicinal plants and herbs, which can be not only used for daily consumption but they can act as remedies to cure various ailments. Of lately, the ancient wisdom of India to cure ailments through herbs and plants known as *Ayurveda;* has gained immense demand in international markets. In the similar manner the wisdom of tribes in Africa can be immensely useful and can have potential demand which through microfinance can be used to uplift the standard of living of the tribes and connect them with the mainstream as well as outer world. Their knowledge of medicines, herbs can provide them livelihood as well as will keep them connected with nature and sustainable practices. "The principles of sustainability are the foundations of what this concept represents. Therefore, sustainability is made up of three pillars: the economy, society, and the environment. These principles are also informally used as profit, people and planet".

Focus on Sustainable and Nature Based Tourism

Nature Based tourism is an emerging concept (Fossgard & Fredman, 2019). Countries like Africa and India have got immense potential to tap resources by promoting tourism. There are so many things which are tourist attraction for both the countries. Both the countries are rich in wildlife, flora, fauna and scenic beauty so tourism sector has a great potential to uplift the standard of living for many people who can become part of service chain. Nature based tourism is basically responsible travel to the various natural areas which can help one to conserve the environment. The main aim of nature based tourism is to improve the welfare of the local people also because when the rural and natural places become an attraction there arise possibilities of small ventures in the local and rural communities. Local communities get involved in nature based tourism activities like helping in photography, stargazing, camping, hunting, fishing or visiting the places. There is immense possibility in both the countries to focus on nature based tourism because many small venture creations are possible in this area. Sustainable microfinance is provided for such projects which can assist and help the nature based tourism activities then the country can also earn and the local communities will also benefit. It can help them to increase their standard of living as well as to connect with the outer world when we talk about the nature based tourism it is basically dependent on the experiences which are directly related with the natural attractions and it also includes eco-tourism. These days adventure tourism has also become famous and it also helps local communities to gain small venture creation.

FUTURE RESEARCH DIRECTIONS

The world is in the midst of a global climate crisis and pandemic. It becomes necessary to address the needs of climate control and the effects of pandemic by following sustainable business practices. Addressing sustainability across all industries is a worldwide priority, and global finance is no exception. The blockchain and digital asset industry will play a critical role in building a sustainable future for global finance. Moreover, Microfinance Institutions (MFIs) work to increase social sustainability by providing more services to particular clientele, while maintaining the financial and operational sustainability of the institutions. There comes a need to explore and research in the areas of increasing social sustainability, and explore the areas for building a sustainable future for global finance.

CONCLUSION

Based on the above discussion we can conclude by saying that microfinance can act as the most reliable as well as sustainable tool to preserve and nurture the natural treasures of Africa. This is owing to the fact that sustainable micro financial activities at one level involves stakeholders from different tribal communities, at another it strengthens their bond with the land, water, forest and other natural resource. Sustainable microfinance also helps eradicate inequitable distribution of financial resources and it becomes evident because of the fact that the credit providing institutions remain keenly sensitive and mindful of the clients sitting on the last step of the economic ladder. The Indian experience concerning microfinance has been richly diverse and varied and it has all the necessary ingredients required to nurture and sustain a continent of African proportion. The key points of discussion above point towards the crucial role that financial institutions play in reaching out to the deprived sections of the society and thereby making them conscious and aware about the natural wealth comprising water, forest and land. The notions of group lending, joint liability system and mentored credit help can play a decisive role in empowering the poor and providing financial sustainability to the rural artisans and people from weaker sections of the society. In addition to that sustainable microfinance can also play a crucial role in ameliorating the poor, removing socio economic disparities, providing paddle push to the poorest of the poor and empowering women belonging to African hinterlands. Such observations is based on powerfully grounded and based on Indian rural and tribal arenas and have been tried and tested over a long period of time. The lending institutions in India present an evidence of the fact that if we are genuinely motivated and sincerely committed to fight for the cause of the deprived and downtrodden, there can be no obstacle in the way of uplifting the poor through sustainable microfinance and provision of microcredit. In addition to micro financial services co-operative ventures can also lend tremendous push to eradicate inequality, disparity and poverty. Another very important aspect of sustainable microfinance is effective communication between the lending financial institutions and the borrowing clients from rural and tribal communities as is the case in Africa. Awareness campaigns, regarding sustainable finance and preserving natural wealth/resources may lead to prosperity in the agricultural sector as well. The awareness campaigns can never lose sight of the importance of those sustainable practices that contribute to preserving the ecology and environment. Therefore sustainable microfinance is undoubtedly the key to achieve various SDG's in the rural and tribal arenas of African society. The Indian experience may certainly serve as an object lesson for Africa to follow from the view point of sustainable microfinance, microcredit, and sustainable practices at the rural and tribal levels.

REFERENCES

Addae-Korankye, A. (2012). Microfinance: A tool for poverty reduction in developing countries. *The Journal of Business and Retail Management Research, 7*(1), 138–149.

Adjei, J., Arun, T., & Hossain, F. (2009). Asset building and poverty reduction in Ghana: The case of microfinance. *Savings and Development, 33*(3), 265-291. Retrieved July 30, 2021, from https://www.jstor.org/stable/41406497

Afazeli, H., Jafari, A., Rafiee, S., & Nosrati, M. (2014). An investigation of biogas production potential from livestock and slaughterhouse wastes. *Renewable & Sustainable Energy Reviews, 34*, 380–386. doi:10.1016/j.rser.2014.03.016

Al-Hamamre, Z., Saidan, M., Hararah, M., Rawajfeh, K., Alkhasawneh, H. E., & Al-Shannag, M. (2017). Wastes and biomass materials as sustainable-renewable energy resources for Jordan. *Renewable & Sustainable Energy Reviews, 67*, 295–314. doi:10.1016/j.rser.2016.09.035

Amoa-Awua, W. K., Ngunjiri, P., Anlobe, J., Kpodo, K., Halm, M., Hayford, A. E., & Jakobsen, M. (2007). The effect of applying GMP and HACCP to traditional food processing at a semi-commercial kenkey production plant in Ghana. *Food Control*, *18*(11), 1449–1457. doi:10.1016/j.foodcont.2006.10.009

Ananth, S., & Öncü, T. (2013). Challenges to Financial Inclusion in India: The Case of Andhra Pradesh. *Economic and Political Weekly, 48*(7), 77-83. Retrieved July 30, 2021, from https://www.jstor.org/stable/23391312

Arora, M., & Singh, S. (2018). Microfinance, Women Empowerment, and Transformational Leadership: A Study of Himachal Pradesh. *International Journal on Leadership*, *6*(2), 23.

Bakhtiari, S. (2006). Microfinance and poverty reduction: some international evidence. *International Business & Economics Research Journal, 5*(12).

Bangoura, L. (2012). Microfinance as an Approach to Development in Low Income Countries. *Bangladesh Development Studies*, *35*(4), 87–111. Retrieved July 30, 2021, from https://www.jstor.org/stable/41968844

Basu, P., & Srivastava, P. (2005). Exploring Possibilities: Microfinance and Rural Credit Access for the Poor in India. *Economic and Political Weekly*, *40*(17), 1747–1756. https://www.jstor.org/stable/4416534

Bhattacharya, S. C., Thomas, J. M., & Salam, P. A. (1997). Greenhouse gas emissions and the mitigation potential of using animal wastes in Asia. *Energy*, *22*(11), 1079–1085. doi:10.1016/S0360-5442(97)00039-X

Boateng, G. O., Boateng, A. A., & Bampoe, H. S. (2015). Microfinance and poverty reduction in Ghana: Evidence from policy beneficiaries. *Review of Business & Finance Studies*, *6*(1), 99–108.

Cheston, S., & Kuhn, L. (2002). Empowering women through microfinance. *Draft. Opportunity International*, *64*, 1–64.

Devaraja, T. S. (2011). *Microfinance in India-A tool for poverty reduction. University of Mysore*. University Grants Commission of India.

Farrelly, D. (1996). *The book of bamboo: A comprehensive guide to this remarkable plant, its uses, and its history*. Thames and Hudson Ltd.

Fossgard, K., & Fredman, P. (2019). Dimensions in the nature-based tourism experience scape: An explorative analysis. *Journal of Outdoor Recreation and Tourism, 28*.

Hudson, S., Krogman, N., & Beckie, M. (2016). Social practices of knowledge mobilization for sustainable food production: Nutrition gardening and fish farming in the kolli hills of India. *Food Security, 8*(3), 523–533. doi:10.100712571-016-0580-z

Javid, A., & Abrar, A. (2015). Microfinance Institutions and Poverty Reduction: A Cross Regional Analysis. *Pakistan Development Review, 54*(4), 371–387. doi:10.30541/v54i4I-IIpp.371-387

Kaladhar, K. (1997). Microfinance in India: Design, Structure and Governance. *Economic and Political Weekly, 32*(42), 2687–2706. https://www.jstor.org/stable/4405979

Kapur, S. (2021). *A Finance Structure That Matches India's Ambitions For Renewable Energy Sector.* Moneycontrol. Available at: https://www.moneycontrol.com/news/business/companies/a-finance-structure-that-matches-indias-ambitions-for-renewable-energy-sector-5467911.html

Khandelwal, A. K. (2007). Microfinance development strategy for India. *Economic and Political Weekly*, 1127–1135.

Khandker, S. R. (1998). *Fighting poverty with microcredit: experience in Bangladesh.* Oxford University Press.

Kumar, A., Kumar, N., Baredar, P., & Shukla, A. (2015). A review on biomass energy resources, potential, conversion and policy in India. *Renewable & Sustainable Energy Reviews, 45*, 530–539. doi:10.1016/j.rser.2015.02.007

Kusters, K., Achdiawan, R., Belcher, B., & Pérez, M. R. (2006). Balancing development and conservation? An assessment of livelihood and environmental outcomes of nontimber forest product trade in Asia, Africa, and Latin America. *Ecology and Society, 11*(2), art20. doi:10.5751/ES-01796-110220

Ledgerwood, J. (1998). *Microfinance handbook: An institutional and financial perspective.* World Bank Publications. doi:10.1596/978-0-8213-4306-7

Leikem, K. (2012). Microfinance: a tool for Poverty Reduction. *Senior Honors Projects. Paper, 300.*

Lewis, J. J., Hollingsworth, J. W., Chartier, R. T., Cooper, E. M., Foster, W. M., Gomes, G. L., Kussin, P. S., MacInnis, J. J., Padhi, B. K., Panigrahi, P., Rodes, C. E., Ryde, I. T., Singha, A. K., Stapleton, H. M., Thornburg, J., Young, C. J., Meyer, J. N., & Pattanayak, S. K. (2017). Biogas stoves reduce firewood use, household air pollution, and hospital visits in Odisha, India. *Environmental Science & Technology, 51*(1), 560–569. doi:10.1021/acs.est.6b02466 PMID:27785914

Leyshon, A., & Thrift, N. (1995). Geographies of Financial Exclusion: Financial Abandonment in Britain and the United States. *Transactions of the Institute of British Geographers*, *20*(3), 312–341. doi:10.2307/622654

Lobovikov, M., Paudel, S., Ball, L., Piazza, M., Guardia, M., Ren, H., ... & Wu, J. (2007). *World bamboo resources: a thematic study prepared in the framework of the global forest resources assessment 2005* (No. 18). Food & Agriculture Org.

Mekhilef, S., Saidur, R., & Safari, A. (2011). A review on solar energy use in industries. *Renewable & Sustainable Energy Reviews*, *15*(4), 1777–1790. doi:10.1016/j.rser.2010.12.018

Midgley, J. (2008). Microenterprise, global poverty and social development. *International Social Work*, *51*(4), 467–479. doi:10.1177/0020872808090240

Minde, G., Magdum, S., & Kalyanraman, V. (2013). Biogas as a sustainable alternative for current energy need of India. *Journal of Sustainable Energy & Environment*, *4*, 121–132.

Mittal, S., Ahlgren, E. O., & Shukla, P. R. (2019). Future biogas resource potential in India: A bottom-up analysis. *Renewable Energy*, *141*, 379–389. doi:10.1016/j.renene.2019.03.133

Morduch, J., & Haley, B. (2002). *Analysis of the effects of microfinance on poverty reduction* (Vol. 1014). New York: NYU Wagner working paper.

Mottaleb, K. A., & Rahut, D. B. (2019). Biogas adoption and elucidating its impacts in India: Implications for policy. *Biomass and Bioenergy*, *123*, 166–174. doi:10.1016/j.biombioe.2019.01.049

Pappu, A., Saxena, M., & Asolekar, S. R. (2007). Solid wastes generation in India and their recycling potential in building materials. *Building and Environment*, *42*(6), 2311–2320. doi:10.1016/j.buildenv.2006.04.015

Rahman, A. (2004). Microcredit and poverty reduction: Trade-off between building institutions and reaching the poor. *Livelihood and microfinance. Anthropological and sociological perspectives on savings and debt*, 25-42.

Rao, P. V., Baral, S. S., Dey, R., & Mutnuri, S. (2010). Biogas generation potential by anaerobic digestion for sustainable energy development in India. *Renewable & Sustainable Energy Reviews*, *14*(7), 2086–2094. doi:10.1016/j.rser.2010.03.031

Song, X., Zhou, G., Jiang, H., Yu, S., Fu, J., Li, W., Wang, W., Ma, Z., & Peng, C. (2011). Carbon sequestration by Chinese bamboo forests and their ecological benefits: Assessment of potential, problems, and future challenges. *Environmental Reviews*, *19*(NA), 418–428. doi:10.1139/a11-015

Surendra, K. C., Takara, D., Hashimoto, A. G., & Khanal, S. K. (2014). Biogas as a sustainable energy source for developing countries: Opportunities and challenges. *Renewable & Sustainable Energy Reviews, 31,* 846–859. doi:10.1016/j.rser.2013.12.015

Thokchom, A., & Yadava, P. S. (2015). Bamboo and its role in climate change. *Current Science, 108*(5), 762–763. https://www.jstor.org/stable/24216487

Udmale, P., Pal, I., Szabo, S., Pramanik, M., & Large, A. (2020). Global food security in the context of COVID-19: A scenario-based exploratory analysis. *Progress in Disaster Science, 7,* 100120. doi:10.1016/j.pdisas.2020.100120 PMID:34173442

Vatta, K. (2003). Microfinance and Poverty Alleviation. *Economic and Political Weekly, 38*(5), 432–433. https://www.jstor.org/stable/4413155

Vijay, V. K., Kapoor, R., Trivedi, A., & Vijay, V. (2015). Biogas as clean fuel for cooking and transportation needs in India. In *Advances in Bioprocess Technology* (pp. 257–275). Springer. doi:10.1007/978-3-319-17915-5_14

KEY TERMS AND DEFINITIONS

Microfinance: Microfinance refers to the financial services provided to low-income individuals or groups who are typically excluded from traditional banking.

Sustainability: Sustainability means meeting our own needs without compromising the ability of future generations to meet their own needs.

Sustainable Development Goals: The Sustainable Development Goals are the blueprint established by United Nations to achieve a better and more sustainable future for all.

Sustainable Practices: Sustainable practices are the processes services employ to maintain the qualities that are valued in the physical environment. Living sustainably is about living within the means of natural systems (environment) and ensuring that our lifestyle doesn't harm other people.

Chapter 5
Analysis of Factors That Affect the Use of Microfinance for Microbusiness Development in Ghana

Yahaya Alhassan
https://orcid.org/0000-0001-6700-635X
University of Sunderland in London, UK

Uzoechi Nwagbara
University of Sunderland in London, UK

Samuel Salia
De Montfort University, UK

ABSTRACT

This chapter examined the factors that affect the use of microfinance for microbusiness development in Ghana. The study employed semi-structured survey questionnaire to determine whether an entrepreneur's personal attributes impede or facilitate microbusiness development in Ghana. Multiple linear regression analysis was conducted to determine the effects of entrepreneur's personal attributes on the monthly sales, number of employees, business assets, and capital stock of microbusinesses that received credit from a microfinance provider in the northern region of Ghana. The findings of the study suggest that micro-entrepreneur prior work experience, occupation, and prior income facilitate the use of microfinance for microbusiness development. These findings have policy implications for the government of Ghana and other agencies that are interested in using microfinance as a catalyst for economic growth in deprived communities in the country.

DOI: 10.4018/978-1-7998-7499-7.ch005

INTRODUCTION

The widespread use of microfinance as a key source of finance for microbusinesses in developing countries and recently in some developed countries has generated several studies that have attempted to determine its impact on microbusiness growth. For instance, Rotich, et al. (2015) found that the provision of microfinance increased the performance of microbusinesses in Sub-Saharan Africa. Similarly, analysis of Mochona (2006) suggests that clients of microfinance institutions in Ethiopia may have improved their level of sales from the use of microfinance. This view is consistent with Cooper (2012) who argues that microfinance services have helped businesses in Kenya to grow their monthly sales from micro to small and from small to medium. Microfinance has also been reported to have made a positive contribution to the development of microbusinesses in Asia. In particular, a study conducted in Malaysia found that microfinance impacted positively on total assets of microbusinesses (Al Mamun, et al., 2012). This may explain why Kondo, et al. (2008) concluded that generally, microfinance increases microbusiness productivity and creates jobs for the poor.

Other narratives from existing microfinance literature suggest that the personal attributes of the micro-entrepreneur may have influenced the growth of microbusinesses in developing countries. Taiwo, et al. (2016) for example, found that businesses owned by male micro-entrepreneurs generate more employment than those owned by their female counterparts. Also, a study conducted in Kenya by Naituli, et al., (2006) found a significant positive relationship between the age of the entrepreneur and the sales revenue of micro and small enterprises. Furthermore, Vikas and Vijayalakshmi (2017) have shown that the educational qualification of micro-entrepreneurs impacted positively on the sales of women enterprises in India. The influence of an entrepreneur's work experience and ethnicity on microbusiness development has also been reported by various researchers. Cabrera and Mauricio (2017) for instance, found a positive relationship between an entrepreneur's work experience and capital stock. Wang and Altinay (2012) have also shown that a significant positive relationship exists between the ethnicity of entrepreneur and microbusiness employment growth. Further evidence from existing literature also suggest that key attributes of a microbusiness such as the type of business, industry sector, location, source of capital and duration of operation may also influence microbusiness development (Mshenga, et al., 2010, Osei-Assibey, et al., 2012, Gill and Biger 2012, Kanyare and Mungai 2017, Li and Rama 2015).

However, further analysis of existing literature suggest that characteristics factors that impede or facilitate the use of microfinance for microbusiness development in developing countries particularly in Ghana has been under research. This raises the question: what are the distinctive factors that impede or facilitate the use of microfinance for microbusiness development in Ghana? The aim of this chapter therefore is to cover this knowledge gap by analysing the distinctive factors that impede or facilitate the use of microfinance for microbusiness development in Ghana.

BACKGROUND

Researchers who have attempted to describe microfinance rather explained the services microfinance institutions provide which in actual sense differ depending on the provider and the context within which such services are provided. Microfinance according to Ledgerwood, et al. (2013) is a combination of financial services made up of loans and savings designed purposely to alleviate poverty. Equally, Ebomuche, et al. (2014) define microfinance as the provision of credit at higher interest rates to individuals who have no access to traditional banks. Moreover, microfinance has been described by Martin, et al. (2002) as the provision of credit, deposits and insurance to financially disadvantaged households and microbusinesses. Perhaps the differences that emerged from the various explanation of microfinance are due to the fairly new nature of the concept of microfinance. Therefore, it is reasonable to suggest that microfinance institutions are still trying different services in order to ascertain the right mix of services for promoting microbusiness growth. Nevertheless, outcomes of analysis and evaluation of the various definitions offer a common basis for understanding microfinance. Overall, the outcomes of the review of the above definitions suggest that microfinance is designed to deliver credit and other financial services to people who have no access to traditional formal banks. It is very essential to note that the concept of microfinance is dynamic and has continued to change from the 18th century to date.

Certainly, the ability of microfinance institutions to effectively provide credit to individuals and groups without collateral has enhanced financial inclusion in deprived communities around the world (Ghosh, 2013). These achievements have been recognised by several international organisations. For instance, the Grameen bank and the founder of the bank (Muhammad Yunus) received the prestigious Noble Peace price in 2006. This award is perhaps a confirmation of the acceptance of microfinance as a financial inclusion strategy for poverty alleviation (Ledgerwood, 2013).

Empirical evidence suggests that microfinance outreach in the world exceeded 135 million customers in the last 20 years (Mia et al., 2019). Likewise, Bondinuba (2020) suggest there were over 10,000 microfinance institutions around the world in 2020. Moreover, despite the recent Covid-19 pandemic about 90 million microfinance borrowers were reached globally in 2020 alone (Oshora et al., 2020). Furthermore, Cull, et al. (2014) found that the Grameen bank solely funded over

8 million microbusinesses in 2011. Another microfinance institution that has been reported to have made significant contributions to the lives of millions of low-income earners and microbusiness development is the Bank Rakyat of Indonesia (Steinwand, 2013). Perhaps it is these positive outcomes that have influenced the Microfinance Summit to suggest that microfinance institutions will reach about 175 million low-income earners including microbusinesses globally by 2025. However, the question is whether microfinance institutions have achieved their intended objectives to justify the huge publicity about their achievements.

Microfinance success stories have also been reported by Ahmed (2009) and Ashcroft (2008). These studies have shown that microfinance institutions played a significant role in poverty alleviation in the last two decades. Against this background, Ghosh (2013) argue that microfinance institutions all over the world provide services that have helped to promote microbusiness development and financial inclusion in deprived communities. In this context, will the provision of microfinance to microbusinesses in Ghana yield similar positive outcomes?

Further analysis of existing literature provide evidence that microfinance has produced positive microbusiness development outcomes which has potential to improve incomes and reduce poverty in poor areas (Rotich, et al., 2015; Masanga and Jera, 2017; Cooper 2012). However, there are other narratives from existing microfinance literature that suggests that the personal attributes of the micro-entrepreneur such as the gender, age, level of education, prior income, work experience, ethnicity and occupation may influence the use of microfinance for microbusiness development.

FACTORS THAT INFLUENCE USE OF MICROFINANCE FOR MICROBUSINESS DEVELOPMENT

Issues, Controversies, Problems

1. Gender of Micro Entrepreneur

Analysis of Monahan, et al., (2011) suggests that entrepreneur gender has a positive impact on microenterprise sales volume in some parts of the United State of America. However, Chirwa (2008) found gender to have no impact on the sales revenue of microenterprises in Malawi. With regards to the impact of gender on employment creation by microbusiness, Taiwo, et al. (2016) found that businesses owned by male micro-entrepreneurs generate more employment than those owned by their female counterparts in Nigeria. Similarly, a previous study conducted in Pakistan by Naeem

(2016) found that microbusinesses operated by male entrepreneurs created more jobs than female operated businesses. However, the outcomes of Atmadja, et al., (2018) suggests that entrepreneur gender has a negative impact on microenterprise employment creation in Indonesia. Besides, Dutta and Banerjee (2018) have also shown that the gender role of women entrepreneurs in Bangladesh forces them to be less risky which often encourage them to invest in low growth businesses which impact negatively on their ability to employ more staff.

With regards to the analysis of prior research on the influence of micro-entrepreneur's gender on the growth microbusiness assets, Morris, et al., (2006) have shown that the gender of microbusiness owners may have no impact on the growth of the business assets. This view is supported by Robinson and Finley (2007) who suggest that the gender of micro-entrepreneur has no impact on the growth of micro business assets. In view of the above mixed outcomes on the impact of gender on microbusiness growth, research in Ghana to explore the role of gender on microbusiness development could enhance our knowledge.

2. Age of Micro Entrepreneur

Evidence from microfinance literature suggests that the age of an entrepreneur may have a significant impact on microbusiness development. In particular, a study conducted in the North and Central Meru districts of Kenya by Naituli, et al., (2006) found that the age of the entrepreneur positively impacts on the sales revenue of micro and small-scale women-owned enterprises. This positive outcome on the impact of age on microbusiness sales appears not to be supported by Chowdhury, et al., (2013) as these researchers found age to have a negative impact on the sales revenue of microenterprises in Bangladesh.

With regards to the possible impact of entrepreneur's age on the number of people employed by a microbusiness, evidence from Tanveer, et al., (2013) appears to suggest that entrepreneur's age positively impact on business success and employment creation. Similarly, Rose, et al., (2006) have shown that the age of the owner(s) of a microbusiness has significant positive implications for the employment creation and success of the business. However, Antoncic (2009) found that an entrepreneur's age has no impact on their ability to employ more people and business success.

The work of Fadahunsi (2012) suggests that the age of an entrepreneur have no correlation with improvement in the assets of small businesses in the United States. This is consistent with Headd and Kirchoff (2009) who also concludes that the age of an entrepreneur may have no impact on business assets and the overall performance of small businesses. However, there are other narratives in the existing literature that suggests that age has a direct influence on business assets and success. For instance, Chowdhury, et al., (2013) found a negative correlation between the age of entrepreneur and business growth including increased business assets. Perhaps these mixed results suggest that the influence of entrepreneur's age on microbusiness growth has not been adequately examined and therefore a study to examine the influence of entrepreneur's age on ethnic minority microbusiness development in Ghana is justified.

3. Micro Entrepreneur Level of Education

The influence of an entrepreneur's level of education on microbusiness development has also been reported by various researchers. For instance, Vikas and Vijayalakshmi (2017) found that the educational qualification of micro-entrepreneurs impacted positively on the sales of women enterprises in India. Similarly, Obebo, et al., (2018) have shown that the tertiary education level of a micro-entrepreneur is key determinants of participation in microfinance and hence the monthly sales performance of the microbusiness.

With regards to the influence of entrepreneur's level of education on employment creation, Barazandeh, et al., (2015) found the entrepreneur's level of education to be positively related to microbusiness development including the number of people employed by the enterprise. Likewise, a study conducted by Chirwa (2008) demonstrates that education is a critical factor in contributing towards women micro-entrepreneurs' performance (measured by profit margin and growth in employment). However, outcomes of Taiwo, et al., (2016) suggests that businesses owned by male micro-entrepreneurs in Nigeria generate more employment than those owned by their female counterparts while employment declined in the enterprises owned by those with no formal education.

Using a cross-sectional design and structured interviews, Mamun (2016) suggests that women microentrepreneurs' level of education have a significant positive impact on microenterprise assets and overall performance in Malaysia. The work of Martin and Alejandro (2016) also suggests that formal education acquired at educational institutions by the entrepreneurs plays a role not only in terms of determining the productivity level across enterprises but also in enhancing long-run productivity. However, evidence from Kiyai, et al., (2019) suggest a negative correlation between increased business assets and entrepreneur's level of education. In view of the inconclusive outcomes on the impact of entrepreneur's level of education on microbusiness growth, research in the United Kingdom to explore the influence of entrepreneur level of education on ethnic minority microbusiness development could enhance our knowledge.

4. Prior Income of Micro Entrepreneur

Analysis of existing literature provides evidence that the entrepreneur's prior income positively impact on microbusiness development. For instance, Qin, et al., (2019) employed a two-stage Hackman model to examine the impact of farmers' family characteristics on use of microfinance and the subsequent impact on the performance of the agribusiness in Northern China. The outcome of their study suggests that farmers' prior income is positively related to the total sales of the micro agribusiness. Similarly, the outcomes of Muthoni (2016) also suggests that borrowers' characteristics such as prior income may have contributed positively to the sales revenue of microenterprises in Kenya. Furthermore, analysis of Nandamuri and Gowthami (2013) suggests that entrepreneur prior income has a profound impact on entrepreneurial resourcefulness and its ability to employ more people. Therefore, a study of the possible impact of entrepreneur prior income on ethnic minority microbusiness growth in the United Kingdom could provide further insight into the relationship between microentrepreneur's income and microenterprise development.

5. Micro Entrepreneur's Work Experience

The influence of an entrepreneur's work experience/occupation on microbusiness development has also been reported by various researchers. For example, Cabrera and Mauricio (2017) found that an entrepreneur's work experience has a positive impact on capital stock. Similarly, Adegbite, et al., (2007) found that micro-entrepreneurs prior work experience has a positive impact on the working capital of microenterprises in Nigeria. The outcomes of Chowdhury, et al., (2013) in Bangladesh support findings above as they too found a positive correlation between prior occupation and microenterprise growth. However, Simpson, et al., (2004) found micro-entrepreneurs work experience to have no impact on business revenue. Perhaps these mixed results suggest that the influence of entrepreneur's work experience/ occupation on microbusiness growth has not been adequately examined and therefore a study to examine the influence of these variables on ethnic minority microbusiness development in the United Kingdom is justified.

6. Ethnicity of Micro Entrepreneur

Entrepreneur's ethnicity has also been reported to have made positive contributions to microbusiness development in several countries. In particular, Monahan, et al., (2011) found micro-entrepreneurs ethnicity to have a significantly positive impact on microenterprise number of employees in the United States. Similarly, using face-to-face interviews, Wang and Altinay (2012) have shown that the ethnicity of entrepreneur has a significant positive impact on microbusiness employment growth.

Furthermore, Scott, et al., (2012) have shown that ethnicity or race of micro-entrepreneur is connected to the growth of microbusiness assets. Likewise, Bagwell (2008) concludes that the ethnic background of the entrepreneur positively relates to the performance of their business. However, Thapa (2015) found ethnicity to have no impact on sales in a study conducted in Nepal. Similarly, Fadahunsi (2012) also argues that the ethnicity of a micro-entrepreneur is unlikely to have any significant impact on the business assets and general growth of the business. In view of the mixed outcomes on the impact of an entrepreneur's ethnicity on microbusiness growth, research in the United Kingdom to explore the influence of ethnicity on ethnic minority microbusiness development could enhance our knowledge.

Methodology

1. Data and study Sample

Semi-structured questionnaire was used to collect data from 275 microbusinesses that received microfinance from a microfinance institution in the northern region of Ghana. The data was used to investigate the impact of entrepreneur's personal characterisrics on use of microfinance for microbusiness development in Ghana. The microbusinesses selected were located in Tamale municipality, Savelugu, Walewale, Salaga, Bimbila, Yendi and Tolon. The 275 microbusinesses were drawn from the database of a microfinance institution based in Tamale with branches in all the areas of the research.

2. Research Variables

This study's main dependent variable is microbusiness development, proxied by capital stock, sales, assets and number of employees. Studies such as (Akingunola, et al., 2018; Naeem, et al., 2015) have used capital stock, sales, business assets and total number of employees to measure microbusiness development. For instance, Akingunola, et al., (2018) adopted capital stock, sales, business assets and total number of employees to measure the impact of microfinance on the growth of small and medium size enterprises in Nigeria. According to Al Mamun, et al., (2012) capital stock, sales, business assets and total number of employees delivers more robust evidence of business growth compared to other measures of microbusiness development. The benefit of using capital stock, sales, business assets and total number of employees as a measure of microbusiness development is that it is easily quantifiable (Naeem, eta al., 2015). The use of these proxies (capital stock, sales, business assets and total number of employees) as a measure of microbusiness development demonstrates the extent to which the performance of a microbusiness

Analysis of Factors That Affect the Use of Microfinance

has improved or worsened over a period of time (Panda, 2016). This chapter's key independent variable is microfinance, measured as the amount of credit provided to entrepreneur to set up a new business or improve existing business. Prior studies that have used this measure to capture microfinance include Akingunola, et al., 2018; Naeem, et al., 2015 and Al Mamun, et al., 2012. In the study, the authors designate the personal characteristics of the entrepreneur as moderating variables. Several studies have used entrepreneur personal characteristics as moderating variables (Chowdhury, et al., 2013; Obebo, et al., 2018 and Qin, et al., 2019). The personal attributes in this chapter include; gender, age, level of education, occupation, work experience, income and ethnic origin.

3. Multiple Linear Regression Model

To achieve the study objective of establishing the factors that impede or facilitate the use of microfinance for microbusiness development, stepwise multiple linear regression technique was used to determine if the personal attributes of the entrepreneurs studied (**see figure 1**) affected the growth of microbusinesses in Ghana. The dependent variables tested include monthly sales, capital, assets and employment creation.

Figure 1. Regression Models for Personal Attributes of Entrepreneur (Authors, 2021)
Source: Created by Author from Ansari and Riasi (2016)

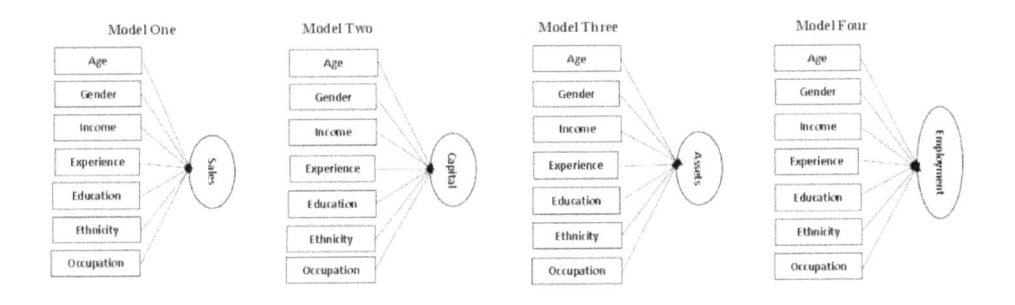

SOLUTIONS AND RECOMMENDATIONS

1. Nexus between Entrepreneur Personal Attributes, use of Microfinance and Microbusiness Sales

Analysis of existing literature provides evidence that microfinance has produced positive microbusiness development outcomes which improve incomes and reduce poverty in poor areas (Rotich, et al., 2015; Masanga and Jera, 2017; Cooper 2012). However, the findings of this study and evidence from existing microfinance literature suggest that the personal attributes of the micro-entrepreneur such as the gender, age, level of education, prior income, experience and occupation may facilitate or impede the growth of the microbusiness. In this regard, this study established that micro-entrepreneurs ethnicity might have negatively influenced the use of microfinance as the results show that the monthly sales of the microbusinesses studied reduced due to their ethnicity. Thus, this study concludes that the ethnicity of the micro-entrepreneur impedes microbusiness development in Ghana. This outcome is inconsistent with Thapa (2015) who found no relationship between ethnicity and sales in a study conducted in Nepal. However, Monahan, et al., (2011) found a significantly positive relationship between micro-entrepreneurs ethnicity and sales volume in the United States. The outcome of this study on ethnicity suggests that microfinance providers should consider the ethnicity of owners of microbusinesses in their review of loan applications.

This study also found a positive impact of micro-entrepreneur's prior occupation on use of microfinance as the monthly sales of the microbusinesses studied improved. This finding is supported by existing literature, for instance, Adegbite, et al., (2007) established a positive relationship between the entrepreneur's prior occupation and sales revenue in Nigeria. The outcomes of Chowdhury, et al., (2013) in Bangladesh also support the findings of this study as they too found a positive correlation between prior occupation and microenterprise growth. The findings of the present study, therefore, suggests that the micro-entrepreneurs prior occupation facilitate microbusiness development in Ghana. This outcome has implication for policymakers. Thus, policies aimed at developing microbusinesses should be designed to encourage individuals working in the private and public sectors to set up businesses either as individuals or groups.

With regards to prior income, this experiment found that prior income of the micro-entrepreneur has a positive impact on monthly sales of the microbusinesses studied. Thus, this study found that the micro-entrepreneur's prior income facilitate the use of microfinance for microbusiness development in Ghana. These findings are consistent with existing microfinance literature. For instance, Qin, et al., (2019) employed a two-stage Hackman model to examine the impact of farmers' family characteristics on use of microfinance and the subsequent impact on the performance of the agribusiness in Northern China. The outcome of their study suggests that farmers' prior income is positively related to the total income of the micro agribusiness. The findings of this study and the Chinese experiment can be very useful to policymakers as the findings provide examples of factors that need to be considered in the design of microfinance services. The outcomes of Muthoni (2016) also support the findings of this research as the study found that borrowers' characteristics such as prior income may have contributed positively to the sales revenue of microenterprises in Kenya. These findings have further implications for policymakers including providers of microfinance services in Ghana. It is recommended that microfinance companies and other financial institutions should always consider the prior income of entrepreneurs in their assessment of microbusiness loan applications as this has been proven to influence loan use and repayment.

With regard to the micro-entrepreneur's gender, age, level of education and work experience, the chapter found no relationships with these four attributes and the monthly sales of the microbusinesses studied. Thus, the entrepreneur's gender, age, level of education and prior work experience neither impede nor facilitate their use of microfinance for microbusiness growth in the Ghana. The outcome of this study on the impact of gender appears to be consistent with Chirwa (2008) who also found no relationship between gender and the sales revenue of microenterprises in Malawi. The result, however, contradicts the outcomes of Monahan, et al., (2011) as they found a significant correlation between gender and microenterprise sales volume in the United States. The outcome of this present study on nexus between age, use of microfinance and monthly sales appears not to be supported by Chowdhury, et al., (2013) as these researchers found a negative relationship between age and sales revenue of microenterprises in Bangladesh. Similarly, a study conducted in the North and Central Meru districts of Kenya by Naituli, et al., (2006) also found a significant relationship between age of the entrepreneur and the sales revenue of micro and small-scale women-owned enterprises. The result of the study on the impact of the entrepreneur's level of education is also inconsistent with recent literature. For instance, Vikas and Vijayalakshmi (2017) found that the educational qualification impacted positively on the turnover of women entrepreneurs in India. Similarly, Obebo, et al., (2018) have shown that the tertiary education level of a micro-entrepreneur is key determinants of participation in microfinance and hence the performance of the microbusiness. Furthermore, this study outcome on the relationship between the entrepreneur's work experience, use of microfinance and microbusiness monthly sales appears to be supported by Simpson, et al., (2004) as they too found no relationship between micro-entrepreneurs work experience and business revenue.

2. Nexus between Entrepreneur Personal Attributes, use of Microfinance and Microbusiness Employment Creation

The findings of this study and previous experiments on use microfinance also suggest that the personal attributes of the micro-entrepreneur such as the gender, age, level of education, prior income, experience, occupation and ethnicity may have a significant relationship with microbusiness employment creation. In this context, this chapter concludes that micro-entrepreneur's ethnicity has a negative impact on use of microfinance as the number of people employed by the microbusinesses studied reduced significantly due to their ethnicity. Similar to the impact of ethnicity on monthly sales, this study thus concludes that the ethnicity of the micro-entrepreneur impedes microbusiness development in Ghana. The outcomes of Monahan, et al., (2011) appears to contradict the findings of this study as they found a significantly positive relationship between micro-entrepreneurs ethnicity and microenterprise number of employees in the United States. Similarly, using face-to-face interviews in the UK, Wang and Altinay (2012) have shown that a significant positive relationship exists between the ethnicity of entrepreneur, use of microfinance and microbusiness employment growth. The findings of this study, therefore, have implications for understanding the role of the ethnic background of micro-entrepreneurs and the employment growth of microbusinesses.

With regard to the micro-entrepreneurs age, level of education, occupation, work experience and prior income, the study found no relationships with these attributes and the number of employees of the microbusinesses studied. Thus, the entrepreneur's age, level of education, occupation, work experience and prior income neither impede nor facilitate their ability to create employment. The finding of this study that the entrepreneur's age has no relationship with the number of people employed by the microbusiness is supported by Antoncic (2009) who found that an entrepreneur's age is not related to their ability to employ more people and business success. However, evidence from Tanveer, et al., (2013) appears to contradict this outcome as they argue that an entrepreneur's age positively relates to business success and employment creation. Similarly, Rose, et al., (2006) have shown that the age of the owner(s) of a microbusiness has significant implications for the employment creation and success of the business. The finding of this study thus has implications for understanding the relationship between micro-entrepreneurs age and business success.

In addition to the above, this study found that the gender of the micro-entrepreneur may have a negative influence on use of microfinance for microbusiness employment creation. This suggests that the gender of the entrepreneurs investigated impede the microbusiness ability to employ more people and the growth of the business. Therefore, the negative relationships found between gender and microenterprise employment creation and development in Indonesia by Atmadja, et al., (2018) are consistent with the findings of this chapter. Besides, Dutta and Banerjee (2018) have also shown that the gender role of women entrepreneurs in Bangladesh forces them to be less risky which often encourage them to invest in low growth businesses which impact negatively on their ability to employ more staff. However, a previous study conducted in Pakistan by Naeem (2016) found that microbusinesses operated by male entrepreneurs created more jobs than female operated businesses. The implication of this rare findings suggests that men utilise services received from microfinance companies better than their female counterparts.

3. Nexus Between Entrepreneur Personal Attributes, use of Microfinance and Microbusiness Assets

Previous experiments on microfinance impact and the findings of this study further suggest that micro-entrepreneur's gender, age, level of education, prior income, experience, occupation and ethnicity may have a significant relationship with microbusiness business assets. In this context, this study found that micro-entrepreneurs ethnicity has a statistically significant negative relationship with use of microfinance and business assets. Similar to the impact of ethnicity on monthly sales and number of employees this study thus concludes that the ethnicity of the micro-entrepreneur, impedes microbusiness development in Ghana. Evidence from existing literature that supports this outcome includes Fadahunsi (2012) who argues that the ethnicity of a micro-entrepreneur is unlikely to have any significant impact on the business assets and general growth of the business. However, Scott, et al., (2012) have shown that ethnicity or race of micro-entrepreneur is connected to the growth of microbusiness assets in the United States. Similarly, Bagwell (2008) concludes that the ethnic background of the entrepreneur positively relates to the performance of their business.

For the entrepreneur's gender, age, level of education, occupation, work experience and prior income, this study found no relationships with these attributes and the assets of the microbusinesses studied. Thus, the ethnic minority entrepreneur's gender, age, level of education, occupation, work experience and prior income neither impede nor facilitate microbusiness assets growth in Ghana. With regards to the gender of the entrepreneur, evidence from existing literature appears to support the finding of this study that gender has no relationship with the growth of microbusiness assets. For instance, Morris, et al., (2006) found that the gender of microbusiness owners may have no impact on the growth of the business assets. This view is also supported by Robinson and Finley (2007) who suggest that the growth of microbusiness assets have no relationship with the gender of the micro-entrepreneur.

The finding of this study on the impact of age on business assets appears to be also supported by prior research. For example, the work of Fadahunsi (2012) suggest that the age of an entrepreneur have no correlation with improvement in the assets of small businesses in the United States. This is consistent with Headd and Kirchoff (2009) who also concludes that the age of an entrepreneur may have no impact on business assets and the overall performance of small businesses. There are other narratives in the existing literature that suggests that age has a direct influence on business assets and success. For instance, Chowdhury, et al., (2013) found a negative correlation between the age of entrepreneur and business access. The outcome of this study on the relationship between entrepreneur's level of education and business assets contradicts the findings of Barazandeh, et al., (2015) who found the entrepreneur's level of education to be positively related to business performance. Similarly, Obebo, et al., (2018) have shown that the tertiary education level of a micro-entrepreneur is key determinants of participation in microfinance and hence the performance of the microbusiness. The results of this study on micro-entrepreneur's prior occupation, work experience and prior income appear to be unique as some researchers have suggested otherwise. For instance, Qin, et al., (2019) found that farmers' prior income positively related to the business assets of the micro agribusiness in China. Similarly, Muthoni (2016) also found that borrowers' characteristics such as prior occupation and income may have contributed positively to the use of microfinance for microenterprise development in Kenya.

4. Nexus between Entrepreneur Personal Attributes, use of Microfinance and Microbusiness Capital Stock

The findings of this study and prior research on microfinance impact also suggest that the micro-entrepreneur's gender, age, level of education, prior income, work experience, occupation and ethnicity may have a significant relationship with microbusiness capital stock. For the micro-entrepreneur's prior work experience, the findings of this study suggest that the entrepreneur's prior work experience has a significant positive relationship with capital stock. This result is consistent with Cabrera and Mauricio (2017) who also found a positive impact of entrepreneur's work experience on capital stock. Similarly, Adegbite, et al., (2007) have also found a positive relationship between micro-entrepreneurs prior work experience and the working capital of microenterprises in Nigeria. This findings and the outcomes of the prior research above have implication for policymakers. Thus, policies aimed at developing microbusinesses should encourage individuals working in the private and public sectors to set up businesses either as individuals or groups.

However, the findings of this study also show that the micro-entrepreneur's gender, age, level of education, occupation, prior income and ethnicity have no impact on microbusiness capital stock. Thus, this study concludes that the entrepreneur's gender, age, level of education, prior occupation and income and ethnicity neither facilitate nor impede microbusiness capital stock. The results of this study suggesting that no relationship exists between an entrepreneur's gender, age and microbusiness capital stock are supported by Chirwa (2008) and Fadahunsi (2012). However, the lack of relationship between micro-entrepreneurs level of education and capital stock established by this study appears not to be supported by existing microfinance literature. For example, Vikas and Vijayalakshmi (2017) have shown that the level of education of women entrepreneur's in India contributed to the amount of capital acquired by their respective businesses which impacted positively on the success of the business. Besides, the work of Obebo, et al., (2018) provides further evidence that the educational level of a micro-entrepreneur is key determinants of the performance of the microbusiness.

Similar to this study outcome on the relationship between capital stock and entrepreneur's level of education, evidence from prior research appears to contradict this study finding that no relation exists between prior occupation and microbusiness capital as Chowdhury, et al., (2013) found a positive correlation between prior occupation and microenterprise capital stock in Bangladesh. Similarly, the outcomes of Muthoni (2016) also appears not to be consistent with these study findings that no relation exists between prior income and capitals stock as he found that borrowers characteristics such as prior income may have contributed positively to the growth of microenterprises in Kenya. However, the finding of this research that suggests that no relationship exists between the ethnicity of the micro-entrepreneurs studied and the capital stock appears to be supported by Thapa (2015) who found no relationship between ethnicity and capital stock in a study conducted in Nepal. Monahan, et al., (2011) however, found a significantly positive relationship between micro-entrepreneurs ethnicity and growth of the working capital of microenterprises in the United States. The findings of this present study and the evidence from existing literature have further implications for microfinance providers as the attributes of beneficiaries of microfinance services have been proven to be mediating factors of use of microfinance services and therefore significant for the growth of microbusinesses.

FUTURE RESEARCH DIRECTIONS

This research was conducted in seven cities of northern region of Ghana. However, since the provision of microfinance to microbusinesses is not limited to these locations in Ghana, conducting similar research at other locations in Ghana to determine the factors that impede or facilitate the use of microfinance for microbusiness development could enhance our knowledge of these factors and how the influence the use of microfinance in different contexts.

Also, this study focused on the automobile, catering, construction, food and grocery, health and beauty and the transportation industry. Thus, the data used in this research was collected from seven industries which suggest that the outcomes may be overly general. In this regard, future research on factors that influence the use of microfinance for microbusiness development in specific industries in Ghana is important for our understanding of the use and impact of microfinance in a specific industry context. Besides, going forward, conducting research on factors that influence the use of microfinance for microbusiness growth in Ghana using a collaborative approach between industry experts and academic institutions could yield more robust and in-depth research outcomes.

Furthermore, future comparative studies on the factors that influence the use of microfinance for microbusiness development in Ghana, other counties in Africa and developed countries could provide wide and comprehensive outcomes that could be explained in the context of both developed and developing countries. Besides, the current study was conducted using one microfinance provider. However, evidence from existing literature suggests that often microenterprises often borrow from multiple providers. In this regard, future investigations on the factors that influence the use of multiple sources of microfinance for microbusiness development in Ghana and elsewhere is required.

Future research on the impact of microfinance on sustainable development in Ghana is required as the current study focused on microbusiness development. Some studies have also examined the factors that influence the use of microfinance for poverty reduction in other developing countries, there is however no evidence of any investigation in Ghana that has investigated the factors that influence the use of microfinance for poverty reduction. Hence, future studies should consider examining the factors influence the use of microfinance for poverty reduction in poorer communities in Ghana which could help policymakers formulate strategies for improving the standard of living in financially excluded communities in the country.

CONCLUSION

To achieve the study objective of establishing the factors that impede or facilitate the use of microfinance for microbusiness development, stepwise multiple linear regression technique was used to determine if the personal attributes of the entrepreneurs studied affected the growth of microbusinesses in Ghana. Accordingly, the following conclusions consistent with the chapter objectives were reached:

With regard to the impact of the micro-entrepreneurs personal attributes on microbusiness monthly sales, findings from the stepwise multiple linear regression analysis established that the micro-entrepreneurs ethnicity has a negative impact on the monthly sales. Thus, this study concludes that the ethnicity of the micro-entrepreneur impedes use of microfinance and growth of monthly sales of microbusinesses. With regard to the impact of the micro-entrepreneurs prior occupation on monthly sales, it was found that a positive relationship exists between micro-entrepreneurs prior occupation and monthly sales. The study, therefore, concludes that the micro-entrepreneurs prior occupation facilitate use of microfinance and the growth of monthly sales of microbusinesses. In respect of the impact of micro-entrepreneurs prior income on monthly sales, this experiment found a positive relationship between prior income of the micro-entrepreneur and monthly sales of microbusinesses. Thus, this study concludes that micro entrepreneur's prior income facilitate the use of microfinance which impacts positively on the monthly sales of microbusinesses. With regard to the impact of micro-entrepreneurs gender, age, level of education and work experience on microbusiness monthly sales, this study found no impact on the monthly sales of microbusinesses. This study, therefore, concludes that entrepreneur's gender, age, level of education and prior work experience neither impede nor facilitate the use of microfinance for improvement of microbusiness monthly sales.

In respect of the impact of the micro-entrepreneurs personal attributes on microbusiness number of employees, it was found that the micro-entrepreneurs ethnicity has a negative impact on microbusiness number of employees. This study thus concludes that the ethnicity of the micro-entrepreneur impedes use of microfinance and microbusiness employment creation. With regard to the impact of micro-entrepreneurs age, level of education, occupation, work experience and prior income on the number of employees, the study found no impact on the number of employees of microbusinesses. Thus, the entrepreneur's age, level of education, occupation, work experience and prior income neither impede nor facilitate use of microfinance and employment creation. It was also found that the gender of the micro-entrepreneur has a negative influence on microbusiness employment creation. Thus, the study concludes that the gender of the entrepreneurs investigated impede use of microfinance and the microbusiness ability to employ more people and the growth of the business.

In the case of the impact of the micro-entrepreneurs personal attributes on microbusiness assets, it was found that the micro-entrepreneurs ethnicity has a statistically significant negative relationship with business assets. This study thus concludes that the ethnicity of the micro-entrepreneur impedes use of microfinance and microbusiness assets growth. For the entrepreneur's gender, age, level of education, occupation, work experience and prior income, the study found no impact on the assets of microbusinesses. Thus, the study concludes that the entrepreneur's gender, age, level of education, occupation, work experience and prior income neither impede nor facilitate use of microfinance and microbusiness assets growth.

With regard to the impact of micro-entrepreneurs personal attributes on microbusiness capital stock, it was found that the micro-entrepreneurs prior work experience has a significant positive relationship with capital stock. The study, therefore, concludes that micro-entrepreneurs prior work experience facilitates use of microfinance and the growth of microbusiness capital stock. The study, however, found that the micro-entrepreneurs gender, age, level of education, occupation, prior income and ethnicity have no impact on microbusiness capital stock. Thus, this study concludes that the entrepreneur's gender, age, level of education, prior occupation and income and ethnicity neither facilitate nor impede use of microfinance and microbusiness capital stock.

ACKNOWLEDGMENT

This research received no specific grant from any funding agency in the public, commercial, or not-for-profit sectors.

REFERENCES

Adegbite, S. A. (2007). Evaluation of the impact of entrepreneurial characteristics on the performance of small scale manufacturing industries in Nigeria. *Journal of Asia Entrepreneurship and Sustainability, 3*(1), 1.

Ahmed, S. (2009). Microfinance institutions in Bangladesh: Achievements and challenges. *Managerial Finance, 35*(12), 999–1010. doi:10.1108/03074350911000052

Akinboade, O. A. (2015). Determinants of SMEs growth and performance in Cameroon's central and littoral provinces' manufacturing and retail sectors. *African Journal of Economic and Management Studies, 6*(2), 183–196. doi:10.1108/AJEMS-03-2013-0033

Akingunola, R., Olowofela, E., & Yunusa, L. (2018). Impact of Microfinance Banks on Micro and Small Enterprises in Ogun State, Nigeria. *Binus Business Review, 9*(2), 163–169. doi:10.21512/bbr.v9i2.4253

Al Mamun, A., Abdul Wahab, S., & Malarvizhi, C. (2010). Impact of Amanah Ikhtiar Malaysia's microcredit schemes on microenterprise assets in Malaysia. *International Research Journal of Finance and Economics, 60*, 144–154. doi:10.2139srn.1946089

Al Mamun, A., Adaikalam, J., & Mazumder, M. N. H. (2012). Examining the effect of Amanah Ikhtiar Malaysia's microcredit program on microenterprise assets in rural Malaysia. *Asian Social Science, 8*(4), 272–280. doi:10.5539/ass.v8n4p272

Antoncic, B. (2009). The entrepreneur's general personality traits and technological developments. *World Academy of Science, Engineering and Technology, 53*, 236–241.

Ashcroft, M. O. (2008). Microfinance in Africa–The challenges, realities and success stories. *Microbanking Bulletin, 17*, 5–11.

Atmadja, A. S., Sharma, P., & Su, J. J. (2018). Microfinance and microenterprise performance in Indonesia: An extended and updated survey. *International Journal of Social Economics*, *45*(6), 957–972. doi:10.1108/IJSE-02-2017-0031

Babajide, A. A. (2012). Effects of microfinance on micro and small enterprises (MSEs) growth in Nigeria. *Asian Economic and Financial Review*, *2*(3), 463–477.

Bagwell, S. (2008). Transnational family networks and ethnic minority business development: The case of Vietnamese nail-shops in the UK. *International Journal of Entrepreneurial Behaviour & Research*, *14*(6), 377–394. doi:10.1108/13552550810910960

Barazandeh, M., Parvizian, K., Alizadeh, M. & Khosravi, S. (2015). Investigating the effect of entrepreneurial competencies on business performance among early stage entrepreneurs Global Entrepreneurship Monitor (GEM 2010 survey data). *Journal of Global Entrepreneurship Research*, *5*(1), 18.

Bondinuba, F. K., Stephens, M., Jones, C., & Buckley, R. (2020). The motivations of microfinance institutions to enter the housing market in a developing country. *International Journal of Housing Policy*, *20*(4), 534–554. doi:10.1080/19491247.2020.1721411

Cabrera, E. M., & Mauricio, D. (2017). Factors affecting the success of women's entrepreneurship: A review of literature. *International Journal of Gender and Entrepreneurship*, *9*(1), 31–65. doi:10.1108/IJGE-01-2016-0001

Chirwa, E. W. (2008). Effects of gender on the performance of micro and small enterprises in Malawi. *Development Southern Africa*, *25*(3), 347–362. doi:10.1080/03768350802212139

Chowdhury, M. S., Alam, Z., & Arif, M. I. (2013). Success factors of entrepreneurs of small and medium sized enterprises: Evidence from Bangladesh. *Business and Economic Review*, *3*(2), 38. doi:10.5296/ber.v3i2.4127

Cooper, J. N. (2012). *The impact of microfinance services on the growth of small and medium enterprises in Kenya* (Doctoral dissertation). University of Nairobi.

Cull, R., Demirgüç-Kunt, A., & Morduch, J. (2014). Banks and microbanks. *Journal of Financial Services Research*, *46*(1), 1–53. doi:10.100710693-013-0177-z

Dutta, A., & Banerjee, S. (2018). Does microfinance impede sustainable entrepreneurial initiatives among women borrowers? Evidence from rural Bangladesh. *Journal of Rural Studies*, *60*, 70–81. doi:10.1016/j.jrurstud.2018.03.007

Ebomuche, N. C., Ihugba, O. A., & Bankong, B. (2014). The impact of Nigeria microfinance banks on poverty reduction: Imo State experience. *International Letters of Social and Humanistic Sciences*, (05), 92–113.

Fadahunsi, A. (2012). The growth of small businesses: Towards a research agenda. *American Journal of Economics and Business Administration*, 4(1), 105–115. doi:10.3844/ajebasp.2012.105.115

Ghosh, J. (2013). Microfinance and the challenge of financial inclusion for development. *Cambridge Journal of Economics*, 37(6), 1203–1219. doi:10.1093/cje/bet042

Gill, A., & Biger, N. (2012). Barriers to small business growth in Canada. *Journal of Small Business and Enterprise Development*, 19(4), 656–668. doi:10.1108/14626001211277451

Headd, B., & Kirchoff, B. (2009). The growth, decline and survival of small businesses: An exploratory study of life cycles. *Journal of Small Business Management*, 47(4), 531–550. doi:10.1111/j.1540-627X.2009.00282.x

Islam, M. A., Khan, M. A., Obaidullah, A. Z. M., & Alam, M. S. (2011). Effect of entrepreneur and firm characteristics on the business success of small and medium enterprises (SMEs) in Bangladesh. *International Journal of Business and Management*, 6(3), 289.

Kanyare, N., & Mungai, J. (2017). Access to Microcredit Determinants and Financial Performance of Small and Medium Retailing Enterprises in Wajir County, Kenya. *International Journal of Finance*, 2(6), 103–136. doi:10.47941/ijf.164

Khan, S. (2015). Impact of sources of finance on the growth of SMEs: Evidence from Pakistan. *Decision*, 42(1), 3–10.

Kondo, T., Orbeta, A. Jr, Dingcong, C., & Infantado, C. (2008). Impact of microfinance on rural households in the Philippines. *IDS Bulletin*, 39(1), 51–70. doi:10.1111/j.1759-5436.2008.tb00432.x

Kristiansen, S., Furuholt, B., & Wahid, F. (2003). Internet cafe entrepreneurs: Pioneers in information dissemination in Indonesia. *International Journal of Entrepreneurship and Innovation*, 4(4), 251–263. doi:10.5367/000000003129574315

Ledgerwood, J. (2013). *Measuring Financial Inclusion and Assessing Impact. The New Microfinance Handbook: A Financial Market System Perspective*. The World Bank.

Masakure, O., Henson, S., & Cranfield, J. (2009). erformance of microenterprises in Ghana: A resource-based view. *Journal of Small Business and Enterprise Development*, *16*(3), 466–484. doi:10.1108/14626000910977170

Masanga, G. G., & Jera, M. (2017). The Significance of Microfinance to Urban Informal Traders in Zimbabwe. *ADRRI Journal (Multidisciplinary)*, *26*(3), 44–61.

Matin, I., Hulme, D., & Rutherford, S. (2002). Finance for the poor: From microcredit to microfinancial services. *Journal of International Development*, *14*(2), 273–294. doi:10.1002/jid.874

Mia, M. A., Lee, H. A., Chandran, V. G. R., Rasiah, R., & Rahman, M. (2019). History of microfinance in Bangladesh: A life cycle theory approach. *Business History*, *61*(4), 703–733. doi:10.1080/00076791.2017.1413096

Mochona, S. (2006). *Impact of microfinance in Addis Ababa: The case of GASHA microfinance institute* (Doctoral dissertation). University School of Graduate studies, Regional and Local Development Studies.

Monahan, M., Shah, A., & Mattare, M. (2011). The road ahead: Micro enterprise perspectives on success and challenge factors. *Journal of Management Policy and Practice*, *12*(4), 113–125.

Morris, M. H., Miyasaki, N. N., Watters, C. E., & Coombes, S. M. (2006). The dilemma of growth: Understanding venture size choices of women entrepreneurs. *Journal of Small Business Management*, *44*(2), 221–244. doi:10.1111/j.1540-627X.2006.00165.x

Mshenga, P. M., Richardson, R. B., Njehia, B. K., & Birachi, E. A. (2010). The contribution of tourism to micro and small enterprise growth. *Tourism Economics*, *16*(4), 953–964. doi:10.5367/te.2010.0018

Muthoni, M. P. (2016). Assessing Borrower's and Business' Factors Causing Microcredit Default in Kenya: A Comparative Analysis of Microfinance Institutions and Financial Intermediaries. *Journal of Education and Practice*, *7*(12), 97–118.

Naeem, A., Khan, S., Ali, M., & Hassan, F. S. (2015). The Impact of Microfinance on Women Micro-Enterprises "A Case Study of District Quetta, Pakistan. *American International Journal of Social Science*, *4*(4), 19–27.

Naeem, A., & Rehman, S. (2016). Gender Based Utilization of Microfinance: An Empirical Evidence from District Quetta, Pakistan. *International Business Research*, *9*(10), 162–168. doi:10.5539/ibr.v9n10p162

Naituli, G., Wegulo, F. N., & Kaimenyi, B. (2006). Entrepreneurial characteristics among micro and small-scale women owned enterprises in North and Central Meru districts, Kenya. *Gender Inequalities in Kenya*, 7-25.

Obebo, F., Wawire, N., & Muniu, J. (2018). Determinants of Participation of Micro and Small Enterprises in Microfinance in Kenya. *Int J Econ Manag Sci, 7*(523), 2. doi:10.4172/2162-6359.1000523

Osei-Assibey, E., Bokpin, G. A., & Twerefou, D. K. (2012). Microenterprise financing preference: Testing POH within the context of Ghana's rural financial market. *Journal of Economic Studies (Glasgow, Scotland), 39*(1), 84–105. doi:10.1108/01443581211192125

Oshora, B., Fekete-Farkas, M., & Zeman, Z. (2020). Role Of Microfinance Institutions In Financing Micro And Small Enterprises In Ethiopia. *Copernican Journal of Finance & Accounting, 9*(3), 115–130. doi:10.12775/CJFA.2020.015

Panda, D. K. (2016). Microfinance Spurs Microenterprise Development: An Exploration of the Latent Processes. *Strategic Change, 25*(5), 613–623. doi:10.1002/jsc.2084

Psaltopoulos, D., Stathopoulou, S., & Skuras, D. (2005). The location of markets, perceived entrepreneurial risk, and start-up capital of micro rural firms. *Small Business Economics, 25*(2), 147–158. doi:10.100711187-003-6456-6

Qin, M., Wachenheim, C. J., Wang, Z., & Zheng, S. (2019). Factors affecting Chinese farmers' microcredit participation. *Agricultural Finance Review, 79*(1), 48–59. doi:10.1108/AFR-12-2017-0111

Robinson, S., & Finley, J. (2007). Rural women's self-employment: A look at Pennsylvania. *Academy of Entrepreneurship Journal, 13*(2).

Rose, R. C., Kumar, N., & Yen, L. L. (2006). The dynamics of entrepreneurs' success factors in influencing venture growth. *Journal of Asia Entrepreneurship and Sustainability, 2*(2), 1–122.

Rotich, I., Lagat, C., & Kogei, J. (2015). Effects of microfinance services on the performance of small and medium enterprises in Kenya. *African Journal of Business Management, 9*(5), 206–211. doi:10.5897/AJBM2014.7519

Salia, P. J. (2014). The effect of microcredit on the household welfare (empirical evidences from women micro-entrepreneurs in Tanzania). *International Journal of Academic Research in Business & Social Sciences, 4*(5), 259. doi:10.6007/IJARBSS/v4-i5/853

Scott, D. M., Curci, R., & Mackoy, R. (2012). Hispanic business enterprise success: Ethnic resources, market orientation, or market exchange embeddedness? *Journal of International Business and Cultural Studies*, *6*, 1.

Simpson, M., Tuck, N., & Bellamy, S. (2004). Small business success factors: The role of education and training. *Education + Training*, *46*(8), 481–491. doi:10.1108/00400910410569605

Steinwand, D. (2013). The Indonesian People's Credit Banks (Bpr). Southeast Asia's Credit Revolution: From Moneylenders to Microfinance, 95-112.

Taiwo, J. N., Agwu, M. E., Adetiloye, K. A., & Afolabi, G. T. (2016). Financing women entrepreneurs and employment generation–a case study of microfinance banks. *European Journal of Soil Science*, *52*(1), 112–141.

Tanveer, M. A., Akbar, A., Gill, H., & Ahmed, I. (2013). Role of Personal Level Determinants in Entrepreneurial Firm's Success. *Journal of Basic and Applied Scientific Research*, *3*(1), 449–458.

Thapa, A. (2015). Determinants of microenterprise performance in Nepal. *Small Business Economics*, *45*(3), 581–594. doi:10.100711187-015-9654-0

Vikas, B., & Vijayalakshmi, B. (2017). Microfinance and Women's Empowerment: An Exploratory Demographic Study in Karnataka, India. *South Asian Journal of Management*, *24*(3), 46–61.

Wang, C. L., & Altinay, L. (2012). Social embeddedness, entrepreneurial orientation and firm growth in ethnic minority small businesses in the UK. *International Small Business Journal*, *30*(1), 3–23. doi:10.1177/0266242610366060

KEY TERMS AND DEFINITIONS

Assets: Resource owned by a business that have significant financial value.

Capital: Any resources both tangible and intangible that confers value or benefit to a business organisation.

Development: Improvement in the performance of microbusiness such as increased amount of capital, sales, assets, and number of people employed.

Facilitate: Makes it easy to use microfinance to for microbusiness development.

Impede: Prevent the use of microfinance for microbusiness growth.

Microbusiness: Any business organisation that directly employs fewer than ten employees.

Microcredit: The provision of small loans to low-income earners to set up or develop their existing businesses.

Microfinance: The provision of small loans and training exclusively to microbusinesses, financially disadvantaged individuals, and low-income families.

Chapter 6
Islamic Social Finance: Integrating Zakah Funds in Microfinance and Microenterprise Support Programs:
Selected Case Studies

Omar Ahmad Kachkar
https://orcid.org/0000-0001-7786-8893
Ibn Haldun University, Turkey

Marwa Alfares
İstanbul Sabahattin Zaim University, Turkey

ABSTRACT

Alleviating poverty and inequality are among the central objectives of zakah in the Islamic economic system. These objectives are also on top of the 17 SDGs of the UN 2030 Agenda. This research argues that microenterprise support programs (MSPs) have been proven as effective tools in combating poverty. However, lack of funds has always been a major challenge for the sustainability of those programs. Channeling zakah funds to MSPs will directly contribute to empowering deprived populations and helping them to lift themselves out of the poverty cycle. Two zakah-based MSPs have been analyzed in this chapter. The first one is the Asnaf Entrepreneurship Program of Lembaga Zakah, Malaysia and the second one is Baitul Maal Muamalat Indonesia (BMMI). According to literature, using zakah in (MSPs) requires a strict implementation of best practices including screening program beneficiaries, providing professional training and monitoring to businesses, and finally applying a graduation scheme.

DOI: 10.4018/978-1-7998-7499-7.ch006

INTRODUCTION

Zakah is one of the most effective tools in the Islamic fiscal policy and economic system that has been introduced to achieve a variety of socio-economic objectives. On top of those objectives are poverty alleviation and wealth redistribution. The former objective is clearly indicated in the *hadith* narrated by *Imam* al-Bukhari when the Prophet (PBUH) commanded Muʿadh bin Jabal, his delegate to govern Yemen: "Inform them (the people of Yemen) that Allah has made a charity obligatory upon them, that is collected from their rich and given back to their poor." (Al-Bukhari, 1422.H); the latter objective –wealth redistribution- is mentioned in Surat (At-Tawbah) "*Zakah* expenditures are only for the poor and for the needy and for those employed to collect [*zakah*] and for bringing hearts together [for Islam] and for freeing captives [or slaves] and for those in debt and for the cause of Allah and for the [stranded] traveller - an obligation [imposed] by Allah. And Allah is Knowing and Wise". Historically, *zakah* has played a significant role in lifting the socio-economic situations of Muslim communities. For instance, at the time of Khalifa Omar bin Abdul-Aziz (RAA), there was a surplus of *zakah* funds which indicate to little poverty, Omar bin Abdul Aziz had enriched people to the extent that they did not find a poor man who would accept *zakah* (As-Sallabi, 2015).

In contrast, currently, estimations of *zakah* amounts that are estimated to be payable by Muslim individuals around the world ranges from US$ 76 billion UNHCR (2019) to as much as US$600 billion (UNICEF, 2019). Other estimations are also found in the literature including the estimation of Shaikh al-Qaradaghi, *zakah* might reaches about 400 billion (Al-Taher, 2017). In addition, the Islamic Development Bank that estimated *zakah* to reach $230 - $560 billion (Modéer, 2018; Kachkar, 2019). Such a huge potential of *zakah* funds, can substantially contribute to closing the widening financial deficit in humanitarian efforts. According to the latest UNHCR reports, a funding gap of over $4.5 billion for 2020. This represents approximately 51% of total funds needed (UNHCR, 2020). No wonder that the UNHCR has recently established the Refugee *Zakah* Fund in attempt to tap on the institution of *zakah* (UNHCR, 2020a). According to the report, in the first six months of 2020 the fund managed to collect $55.2 million in Zakah and *Sadaqah* funds. The funds are expected to help over 1.8 million IDPs and refugees by the end of 2020 (UNHCR, 2020a). Since its onset in 2016 to 2019 the fund has managed to raise and distribute around $14.4 million to approximately 6,888 families located in Lebanon, Jordan, and Yemen (UNHCR, 2019).

Zakah is also considered one of the key sources of funds to financing the proposed UN 17 SDGs for 2030. These goals were unanimously agreed upon by world leaders in September 2015 at an historic UN Summit and subsequently came into effect in January 2016. The core objectives of the UN SDGs are to tackle the major challenges facing humanity and the planet. Accordingly, it was understood that "over the next fifteen years all, countries will mobilize efforts to end all forms of poverty, fight inequalities and tackle climate change, while ensuring that no one is left behind" (https://www.un.org). However, for the achievement of the mandated SDGs, billions of US dollars are direly needed particularly, in developing countries including many of Muslim-majority states. Thus, the role of *zakah* as a potential source of funding is very much appreciated along with other components of Islamic social finance. In other words, *zakah* is strongly aligned with the SDGs, including SDG No.1 no poverty, SDG No.2, zero hunger, and SDG No.10, reduced inequalities, and others.

It is believed that serious collaboration with *zakah* donors and administrators could substantially enhance the effort to reach the goals (SDG 17) (A Rehman, 2018). A case in point is the collaboration between UNDP and BAZNAS Indonesia (the national *Zakah* collection body) to employ *zakah* funding for SDG (A Rehman, 2018). To accomplish the above-mentioned SDGs, an integrated microenterprise-*zakah* support programs could potentially hit two birds with one stone; on one hand, it will achieve the SDG on poverty alleviation and on the other hand, it will secure the financial sources needed to achieve that purpose. Empowering the poor is recommended in Islam. A practical example on that is found in one of the traditional hadith of prophet Muhammed (PBUH) as narrated by Anas ibn Malik in Sunan Abu Dawud, "when a man from the Ansar came to the Prophet (PBUH) begging for financial assistance. The Prophet (PBUH) asked the man to bring what can be sold from his own property, the Prophet (PBUH) took them and sold them for two dirhams in an auction in the masjid, the Prophet (PBUH) gave them to the Ansari and said: buy food with one dirham for your family and ordered the man to buy an axe with the other dirham. The man brought the axe to the Prophet (PBUH). The Messenger of Allah (PBUH) fixed a handle on it with his own hands and said: Go, gather firewood, and sell it, and do not let me see you for a fortnight. The man went away and gathered firewood and sold it. When he had earned ten dirhams. The Messenger of Allah (PBUH) then said: This is better for you than that begging should come as a spot on your face on the Day of Judgment" (Abu Dawud, 2008). The hadith is an explicit reference on empowerment of the poor and underprivileged people rather than encourage them to receive cash assistance that will never improve their self-reliance but will push them into deeper poverty.

This paper explores the viability of using *zakah* funds as a source of funding in Micro Enterprise Support Programs (MSP). It further aims at highlighting the best practices of using *zakah* to support microenterprises programs. The later objective is undertaken through examining two case studies of actual microenterprise support programs from Malaysia and Indonesia.

BACKGROUND

Definition Of Social Finance

Social finance is generally known as an impact investment or social investment, in other words, it is a financial strategy to overcome social and environmental problems and to generate both social and financial returns. more specifically, social finance is defined as "An approach to managing investments that generate financial returns while including measurable positive social and environmental impact" (Deloitte, 2019). It is believed that social finance may be an effective solution to tackle some of societies' greatest challenges in an efficient and innovative way. By providing capital and fund to social organizations and enterprises, it offers an alternative way to mobilize funding to provide them with financial sustainability and the opportunity to run their projects in the long-term. Social finance may generate a financial return, but the social returns are described as a priori and are not an incidental side effect of a commercial deal (Brown and Swersky, 2012: 3).

Scope Of Social Finance

From the definition above, the scope of social finance is possibly divided into three aspects:

First: to address social and environmental issues.
Second: to generate a positive impact on society and the environment
Third: to achieve a positive social and environmental impact while at the same time generating financial returns (Weber, 2012).

Islamic Social Finance

Combining faith and social purposes in finance is known as 'Islamic social finance'. It is an innovation investment that aims at bringing about a difference in the fight against poverty. Traditionally, Islamic social finance sector generally comprises Islamic institutions based on philanthropy e.g., *zakah*, *sadaqah* and *awqaf*; in addition to institutions based on cooperation e.g., *qard* and *kafalah*; and finally contemporary Islamic microfinance institutions. Through a verity of instruments, Islamic social finance can potentially add extra sources of financing to address the huge gap in funding humanitarian projects (Islamic Social Finance Report, 2020). It has been argued that Islamic social finance should be included in the definition of Islamic finance, this inclusion in turn achieves three main advantages:

First, it significantly expands the sector's scale in other words by adding the potential of *zakah* and *awqaf* funds which is estimated by US$1 trillion for the former and US$2.5 for latter.

Second, social finance is far more inclusive and widely adopted.

Third, social finance embodies key values, such as generosity and concern for others (Rehman, 2019).

Components of Islamic Social Finance

According to the Islamic Social Finance Report (2014), Islamic Social Finance involves the traditional Islamic institutions based on philanthropic acts of *zakah*, *sadaqah*, and *waqf* and many other instruments. However, this research will focus on the three main instruments in Islamic Social Finance, i.e., *waqf*, *sadaqah* and *zakah*. These three instruments have been very effective in providing the basic needs of Muslim communities throughout Islamic history.

Waqf (Endowment)

Waqf is the Arabic word for a civic endowment that is usually devoted to the benefit of the community. More specifically waqf has been defined by Kahf (1998) as "an action that involves investment for the future and accumulation of productive wealth that benefits future generations." The Accounting and Auditing Organization for Islamic Financial Institutions (AAOIFI), in its Shariah Standard No. 33 on waqf 2008, has defined waqf as "the confinement of a certain property against any disposition that may lead to transfer its ownership, and donating the usufruct of that property to certain beneficiaries" (AAOIFI Shariah Standards, 2009:444). In North and West Africa *waqf* is also known as *habs* (Kahf, 2003). For Westerners, the traditional waqf can also be equivalent to the non-profit trusts (Cizakca, 2011). Waqf is a philanthropic institution that deeply rooted in the Islamic history and has been used to cater social protection and social services for the community in all education and health sectors. It is believed that waqf is originally derived from the famous prophetic saying of the Prophet Muhammad (PBUH) as reported by Muslim collection of sound Hadith under the chapter of *Wasiyyah* (will) that when the son of Adam passes away his book of deeds closes except from three sources: a perpetual charity, a heritage of knowledge that benefits people at large and a pious child who constantly pray to Allah to have mercy upon the dead person. So, in the preceding Hadith, the perpetual charity, which typical to waqf, is considered among the deeds whose benefits will not be stopped. In the Islamic history, the first known Waqf in Islam is the mosque of *Quba'* in the city of Medina. It was established by the initiative of the Prophet Muhammad (PBUH) when he asked for someone to buy the water well of *Bayruha'* and to designate it as a free public utility for drinking water. in another similar case the Prophet (PBUH), advised 'Umar to assign his land in *Khaibar* as a *waqf* for the poor and needy. Later on, a new type of *waqf* which is (family waqf) has been introduced by the companions of Prophet (PBUH), during the reign of 'Umar (RAA) (Kahf, 2003).

Sadaqah (Charity)

In Islam, *sadaqah* is a comprehensive term that encompasses all aspects of life including religious, legal, spiritual, moral, social, economic, and political. Any act of giving either financial or non-financial is considered an act of charity. In Islam Muslims are encouraged to help others. The more helpful and charitable individuals are the closer they become to Allah and the more successful to become in this life and in the hereafter. Through the sharing of one's resources with the other underprivileged people, *sadaqah* helps improve the social conscience but also promotes social cohesion and harmony (ISRA, 2012).

Zakah (Almsgiving)

The Islamic fiscal system has a pioneer mechanism that can maintain the balance between society's strata. *Zakah* purifies not only wealth but also the spirit, it is considered an obligatory religious tax imposed on all wealthy Muslims who are eligible to pay a certain rate of their wealth upon achieving certain thresholds, these thresholds vary according to the type of wealth.

Types of *Zakah*

Islam has determined two types of zakah:

Zakah al-mal is an annual levy on the wealth of a Muslim above a certain level (ISRA 2012).

Zakah al-fitr (*zakah* of ending the month of fasting), this *zakah* is payable by every Muslim who has the financial capability to pay this *zakah* at the end of the month of Ramadan.

Zakah Estimation

Estimation of total *zakah* amounts payable by Muslims around the world ranges from US$ 76 billion UNHCR (2019) to as much as US$600 billion (UNICEF, 2019) and in between several estimation are found in the literature including the estimation of Shaikh al-Qaradaghi, (2014) that reaches about 137.5 billion and the estimation of the Islamic Development Banks that estimated *zakah* at to reach $230 - $560 billion (Modéer, 2018).

SHARIA LEGALITY OF USING *ZAKAH* FUNDS TO BACK MICRO-ENTERPRISES AND MICROFINANCE PROGRAMS

Bearing in mind the great potential of mobilizing *zakah* funds to financing relief and humanitarian operations and projects, there is a widespread misconception on the permissibility of using *zakah* funds in development and empowerment projects. This misconception is due to the well-known condition of *tamleek*. The concept of *tamleek* refers to the obligation of the full transfer of ownership of property (cash or non-asset) from the *zakah* payer to the *zakah* beneficiary (Al-Gamal, 2021). This research maintains that the condition of *tamleek* is absolutely satisfied in microfinance and microenterprise programs in one of the following forms:

1. Grant payment from the microcredit/microfinance institution to the beneficiary,
2. Debt/default settlement made by the microcredit/microfinance institution on behalf of the indebted beneficiary
3. Purchase of business equipment and professional tools or raw materials with the full transfer of ownership of those materials and equipment to the beneficiary entrepreneurs.
4. Payment of arrears for the beneficiary such as bills and rental payments.
5. Setting up a takaful (insurance) fund to mitigate any business or non-business-related risk.

At this juncture, it must be admitted that another Shariah question might arise in relation to paying *zakah* in kind and in commodities rather than in cash. This is particularly relevant to form no. 3 above. Opinions of shariah scholars vary in this regard; according to the famous opinion in Maliki *mazhab* (school of *fiqh*) and one account in the Hanbali *mazhab*, it is permissible to use *zakah* funds to purchase army tools and equipment and grant them to the military members (Ibn Qudamah, 1997). Additionally, according to Imam Abu Hanifah, in general it is allowed to pay the value of *zakah*, moreover, the Hanafi school allowed for the Imam to borrow the money of *zakah* from the *zakah* house, to settle the expenses of the state and to return the money back as a borrower (Ibn 'Abidin, 2011). Furthermore, the Maliki, Shafi'i and Hanbali schools allowed the sale of *zakah* commodities and goods in the cases of necessity, they moreover, allowed the conversion of *zakah* funds or properties into another type or category contingent on the *maslaha* and interest of the poor. A case in point, is when a serious risk is feared on *zakah* properties, such as the probable risk that might encounter the sheep cattle on the way to the *zakah* center (Al-Uthman and Hamzah, 2012). Last but not least, the International Islamic Fiqh Academy allowed using *zakah* funds in profit generating projects. The permissibility resolution was issued as early as 1986 in its third session held in Amman, Jordan. The resolution states: "It is permissible, in principle, to put *zakah* funds in investment projects which eventually lead to be owned by those who are deserving of *zakah*, or which are under the control and administration of the entity which is responsible and has the jurisdiction over collecting and distributing *zakah*, provided that it is done after satisfying the basic and immediate needs of the beneficiaries and with proper guarantees against loss." (Resolutions and Recommendations of the Council of the Islamic Fiqh Academy 1985-2000, 2000).

Leveraging *Zakah* funds to achieve SDGs

In September 2015, World leaders gathered at United Nations Headquarters in New York and officially adopted the 2030 Agenda for Sustainable Development and the global 17 Sustainable Development Goals (SDGs) with the 169 related targets grouped under five major topics: finance, information and communications technology (ICT), capacity building, trade, and systemic issues, as shown in *Figure* 1.

Figure 1. Sustainable Development Goals (SDGs)
Source: https://sdgs.un.org/goals

Financing the SDGs requires the mobilization of huge amounts of financial resources. One report published by the World Bank in 2019 found that the costs for new SDG related infrastructure could range from $637 billion (or 2 percent of GDP) to $2.74 trillion (8 percent of GDP) in low- and middle-income countries

(LMICs) depending on the spending efficiency and the quality of services delivered (Rozenberg and Fay, 2019).

Figure 2. Estimated annual cost to achieve the SDGs 2015-2030
Source: Doumbia And Laurids, (2019)

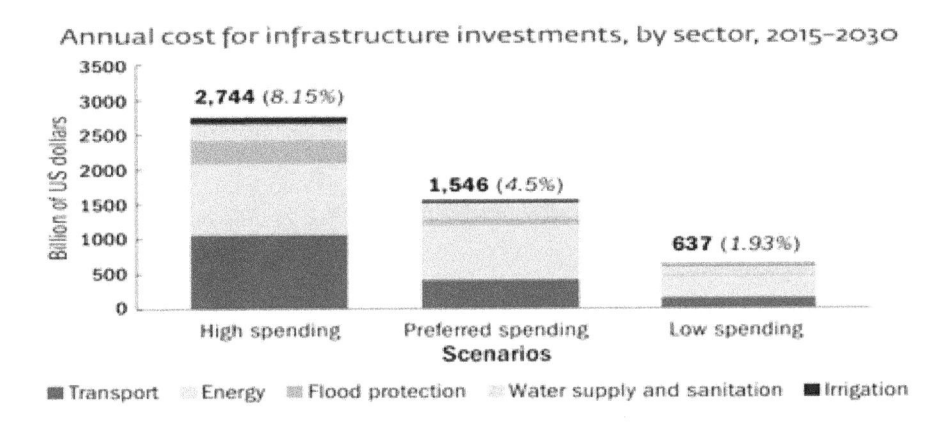

Annual cost for infrastructure investments, by sector, 2015-2030

[Bar chart showing three scenarios:
- High spending: 2,744 (8.15%)
- Preferred spending: 1,546 (4.5%)
- Low spending: 637 (1.93%)
Billion of US dollars on y-axis. Categories: Transport, Energy, Flood protection, Water supply and sanitation, Irrigation]

The three scenarios highlighted in the *Figure* 2 above can be explained as follow: high spending scenario refers to ambitious goals and low efficiency; preferred spending scenario refers to ambitious goals and high efficiency; and low spending scenario refers to less ambitious goals and high efficiency (Doumbia and Laurids, 2019).

In the context of Africa, the progress on SDG achievements is even more serious. Taking as an example the first SDG on poverty, the year 2015 and afterwards, COVID-19 adjusted forecasts reveal that nearly 460 million Africans are projected to remain poor by 2030. This translates into 8 in 10 of the world's poor will be living in the African continent, nearly two-thirds of them are living in rural areas (Africa 2030, 2021). To give a more accurate information of the SDG achievement across the globe, Cambridge University issued a global report in June 2020 measuring the progress in achieving the SDGs. The report contains in part 2 the SDG Index and Dashboards. SDG Index tracks country performance on the 17 SDGs, with equal weight to all 17 goals. The score signifies a country's position between the worst (0) and the best target (100) (Sustainable Development Report, 2020). The SDG index highlight the top countries in SDG performance. Unfortunately, non- of the African countries has any place in the top 50 performing countries, Egypt came 83 in the index with 68.8 as in *Figure* 3.

Figure 3. Top performing countries in SDG Index
Source: Sustainable Development Report (2020),

Rank	Country	Score	Rank	Country	Score
1	Sweden	84.7	43	Greece	74.3
2	Denmark	84.6	44	Luxembourg	74.3
3	Finland	83.8	45	Uruguay	74.3
4	France	81.1	46	Ecuador	74.3
5	Germany	80.8	47	Ukraine	74.2
6	Norway	80.8	48	China	73.9
7	Austria	80.7	49	Vietnam	73.8
8	Czech Republic	80.6	50	Bosnia and Herzegovina	73.5
9	Netherlands	80.4	51	Argentina	73.2
10	Estonia	80.1	52	Kyrgyz Republic	73.0
11	Belgium	80.0	53	Brazil	72.7
12	Slovenia	79.8	54	Azerbaijan	72.6
13	United Kingdom	79.8	55	Cuba	72.6
14	Ireland	79.4	56	Algeria	72.3
15	Switzerland	79.4	57	Russian Federation	71.9
16	New Zealand	79.2	58	Georgia	71.9
17	Japan	79.2	59	Iran, Islamic Rep.	71.8
18	Belarus	78.8	60	Malaysia	71.8
19	Croatia	78.4	61	Peru	71.8
20	Korea, Rep.	78.3	62	North Macedonia	71.4
21	Canada	78.2	63	Tunisia	71.4
22	Spain	78.1	64	Morocco	71.3
23	Poland	78.1	65	Kazakhstan	71.1
24	Latvia	77.7	66	Uzbekistan	71.0
25	Portugal	77.6	67	Colombia	70.9
26	Iceland	77.5	68	Albania	70.8
27	Slovak Republic	77.5	69	Mexico	70.4
28	Chile	77.4	70	Turkey	70.3
29	Hungary	77.3	71	United Arab Emirates	70.3
30	Italy	77.0	72	Montenegro	70.2
31	United States	76.4	73	Dominican Republic	70.2
32	Malta	76.0	74	Fiji	69.9
33	Serbia	75.2	75	Armenia	69.9
34	Cyprus	75.2	76	Oman	69.7
35	Costa Rica	75.1	77	El Salvador	69.6
36	Lithuania	75.0	78	Tajikistan	69.4
37	Australia	74.9	79	Bolivia	69.3
38	Romania	74.8	80	Bhutan	69.3
39	Bulgaria	74.8	81	Panama	69.2
40	Israel	74.6	82	Bahrain	68.8
41	Thailand	74.5	83	Egypt, Arab Rep.	68.8
42	Moldova	74.4	84	Jamaica	68.7

On the contrary, many of the African countries came at the bottom of the list of the least performing countries. *Figure* 4 illustrates the gloom picture of African countries clearly.

Figure 4. Least performing countries in SDG Index
Source: Sustainable Development Report (2020),

Rank	Country	Score	Rank	Country	Score
85	Nicaragua	68.7	126	Syrian Arab Republic	59.3
86	Suriname	68.4	127	Senegal	58.3
87	Barbados	68.3	128	Côte d'Ivoire	57.9
88	Brunei Darussalam	68.2	129	The Gambia	57.9
89	Jordan	68.1	130	Mauritania	57.7
90	Paraguay	67.7	131	Tanzania	56.6
91	Maldives	67.6	132	Rwanda	56.6
92	Cabo Verde	67.2	133	Cameroon	56.5
93	Singapore	67.0	134	Pakistan	56.2
94	Sri Lanka	66.9	135	Congo, Rep.	55.2
95	Lebanon	66.7	136	Ethiopia	55.2
96	Nepal	65.9	137	Burkina Faso	55.2
97	Saudi Arabia	65.8	138	Djibouti	54.6
98	Trinidad and Tobago	65.8	139	Afghanistan	54.2
99	Philippines	65.5	140	Mozambique	54.1
100	Ghana	65.4	141	Lesotho	54.0
101	Indonesia	65.3	142	Uganda	53.5
102	Belize	65.1	143	Burundi	53.5
103	Qatar	64.7	144	Eswatini	53.4
104	Myanmar	64.6	145	Benin	53.3
105	Honduras	64.4	146	Comoros	53.1
106	Cambodia	64.4	147	Togo	52.7
107	Mongolia	64.0	148	Zambia	52.7
108	Mauritius	63.8	149	Angola	52.6
109	Bangladesh	63.5	150	Guinea	52.5
110	South Africa	63.4	151	Yemen, Rep.	52.3
111	Gabon	63.4	152	Malawi	52.2
112	Kuwait	63.1	153	Sierra Leone	51.9
113	Iraq	63.1	154	Haiti	51.7
114	Turkmenistan	63.0	155	Papua New Guinea	51.7
115	São Tomé and Príncipe	62.6	156	Mali	51.4
116	Lao PDR	62.1	157	Niger	50.1
117	India	61.9	158	Dem. Rep. Congo	49.7
118	Venezuela, RB	61.7	159	Sudan	49.6
119	Namibia	61.6	160	Nigeria	49.3
120	Guatemala	61.5	161	Madagascar	49.1
121	Botswana	61.5	162	Liberia	47.1
122	Vanuatu	60.9	163	Somalia	46.2
123	Kenya	60.2	164	Chad	43.8
124	Guyana	59.7	165	South Sudan	43.7
125	Zimbabwe	59.5	166	Central African Republic	38.5

Tapping *zakah* funds for development in general, and through supporting microenterprises and microfinance programs particularly, can help many of the

African countries especially the Muslim majority member states. Especially when we know that near to half (27 states) of the OIC 57 member states are also members of the African Union (55 states). Rehman and Pickup (2018) maintains that four tips need to be observed when considering *zakah* for the UN SDGs.

Tapping zakah funds for development in general, and through supporting microenterprises and microfinance programs particularly, can help many of the African countries especially the Muslim majority member states. Especially when we know that near to half (27 states) of the OIC 57 member states are also members of the African Union (55 states). Rehman and Pickup (2018) maintains that four tips need to be observed when considering zakah for the UN SDGs:

- Zakah is a philanthropic pool too large to ignore;
- Zakah is highly aligned with the SDGs;
- UNDP has already begun harnessing zakah for SDG projects; and
- Engaging with zakah is an opportunity for a wide range of stakeholders.

United Nations Development Programme (UNDP) in Indonesia has already started tapping zakah funds for developmental projects. In April 2017 BAZNAS (the national zakah collection body) and UNDP signed a Memorandum of Understanding (MoU) in Jakarta with the objective of developing Sustainable Development Goals (SDGs). (http://pusat.baznas.go.id) Here's how the partnership works:

- BAZNAS collects funds as per its organizational mandate
- BAZNAS makes grants to the UNDP to implement projects, and
- The UNDP implements projects in accordance with the UN Charter and the UNDP's global policies (Rehman and Pickup (2018).

Areas of collaboration between UNDP and BAZNAS can possibly include supporting livelihoods project in remote and rural areas, improving their access to electricity among other instances. Zakah potential can also be utilized to support productive capacities of individuals and communities instead of focusing on just consumptive or humanitarian activities such as the payment of hospital bills and disaster relief. Furthermore, the UNDP can also provide much-needed technical assistance to BAZNAS and other zakah organizations and to governments as well to enhance the effectiveness of zakah collection and administration, and to link zakah plans with the overall SDG strategies (Rehman and Pickup, 2018). The first major collaboration between BAZNAS and the UNDP was the installation of micro hydropower plants, which bring electricity to more than 4,500 people in four remote communities. This is part of a larger renewable energy project supported by the Global Environment Facility (https://www.undp.org/blog/zakah-sdgs). Another example of the collaboration between UNDP and BAZNAS is the implementation of four micro hydro power plants in two districts in Jambi Province of Sumatra. BAZNAS contributed $350k in zakah funds and the provincial state-owned Bank Jambi also contributed $281k to the partnership. The projects are part of Global Environment Facility (GEF) to support renewable energy in Indonesia (Buana, 2018).

USING ZAKAH FUNDS TO SUPPOT MICROFINANCE AND MICROENTERPRISES PROGRAMS

Islamic literature has excessively explained that alleviating hunger, poverty, and inequality, promoting peace and protecting the environment could possibly fall under the fundamental purposes of maqasid (objectives) Shariah. Likewise, microfinance has emerged as an important tool for poverty alleviation in the developing countries (Yonis, 2012). Microfinance is more appreciated when it is used to improve the socio-economic situations of poor and low-income people. The exiting literature is full of articles and studies that describe several success stories for using zakah in microfinance and microenterprises support programs (Ahmed, 2015; Yudha and Lathifah, 2018; Ibrahim and Ghazali, 2014; Din, 2014; Possumah and Ismail 2011). The next part of this paper will discuss two case studies in which zakah has been used in microfinance and microenterprise programs, one program is from Malaysia and the other one is from Indonesia.

MICROFINANCE AND MICROENTERPRISE PROGRAMS

Microfinance is widely known as the financial enablement for poor and needy who suffer from lack of collateral, financial records, and credit history; therefore, these populations are often aided with small amounts of credit to help them start their businesses. Unprecedentedly, many developing and developed countries have started to use microfinance as a magical tool that can contribute directly to alleviate poverty and ensure livelihood development and wellbeing of poor. Thus, enhance job opportunities, which is the main goals for the socioeconomic development (Thai-Ha, 2021).

Malaysia was a pioneer in this field starting from 1966, the formal microcredit institutions were lunched in Malaysia as the Rural Industrial Development Authority (RIDA), the main target for RIDA was to provide economic assistance and to support Malay farmers and rural inhabitants (Haque, &Siwar, 2019). In 1987 Malaysia initiated microcredit programs and strategies to eradicate poverty problem in the country (Suraya, 2011). Amanah Ikhtiar Malaysia (AIM) was the first microfinance institution established by two social scientists, Dr. David Gibbon and Prof. Sukor Kasim (Siwar and Quianones, 2000). Then many initiatives have followed, such as Yayasan Usaha Maju (YUM) and the Economic Fund for National Entrepreneurs Group (TEKUN). The fundamental goal for all these initiatives was to provide funds for poor households who lack the required collateral. (AIM) provides free interest loan, however clients have to pay 10% as operational and management fees with 2% as a compulsory saving. In 2013 AIM's market share of the microfinance industry stands at 40 percent and is expected to increase to 50 percent in the next 5 years (Nor Fazidah, 2011). Remarkably, (AIM) considered the prominent MFI in Malaysia, which services approximately 82 percent with 222,557 of Malaysian poor households (Omar, Noor, & Dahalan, 2012) with highest loan repayment rate in the world which reached 99.2 percent (Monitor, 2010). AIM chairman, Datuk Dr Zubir Harun said "only less than 1.8 per cent of the total 326,009 borrowers nationwide failed to fully settle their outstanding amounts" also he added that "98.22 per cent of the total borrowers, who received loans worth RM18.44 billion at 134 AIM branches nationwide had fully settled their loans (David, 2017). Aim shifted from qard hasan (interest-free loan) to tawarruq (sell and buy back arrangement) financing in 2013 (Engku Ali, 2019).

Table 1. Active MFIs in Malaysia

Name of MIFs	Date of Birth	Status	Location/Scale
Federal and Authority (FELDA)	1956	Governmental	National
Majlis Amanah Rakyat (MARA)	1966	NGO	National
Credit Guarantee Corporation (CGC)	1972	Governmental	National
Farmers Organization Authority (LPP)	1973	Governmental	National
National Savings Bank (BSN)	1974	Governmental	National
Amanah Ikhtiar Malaysia (AIM)	1987	NGO	National
Koperasi Kredit Rakyat	1988	NGO	Selangor
Tabung Ekonomi Kumpulan Usaha Negara (TEKUN)	1988	NGO	National
Yayasan Usaha Maju	2002	NGO	Sabah
Bank Pertanian Malaysia (BPM)	2003	Governmental	National

Source: (APEC, 2015)

It is observed that microfinance in Malaysia is over six decades old. non-government sector seems to play an effective role in providing microfinance with five NGOs. The vast majority of microfinance providers are national institutions with only two local institutions operating on the state level, namely in Selangor and Sabah.

SOCIAL-ECONOMIC EFFECT OF MICROFINANCE AND MICROENTERPRISE SUPPORT PROGRAMS

Microcredit programs have proven to be an effective measure in freeing people from poverty toward more economic inclusive in the society. It has been argued that such programs are potential tools that can positively impact poverty reduction, enhance employment rate, and develop the community and national welfare (Terano et al., 2015).

The Malaysia's report on Millennium Development Goals indicated that employing microcredit schemes has major impact in increasing the income of the poor people in Malaysia particularly among the women. To be more specific, the extreme poverty rate in Malaysia had noticeably dipped from 16.5% in 1990 to 0.6% in 2014. In other words, Malaysia have successfully improved the socioeconomic status of women by implementing several programs such as microcredit scheme, women entrepreneurship programs, tax incentives and re-employment program for the women. According to Che Supian, and Norziani (2012), Kedah state in Malaysia has shown that the average income of the borrowers increased from RM1,286.77 before joining microcredit to RM2,703.63 after joining the programs, this represents an increment rate of about 110% or RM1,416.86 to their income before joining the program. The group of "extreme poverty" fell from 12.8% (before) to 2.3% (after). The group of "poor" dropped from 19.8% (before) to 5.2% (after), and those who were in the category of "low income" fell from 54.1% (before) to 44.8% (after). The later figures and statistics indicated that microcredit has a positive effect on increasing the income of the borrowers, thus reducing the poverty rate.

ZAKAH-BASED MICROENTERPRISE SUPPORT PROGRAMS: TWO SELECTED CASE STUDIES

Case One: Malaysia- Selangor *Zakah* Board (Lembaga Zakah Selangor- LZS)

In Malaysia, the Administration of *zakah* funds falls under the State Islamic Religion Councils (SIRCs). A total of 14 SIRCs over Malaysia where 13 of it is belong to the state and one for Wilayah Persekutuan Kuala Lumpur (Razimi et al., 2016). Furthermore, *zakah* in Malaysia is under the mandate of the Department of *Wakaf*,

Zakah, and *Hajj* (JAWHAR). JAWHAR was set up on March 27, 2004 by former Prime Minister Tun Abdullah Ahmad Badawi (JAWHAR, 2020). Collections of *zakah* in Malaysia has increased over the past decade. Remarkably, the amount of *zakah* funds vary from state to state. However, a remarkable increase in *zakah* funds occurred between 2007 and 2016. In Selangor state for instance, *zakah* funds reached approximately RM 673.7 million in 2016 compared to 202.2 million RM in 2007 (exchange rate is RM 4.17 for one US$). Figure 5. illustrates the zakah collection in all Malaysian states between 2007 and 2016.

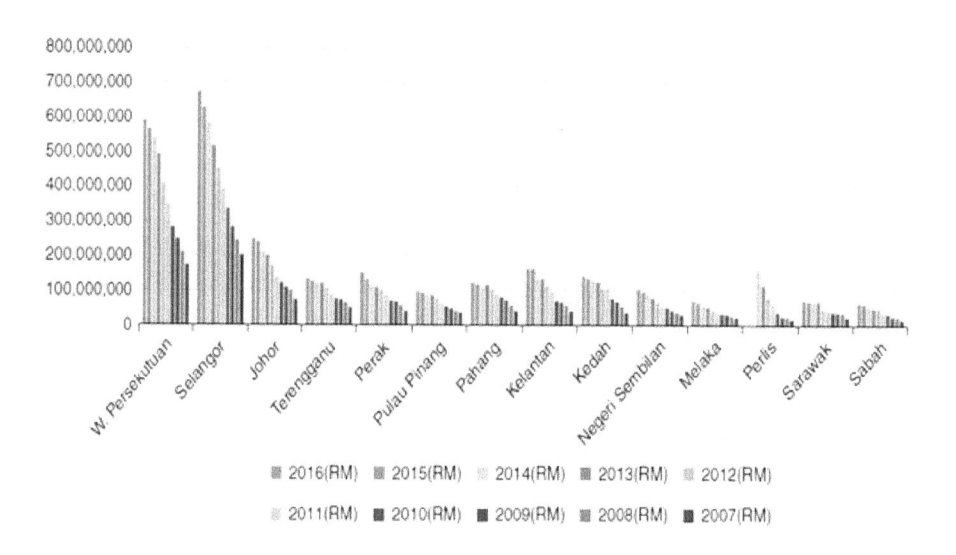

Figure 5. Zakah collections in Malaysia by states between 2007–2016
Source: JAWHAR/ State Religious Authority/ (Abdul Razak, 2019)

According to the figure above, two states i.e., Selangor and the Federal Territory jointly contributed about 50 per cent to the total collected amounts, that is approximately RM1.262bn out of the total RM2.631bn collected by all the states excluding state of Perlis (Abdul Razak, 2019). Table 2 below illustrates the details of the collected *zakah* funds in all Malaysian states.

Table 2. Zakah collection in Malaysia (2007- 2016)

State/year	2007	2008	2009	2010	2011	2012	2013	2014	2015	2016
Federal territory	173.8	211.4	248.8	282.7	348.9	410.4	492.4	540.8	565.8	589.3
Selangor	202.2	244.4	283.6	336.9	394.1	451.3	517.3	582.1	627.2	673.7
Johor	73.3	100.7	109.2	122.3	137.5	171.9	200.6	212.8	239.9	250.4
Terengganu	51.4	66.2	73.5	76.4	88.3	107.1	120.9	120.1	126.6	133.4
Perak	41.3	57.0	67.2	69.6	86.1	99.6	109.8	114.6	132.6	151.2
PPinang	37.1	41.8	48.0	53.2	62.3	76.5	86.0	87.9	92.8	96.8
Pahang	41.5	57.9	71.9	80.9	88.6	102.9	115.8	109.3	118.0	122.2
Kelantan	40.2	58.2	66.5	70.4	94.1	113.2	134.2	133.3	161.9	162.7
Kedah	36.7	53.2	67.6	76.9	106.1	106.2	122.7	128.4	133.9	140.4
NSembilan	29.4	37.4	42.3	50.2	57.9	65.4	78.9	88.2	95.2	104.8
Melaka	22.1	26.9	30.7	34.0	37.9	54.0	53.1	58.3	66.0	70.5
Sarawak	23.1	36.1	36.9	39.1	44.1	50.8	69.5	67.3	68.6	72.1
Sabah	17.5	23.8	25.4	32.9	33.9	48.9	49.2	52.8	61.8	63.7
Perlis	16.7	23.1	25.3	38.1	61.4	78.9	115	162.3		
Total	806.3	1,038.1	1,196.9	1,363.6	1,641.2	1,937.1	2,265.4	2,458.2	2,490.3	2,631.2

Source: (Lembaga Zakah Selangor, 2020).
https://drive.google.com/file/d/18sxTJL3Mw3meCv6RxRzJMLr6GIcw2Vci/view

Interestingly, the total amount of *zakah* funds has soared from RM 806.3 million in 2007 to over RM 2,631.2 million in 2016 excluding the state of Perlis. This translates into a cumulative annual growth rate of 47.5 per cent for the period from 2007 to 2016.

Figure 6. Total distribution & collection of zakah from 1 January to 31 May 2020
Source: (Lembaga Zakah Selangor, 2020)

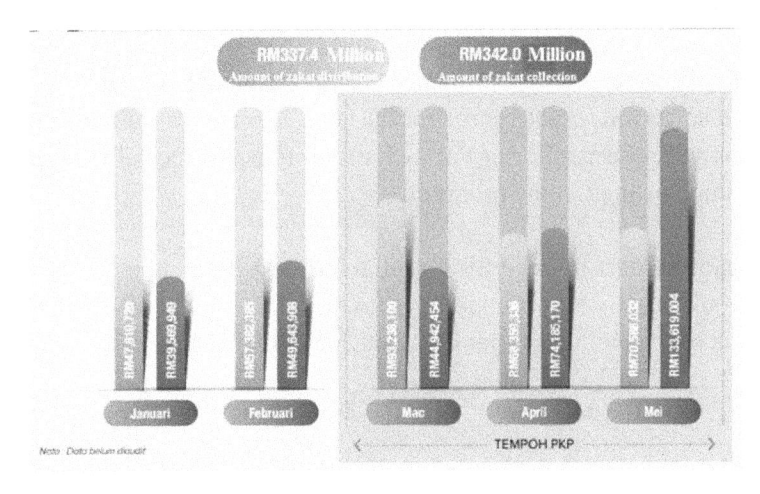

During the COVID-19 pandemic lockdowns, Selangor *Zakah* Board (MAIS) has distributed a total of RM232.2 million to eight *asnaf* (*zakah* beneficiaries) groups including more than 57 thousand *asnaf* families as well as more than 6 thousand converts. Nonetheless, *zakah* collection in Selangor shows a decrease of 0.1% from RM253.1 million (2019) to RM252.7 million (2020) for the same period; this decrease can possibly be attributed to covid19 lockdown and its impacts on businesses.

Moreover, among the efforts to assist affected business and families during the COVID-19 pandemic, the Selangor *Zakah* Board (LZS), has assigned approximately MYR 15 million as an emergency relief fund to assist the small vendors and hawkers who are affected by the thirteen-day movement control order (MCO) imposed in the country (IM Insights, 2020).

Selangor Zakah Board (LZS) Programs for Microenterprises

LZS is the official authority that is in charge of managing *zakah* affairs in the state of Selangor in Malaysia. LZS is also one of the prominent institutes in the Department of *Wakaf*, *Zakah*, and *Hajj* (JAWHAR). LZS has utilized its creative and innovative system combined with technology to achieve ideal *zakah* management (collection and distributed). Its method becomes the benchmark for other *zakah* offices in Malaysia. LZS has initiated some programs to support micro-entrepreneurs with capital assistance and aids them with extra skills in business management. Such skills include professional training and marketing. For this purpose, LZS cooperates with many other agencies, such as the Malaysian Agricultural Research and Development Institute, and the Small and Medium Industries Development Corp. According to the innovative LZS system, the traditional eighth categories of *zakah* recipients have been classified into two main categories: productive and non-productive groups. this classification has been adopted in consideration to recipients' physical skills and abilities. Thus, the distribution of funds has been classified into consumption and productive purposes; in our context, the latter one is the subject matter, and it is known as *zakah* microfinance (Ibrahim and Ghazali, 2014).

Interestingly, the *zakah* microfinance program contains not only the provision of capital seed to micro entrepreneurs but also it provides training on business management and close monitoring throughout the program. The following procedures have been implemented in the program:

1. Provision of start-up fund for potential business project.
2. Rigorous examination is undertaken to the applicants to ensure the eligibility criteria which include proper skills, business interest and desire to learn along with the physical capabilities.

3. Provision of the required knowledge and guidance to the recipients before and during the conduct of business.
4. Capital is given in the form of equipment and working capital such as machinery and rental premises.
5. Recipients are given a basic course of business, including financial management and motivation before starting a business.
6. LZS provides spiritual knowledge and religious practices such as trust, honesty, and sincerity.
7. Monitoring of applicants and their business. Each 40 recipients are assigned to one *zakah* officer. Monitoring includes not only business performance but also spiritual aspects, daily necessities, housing conditions and income (Ibrahim and Ghazali, 2014; Kachkar, 2019).

From 2008 to 2010 the total number of recipients reached 1054 and the funds distributed reached RM 6.862.938 the details are in the table below.

Table 3. Number of recipients of capital assistance 2008-2010

Program	Number of Recipients 2008	Number of Recipients 2009	Number of Recipients 2010	Total 2008 – 2010
Business Capital Assistance	299	234	356	889
Fishery Capital Assistance	21	8	50	79
Livestock Capital Assistance	8	12	11	31
Agricultural Capital Assistance	15	22	18	55
Total Recipient	343	276	435	1054
Total Distribution (RM)	1,806,753.	2,593,854	2,462,331	6,862,938
Average amount of distribution per recipient	5,267.50	9,398.02	5,660.53	6,511.33

Source: (Ibrahim and Ghazali, 2014).

Looking at the segments assisted by LZS program, assistance to businesses occupies the top of the list by 299 recipients with livestock the least with only 8 beneficiaries. The number of recipients has decreased about 20% in 2009 before taking off again in 2010 to increase about 22% from 2008 and 37% from 2009 respectively.

LZS Asnaf Entrepreneurship Program (AEP)

Asnaf is the Arabic word to denote the eight categories of *zakah* recipients highlighted in *Surah At-Tawba* (9:60). Through Asnaf Entrepreneurial Program (AEP), LZS endeavors to aid the poor in order to become entrepreneurs and to enhance their social and economic life. The program can be divided into four core elements which are (1) entrepreneurship development program, (2) skill development program (3) administrative and monitoring and (4) distribution program. In addition to start-up capital (Shiyuti and Al-Habshi, 2018). To this effect, LZS collaborates with some other institutions such as Institute Keusahawanan Negara (INSKEN) and Institute Latihan Islam Malaysia (ILIM) within the scope of training and skill improvements among entrepreneurs (Din et al., 2019). *Asnaf* program is in line with the core objectives of *zakah* that aims to "empower the productive *asnaf* to generate income up to the level of graduation from the *asnaf* status" (Qardawi,2009). Eligibility criteria taken into account when selecting the eligible *asnaf* to become entrepreneurs are commitment, hardworking, mental and physical capability, and shows interest in entrepreneurship (Mohamed, et al., 2018). *Asnaf* program is quite important and has many advantages for many reasons, for instance:

1. The *zakah* institution provides capital assistance to *asnaf* entrepreneurs in order to fulfill self-confidence and productivity in running the business.
2. In addition, this capital will add and enhance the social and morale in the societies,
3. Also, it has a positive impact on the economy (Din et al., 2019).

In 2015, *zakah* institutions supported around RM 9,000,0000 to *asnaf* who are under this program covered in terms of training, capital and monitoring to become entrepreneurs (Asnaf MAIS, 2015).

Lembaga *Zakah* Selangor (2016) has identified three types of *zakah* receipts under AEP program, first type is *asnaf* who has no professional skills and cannot run any type of business; second type is *asnaf* who is in need of one-time assistance to cope or get out of the poverty; and the third type is *asnaf* which is currently struggling with hardship but has the potential to develop, grow and graduate from *asnaf* (Din, et al., 2019).

According to (Din,et al., 2019) the AEP program consists of many processes as follow:

1- Identifying the inputs by selecting the possible entrepreneurs who are complying with Islamic ideas.

2- Transformation process, which is transforming the training and project preparation to the outputs such as goods, services, ideas, and entertainment based on the outputs it will achieve the goals that is rapidly national growth.

LZS *Asnaf* Entrepreneurship Program (AEP) has two manners of financial assistance granted to recipients. The first is the distribution of start-up financial assistant based on the request made by the recipients to run their own business. Secondly, LZS also offers capital assistance to businesses selected by LZS management. Consequently, two categories are identified, the first category includes micro-entrepreneurs of *zakah* beneficiaries who run micro enterprises of value less than RM5,000, such as selling nasi lemak (traditional Malaysian food), fried banana and others. The second category include business with value varies between RM5,000 to RM50,000, such as restaurants, laundry shops and others (Mohamed et al., 2018).

Figure 7. Turning over model
Source: (Din, Rosdi, Ismail, Muhammad, & Mukhtar, 2019)

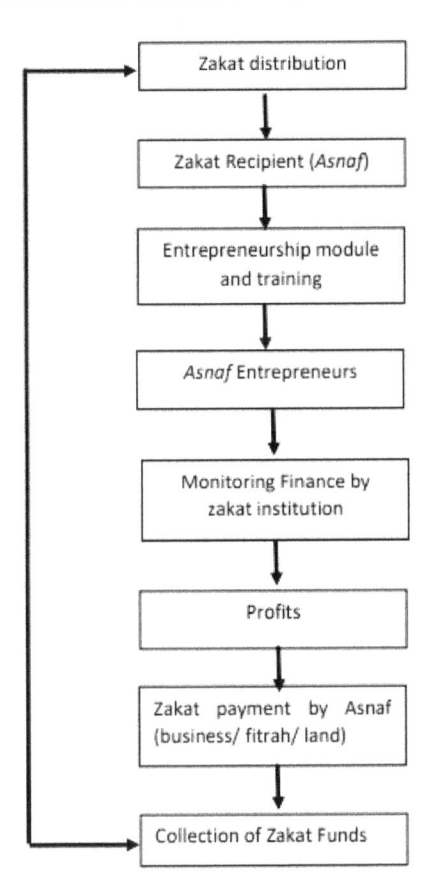

```
Zakat distribution
      ↓
Zakat Recipient (Asnaf)
      ↓
Entrepreneurship module
and training
      ↓
Asnaf Entrepreneurs
      ↓
Monitoring Finance by
zakat institution
      ↓
Profits
      ↓
Zakat payment by Asnaf
(business/ fitrah/ land)
      ↓
Collection of Zakat Funds
```

Turning Over Model

According to (Sabri & Hasan, 2006), the Turning Over Model is innovative *zakah* distribution to potential *asnaf* in business. Under the supervision of *zakah* institution, Asnaf will enter sequences process of forming and enhancing the business with the aid of *zakah* and the main purpose of this is to provide *asnaf* with a better opportunity to work and earn a better income which could turn them from *asnaf*, i.e., *zakah* receivers to the source of *zakah* who are able to pay *zakah*. So, they will stop relying on *zakah* funds to achieve more productive societies.

As of 2016, LZS has assisted 175 *asnaf* entrepreneurs to graduate from the program and to become self-sufficient (Izwan, 2017).

Case Two: Baitul Maal Muamalat Indonesia (BMMI)

Indonesia is considered as a significant key player in poverty alleviation, since Indonesia is the biggest Muslim country which is 85 percent of total population in Indonesia or 216.66 million populations (BPS, 2015), Indonesia has several *zakah* institutions such as, BAZNAS, BAZNAS Province, BAZNAS Regency/City and certified *zakah* institutions (LAZ) as elaborated in Table 4. The National Board of *Zakah* (BAZNAS) is the coordinator which is responsible for managing *zakah* funds in Indonesia. In addition, BAZNAS has a responsibility to collect a regular report from Certified *Zakah* Institution (LAZ). Minister of Religious Affairs Decision (KMA) No. 333/2015 about guidelines for licensing Certified Zakah Institutions (LAZ) which led The National Board of *Zakah* (BAZNAS) has an authority to recommend The Certified *Zakah* Institutions to have official license (Indonesia *Zakah* Outlook, 2019).

Table 4. *The effective collection and distribution of zakah funds in 2107 through zakah institution (figures in Indonesian Rupiah IDR, one $UD is equal to IDR14,185)*

No	Sectors	Collection	%	Distribution	%	Absorption
1	BAZNAS	153,542,103,405	2.47	131,917,747,764	2.71	85.92%
2	Provincial BAZNAS	448,171,189,258	7.20	388,168,225,347	7.99	86.61%
3	Regency/City BAZNAS	3,426,689,437,619	55.05	2,629,588,214,952	54.11	76.74%
4	LAZ	2,195,968,539,189	35.28	1,710,481,136,382	35.19	77.89%
	TOTAL	6,224,371,269,471	100	4,860,155,324,445	100	78.08%

Source: (Indonesia Zakah Outlook 2019).

Table 4 compares the amount of *zakah* collected by *zakah* institutions in 2017. It is illustrating that the total *zakah* funds collection reached approximately 6.2 trillion Rupiahs in 2017. Whereas the distribution amount was almost 4.8 trillion Rupiahs. Therefore, the national absorption rate is estimated at around 78.08% which indicates that the fund's absorption in 2017 is "effective." (BAZNAS, 2019).

Baitul Maal Muamalat Indonesia (BMMI)

The second case study to be highlighted in this section is the program of Baitul Maal Muamalat Indonesia (BMMI). BMMI is a licensed *zakah* organization in Indonesia that collects Islamic charities (*zakah, sadaqa* and *waqf*) and disburses the funds for the society purposes. It was established in 2000 as a social subsidiary of Bank Muamalat Indonesia that collects Islamic charity from Bank Muamalat's clients and distributes this charity for social purposes. Seventy percent of its funds are distributed for economic empowerment through microfinance programs (Yumna, 2019). BMMI in Indonesia has three major programs to include the poor within the microfinance system. One particular program for micro entrepreneurs called Komunitas Usaha Mikro Muamalat Berbasis Masjid (Micro entrepreneur community based on mosques/KUMMM), were initially developed in 2007. This KUMMM program is especially designed for micro entrepreneurs who actively participate in the local mosque. The key objectives of the program are firstly, to work toward economic empowerment of the poor and secondly to support religious education for society. This second objective is translated into the institution's mission statement as an intention to develop an individual character with strong religious beliefs, a determined commitment to grow, and with the capacity to empathize with others. All BMMI KUMMM microfinance program activities, are conducted in mosques including client selection, mentoring and loan repayment arrangements (Yumna, 2019). The main objective of conducting the activities in the mosque is the institution's intention to be able to choose clients who are motivated towards and committed to the adoption of positive attitudes and values. These client characteristics may go some way to reduce asymmetric information and moral hazard problems (Yumna, 2019). One interesting feature of the program is that it has a graduation concept for participants. Successful graduates manage their own cooperatives and begin to participate in commercial microfinance (Yumna, 2019).

The data on the program is available only for the year 2011 and 2012. It indicates that in 2011 the program has dispersed around IDR6,101,367,487.54 ($435,811) and in 2012 it dispersed about IDR 3,309,973,000.00 ($236,426) ($1= RP 14,090), this indicates a decrease of about 50% from the previous year. Unfortunately, the available data and information does not provide any explanation to this serious decrease. As for the repayment rate and non-performing financing, the data reveals that in 2011 around 56% of loans were repaid by the clients, non- performing financing reached in the same year about 43%, however, this low rate of repayment became even worse in 2012 with a repayment rate of only 20% and non-performing financing about 80%. The low repayment rate in fact undermines the whole idea of mosque centralisation and commitment etc. However, it is believed that low repayment rate is attributed to two factors:

1. lack of human resources, i.e. no enough field workers to monitor the clients, in turn, the lack of human resources can often be put down to severe cuts to the institution's operating budget.
2. public perceptions of *zakah* as social organizations that simply disperse charitable funding directly to those in dire need, without an expectation that this funding be repaid (Yumna, 2019).

In fact, this is a very low repayment rate compared to other similar microfinance institution. In Malaysia, Amana *Ikhtiar* Malaysia reported in 2012 very high repayment rate of 99.35% (Abdul Rahman et.at. 2013). no doubt that non-performing loans are among the top challenges that encounter humanitarian agencies when providing commercial financial services.

SOLUTIONS AND RECOMMENDATIONS

The core objective of this research is to identify the best practices of the cited microenterprise support programs MSPs. It attempts to extend such applications to many developing and underdeveloped countries, including many African countries. As discussed in the early sections, the best practices in microenterprise support programs start with the participants' selection process. Screening the targeted clients is essential for the success of MSPs. This is to ensure eligibility of participants to the program. It is already acknowledged that not all poor and needy persons are potential entrepreneurs. Additionally, best practices in MSPs means that microenterprise programs must include both financial and non-financial services. The later set of services are believed to be equally important of the former set of services. Non-financial services Include business management training, skill upgrading, monitoring, counselling. It is interesting that the LZS program in Malaysia includes also religious and spiritual training and sessions to encourage participants on Islamic ethics and values that are believed to enhance the commitments of the participants and the repayments of their liabilities. BMMI KUMMM program has also conducted their activities and periodic meetings in the mosques. Another point of best practices as adopted in the LZS program is that cash is not provided to participants, but capital is offered in the form of equipment and working capital such as machinery and rental premises. The last point to be highlighted pertains to the concern on the very low repayment rate in the BMMI KUMMM program about 20% and non-performing financing about 80%. As discussed earlier, possible reasons could be the misperception on the program among participants. For that reason, it is strongly advised that participants in *zakah*-based programs and the alike must not be informed on the source of funding, this is to avoid the moral hazard that consequently happened by the participants and could possibly demotivate them to pay back their liabilities.

FUTURE RESEARCH DIRECTIONS

With the gloomy picture depicted above on sustainable development in majority of African countries, the importance of this book cannot be over emphasized. This research attempts to contribute to the book and to the existing literature on sustainable development in Africa by highlighting two examples of actual institutions that are using zakah funds to support microenterprise. The role of zakah can be further explored in future research to investigate the long-term outcome of *zakah*-based programs. That can include analyzing the impact of such programs on the socio-economic situations of beneficiaries. The serious issue of low repayment rate in the BMMI KUMMM microfinance program can be another area of future studies. Learning from the practices of successful programs like the Amanah Ikhtiar Malaysia could be one of the recommendations to address this issue. One more possible area of research is to analyses the views of zakah payers on channeling their *zakakh* payments to such microfinance programs. Finally, a feasibility study on using zakah fund in selected African countries is one of the potential areas of research.

CONCLUSION

This research draws on the basic premises that together can constitute the theoretical framework and rationale for this research. Premise one is built on the importance of microenterprises in bringing about a real change in the socioeconomic situations of millions of poor and underprivileged households. In many countries, microenterprises represent the backbone of the economy. In Cambodia for instance, according to the survey conducted by the Cambodia Intercensal Economic in 2014, there were 512,871 enterprises established in Cambodia, among them, 501,612 were micro enterprises, and 11,259 were small and medium enterprises combined (UN-DESA, 2020). This premise is well established in the literature and supported by many empirical studies (International Labor Organization, 2017; Mustapha et al., 2018; Khan and Quaddus, 2015, Akram et al., 2015). Enhancing the living standard of poor populations through supporting their microenterprises can at least contribute significantly to achieving eight goals of the 17 SDGs. These goals are related to the 1. SDG: no poverty, 2. SDG: Zero hunger, 3. SDG: Good health and well-being, 4. SDG: quality education 6. SDG: clean water and sustainability, 8. SDG decent work and economic growth 10. SDG: reduce inequality and finally 16. SDG: peace justice and strong institutions.

Premise two, lack of financial resources is a major challenge for small and micro businesses as well as for NGOs and government entities that intends to support such micro businesses. This is another fact that is well documented in the literature on microenterprises (Bartsch, 2003; Ranalli, 2013; the Women's Refugee Commission (WRC), (n.d.) and Jacobsen and Titus, 2004). The governments of both developing countries as well as developed countries encounter the lack of financial resources. In Bangladesh for instance, it is estimated that the total demand for ME loans in 2015 is Tk. 737 billion (one USD is equal to 85 Bangladesh Takas (TK)). Total ME loan outstanding by MFIs is Tk. 123.27 billion and that of banks is Tk. 176.65 billion. So, total loan supply to MEs is Tk.299.92 billion and therefore the demand-supply gap is Tk. 437.39 billion, that is, around 60% of the demand is unmet (Khalily et al., 2017). According to a recent study funded by the European Commission, the funding gap for EFTA region is EUR 12.9 billion, which corresponds to 92.3% of the constrained demand. EFTA region include in addition to EU member states Albania, Iceland, Montenegro, North Macedonia, Norway, Serbia, and Turkey. In the EU alone, the funding gap is for 53.9% (European Commission, 2020). Premise three, *zakah* funds represent a huge potential source of funding to be channelled into microfinance and microenterprises programs. Importance of *zakah* funds becomes clear with the fact that the majority of Organization of Islamic Cooperation member states are in dire needs for financial resources to fund their financial needs for socio-economic development and to achieve the SDGs as discussed in earlier sections. In order to meet the SDGs by 2030 in five priority areas of education, health, roads, electricity, and water and sanitation, it is estimated that an additional private and public annual spending of $528 billion is required for low and lower middle-income countries and $2.1 trillion for Emerging countries (Doumbia and Laurids, 2019). The aim of this research is to spot the light on the importance of Islamic social finance in bridging the gap in financial resources. Particularly, this research brought two of the actual projects where *zakah* funds are practically implemented in the provision of microenterprise support programs. From the two programs of microenterprise support, it can be deduced that *zakah* funds constitute a great potential of funds that can significantly contribute to address the lack of financial resources to financing such programs. However, best practices of offering microfinance to potential microentrepreneurs, as discussed e earlier, must be strictly observed.

REFERENCES

Abdul Rahman, R. K., Siwar, C., Ismail, A. G., Bahrom, H., & Khalid, M. M. (2013). Zakah and microfinance. *International Proceedings of Economics Development and Research*, *61*(3), 10–13. 10.7763

Abdul Razak, H. (2019). Zakah and waqf as instrument of Islamic wealth in poverty alleviation and redistribution: Case of Malaysia. *Malaysia International Journal of Sociology and Social Policy*, *40*(3/4), 249–266. doi:10.1108/IJSSP-11-2018-0208

Abu Dawud, S. (2008). *Sunan Abi Dawud*. Dar Al- Kotob Al- Ilmiyah.

Adawiah, E. R. (2019). Successful Models of Social Finance Initiatives: Lessons from Amanah Ikhtiar Malaysia (AIM). In S. Kassim, A. H. Othman, & R. Haron (Eds.), *Handbook of Research on Islamic Social Finance and Economic Recovery After a Global Health Crisis*. IGI Global.

African 2030. (2021). *Africa 2030: SDGs within Social Boundaries Leaving No One Behind Outlook*. https://sdgcafrica.org/wp-content/uploads/2021/07/20210721_Full_Report_Final_Web_En.pdf

Ahmed, H. (2015). *Zakah, Macroeconomic Policies, and Poverty Alleviation: Lessons from Simulations on Bangladesh*. https://ibtra.com/pdf/journal/v4_n2_article4.pdf

Al-Gamal, M. (2020). Shart Tamleek al-Zakah wa 'Atharuhu fi Kayfiyat Tawzi'iha. *Dirasat: Ulum al-Shariah waAlqanun*, *47*(3), 30-42. https://journals.ju.edu.jo/DirasatLaw/article/download/104603/11635

Al-Qaradaghi, A. (2014). المقال داعي وعدي الحكومات الإسلامية لإخراج زكاة ثرواتها وخُمس النفط لإغناء الفقراء. https://arabic.cnn.com/middleeast/2014/07/17/ali-qaradahji-islamic-finance

APEC. (2005). *The Need and Availability of Micro Finance Service for the Micro Enterprise: Bringing multi-level Good Practices into Local Context*. https://www.sica.int/documentos/the-need-and-availability-of-micro-finance-service-for-micro-enterprise-bringing-multi-level-good-practices-into-local-context_1_86513.html

As-Sallabi, A. (2015). *Umar Bin 'Abd- 'Aziz*. Dar Ibn Katheer.

Asnaf, M. A. I. S. (2015). *Bersama kami membantu Asnaf*. Lembaga Zakah Selangor.

Badan Pusat Statistik (BPS). (2016). *Gini Ratio Maret 2016*. BPS Official News. https://bali.bps.go.id/

Balwi, M. A., & Halim, A. H. A. (2008). Mobilising zakah dalam pewujudan usahawan Asnaf: Satu tinjauan. Shariah Journal, 16, 567-584.

Brown, A., & Swersky, A. (2012). *The First Billion, A forecast of social investment demand*. The Boston Consulting Group and Big Society Capital. http://impactstrategist.com/wp-content/uploads/2015/12/First-Billion-forecast-demand.pdf

Buana, G. K. (2018). *Innovative financing for SDGs: Mobilizing ummah's potential to leave no one behind*. https://www.asia-pacific.undp.org/content/rbap/en/home/blog/2018/innovative-financing-for-sdgs.html

Bukhari, M. (1422H). *Al-Jami' al-ṣaḥiḥ al-mukhtaṣar min umur rasuli Llah wasunanihi waayyamihi* (Ṣaḥiḥ al-Bukhari) Dar Tawq al- Najah, 14(22), 1331.

Cizakca, M. (2011). *The Waqf, its Contribution and Basic Operational Structure*. http://www.iqra.org.my/slide/Iqra%20Waqf%20101.pptx

David, A. (2017). Amanah Ikhtiar willing to give more loans to women entrepreneurs. *New Straits Time*. https://www.nst.com.my/news/nation/2017/10/297067/amanah-ikhtiar-willing-give-more-loans-women-entrepreneurs

Din, N. M., Rosdi, M. S. M., Ismail, M., Muhammad, M. Z., & Mukhtar, D. (2019). Contributions of Asnaf Entrepreneurs in Zakah of Business: A Revisiting Based on Turning over Model. *International Journal of Academic Research in Business & Social Sciences*, 9(9), 744–752.

Doumbia. D. & Lauridsen, M. (2019). *Closing the SDG Financing Gap—Trends and Data*. Note 73.

European Commission. (2020). *Microfinance in the European Union: Market analysis and recommendations for delivery options in 2021-2027*. https://ec.europa.eu/social/BlobServlet?docId=23029&langId=en

Fox, M. (2010). *Micro capital Brief: Malaysian Microfinance Institution (MFI), Amanah Ikhtiar Malaysia (AIM), Claims "World's Highest" Microcredit Repayment Rate of 99.2 Percent*. http://www.microcapital.org/microcapital-brief-malaysian-microfinance-institution-mfi-amanah-ikhtiar-m

Geetha, C., Savarimuthu, A., & Majid, A. (2017). Assessing Financial Returns on Microloans from Socioeconomic, Social and Environment Impact: A Case in Kota Kinabalu. *Malaysian Journal of Business and Economics.*, 4(2), 7–29.

Haque, T., Siwar, C., Bhuiyan, A. B., & Joarder, M. H. (2019). Contributions of Amanah ikhtiar Malaysia (AIM) in microfinance to economic empowerment (EE) of women borrowers in Malaysia. *Economia e Sociologia*, 12(4), 241–256. doi:10.14254/2071-789X.2019/12-4/15

Harij, K., & Hebb, T. (2010). Investing for Impact: Issues and Opportunities for Social Finance in Canada. In *ANSER Conference*. Carleton Centre for Community Innovation.

Ibn 'Abidin, M. (2011). *Hashiyat ibn 'Abidin: radd al-muhtar 'ala al-Durr al-mukhtar*. Dar al-Ma'rifah.

Ibn Qudaamah, M. (1997). *Al-Mughni*. Dar Alam al-Kutub.

Ibrahim, P., & Ghazali, R. (2014). Zakah As an Islamic Micro-Financing Mechanism to Productive Zakah Recipients. *Asian Economic and Financial Review*, 4(1), 117–125.

Indonesia Zakah Outlook. (2019). *Centre of Strategic Studies the National Board of Zakah, Republic of Indonesia (BAZNAS)*. https://www.puskasbaznas.com/publications/outlook/indonesia-zakat-outlook-2019

Insights, I. M. (2020). *Malaysia's Selangor State Zakah Board Allots MYR 15 Million Fund to Assist Small Business Vendors*. https://islamicmarkets.com/articles/malaysia-s-selangor-state-zakah-board-allots-myr-15-million-fund

International Labour Organisation. (2017). *Growing microenterprises: how gender and family can impact outcomes – evidence from Uganda, Issue Brief No 2, March 2017*. Author.

Islamic, S. F. R. (2014). *Islamic Research and Training Institute, Islamic Development Bank, Jeddah*. https://irti.org/product/islamic-social-finance-report-2014/

ISRA. (2012). Islamic Financial System: principles and Operations. International Shari'ah Research Academy for Islamic Finance (ISRA).

Jawhar. (2020). *Department of Awqaf, Zakah & Hajj (Jawhar)*. = https://www.jawhar.gov.my/en/profil-jabatan/mengenai-jawhar/sejarah-jawhar/

Kachkar, O. (2019). Islamic social finance: Mobilizing Zakah (almsgiving) funds to support refugees' microenterprises pogroms. *International Congress of Islamic Economy, Finance & Ethics*.

Kadri, F. (2011). The Role of Microfinance in Poverty Alleviation: AIM's Experience. The 2nd Working Group on the Development of Islamic Financial Service Industry, Jakarta.

Kahf, M. (1998). *Financing the Development of Awqaf Property*. The Seminar on Development of Awqaf.

Kahf, M. (2003). The role of waqf in improving the Ummah welfare. In *The International Seminar on Waqf as a Private Legal Body*. Islamic University of North Sumatra.

Kaleem, A., & Ahmed, S. (2011). The Quran and Poverty Alleviation: A Theoretical Model for Zakah-Based Islamic Microfinance Institutions. *Nonprofit and Voluntary Sector Quarterly, 39*(3), 409–428. doi:10.1177/0899764009332466

Khalily, B., Mujeri, M., Hasan, M., & Muneer, F. (2017). *Diagnostics of Micro-enterprise (ME) Lending by MFIs in Bangladesh: Opportunities and Challenges.* http://inm.org.bd/wp-content/uploads/2017/07/Policy-Brief_ME_English.pdf

Khan, E., & Quaddusm, M. (2014). Examining the influence of business environment on socio-economic performance of informal microenterprises Content analysis and partial least square approach. *The International Journal of Sociology and Social Policy, 35*(3/4), 273–288. doi:10.1108/IJSSP-02-2014-0016

Modéer, U. (2018). *Unlocking Islamic Social Finance to Help Communities Address Vulnerability and Inequality.* https://www.undp.org/content/undp/en/home/news-centre/speeches/2018/Unlocking_Islamic_Social_Finance_to_Help_Communities_Address_Vulnerability_and_Inequality.html

Mohamed, N., Mastuki, N., Yusuf, S., & Zakaria, M. (2018). Management Control System in Asnaf Entrepreneurship Development Program by Lembaga Zakah Selangor [Sistem Kawalan Dalamanbagi Program Pembangunan Usahawan Asnaf di Lembaga Zakah Selangor]. *JurnalPengurusan, 53*, 13–22.

Mohamed, Z. O., Che Supian, M. N., & Norziani, D. (2012). The economic performance of the Amanah Ikhtiar Malaysia rural microcredit program: A case study in Kedah. *World Journal of Social Sciences, 2*(5), 286–302.

Monitor Institute. (2009). *Investing for Social and Environmental Impact, A Design for Catalyzing an Emerging Industry.* http://monitorinstitute.com/what-wethink/#

Mustapa, W. N., Mamun, A., & Ibrahim, M. (2018). Development Initiatives, Micro-Enterprise Performance and Sustainability. *International Journal of Financial Studies, 6*(3), 74. doi:10.3390/ijfs6030074Omar, M. Z., Noor, C. S. M., & Dahalan, N. (2012). The economic performance of the Amanah Ikhtiar Malaysia rural microcredit programme: A case study in Kedah. *WORLD (Oakland, Calif.), 2*(5).

Qardawi, Y. (2009). A comparative study of *Zakah*: Regulations and Philosophy in the light of qur'an and sunnah. *Fiqh Al Zakah, I*, 1–309.

Razimi, M., Romle, A., & Erdris, M. (2016). Zakah Management in Malaysia: A Review. *American-Eurasian Journal of Scientific Research, 11*(6), 453–457.

Rehman, A. (2019). *Islamic finance for social good.* https://www.undp.org/content/undp/en/home/blog/2019/IFN_ANNUAL_GUIDE_2019_Islamic_Social_Finance.html

Rehman, A., & Pickup, F. (2018). *Zakah for the SDGs.* https://www.undp.org/blog/zakah-sdgs

Rehman, A., & Pickup, F. (2018). *Zakah for the SDGs.* https://www.undp.org/content/undp/en/home/blog/2018/zakah-for-the-sdgs.html

Remenyi, J., & Quiñones, B. (2000). *Microfinance and poverty alleviation: Case studies from Asia and the Pacific.* Routledge.

Rozenberg, J., & Fay, M. (2019). *Beyond the Gap How Countries Can Afford the Infrastructure They Need while Protecting the Planet.* https://openknowledge.worldbank.org/handle/10986/31291

Sabahat, A., Imran, S., & Safina, M. (2015). Socio-Economic Empowerment of Women Through Micro Enterprises: A Case Study of Ajk. *European Scientific Journal, 11*(22).

Sabri, H., & Hasan, Z. (2006). *Zakah: Instrumen penyumbang pembentuk anusahawan. In Prosiding Seminar Kebangsaan Pengurusan Harta Dalam Islam. Jabatan Syariah.* Universiti Kebangsaan Malaysia.

Shiyuti, H., & Al-Habshi, S. (2018). An Overview of *Asnaf* Entrepreneurship Program by Lembaga Zakah Selangor. *Malaysia 6 th ASEAN Universities International Conference on Islamic Finance (AICIF).*

Terano, R., Mohamed, Z., & Jusri, J. (2015). Effectiveness of microcredit program and determinants of income among small business entrepreneurs in Malaysia. *Journal of Global Entrepreneurship Research, 5*(22), 22. doi:10.118640497-015-0038-3

Thai-Ha, L. (2021). *Microfinance and Social Development: A Selective Literature Review.* Background Note. https://www.adb.org/sites/default/files/institutional-document/691951/ado2021bn-microfinance-social-development.pdf

UN-DESA. (2020). *Supporting Micro-, Small and Medium-sized Enterprises (MSMEs) to Achieve the Sustainable Development Goals (SDGs) in Cambodia through Streamlining Business Registration Policies.* https://sdgs.un.org/publications/supporting-micro-small-and-medium-sized-enterprises-msmes-achieve-sustainable

UNHCR. (2019). *Refugees: The Most in Need of zakah Funds UNHCR Zakah Program:2019, Launch Report.* https://zakah.unhcr.org/wp-content/uploads/2019/04/UNHCR-Annual-Zakah-Report-2019-En.pdf

UNHCR. (2020). *Consequences of underfunding in 2020.* https://www.unhcr.org/underfunding-2020/wp-content/uploads/sites/107/2020/09/Underfunding-2020-Full-Report.pdf

UNHCR. (2020a). *UNHCR's 2020 Islamic Philanthropy Mid-Year Report Winter Edition.* https://zakah.unhcr.org/wp-content/uploads/2020/11/UNHCR-2020-Mid-Year-Islamic-Philanthropy-Report-English-Compressed.pdf

UNICEF. (2019). *UNICEF and the Islamic Development Bank launch first global Muslim philanthropy fund for children.* https://www.unicef.org/press-releases/unicef-and-islamic-development-bank-launch-first-global-muslim-philanthropy-fund

Weber, O. (2012). *Social Finance and Impact Investing.* Working Paper, University of Waterloo.

Yonis. B. (2012). *Islamic Microfinance System and Poverty Alleviation in Somaliland.* BBA research paper presented to the of Hargeisa.

Yudha, A. T., & Lathifah, N. (2018). Productive Zakah as a Fiscal Element for the Development and Empowerment of Micro Enterprises in East Java Province. *The International Conference of Zakah (ICONZ).* https://www.iconzbaznas.com/submission/index.php/proceedings/article/view/123/68

Yumna, A. (2019). Islamic charity based micro-finance: lessons from Indonesia. *The Third International Conference on Economics Education, Economics, Business and Management, Accounting and Entrepreneurship (PICEEBA 2019).* 10.2991/piceeba-19.2019.18

KEY TERMS AND DEFINITIONS

Baitul Maal Muamalat Indonesia (BMMI): A licensed *zakah* organization in Indonesia that collects Islamic charities (*zakah*, *sadaqa* and *waqf*) and disburses the funds for the society purposes.
BAZNAS: The National Board of *Zakah* that is responsible for managing *zakah* funds in Indonesia.
Islamic Social Finance: The Islamic perspective of managing investments that generate financial returns with positive social and environmental impact.
JAWHAR: The Department of Wakaf, Zakah, and Hajj in Malaysia.

Lembaga Zakah Selangor (LZS): The official authority that oversees managing *zakah* affairs in the state of Selangor in Malaysia.

Microenterprises: Small businesses that are often targeted by microcredit and microfinance programs.

Microfinance: Refers to providing micro-credit or low amounts of money to people who are typically excluded from traditional banking and financial services.

SDGs: The Sustainable Development Goals (SDGs) represent an urgent call for action by all countries, developed and developing, in a global partnership. SDGs provide a shared blueprint for peace and prosperity for people and the planet, now and in the future.

Zakah: A religious obligation to contribute a certain portion of one's wealth in support of the poor or needy.

Chapter 7

Investigating Entrepreneurial Success Factors of Businesses Owned by Nigerian Women in the UK

Victoria Temitope
University of Sunderland in London, UK

Seema Sharma
University of the West of Scotland, UK

ABSTRACT

The aim of this study is to investigate the entrepreneurial success factors of Nigerian women entrepreneurs based in the UK. An exploratory case study approach was used to gather the primary data from 15 small businesses run by Nigerian women entrepreneurs in the UK. The data collection was conducted through face-to-face semi-structured interviews, observations, and published sources. The data was thematically analysed using NVivo. The main findings indicated that Nigerian women entrepreneurs in the UK primarily depend on personal traits, self-funding, work experience, personal satisfaction, physical networking, and family support for business success. The most significant entrepreneurial success factor was the personal success factor. The study provided feasible recommendations for Nigerian women entrepreneurs based in the UK to put emphasis on environmental success factors and online networking, taking advantage of social media platforms for easy and quicker reach of more customers and business partners.

DOI: 10.4018/978-1-7998-7499-7.ch007

INTRODUCTION

This chapter aims to analyse the entrepreneurial success factors of Nigerian women entrepreneurs based in the UK and make recommendations to them on how they can increase the level of success in their business to help sustain their existence in the market. The knowledge in this chapter will be useful to both existing and new Nigerian women entrepreneurs.

BACKGROUND

Entrepreneurship is a means of economic development in both developing and developed countries, while entrepreneurs are the individuals who initiate and run businesses with the aim of making profits while taking financial risks (Georgios and Seemab 2017; Parker, 2018; Arsalan and Ali 2020). Entrepreneurship is the process of creating and putting new ideas together or vitalising discovered opportunities to generate profit, which most times involves taking financial risks (Temitope and Sharma, 2019). According to Amodu et al. (2015) there are new businesses stimulated by women in both developed and developing economies, and the entrepreneurial success is empirically associated with several factors such as government support, physical and environmental factors in addition to their entrepreneurial skills.

Focusing on the UK, this is the most entrepreneurial country in Europe, and it is well beyond economic giants like Germany and France when it comes to entrepreneurship. Also, UK does well in entrepreneurship because of the support that is accorded to small businesses in the country, by the government (Ellis and Borsworth, 2015; Burns, 2016; Arsalan and Ali 2020). Surprisingly, women who are entrepreneurs in the UK make up just one third of all entrepreneurs running businesses in the country which is due to major reasons like: funding, difficulty in work-life balance and a poor support system. Moreover, Nigerian women entrepreneurs running businesses in the UK are part of these women entrepreneurs (Ipek et al., 2017; Raghunandan, 2018; Arsalan and Ali 2020). According to Susan et al. (2016) and Donthu, (2020), the economic development of the UK would be partial without women being wholly involved in economic development through entrepreneurship. Also, the frame of reference for the Nigerian female entrepreneurs in Britain is tenuous, and this is because many of the research focuses on the generic Afro-Caribbean entrepreneurship that tends to generalize Black entrepreneurs as a single categorical group. However, knowing the differences in these categories can help give tailored support for business success (Ojo, 2013: Sanya 2018, Temitope, 2020). The research objectives are:

- To explore the determinants of entrepreneurial success for Nigerian women entrepreneurs in the UK.
- To analyse how the key entrepreneurial success determinants assisted their businesses.

ENTREPRENEURIAL SUCCESS FACTORS FOR NIGERIAN WOMEN ENTREPRENEURS

Jodyanne (2016), Michela et al., (2016) and Marina et al., (2019) found that female entrepreneurship represents an important economic driver, which recently is leading scholars to strongly advocate for the need to shift the female entrepreneurship research focus from only analysis of women business owners' characteristics, to the investigation of those specific factors such as government support, physical and environmental factors which are able to directly affect female business activities. These entrepreneurial success factors as shown in figure 1 are critically evaluated in the following section.

Personal Success Factors for Women Entrepreneurs

The personal factors necessary for business success include psychological factors such as personal traits and motivation that enable the women to overcome the barriers in pursuing entrepreneurial activity (Namrata and Anita, 2018). This section reviews the personal success factors for women entrepreneurs.

Personal Traits and Motivation

Women have an entrepreneurial spirit permeating their lives that is not immediate but within them from the moment they wake up and need to manage all their infinite tasks, which are part of their daily life (Michela et al., 2016). According to Ismail et al. (2016) and Ajuna et al. (2018), women entrepreneurs reflect a continuous commitment enhanced by their restlessness, dreams and desire to do more and better regardless of the hurdles. Additionally, as a virtuous cycle, each step taken by women entrepreneurs leads towards new challenges, but their commitment drives their energy and ability to execute and overcome the challenges. Another personal trait of entrepreneurial women, apart from commitment and passion, is the ability to take risks and overcome challenges. It has been identified by Bulanova et al. (2016), that entrepreneurial women are not afraid of work but understand the possibility of managing their time as a critical success factor. Women recognise that their workload may be higher than that of others, but they value the fact that they have flexibility and the ability to overcome the challenge.

Level of Education / Formal Training

The study conducted by Bullough et al. (2015), shows that women entrepreneurs have limited entrepreneurial training. Additionally, they sometimes lack resources to continue their education and get private education for entrepreneurial training. This also has been identified by Chinomona and Maziriri (2015), that the lack of experiences and skills among the women entrepreneurs is because there is limited support available for them. It is also argued that there are limited professional agencies which are not efficient in disseminating information to entrepreneurs regarding the training and assistance to thrive (Michela et al., 2016 and Marina et al., 2019). Also, research in this context has been undertaken by Idrus et al. (2014), who found that training of women entrepreneurs is essential for successful entrepreneurs, but women have limited awareness about the programmes and institutes that offer them training to start their own business. Notably, Gough and Langevang (2016) have pointed out that the reason women entrepreneurs are thriving in the less developed countries is because they have basic needs. Moreover, they are mostly social entrepreneurs who are working for social good and they also get support from society.

Work Experience

Most of the women who become entrepreneurs in developed countries are in the second phase of their work cycle where they have education and knowledge to set up their own business. This has been confirmed in the study conducted by Schaper (2016) who argued that women who have limited knowledge and are in an early phase of employment are less likely to pursue entrepreneurship in comparison to those with work experience of more than five years. Additionally, it has been claimed that the women who mostly engage in entrepreneurial activities have significant work experience and technical knowledge which enables them to start up their own business. This finding is also relevant in Avolio (2017) who found that such women choose entrepreneurship because they find their salary insufficient and have higher education to support their entrepreneurial idea.

Family Support

Social support that women obtain from loved ones in the form of both real help and small financial support has a stronger relationship with the fate of their companies than with men. In this perspective, Kabasakal et al. (2016) argued that women without support from family do worse than men, whereas women who are supported have been observed to be successful in their entrepreneurial journey. Dalborg et al. (2015) suggested that for women, it is crucial to enter associations and participate in meetings organised by enterprising women because they can get support for their entrepreneurial ideas. Additionally, they can contact women who manage to run their own business, build a network of contacts and, therefore, more willingly decide to start their own business (Dalborg et al., 2015). Having the business itself was perceived by women as a career option that led to a greater balance between roles at work and in the family; entrepreneurship could offer certain characteristics of work, such as autonomy and flexible hours, which, in a woman's perception, should lead to this equilibrium.

However, the research findings of Arregle et al. (2015) pointed to a significant increase in conflicts between work and family, precisely because of the freedom and flexibility found by women entrepreneurs. The authors defined the work-family conflict as the form of conflict in which the dominant pressures of work and family are mutually incompatible. Additionally, they found that there were increasing work-family conflicts between couples with different professions, especially if men found that their wives aspire to achieve professional success (Arregle et al., 2015). Nevertheless, it has also been argued by Chasserio et al. (2014) that women believe entrepreneurship to be an opportunity to reconcile work and family due to the flexibility of schedules they organise themselves.

Environmental Success Factors for Women Entrepreneurs

Access to Bank Loans and Start-Up Capital

It has been argued by Adom et al. (2016) and Tambunan (2016) that for an entrepreneurial activity, financing and capital is one of the most challenging factors that the entrepreneur must overcome. There are various possible ways that entrepreneurs can access funds for their businesses and that include bank debt, equity-based capital, crowdfunding and grants (Inman, 2016). Each type of funding has its own advantages and disadvantages. The debt from a bank enables the individual to have full control over the business whereas equity-based capital enables limited control. On the other hand, crowdfunding and grants can also be used as a source of funding, but they are difficult to access where crowdfunding requires information to be disclosed that exposes such information to competitors. Moreover, grants are very specific (Ahl and Nelson, 2015). The women entrepreneurs who have a vision and a plan to implement a business tend to access bank loans which they can repay after building their new venture.

Chinomona and Maziriri (2015) argued that women entrepreneurs in developed countries have their own funds or they tend to engage in partnerships for equity as well as borrowing from friends and family. On the other hand, women in developing countries and those in rural areas have limited access to funds and loans. Adom et al. (2016) argued that this is mainly due to their limited awareness and understanding of the formal financial sector that can lend money for their business. It has also been added by Heuer (2017) that women entrepreneurs also encounter issues with access to loans because of their limited knowledge and understanding about the informal nature of the business and neither have they determined their turnover and equity. Besides, they have limited access to funds because of inadequate documentation in terms of accounting and business records to determine their borrowing capacity (Michela et al., 2016; Marina et al., 2019; Temitope 2020). As a result, they fail to avail of loans and cannot implement their entrepreneurial ideas and ventures.

Access to Market and Customers

It is important for the women entrepreneurs to get access to customers and new markets; this is associated with the development of new product or services in a new region or country (Adom et al. 2016). This can be done through the implementation of market strategies in obtaining access to a new market. Meaning, getting access to a new market requires a business entrepreneur to conduct market research which involves business planning. Gaining access to a new market and customers enables women entrepreneurs to expand their business focus and increase their business capacity to increase sales and retain more customers (Warnecke, 2016). To ensure a smooth transition of business, management needs to develop strategies for promoting, advertising and other activities to attract a new segment of customers (Michela et al., 2016 and Marina et al., 2019). In relation to this, market research includes two different parts: target market research and competitive market research (Inman, 2016). This supports the entrepreneurs to identify the nature of customers and their needs to gain competition advantage.

Support for Women Entrepreneurs

Support From NGOs

There is a significant role played by NGOs to support women entrepreneurs because they create employment and benefit the economy as well as the business (Adom et al. 2016; Temitope and Sharma, 2019). NGOs support women with different financing schemes, guarantee programmes, exhibition forums, training and advisory plans (De Vita et al., 2014; Warnecke, 2016). For instance, the support offered by

NGOs in Nigeria is very low in comparison to other countries like Mexico that support women entrepreneurs to successfully find their way into the business sector. According to Haugh and Taneja et al. (2016), NGOs support women with training to be excellent administrators of resources due to being housewives and mothers of families. Additionally, there is a greater likelihood that the money that reaches women will be used for their children, which has a greater impact on the well-being of their family. Apart from that, Brau et al. (2015) and Sabouri et al., (2016) also argued that women entrepreneurs are supported by NGOs mainly in the form of loans, and the authorisation of the programmes is based on a vote of confidence from their clients, who mostly belong to the low-income population sector.

Access to Government Authorities

Many women become successful at finding appropriate funding opportunities and gaining access over capital markets. It has been identified that during the recent financial crisis, it became difficult for women entrepreneurs to get access to funding compared to men (Brau et al., 2015 and Sabouri et al., 2016). In this respect, the focus of government is on the development of women entrepreneurs through the development of different financing programmes to promote women in the field of business. Moreover, different federal programmes have provided grants to various agencies which allocate around 5% of overall funding to provide financing to women entrepreneurs.

Less/ No Bureaucratic Hurdles

The bureaucratic hurdles encountered by women entrepreneurs depend on their geographical location (Warnecke, 2016; pek et al., 2017). Developed countries, for example, where women entrepreneurs have knowledge about the policies and business, tend to face limited bureaucratic hurdles that help in their business success (Devine and Kiggundu, 2016). Conversely, women from the less developed countries tend to face more bureaucratic hurdles because they have limited knowledge on how to overcome bureaucratic hurdles and access to information. In this context, Sabouri et al. (2016) and (Haugh and Talwar, 2016) emphasized the economic factor whereby women in underdeveloped countries have limited economic freedom and limited accessibility to monetary resources to engage in entrepreneurial activities. Figure 1 shows the conceptual framework of the chapter.

Figure 1. Conceptual framework
Sources: Namrata and Anita (2018), Heuer (2017), Tambunan (2016), Garba (2017) Ajuna et al. (2018), Warnecke (2016)

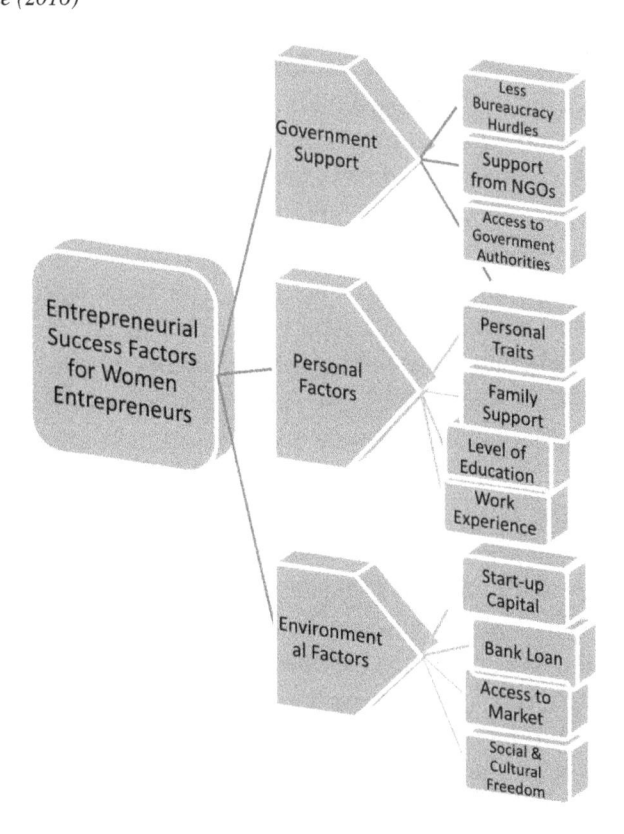

RESEARCH METHODOLOGY

This study used a qualitative research methodology and adopted a case study approach to be able to gather holistic data on the life experiences of Nigerian women entrepreneurs to understand their determinants of entrepreneurial success in the UK. In choosing the size of the sample for qualitative research using interviews, Holliday (2007) and Yin (2014) stated that the researcher needs to consider data saturation, and this is reached when there are no longer new themes or information from the research participants or with additional data collection. In their contribution to research sample size, Green (2009) and Robson (2016) found that after interviewing 20 people, most qualitative researchers collected little to nothing new from their transcripts.

Thus, the sample size of this study consisted of 15 businesses run by Nigerian women entrepreneurs in London with a minimum of 5 years entrepreneurial experience. The researcher formulated criteria for selecting these women entrepreneurs and the first three potential participants were found in the database of Lionesses of Africa, a website with an up-to-date list of the top African women entrepreneurs in the world. The population of this research was Nigerian women entrepreneurs based in the UK. This research used the non-probability sampling technique by using snowball sampling to select firms run by Nigerian women entrepreneurs in the UK. Snowball sampling helped the researcher to reach out to the study sample from the large population of women entrepreneurs in the UK, thereby creating access to a hard-to-reach population, to suit the data collection duration, and analysis process (Creswell, 2013; Wilson 2014). This study used semi-structured interviews, published documents and field texts such as lived experiences, stories, field notes, conversations, past family stories, autobiographies and artefacts, letters, and observations to understand the perceptions of the participants regarding entrepreneurial success factors so that the meanings of their lived experiences can be created as a case study (Yin, 2014; Creswell, 2017).

Thematic analysis of data was conducted using NVivo 12 for coding and nodes. Thematic analysis is a phase in the research study which involves the use of word interpretation of the data collected (Saldana, 2016).

For confidentiality, validity and credibility of data received, a pilot study was conducted; also, the researcher used member checking for the data collected which involve second author verification. A participant information sheet and consent form were also requested to be completed by participants for the purpose of achieving transparency. The interview schedule was subject to critiques by co-author and two Nigerian women entrepreneurs in London. For this study triangulation, existing research by scholars on women entrepreneurship were used for the secondary data. The findings from the pilot study were compared to this research's key findings from the interviews and published reports on the business websites of the participants, to give reliable and unbiased information (Wilson, 2014; Creswell, 2015). Another recommendation in triangulation is the use of the analyst method (Yin, 2014), which employs the use of several researchers to observe the discovered data and this was achieved by the researcher by attending relevant academic conferences to get feedback from scholars on the data collected (Bosma, 2013; Yin, 2014).

ANALYSIS OF RESULTS

Entrepreneurial Success Factors

Theme 1: Personal Success Factors

Personal success factor was the first major theme that emerged from the participants' responses. All the participants from selected firms mentioned what their different personal success factors are and expressed how these factors have assisted in their business success in the UK. Although participants from case studies (CS) 1, 10 and 13 stated that being interactive, passionate, empathetic, having the ability to influence, and pay attention to details only contribute to their business success by helping to keep their present clients, that is, making their customers loyal. But these personal success factors do not necessarily bring new clients like other entrepreneurial success factors do. Moreover, they said the mentioned personal traits is not their major entrepreneurial success factors. However, the remaining 12 firms believe that their entrepreneurial success is a result of their personal success factors. They informed that their business succeeds only because of their honesty, integrity, personal saving, personal satisfaction, hard work, creativity and commitment. They further explained how these personal success factors make them deliver quality services and products according to their customers' needs, even before deadlines. The following quotes of the women entrepreneurs support the above-mentioned points.

The first firm (CS 1) in their explanation stated that personal success factors do contribute to their entrepreneurial success.

Being Interactive and Passionate

"Being interactive and passionate (enthusiasm) help ease the business communication process with my customers which makes them feel more comfortable to buy from me." (CS1). An entrepreneur needs to be a good communicator to keep their customers and this is easy to develop when the entrepreneur is passionate about the business. This enthusiasm reflects in the communication with each customer and create strong communication relationship between the seller and the buyer. Among other factors, good communication is the first step to good business transactions that will determine if the customer will keep coming back.

Firms 10 and 13 also agreed that their personal traits are more important to increase sales.

Ability to Influence and Empathize

"Ability to influence and empathise help to convince customers and prioritise needs which in turn increase sales" (CS10). Influencers are likely to be good entrepreneurs, because they can make the customer buy more than they plan to purchase, and this also links back to being a good communicator. Another point mentioned by CS 10 was empathy; this trait helps to prioritise customer needs which in turn increase sales of their products and service. So, to achieve entrepreneurial success, you need to learn to prioritise and stock your business with what your customers' need, and not just what you prefer selling, then you can influence customers to buy more from you.

Ability to Pay Attention to Details

"My ability to pay attention to details help me to know and meet the needs of my customers." (CS7). Paying attention to details can be in form of giving attention to your speed of delivery, business environment, types of staff, packaging, product contents, and even your communication. Creating quality service and products that can make your clients return to you requires your ability to pay attention to every little part of the needs of your customers or clients. When keen attention is paid, to all these put together, it can increase the level of business success. Unlike the 3 previous firms that said their personal factor contributed to their entrepreneurial success, the remaining 12 firms believed they achieved entrepreneurial success solely because of their personal success factors. Meaning personal success factor is their only entrepreneurial success factor.

Hard Work, Creativity and Commitment

"Basically, I will say my personal traits which are being hardworking, creative and committed are the only reasons why this business has progressed to this level, because I work alone as I only have few volunteers no employees yet, this can be lonely and demanding sometimes because I bake, clean, and sometimes I do delivery depending on customers' request". Another thing I can say is I have come this far in business journey because of God's grace." (CS4).

To achieve entrepreneurial success, it is necessary for the entrepreneur to possess personal success factors in form of commitment, motivation, personal trait and being creative. These important personal traits can help keep your customers coming back for your products and service. Also, personal savings help reduce borrowing money for the sustenance of the business. The above responses can be clearly connected to the trait theory in entrepreneurship which explains that entrepreneurs are born, implying that entrepreneurs are usually mystified as individuals with personality traits (Ferreira et al., 2015; Ajuna et al., 2018). That is, women entrepreneurs should be interactive, pay attention to details, and have strong self-confidence, ready to take risk, have capacity of taking initiatives as well as creativity.

Integrity and Honesty

"I thank God for this business, my integrity and honesty are what bring me more customers," "my level of education and work experience really help my business progress, as the courses I offered in university is helping my marketing strategies, operations and accountability. Also, my work experience as administrator help my customer service skills like responding to calls and emails. So, the better this is, the more customer orders I receive also it helps to be able to handle computer. So, it is good to be educated as well. But when everything fails, your personality is the only thing you are left with to succeed." (CS5).

The above quote shows that in operating a successful business, what the participant needed the most was her honesty, integrity, formal education and work experience. These are good traits and factors every entrepreneur should have, but if she needs to pass this business on to someone without same work experience and personal traits, that means the business may not be successful. She needs to consider other entrepreneurial success factors such as environmental factors and external supports to increase the business success. This is because not all entrepreneurs have the privilege of formal education and individual have different traits. So, she needs to build networks and seek government or NGO support that any volunteer and successor can benefit from. Also, this will be added advantage to quickly increase the number of business clients.

For firms 4 and 5 (CS4 and CS5) that attribute part of their entrepreneurial success to their God, this evidently shows the connection between entrepreneurial orientations and theocentric orientation. This exhibits that they gauge their success in business as a matter of divine intercession other than a result of factor or strategic planning. However, when this religious belief is viewed from another perspective, a new aspect such as submissiveness towards the institutional failures experienced can be identified. Another element was also identified, such as hopelessness in sustaining a promising start up with a consequence for simulation of activities and entrepreneurial orientations. This can be related to using personal saving for running business, although personal success factors in form of commitment, motivation, personal trait and personal saving are essential for business success as good personal trait can help you keep your customers coming back for your products and service. Also, personal savings help reduce borrowing money for keeping up with business. But this should not be the only factor on which a business success is hinged.

Theme 2: Environmental Success Factors

The next entrepreneurial success factor that resulted from the data analysis was environmental success factors. These are factors mainly related with human capital, and social capital, which have common characteristic that has been observed to stimulate entrepreneurial success regardless of gender, personal traits and location. These factors comprise of partnership, online networking, physical networking, access to market, digital stores, mentorship and award winning. But responses from the participants indicated that firms 2, 3, 4, 5, 8, 9, 11, 12, 14, and 15 still have not taken full advantage of these environmental success factors as they believe it is their personal success factors that is most important for business success. This is true to some extent, but then personal success factors limit your business success to only your present customers becoming loyal to you and it makes you wait on word of mouth for business expansion, whereas the environmental success factors help you to reach new customers quicker and easier. Moreover, it can help get access to network of business partners that provide you with right information needed for your entrepreneurial success, even without you meeting them physically.

Networking, Partnership, and Access to Customers

"Online networking helped in securing contacts for this business. Networking and partnerships led to more exposure, giving my business a wider reach and more impact; take for example on partnership, a company called Moneywise used the game to promote financial education in schools for the last two consecutive years. You can use the link provided to confirm. Also, you do not really need to have much capital to start a business, but you sure need access to customer for a successful business." (CS1).

CS1 stated that online networking and partnership led to the exposure of their business and gave them wider reach and more impact on sales. Further, in her response, she explained that access to customers is very important for a business to be successful. When starting a business, it is more important to have ready access to customers before thinking about how to get financial support, because your customer size determines your business sales and profits. CS7 interviewees also quoted importance of networking and partnership which was similar to participants from CS1.

"You need to network to meet business partners. Networking helps build partnership. Honestly, I didn't really need much capital to start up my business, so I will say access to market/customers is more important in determination of my entrepreneurial success, because the more customers I get online, the more money I make to now expand my business." (CS7).

CS7 further explained how online networking and partnership have assisted their business to rise to this level of entrepreneurial success. "partnership does not necessarily mean partnering with individuals to start business but partnering with professional bodies, for instance, registering my business with awarding bodies to get accreditation for some of my professional business courses. This really helps in my business success, because when people see that you are an accredited centre, they come to you. If I need tutors or if they also need me, they ask for my service as a tutor at a cheaper rate, so also, I can ask for their help at a cheaper rate. My business has been surviving on networking; I will say most especially networking on social media because 99% of our customers are from online networking majorly contacts online." (CS7).

These responses show that online networking and partnership are significant contributors to entrepreneurial success. Some of the roles of partners indicated were cost sharing, offering administrative directions, improving on ideas, and developing enough capital. Partnering with colleagues would not only lower the expenses for service delivery but also offer a forum for discussing challenges, improvements and improvement techniques among peers. Also, online networks, customers and business partners are transferable to business successors unlike the personal traits of the entrepreneur which may be present only in the business owner.

Not all businesses indicated the benefits of networking and partnership. For example, interviewee from CS5 mentioned that most women entrepreneurs feared partnership for fear of sharing profits, uncertainty in losing control over their business, and fear of losing the power to decision making.

"I have never partnered with anyone because I am afraid of the downside of partnership, like sharing income, and I don't think there is government rule in place regarding partnership rights." (CS5).

This response was an accurate indicator of lack of trust in entrepreneurial partners and low confidence in government legislation enacted to guarantee sound partnership rights. On the negative side, failure to develop strong partnership put the business at the risk of collapsing. Although most companies, indeed, thrive without partnership, it is undeniable that securing stronger partners boost business finances, improves the customer base, and reduce business risks due to cost sharing. Most firms cited out that they depended solely on themselves and were not able to land a stable partnership. Although two of the firms agreed to the importance of partnership from the statement of CS 4 and CS 6 who when asked about partnership and networking stated the following.

"Both physical and online networking, I will say yes, but not partnership. I use friends, family and social media. So, no business partners for now." (CS6). Her statement indicated that she and most of her colleagues felt safer if they would partner with family members or close friends. The idea presented a dilemma as friends and family members may lack adequate capital, skills or interest to enter into a partnership. On the other hand, professional partners mostly have enough starting capital, management skills, and a common interest to venture into business but are untrusted. The dilemma that arises is whether to encourage women entrepreneurs to partner with family members and friends who may have little impact on the market or promote partnering with other interested persons who may not be trusted.

Winning Awards and Access to Customers

"Access to increasing clients/customers, online networking, winning awards, help in promoting and increasing visibility, also access to customers give us more service, we need more customers and partners to get started. So more of customers is needed to increase our service and thereby grow impact and income not really money." (CS6).

From the responses of participants of CS6 regarding how winning awards can be useful, it was indicated that it led to credibility and exposure of the business which created better visibility for business partners and investors. Another important information from the findings identified that a significant number of these women are staunch believers who regularly visited their worshipping centers, which were churches and mosques. When they hold meetings in these places, some of these women entrepreneurs use that medium to expand their social networks to enhance their entrepreneurship opportunities. It was also found that some entrepreneurs can even go further and join other socio-cultural associations in the surrounding communities to mobilize resources for their entrepreneurial success.

However, other female entrepreneurs from CS 10 did not prefer joining any social associations to gain ideas to grow their businesses. Instead, they preferred to stay away from such and expanded their businesses based on their experience, own purposes and individual research. They could even go to the extent of paying a specialist to do a specific adjustment in their business premises rather than spending time in those social clubs to listen to their fellow entrepreneurs. Those female entrepreneurs who depended on their fellow entrepreneurs' ideas and suggestions for the growth of their businesses confirmed that back in Nigeria, most female entrepreneurs depend on their social networks to grow their businesses. However, most of the women confirmed that the commencement of their businesses was a success due to the excellent support they received from their close social network contacts.

Theme 3: Support Mechanisms for Entrepreneurial Success

From responses on support mechanism for entrepreneurial success of the firms run by Nigerian women entrepreneurs in the UK: Firms CS 1, 10 and 13 stated that they had mixed support from the government and NGOs. However, they felt different on the issue of government support.

Government and NGO Support

Firm CS1 stated how NGOs have been supportive of her business by giving her free space.

"NGOs have really been helpful in my business success, for instance the space we are using as office base was given to us at a low rate by another social enterprise in the community. Although, NGO support is mostly in form of collaboration than financial, they help to amplify the spreading of important messages about the mission of our businesses to their network, which in turn help us reach more clients or new customers." (CS1).

Firm CS10 also stated that though no monetary support was received from government but she uses government facilities freely: "I receive government support in term of facilities, because I visit public libraries for research, but in term of grant/loan, I have never received grant from government for this business, but I know there are government grants for authors." (CS10).

One of the interviewees from CS13 also stated the following.

"Government support contribute to my business success, because my start-up capital was a government loan, so without that, I don't think I can get enough money to start. The country bureaucracy does support start-ups, with loads of information and finance. In general, UK rules and regulations encourage starting up a business." (CS13). All the three quotes suggested that support mechanisms are important factors to be considered for entrepreneurial success as these supports help in reducing the use of personal savings for setting up and running business. Moreover, government support in form of fund help these three women entrepreneurs (CS1, 10, 13) to establish their businesses on a large scale, not just setting up businesses to serve only their local community, but it allows expansion into mainstream market. Still on the support mechanisms, the response from one of the interviewees in CS1 indicated that the support received from NGOs do help avoid the wait on government for funding and approval of agreement for use of spaces as shop or office.

Inability to secure government support was an important sub-theme that emerged in the current study. Almost every firm presented the issue of financial support from the government. Though women entrepreneurs did not arm-twist the government into helping them directly, they indicated that the improvement of working conditions would boost their businesses.

Firm CS4 expounded that: "Although I have received a loan from the bank, but that was personal effort. Most of the country rules and regulation are difficult to abide by, for instance, I find it hard to employ workers because the country bureaucracy says you need to have pension port for each employee, of which as the business owner, I just started my pension port, so that means I cannot afford to have employee for now. Sometimes, they make rules that seem nice, but then, when you want to go that route, they come up with something new and difficult to apply to small business. Another one is the tax man, once you declare the amount you make in a year, they will start sending debt letter. One needs to be in the know and current about news to access some of the country's opportunities." (CS4)

The inability of this lady to forecast her business income may be as a result of not networking with other women entrepreneurs to get information on how to do a business income forecast, or she may need training on this issue of income forecast. Most Firms were quick to ascertain that they did not receive government support. Some of the issues surrounding their evidence-based arguments included age limits in the allocation of opportunities, government abandonment of businesses which are thought not to require any form of support. Although, some of the firms had mixed reactions about government support, the consensus was that government need to do more to support women entrepreneurs. Some of the issues where women entrepreneurs felt required improvement included the ending of gender discrimination, access to mass market, elimination of exploitative bureaucracies that hinder easy business start-up, and increment in financial support.

Family Support

On the question of support mechanism for Nigerian women entrepreneurs in the UK, eleven firms said that they depend on support from family and friends. Although, they lacked other business partnership, they explained that family members were always there to provide emotional and financial support.

"The only support receive is family support, because my family form part of my physical network. No NGO supports or government support." (CS4). "Being an author, most time I write, my husband takes care of our kids, also my in-laws have been supportive, they help take the kids for timeout because I cannot afford a nanny, and for instance I just completed a masters in creative writing, this require me being in library late nights and so I need family to help watch over the kids for my business to be successful." (CS6).

Some of these firms took government support in the form of public facilities they had access to for free; it can be in form of business advice and even legal support provided for businesses in the UK. Also, the cause of not been able to access government and may be NGO supports can be due to lack of access to information or networking with the right people. Nigerian women entrepreneurs need to consider not just physical networking but also online networking for quicker access to information that can help their business success.

SUMMARY OF FINDINGS

Nigerian women entrepreneurs who wants to penetrate the UK entrepreneurship sector successfully should have enough resources to run their businesses, and these resources include social capital, financial capital, cultural capital and human capital (Namrata and Anita 2018; Porter and Kramer 2018; Temitope and Sharma 2019). However, financial capital seems to be the biggest challenge among most female entrepreneurs. They, therefore, end up setting small and medium-sized enterprises (SMEs). This is the same case even for the highly educated and qualified females who are in entrepreneurship. This is one of the reasons it is so hard to find many Nigerian female entrepreneurs in the bulk production and distribution markets in the UK.

Figure 2. Entrepreneurial Success factors for Nigerian women entrepreneurs in the UK
Source: Authors (2020)

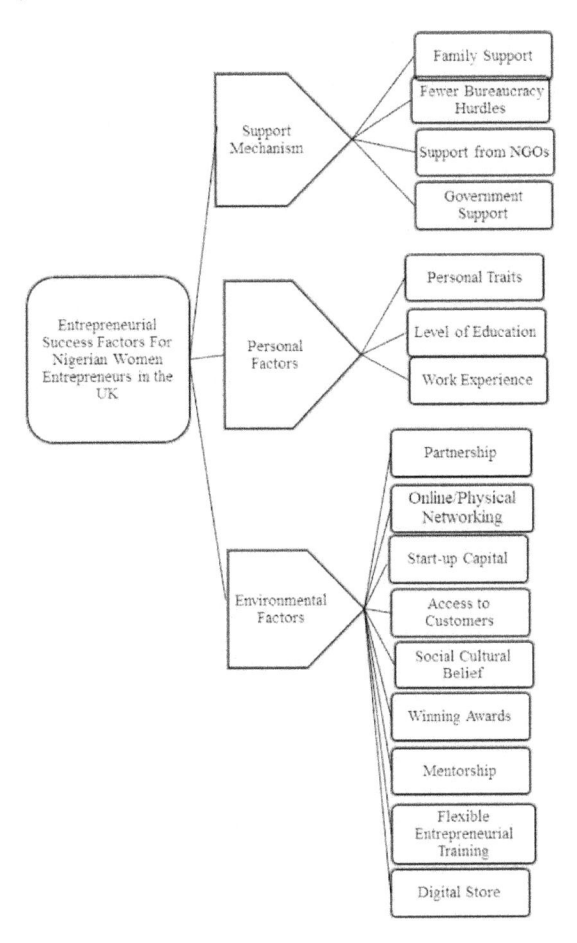

The key findings of this research were categorized under personal success factors, environmental success factors and entrepreneurial support mechanism with recommendations emphasizing that Nigerian women entrepreneurs in the UK should use more of their environmental success factors for business success. The recommendation made was based on the research findings that established that Nigerian women entrepreneurs based in the UK do not use in efficient their environmental success factors; online networking, partnership, digital stores, entrepreneurship webinar/trainings, winning awards and mentorship. The findings further show that creativity, perseverance, self-efficacy, optimism, and communicated vision were directly related to entrepreneurial success, while tenacity was seen to be related to developing resource skills. Analysis of the entrepreneurial success factors, therefore, show how personality traits, environmental success factors and support mechanism combined to ensure the success of some of the Nigerian women entrepreneurs in the UK. Figure 2 shows a summary of the entrepreneurial success factors of Nigerian women entrepreneurs in the UK.

SOLUTIONS AND RECOMMENDATIONS

To achieve the aim of this research, during the interview the research participants were lastly asked to mention their key entrepreneurial success factor and why it is their major determinant of business success. Thus, building on earlier work by Namrata and Anita (2018) on entrepreneurial success factors for women entrepreneurs, using the case study strategy through analysis of the data gathered from the in-depth face-to-face semi-structured interviews with the Nigerian women entrepreneurs in the UK, the author put forward a set of feasible recommendations on entrepreneurial success factors which can help both existing and new women entrepreneurs to start-up and scale-up their businesses respectively.

Prioritising Online Networking

Nigerian women entrepreneurs in the UK should make use of online networking for sharing vital business information, easier reach of new customers and best practice experience from fellow women in business, moral support and to know how to solve social cultural challenges.

Who is most appropriate for web-based systems administration and online networking? From one perspective, the proper response is self-evident: anyone with a personal computer (PC) and an internet connection can reach a number of interpersonal interaction sites on the web. The more subtle answer, notwithstanding, depends on you and your interactive time management inclinations. Do you appreciate investing time using your PC? Some personality types maintain a strategic distance from PC-based interactions as much as possible, while others appear to be attracted to their screens, tablets, and cell phones like moths to lights. There's no set-in stone approach to it, only degrees of inclination. The more you like browsing the web, communicating using email and generally working digitally, the surer you are to find online networking which is a good fit.

Consider ahead of time the amount of your time - as in how long every day or week - you're genuinely eager to dedicate to online networking, just as how you prefer to utilise that time (i.e. reviewing interactions in online forums, keeping your profiles refreshed, posting on your blog, perusing and responding to remarks, reading other individuals' blogs, tweeting, e.t.c). Which online networking platform is best for you? Pick the one(s) where your target audience hangs out the most. At the time of writing, Facebook, LinkedIn, Instagram, Google Plus, and Twitter are the places to go. Regardless of what number of sites you're active on, be clear with yourself - and with others - about your intentions and objectives. Remain positive, useful, and worth-oriented. Look at the distinction between interactions that move you and your online network individuals toward beneficial relationship building and those that waste time and vitality. Most importantly, similarly as with any business networking, your goal is to create social capital. Here's an inquiry you'll need to stand up to in the online world: will your investment of time, energy and care in the interest of other networkers be reciprocated in ways that you find significant? Only you can characterise what necessary means to you, and you alone can choose whether your venture is profitable. On the part of institutions, they can expand existing networking opportunities; the private and public sector organisations should come up with a new centralized networking programme and share the most effective practices on networking opportunities.

Prioritising Digital Store/Website

Nigerian women entrepreneurs in the UK should take their time to understand the effects and benefits of ecommerce to improve their retail store online. With proper guidance and help from professional ecommerce consultants, less internet savvy businesswomen will find it a smooth migration process from offline to online. Some of the benefits ecommerce would bring to women entrepreneurs include but are not limited to increased business reach, ease of product tracking, low operational costs, timing flexibility, and customer reviews. Besides, automated product delivery solutions are also available online through courier services.

Prioritising Winning Awards

Since the study results indicate that Nigerian women entrepreneurs in the UK still depend more on entrepreneurial success factors like their personal traits, self-funding, and family support for business success, women should now embrace modern ways of improving business sales, marketing and other entrepreneurial factors such as winning awards. When women concentrate on winning awards, they will improve their social customer relationship, business popularity and brand quality. The competition of enterprises in the same field will directly influence quality improvement, better customer relationships, and innovation.

Rewards are wide ranging from relating to business recognition, environmental conservation and innovation to quality of products. Considering these range of areas that giv various rewards and recognition, Nigerian women entrepreneurs in the UK should guide their enterprise into competing with similar ones for marketing, quality improvement, customer satisfaction, supporting environmentally friendly initiatives, innovativeness and all other areas that improve the client base and entrepreneurial success.

Prioritising Entrepreneurial Training

Entrepreneurial training improves business management, builds constructive competition, and ensures that more SMEs grow into bigger successful companies. In the long run, all resources used to empower women entrepreneurs will return to the government as a result of more taxes paid, more innovations that put the UK on entrepreneurial world maps, and an overall improvement of the standard of life, poverty reduction and an increment in the population's buying powers. On the other hand, women entrepreneurs should be given more support not only in the form of finance but also in terms of providing flexible motivational workshops and technical skills through training to increase their entrepreneurial confidence and get them ready for challenges and business competition. Flexible online training should also be developed so it can fit into their busy schedules. Webinars on business management would be very helpful to the women as well, and they do not have to leave their houses to attend these webinar sessions as they have an online base.

Mentorship

The absence of mentorship can be a very demotivating factor in business. Mentorship plays a longstanding role in the success of new entrepreneurs. Strong mentorship provides an invaluable opportunity to learn from someone who has experienced similar obstacles and hurdles along their professional path. An entrepreneur's most valuable person is a mentor and the partnerships that relationship between the entrepreneur and their mentor draws are very important.

On the off chance that you are to request that business visionaries describe their mentors, you'll hear words like counsellor, advocate, benefactor, devotee, advisor, mentor, inquisitor, pundit, team promoter, and mother straight through the letter set from A-Z. While much is made of the fundamental significance of finding a guide, the term can appear to cover a full range of human relationships and connections. Most, if not all, mentors are people who focus on the entrepreneur first and the business second. A mentor is someone who will take an active interest in the entrepreneur and look to develop their career. They will get their fingernails dirty, act as a guardian angel, and can say "Yes, I have seen that pattern before, so let us help you avoid it." They are primed and ready, at the right hand of the entrepreneur, for any situation that may develop, whether constructive or antagonistic.

The mentor does not necessarily have to be of Nigerian origin; it is even best to go for a mentor in the mainstream and from another nationality to get a vast business knowledge. To find a mentor and guide, you may need to put in the legwork starting from online. This implies going to volunteer occasions, investigating different college scenes, and checking with your nearby chamber of business. Lastly, peer-to-peer mentorship, too, provides perspective and encourages collaboration, amongst other things. Even when peers in specific niches or industries differ, the issues in technology, management, and human resources often overlap. I strongly recommend that the Nigerian women entrepreneurs find themselves a reliable entrepreneurial mentor as this will help improve their business quality and size even faster.

Prioritising Partnership

There are various ways these women entrepreneurs can collaborate. One of which is partnership; this can be in the form of someone helping you to handle your marketing or online presence while you are busy with the baking or cooking for clients. It can also be in the form of sharing a business platform whereby the woman selling clothes in bulk for ceremonies can introduce the woman cooking for events to help handle the catering for such ceremonies, and vice versa which gives both opportunities for ready business. Some of these women lack trust in entrepreneurial partners and have low confidence in government legislation enacted to guarantee sound partnership rights. On the negative side, failure to develop strong partnership puts the business at risk of collapsing. Although most companies indeed thrive without partnership, it is undeniable that securing stronger partners boosts business finances, improves the customer base, and reduces business risks due to cost sharing. Most firms cited that they depended solely on themselves and were not able to land a stable partnership. Having business partners is a great entrepreneurial success factor, because these business partners do have enough starting capital, management skills, and a common interest to venture into business. The dilemma that arises is whether to encourage women entrepreneurs to partner with family members and friends who may have little impact on the market or promote partnering with other interested persons who may not be trusted. To increase their entrepreneurial success, Nigerian women entrepreneurs in the UK need to start partnering or collaborating with people who have similar business ideas, or people they are in the same business sector with and whom they see as competitors.

FUTURE RESEARCH DIRECTIONS

This study contributes to the ongoing research on women entrepreneurship by illuminating the entrepreneurial success factors of Nigerian women entrepreneurs in the UK. Practically, this research provides feasible recommendations to current and future women entrepreneurs and business advisors, on how they can increase their level of entrepreneurial success.

Further studies can compare the results of this research to that of other western countries where Nigerian women own and run businesses. This comparison can reveal some important information that can provide workable solutions to nations involved. Also, further research can be on the measure of impact of environmental success factors on businesses. In addition, further research can investigate the current entrepreneurial challenges of women entrepreneurs in the UK and Africa.

CONCLUSION

The influence of personal and environmental factors on entrepreneurs' success can never be brushed aside, as business success is impacted more by a variety of environmental factors, from access to capital, access to technology, access to clients, mentorship, winning awards to partnership. Businesses will succeed or fail based on the entrepreneurs' ability to make maximum use of the available environmental factors. Besides, unanticipated changes in the environment can cause even the well-managed and smoothly proceeding businesses to lose momentum. So, for entrepreneurial success, it is important for Nigerian women entrepreneurs in the UK to use more environmental success factors.

From this study's findings, the researcher strongly recommends that the Nigerian women entrepreneurs in the UK place more emphasis on environmental factors for their entrepreneurial success as expounded above. While physical networking seems to be the best way to grow your network of solid relationships, the researcher would advise Nigerian women entrepreneurs in the UK not to ignore online networking; they need to take advantage of this to help them leverage social media platforms to easily reach more customers, business partners and possible investors right at the corner of their houses.

REFERENCES

Adom, K., & Asare-Yeboa, I. T. (2016). An evaluation of human capital theory and female entrepreneurship in sub-Sahara Africa: Some evidence from Ghana. *International Journal of Gender and Entrepreneurship*, *8*(4), 402–423. doi:10.1108/IJGE-12-2015-0048

Ahl, H., & Nelson, T. (2015). How policy positions women entrepreneurs: A comparative analysis of state discourse in Sweden and the United States. *Journal of Business Venturing*, *30*(2), 273–291. doi:10.1016/j.jbusvent.2014.08.002

Ajuna, A., Ntale, J., & Ngui, T. (2018). Impact of training on the performance of women entrepreneurs in Kenya: Case of Meru Town. *International Academic Journal of Innovation, Leadership and Entrepreneurship*, *2*(2), 93–112.

Amodu, Aondoseer, & Audu. (2015). Effects of gender and cultural beliefs on women entrepreneurs in Nigeria. *Journal of African Business*, *12*(2), 64–83.

Arregle, J. L., Batjargal, B., Hitt, M. A., Webb, J. W., Miller, T., & Tsui, A. S. (2015). Family ties in entrepreneurs' social networks and new venture growth. *Entrepreneurship Theory and Practice*, *39*(2), 313–344. doi:10.1111/etap.12044

Arsalan, S., & Ali, S. (2020). Key determinants of SMEs' export performance. *Journal of Business and Industrial Marketing*, *35*(4), 635–654.

Avolio, B. (2017). Why women enter into entrepreneurship? An emerging conceptual framework based on the Peruvian case. *Journal of Women's Entrepreneurship and Education*, (3-4), 43–63.

Bastian, B. L., Sidani, Y. M., & El Amine, Y. (2018). Women entrepreneurship in the Middle East and North Africa: A review of knowledge areas and research gaps. *Gender in Management*, *33*(1), 14–29. doi:10.1108/GM-07-2016-0141

Brau, J. C., Cardell, S. N., & Woodworth, W. P. (2015). Does microfinance fill the funding gap for microentrepreneurs? A conceptual analysis of entrepreneurship seeding in impoverished nations. *International Business Research*, *8*(5), 30. doi:10.5539/ibr.v8n5p30

Bulanova, O., Isaksen, E. J., & Kolvereid, L. (2016). Growth aspirations among women entrepreneurs in high growth firms. *Baltic Journal of Management, 11*(2), 187–206. doi:10.1108/BJM-11-2014-0204

Bullough, A., De Luque, M. S., Abdelzaher, D., & Heim, W. (2015). Developing women leaders through entrepreneurship education and training. *The Academy of Management Perspectives, 29*(2), 250–270. doi:10.5465/amp.2012.0169

Burns, P. (2016). *Entrepreneurship and small business*. Palgrave Macmillan Limited. Available at: https://uws-primo.hosted.exlibrisgroup.com/

Chasserio, S., Pailot, P., & Poroli, C. (2014). When entrepreneurial identity meets multiple social identities: Interplays and identity work of women entrepreneurs. *International Journal of Entrepreneurial Behaviour & Research, 20*(2), 128–154. doi:10.1108/IJEBR-11-2011-0157

Chinomona, E., & Maziriri, E. T. (2015). Women in action: Challenges facing women entrepreneurs in the Gauteng Province of South Africa. *The International Business & Economics Research Journal (Online), 14*(6), 835. doi:10.19030/iber.v14i6.9487

Creswell, J. W. (2013). *Research design: Qualitative, quantitative, and mixed methods approaches*. SAGE Publications Ltd.

Creswell, J. W. (2015). *A concise introduction to mixed methods research*. SAGE Publications Ltd.

Creswell, J. W., & Poth, C. N. (2017). *Qualitative inquiry and research design: Choosing among five approaches*. SAGE Publications Ltd.

Dalborg, C., von Friedrichs, Y., & Wincent, J. (2015). Risk perception matters: Why women's passion may not lead to a business start-up. *International Journal of Gender and Entrepreneurship, 7*(1), 87–104. doi:10.1108/IJGE-01-2013-0001

De-Vita, L., Mari, M., & Poggesi, S. (2014). Women entrepreneurs in and from developing countries: Evidences from the literature. *European Management Journal, 32*(3), 451–460. doi:10.1016/j.emj.2013.07.009

Devine, R. A., & Kiggundu, M. N. (2016). Entrepreneurship in Africa: Identifying the frontier of impactful research. *Africa Journal of Management, 2*(3), 349–380. doi:10.1080/23322373.2016.1206802

Donthu, N. (2020). Effects of Covid-19 on businesses and research. *Elsevier Public Health Journal, 117*, 284-289. Available at https://www.ncbi.nlm.nih.gov/pmc/articles/PMC7280091/ doi:10.1016/j.jbusres.2020.06.008

Ellis, V., & Bosworth, G. (2015). Supporting rural entrepreneurship in the UK microbrewery sector. *British Food Journal, 117*(11), 2724–2738. doi:10.1108/BFJ-12-2014-0412

Gough, K. V., & Langevang, T. (Eds.). (2016). *Young entrepreneurs in sub-Saharan Africa.* Routledge. doi:10.4324/9781315730257

Green, J., & Thorogood, N. (2010). Qualitative Methods for Health Research (3rd ed.). London: Observational Methods, SAGE Publications Ltd.

Haugh, H. M., & Talwar, A. (2016). Linking social entrepreneurship and social change: The mediating role of empowerment. *Journal of Business Ethics, 133*(4), 643–658. doi:10.100710551-014-2449-4

Heuer, A. (2017). Women-to-women entrepreneurial energy networks: A pathway to green energy uptake at the base of pyramid. *Sustainable Energy Technologies and Assessments, 22,* 116–123. doi:10.1016/j.seta.2017.02.020

Holliday, A. (2007). *Doing and Writing Qualitative Research.* SAGE Publication Ltd. doi:10.4135/9781446287958

Idrus, S., Pauzi, N. M., & Munir, Z. A. (2014). The effectiveness of training model for women entrepreneurship program. *Procedia: Social and Behavioral Sciences, 129,* 82–89. doi:10.1016/j.sbspro.2014.03.651

Inman, K. (2016). *Women's resources in business start-up: A study of black and white women entrepreneurs.* Routledge. Available at: https://uws-primo.hosted.exlibrisgroup.com/

Ismail, I., Husin, N., Rahim, N. A., Kamal, M. H. M., & Mat, R. C. (2016). Entrepreneurial success among single mothers: The role of motivation and passion. *Procedia Economics and Finance, 37,* 121–128. doi:10.1016/S2212-5671(16)30102-2

Kabasakal, H., Karakaş, F., Maden, C., & Aycan, Z. (2016). 15 Women in management in Turkey. Women in Management Worldwide: Signs of Progress, 2000(2014), 226.

Mari, M., Poggesi, S., & De Vita, L. (2016). Family embeddedness and business performance: Evidences from women-owned firms. *Management Decision, 54*(2), 476–500. doi:10.1108/MD-07-2014-0453

Marina, S., Tatiana, I., & Anna, T. (2019). Motivation of female entrepreneurs: A cross-national study. *Journal of Small Business and Enterprise Development, 26*(5), 684–705. doi:10.1108/JSBED-10-2018-0306

Namrata, G., & Anita, M. (2018). Investigating entrepreneurial success factors of women owned SMEs in UAE. *Management Decision, 56*(1), 219–232. doi:10.1108/MD-04-2017-0411

Ojo, S. (2013). *Diaspora entrepreneurship: A study of Nigerian entrepreneurs in London* (PhD thesis). University of East London, UK.

Ojo, S. (2018). Identity, Ethnic Embeddedness, and African Cuisine Break-Out in Britain. *Journal of Foodservice Business Research, 21*(1), 33–54. doi:10.1080/15378020.2016.1263058

Outsios, G., & Farooqi, S. A. (2017). Gender in sustainable entrepreneurship: Evidence from the UK. *Gender in Management, 32*(3), 183–202. doi:10.1108/GM-12-2015-0111

Parker, S. C. (2018). *The economics of entrepreneurship*. Cambridge University Press. doi:10.1017/9781316756706

Porter, M. E., & Kramer, M. R. (2018). Creating shared value. In *Managing Sustainable Business* (pp. 327–350). Springer.

Raghunandan, V. (2018). Changing Equations: Empowerment, Entrepreneurship and the Welfare of Women. *Journal of International Women's Studies, 19*(3), 187–198.

Ramadani, V. (2015). The woman entrepreneur in Albania: An exploratory study on motivation, problems and success factors. *Journal of Balkan & Near Eastern Studies, 17*(2), 204–221. doi:10.1080/19448953.2014.997488

Robson, C., & McCartan, K. (2016). *Real world research*. John Wiley & Sons.

Sabouri, M. S., Saberiyan, M., & Arayesh, M. B. (2016). The Role of Socio-economic Factors of Micro-credit Funds in Improving Rural Women Entrepreneurship Development. *Journal of Sustainable Development, 9*(5), 187. doi:10.5539/jsd.v9n5p187

Saldana, J. (2016). *The Coding Manual for Qualitative Researchers*. SAGE Publication Ltd.

Schaper, M. (Ed.). (2016). *Making ecopreneurs: developing sustainable entrepreneurship*. CRC Press. doi:10.4324/9781315593302

Susan & Ozkazanc-Pan. (2016). A Gender integrative conceptualization of entrepreneurship. *New England Journal of Entrepreneurship, 18*(1), 27–40.

Tambunan, T. T. (2015). Development of Women Entrepreneurs in Indonesia: Are they being Pushed or Pulled? *Journal of Socio-Economics, 2*(3), 131–149.

Taneja, S., Pryor, M. G., & Hayek, M. (2016). Leaping innovation barriers to small business longevity. *The Journal of Business Strategy, 37*(3), 44–51. doi:10.1108/JBS-12-2014-0145

Temitope, A., & Sharma, S. (2019). Entrepreneurial Challenges faced by Nigerian Women entrepreneur in UK. *International Journal of Entrepreneurship Management Innovation and Development, 3*(2), 57–69.

Tuzun, I. K., & Takay, B. A. (2017). Patterns of female entrepreneurial activities in Turkey. *Gender in Management, 32*(3), 166–182. doi:10.1108/GM-05-2016-0102

Venkatesh, V., Shaw, J. D., Sykes, T. A., Wamba, S. F., & Macharia, M. (2017). Networks, Technology, and Entrepreneurship: A Field Quasi-experiment among Women in Rural India. *Academy of Management Journal, 60*(5), 1709–1740. doi:10.5465/amj.2015.0849

Warnecke, T. (2016). Informal sector entrepreneurship for women in China and India: Building networks, gaining recognition, and obtaining support. *Journal of Small Business and Entrepreneurship, 28*(6), 479–491. doi:10.1080/08276331.2016.1202092

We-Fi Secretariat. (2020b). *Women entrepreneurs amidst COVID-19 crisis: balancing family and work. Women Entrepreneurs Finance Initiative.* Women Entrepreneurs Finance Initiative. Available at: https://we-fi.org/women-entrepreneurs-amidst-covid-19-crisis/

Wilson, J. (2014). *Essentials of Business Research* (2nd ed.). SAGE Publication Ltd.

World Bank. (2020). *Supporting Women Throughout the Coronavirus (Covid-19) Emergency Response and Economic Recovery.* Available at: https://openknowledge.worldbank.org/bitstream/handle/10986/33612/Supporting-Women-Throughout-the-CoronavirusCovid-19-Emergency-Response-and-Economic-Recovery.pdf?sequence=5&isAllowed=y

Yin, R. K. (2014). *Case Study Research: Design and Methods* (5th ed.). SAGE Publication Ltd.

Chapter 8
Analysis of the Performance of Microfinance Institutions in Sub-Saharan Africa:
Observations and Perspectives

Lawrence Jide Jones-Esan
https://orcid.org/0000-0002-9493-006X
University of Sunderland in London, UK

ABSTRACT

This chapter examines the performance of microfinance institutions in Sub-Saharan Africa through observations from different perspectives. It examined the effects of microfinance institutions in Sub-Saharan Africa. Relevant literature on the sustainability and outreach of microfinance institutions are also analysed in this chapter. Sub-Saharan Africa's future achievement of necessary economic growth is very likely to depend partly on its ability to develop its economic and financial sectors to be more inclusive of small and medium enterprises in a more comprehensive way. Currently, microfinance directly promotes the development of the intermediate financial sector in Africa, which is positively correlated with economic growth. Despite the worsening of the current industrial crisis, microfinance is seen as an essential developmental tool and continues to grow in Sub-Saharan Africa.

INTRODUCTION

Microfinance institutions are seen as a bridge between the financial and banking sectors, especially in post-conflict African countries. Some Sub-Saharan countries are

DOI: 10.4018/978-1-7998-7499-7.ch008

developing MFIs for traditional bank loans due to their positive impact on economic growth. Compared with research on conventional banks, research on improving the growth rate of microfinance institutions has made significant progress.

The importance of microfinance and of MFIs is that microfinance is becoming recognised as one of the most effective tools for reducing poverty in developing economies. Matin et al. (2002) highlighted that MFIs, often major foreign institutions, are present in Sub-Saharan African countries, providing small direct personal loans to customers like villagers, small entrepreneurs, poor women, and low-income families. MFIs may seem like traditional banks. However, MFIs operate differently from banks, particularly when they are registered as mutual funds, non-profits, or cooperatives. These institutions carry out a similar business type and have lower capital requirements for expanding small businesses. Many MFIs are very popular, operate well, and have an excellent record of success, and many are operational and self-sufficient.

The role of microfinance in economic development has been to bring about financial inclusion in the economy to millions of rural families and women of economically marginalised groups. Ledgerwood and White (2006) stated that the purposes of microfinance are to improve the lives of the poor (and those close to the poverty line), to improve healthcare, to improve housing, and to encourage the creation of small and medium enterprises, which should be undertaken in Sub-Saharan Africa to promote economic development and raise funds for marginalised groups. According to Felsenthal (2010), approximately two million people around the world do not have access to financial services. The World Bank Group, with 189 member countries, is committed to combatting poverty in all its dimensions, reducing poverty, and building shared prosperity in developing economies like those in Sub-Saharan Africa. Another purpose of MFIs is to provide necessary financial services to poor and low-income families, entrepreneurs, and early-stage businesses who cannot otherwise access these services. MFIs also make small loans to people who cannot otherwise get credit. This chapter therefore aims to analyse the outreach performance of microfinance institutions (MFIs) in their provision of significant services for the poor using innovative lending techniques within controlled environments.

BACKGROUND

Microfinance refers to mid-term, emergency, and individual loan products designed to meet the low-income group's very diverse personal needs, such as fixed loans and group guarantees (Saba, 2021). MFIs are, as their name suggests, bankers and financial institutions that provide microfinance services to the poor. Microfinance was founded in 1970 by the Bangladeshi economist Muhammad Yunus, who is often referred to as the 'poor banker'. Yunus established the Grameen Bank in Bangladesh in 1976 to provide 'microloans' (Engler, 2009). At the time, microfinance was about expanding loan services to small business owners. Beforehand, banks generally only made loans to middle-class, high-net-worth clients. Yunus's concept of microfinance quickly spread in the microcredit sector in Bangladesh. It became very popular, leading to the establishment of similar microfinance organisations around the world, and it eventually became what is today's microfinance (Yunus, 2008). Yunus won the 2006 Nobel Peace Prize for his efforts. Indeed, while jointly granting Yunus and his bank the prize, the Nobel Committee also paid tribute to Yunus and his bank for their 'bottom-up efforts to create socio-economic development' – fast. In other words, the committee saluted Yunus's philosophy of creating financial opportunities for people in need.

According to Neumann (2012), microfinance enhances the capabilities of the poor by providing funds to entrepreneurs and small businesses who cannot otherwise obtain traditional business financing due to their limited financial resources, financial status, or credit history. It refers to the credit practice of doing so. Small traditional or professional credit provided by banks and cooperatives is an alternative to other informal sources of credit, such as loans provided by community members or small business owners.

Olaosebikan and Adams (2014) found that small loans can be classified in a variety of ways, including loan applications with business subsidies provided. For example, applicants for small loans can be groups or entrepreneurs. Providing credit to a group is called group financing. In this case, each group member can provide collateral or a group pledge to guarantee the loan. Then, each lender only provides a loan to one customer who is responsible for repaying the loan. A small loan can also be classified as such according to the activities carried out by MFIs in order to obtain benefits like savings to help families build resources to finance school fees, get better homes, and attain their life goals. For example, microcredit obtained from specialised banks can be called agricultural credit or utility credit in Sub-Saharan Africa.

Ssewamala et al. (2010) explained that microloans are small loans, education loans, and other resources provided to poor entrepreneurs to ensure the success and fundraising of small businesses. Unlike people who get financial support from the government and charitable organisations to provide funds to poor communities as needed, small business owners provide microloans on the premise that they will repay the principal and interest of the loan from the financial institution. Receiving a small loan in a certain period can be as low as USD 100, and the interest rates can be as high as more than 100%. An applicant for a retail loan must meet the educational and planning eligibility criteria before considering the loan application. This is a clear advantage, because it sends a clear signal to the financial institution to which the applicant is applying that they are taking it seriously. In addition, a person's business education will benefit their company. Every small business development organisation has loan and credit requirements. Usually, a loan requires some type of collateral, and so does the financial stability of the applicant.

The MFI was a pioneer, delivering loans and contribution savings and additional financial services in some of the most distant markets in the world. MFIs empower people to start their own businesses, create employment opportunities, and improve their quality of life. The many types of MFI services include group loans, individual business loans, agricultural loans, insurance, money transfers, energy accounts, and savings accounts. Hermes and Lensink (2007) explained the methods of the microfinance system and how it leads to the alleviation of poverty. They agreed that the financial goal of an MFI is to serve as many poor people as possible, but the methods of doing so vary. The main question is whether the creation of interest rates is reasonable, and it seems appropriate to quote Hermes and Lensink (2007, p. 7): 'economic sustainability as a prerequisite for institutional sustainability'. Hollis and Sweetman (1998) highlighted those financial aspects, such as interest rates, that are prerequisites for the sustainable development of an MFI. The financial sustainability of MFIs is a necessary condition for institutional sustainability (Hollis and Sweetman, 1998).

Without money, a company cannot continue its activities. Institutional sustainability refers to the ability of an organisation to survive, create sustainable communities, and become a viable financial institution – for MFIs, this means providing financial support and basic facilities for the poor (mainly women). As a viable and effective income-generating company, mobilising resources to provide services, the MFI is a necessity. It is crucial to learn and evaluate how poverty can be eradicated faster. There must be a possibility of self-reliance and employment prospects for the needy. Microfinance funding to support low income people in rural areas to acquire necessary skills will help them make use of the financial resources available to them. In other words, such support can contribute to employment and income generation in Sub-Saharan Africa.

Alshebami and Khandare (2015) explained that MFIs have improved in recent years. Traditionally, the importance of microfinance has always been to play a key role in alleviating poverty. According to Dichter (1996), for many years, microfinance has had these key social objectives, so traditional MFIs only comprise non-governmental organisations (NGOs), professional MFIs, and public-sector banking institutions.

The primary role of microfinance in economic development is to help communities that barely have access to financial services to be helped out of poverty. Sustainability, which refers to the capability of an MFI to merge the costs of interest and other income paid by its customers, is a keystone of sound microfinance. MFIs are often non-profit organisations or government agencies dedicated to helping the poor. Profit has never been the end goal of MFIs.

This situation has changed recently. Dichter (1996) pointed out that some non-profit MFIs are transforming into for-profit organisations in order to gain more strength and sustainable development in the marketplace. They currently participate in the microfinancial market through consumer finance companies.

Most MFIs still consider poverty alleviation their primary goal, for consumers and small business owners, but selling additional products to more clients may be the primary motivation for some new market entrants. Today's MFIs are a combination of government banks and non-profit NGOs. Large MFIs strive to meet the financial needs of millions of consumers living in or near poverty in Sub-Saharan Africa.

PERFORMANCE OF MFIS IN SUB-SAHARAN AFRICA

The Role of Microfinance

The role of microfinance in economic development has been to bring about financial inclusion in the economy to millions of rural families and women of economically marginalised groups. Ledgerwood and White (2006) stated that the purposes of microfinance are to improve the lives of the poor (and those close to the poverty line), to improve healthcare, to improve housing, and to encourage the creation of small and medium enterprises, which should be undertaken in Sub-Saharan Africa to promote economic development and raise funds for marginalised groups. According to Felsenthal (2010), approximately two million people around the world do not have access to financial services. The World Bank Group, with 189 member countries, is committed to combatting poverty in all its dimensions, reducing poverty, and building shared prosperity in developing economies like those in Sub-Saharan Africa. Another purpose of MFIs is to provide necessary financial services to poor and low-income families, entrepreneurs, and early-stage businesses who cannot otherwise access these services. MFIs also make small loans to people who cannot otherwise get credit.

Similarly, the importance of microfinance and of MFIs is that microfinance is becoming recognised as one of the most effective tools for reducing poverty in developing economies. Matin et al. (2002) highlighted that MFIs, often major foreign institutions, are present in Sub-Saharan African countries, providing small direct personal loans to customers like villagers, small entrepreneurs, poor women, and low-income families. MFIs may seem like traditional banks. However, MFIs operate differently from banks, particularly when they are registered as mutual funds, non-profits, or cooperatives. These institutions carry out a similar business type and have lower capital requirements for expanding small businesses. Many MFIs are very popular, operate well, and have an excellent record of success, and many are operational and self-sufficient.

Many researchers believe that microfinance is a tool for reducing poverty (Musanganya et al., 2017). Furthermore, MFIs allow for reconciliation between lenders and financial institutions, especially in post-conflict African countries. Musanganya et al. (2017) explained the impact of traditional bank financing by MFIs on economic development in some Sub-Saharan African countries. This development, therefore, confirms that a huge number of financial institutions provide micro financial services and that markets have developed in such a way that individuals and companies are able to diversify their savings and new businesses can raise capital beyond bank loans. However, although bank loans increase investment, microfinance does not generally seem to do so.

In contrast, other researchers have clearly emphasised that microfinance can help reduce poverty and provide better financing channels for global start-ups, like Canva and Giphy. These results show that, although microfinance is mainly present in developing countries (without physical capitalisation), MFIs can still increase total factor productivity, while banks provide funding for bad investments. Here, we emphasise the impact of MFIs on the economic growth of developing countries and show how an integrated microfinance system in rural areas has improved the lives of the poor in Sub-Saharan Africa.

Adams and Tewari (2020) showed that, with the emergence of MFIs, there is a strong interest in mobilising people's deposits, and the supervision of this sector is becoming an important issue. The study used 551 observations from 71 MFIs in 10 countries over 10 years in order to understand the impact of MFI supervision on the sustainability and performance of MFIs disclosed by selected countries in Sub-Saharan Africa. The researchers used a dynamic method for estimating the generalised method of moments – a statistical method that combines observed economic data – and they found empirical evidence that regulation has a positive and significant impact on the sustainability of MFIs and on how far they can expand their services. In terms of scale, the impact on sustainability needs to incorporate all three dimensions in order for us to better understand the performance of a process, product, or system on ecological, financial, and societal factors. The study recommended that the managers and boards of directors of unregulated MFIs should take action to monitor the relevant policies and regulations by using an appropriate budget to meet the minimum capital requirements for regulatory costs and thereby strengthen cooperation with regulatory agencies. In addition, the supervisory authority (the central bank) should strengthen supervision to ensure that MFIs fully comply with supervisory guidelines and protect depositors and the entire financial system.

Ibrahim and Abdisamad Mohamed (2020) explained that an MFI is a type of financial institution that provides financial services to the poor, the unemployed, and those who cannot afford traditional banking financial services. Most MFIs strive to maintain a balance of profitability when dealing with self-sufficiency and a large number of poor people. The purpose of the research was to investigate the internal and external determinants of the services and performance of MFIs in Sub-Saharan Africa. This quantitative research was conducted using secondary data collected from mixed markets and The World Bank. In addition, it determined which MFI collects what data from the 43 MFIs who participated in the sample – based on five phases of data migration between 2013 and 2017. The researchers used EViews software to quantitatively analyse the panel data. They found that the size of an MFI is the main determinant of its social and financial performance. However, GDP growth was not found to be an important factor in an MFI's wellbeing and financial performance. The research recognised the factors that contributed to the success of MFIs and conveys important information to MFI stakeholders.

The Aims of Microfinance Institutions in Sub-Saharan Africa

According to Singh and Yadav (2012), microfinance is asymmetric, and its purpose is to assist people with low and unpredictable income. Traditional banking primarily aims to provide financial facilities by borrowing and lending money. The banks take customer deposits in return for paying customers an annual interest payment. The bank then uses most of these deposits to lend to other customers for a variety of loans. On the other hand, microcredit helps disadvantaged families and entrepreneurs access affordable financial services, provides funds for income-generating activities, builds wealth through investments, helps them meet their household needs, and protects them from the unexpected risks associated with daily life, including disease. It is designed to provide crucial support for families in cases of death, theft, and natural disasters.

According to Van Rooyen et al. (2012), microfinance primarily aims to help families living below or just above the poverty line. Most microfinance loans go to female farmers and traders who carry out micro-projects. This idea has its roots in Sub-Saharan Africa. Microfinance is a financial service that provides low returns or unemployment returns through loans or other small business loans for needy people.

The Benefits of Microfinance in Sub-Saharan Africa

Microfinance activities can bring a variety of benefits to people in Sub-Saharan Africa. Microfinance projects can effectively address the income needs of the impoverished, fund shortfalls, provide basic public services, and improve people's quality of life.

Consequently, the benefits of microfinance can have a direct or indirect effect on ineligible businesses. Pronyk et al. (2007) found that microfinance, on a personal level, can effectively solve the problem of non-material poverty. Here, there are social and psychological effects of poverty, which prevent people from reaching their full potential. Over the past three decades, the economic performance of Sub-Saharan Africa and that of Central Africa have been closely related.

The rates of return on both resources and employment, as well as the overall efficiency of the Sub-Saharan African economies, stay low. This is due to various distortions and institutional deficiencies. Following Abdulai and Tewari (2017), statistical data can be used to evaluate the savings and production decline effects of the three methods, using methods like geographical analysis, economic analysis, and sustainability analysis. In the modern economic environment of continuing global financial and economic change, microfinance is at the heart of Africa's efforts at performing inclusive socioeconomic development. Microfinance could offer significant opportunities for Sub-Saharan African countries to fully unleash the private sector's potential and help to provide long-lasting economic growth and to combat other related challenges, such as poverty, income imbalance, large levels of unemployment (especially among the youth), and the achievement of the UN Millennium Development Goals.

According to Suma (2007), economic growth depends on a significant level of capital accumulation. Sub-Saharan Africa is characterised by its heavy dependence on external savings to fill the investment savings gap, which represents an average of 25% of its GDP (Asongu et al., 2019). Subject to restrictions or binding loan agreements faced by Sub-Saharan African countries in the international capital market, as well as external equilibrium conditions imposed by external donors, is hampering the prospects and growth sustainability. Agénor (2000) argued that the one strategy that can ease the reduction of Sub-Saharan Africa's dependency on aid is implementing clear policies and establishing institutions that promote savings. In Sub-Saharan Africa, the total savings are very small, and, to make matters worse, some of them are converted into financial savings. MFIs are in a bigger position than the banks to assemble savings from the poor. The regular financial sector has a comparative advantage in preparing a much higher volume of savings from the economy, including the MFIs (Diaw, 2018), showing that the official financial sector has difficulties in mobilising funds and providing financial services, especially for the poor. MFIs can play an important role in meeting the financial needs of low-income households and small and medium enterprises. In addition, microfinance can also help reduce poverty by providing well-funded savings plans. On the supply side, microfinance is the best way to eliminate poverty, relax investment restrictions, open the door to new investments, and use good money to meet the urgent needs of the poor over time. According to Oluwaseyi (2016), on the demand side, empirical evidence shows that a large proportion of the disadvantaged groups are investors, and MFIs safely manage their investments and help them earn interest from their investments. Microfinance helps low-income households to become stable in their income flow and save for potential needs. It allows poor people to prepare for their prospects and send more of their children to school for longer. Technical, political, and social factors affect an MFI's performance, so there is an increasing need to combine the advantages of traditional and modern microfinance methods.

Ndambiri et al. (2012) found that, in Sub-Saharan Africa, microfinance has hundreds of advantages, but one of the most important advantages is its role in economic development, which may lead to future investment projects. Microfinance aims to break the cycle of poverty by providing more funds to the poor and those in need. When people's basic needs are met, they can invest in better housing, healthcare, and, ultimately, in small businesses, thereby averting the vicious cycle of poverty. In Nigeria, microfinance is almost risk-free and sustainable. A small amount of USD 100 is enough to free entrepreneurs in Sub-Saharan Africa from the cycle of intergenerational scarcity. Most international lenders believe that a USD 100 loan may be enough to start a small business in a developing country. Technological innovation and invention diversification can add further vitality in microfinance and improve its growth and impact on the alleviation of poverty. Microfinance can create employment opportunities, enabling young entrepreneurs in poor communities in developing countries to create new employment prospects for others. Sponsors can be trained how to take returns and save money for a better tomorrow. There is evidence that, if people's basic needs are met, they will naturally tend to save excess income for the future. Even if the income level of some branches remains very low, microfinance can also provide significant financial benefits. The huge benefits to be gained from participating in microfinance programmes include better nutrition, higher levels of spending, and, ultimately, the development of the financial system – even in small, marginalised communities.

Microfinance can also lead to better loan repayments. According to Adams (2009), it is women who mainly benefit from microfinance, as many MFIs target female clients. Microfinance also enables women and decreases their marginalisation. Microfinance can enhance the living conditions by creating an additional income source related to supply food and send the children to school, among the basic requirements. Most families receiving microfinance services are unlikely to let their children drop out of school for financial reasons.

Yahie (2000) found that microfinance may only involve small-scale loans and financial services, but it has had a global impact in the past 50 years. For example, for small businesses that need a little extra money or credit to get new opportunities, microcredit can be just a label. For microfinance and the banking industry to find new opportunities, microfinance provides a world of opportunities. One microloan or financial service at a time can change the story of an entire community.

Financial Sustainability and Portfolio at Risk

According to Chikalipah's (2017a) analysis of a 2014 survey, only 60% of MFIs are financially sustainable. The data also shows that, although most of these MFIs are supervised by financial authorities, they are all stable. To achieve financial sustainability in Sub-Saharan Africa, Zikaripa (2005) suggests that reducing borrowing costs is critical. Other factors that can improve financial sustainability include increased loans, increased interest rates, and increased returns on total assets. These results provide strong evidence to support the idea that the quality of the portfolio achieved by a portfolio at risk can be improved. Financial loans should be targeted at improving the economic sustainability of communities. Chikalipah (2017b) also found that GDP growth can improve economic sustainability, especially in Sub-Saharan Africa, while an increase in deposits reduces financial sustainability.

The analysis also found that increasing awareness and depth of the financial sustainability of MFIs in developing countries can positively affect the depth of awareness that financial performance produces and increase the possibility of achieving financial sustainability. In addition, microfinance and financial loans are positively affected by sustainable economic development. Therefore, the average loan and the number of companies that assert operationally appropriate are less than unlisted companies.

A study undertaken by Sekabira (2013) shows that the size of an MFI's assets and its capital framework are related to its performance in terms of sustainability and public awareness. Grants represent a large proportion of an MFI's assets, which is negatively related to sustainability but positively related to the MFI's cost of each loan. However, there is evidence that the use of subsidies reduces operational self-sufficiency. According to Hartarsk and Nadolnyak (2007), economic performance is affected by the equity index. Lower-leveraged MFIs have healthier working capital in such a situation. Another study undertaken by Lafourcade et al. (2005) shows that MFIs use intermediary microfinance to expand their wellbeing and provide services to more customers. The more MFI borrowers they have, the more economies of scale and scope they can take advantage of, thereby reducing the cost per borrower. Their study also found that, as a function of the reduction in the total loan portfolio, the repayment rate reduces the ability to earn loan interest and reduces the income of the MFI. If the profit is low, the operating self-sufficiency rate will be flat.

Credit Loans and Credit Subsidies in Sub-Saharan Africa

For an MFI to engage in credit loans and credit link subsidy scheme services and to simultaneously maintain financial sustainability, it must impose higher interest rates and pay more for loans (Quayes, 2012). There are three main approaches to microfinance interest rates. People on a low income are not able to pay interest on market prices after receiving a credit link subsidy loan from an MFI.

Moyo et al. (2014) argued that a credit loan rate would be applicable to small businesses, which applies to microfinance and reflects a decline of 1% in the normal rate. Microfinance loans are given to settle debts at a higher-cost from the informal bankers, thus obtaining a discount on their interest rate could create values additions. These models are only possible with subsidies. Another method is to apply a slightly lower interest rate than commercial banks, which is more feasible because financial institutions benefit from credit subsidies and international aid. The third method is mostly attributed to organisations that are financially self-sufficient, as they have the highest interest rates of the three options. The last option can have very high interest rates. Interventions during the delivery of microfinance services are measured as one of the policy instruments of their government to eliminate poverty (Tehulu, 2013). According to Bogan (2012), from basic to protective, MFIs are applying nominal interest rates of 30% to 60%. This interest rate can cover operating costs but is not ideal for expanding service activities in poor communities. However, empirical studies have demonstrated that MFIs with the highest interest rates are the most successful, most efficient, and most economically sustainable types of MFI.

According to Misati and Nyamongo (2012), the trade-off inbuilt in this customer relationship creates incentives for MFIs to move upmarket and left from their traditional poor customer's base. Poverty can also be decreased because of access to finance, in the form of credit in the hands of the poor, can also empower them to run microenterprises and develop their assets. Access to adaptable, comfortable, and affordable financial assistance empowers and equips the poor with the ability and means to make their own decisions and find their way out of poverty in a supported and self-determined way. However, evidence shows that there are some fluctuations in interest rates among MFIs in Sub-Saharan Africa for the same loan products, like agricultural loans and working capital business loans. Some say that poor borrowers have higher recovery rates, but this challenges the negotiating principle. Marson and Savin (2015) highlighted that MFIs impose market-based interest rates using many innovative lending methods to compensate for the higher costs associated with running such a business. Interest rates include loan screening, oversight, and execution costs. These results suggest that MFIs need to implement a thorough proactive loan review system that can assess the creditworthiness of borrowers and reduce the interest rates of loans to and from MFIs.

Government Contributions and Future Microfinance Success in Sub-Saharan Africa

According to Calgagovski (1990), Sub-Saharan African microfinance is as diverse as the African continent. In traditional group-based systems, various methods are used, including banks and professional loans funded by non-governmental international financial intermediaries. The example of microfinance in Africa provides a series of lessons about what works and what does not. The Open Security Controls Assessment Language (OSCAL) thus developed a microfinance model based on the following principles:

1. People's wealth should be pooled together.
2. People's knowledge should be relied upon.
3. Microfinance should be reinforced to authorise the African private sector.
4. The model must be field tested.
5. The model seeks to recognise a microfinance methodology model personalised to Sub-Saharan Africa.

Microfinance and Microenterprise Growth

Walter and Courtois (2009) highlighted that the Richmond Federal Reserve considers many companies with fewer than five employees as microenterprises, accounting for 87.4% of all US companies. These are defined as companies that require less than USD 35,000 in start-up capital and cannot obtain traditional bank loans. Small business development organisations are filling this gap. According to Datar et al. (2010), in *The New York Times'* 'Net Opinion' column, David Bornstein described the microfinance industry as a USD 25 billion industry. Bornstein also estimated that MFIs have 100 million clients who benefit from microfinance products, such as microcredit, small savings, and micro-insurance products. The microfinance industry comprises informal credit sources, such as NGOs, professional microfinance banks, public sector banks, consumer finance companies, pawnshops, and members of the 'lender' community.

According to Rhyne (2009), microfinance began by providing small loans, savings accounts, and insurance, which enabled people in developing countries to start small businesses or participate in other economic activities to overcome poverty. Now, entrepreneurs and small businesses in Sub-Saharan Africa can use microfinance. These enterprises and small businesses either have no available financial resources or have been adversely affected by the reduced supply of loans. The idea behind microcredit and microfinance is to help small businesses run by the poor and to foster self-sufficiency among individuals, families, and communities. This means that small credit insurance companies and banks provide financial options for the poor. Microcredits are a form of microcredit by which entrepreneurs who run small businesses obtain funds in exchange for the promise to repay the principal and interest on the loan within a specified term. According to Doyle and Black's (2001) study, based on data from the Aspen Institute Microenterprise Fund for Innovation, Effectiveness, Learning, and Dissemination, there are approximately 700 small business development organisations in the US that provide 362 small loans. The field report indicated that if these organisations raised USD 101 million in 2008, and many loans were as small as USD 500, they should also work in Sub-Saharan Africa.

SOLUTIONS AND RECOMMENDATIONS

Microfinance is considered an important economic development tool. Despite the current unemployment crisis, the industry continues to develop in Sub-Saharan Africa. The effectiveness of microfinance in achieving social goals should be used to observe and evaluate the relevance of microfinance. Microfinance compares favourably to other interventions, especially cost-effectiveness and prospects. An advantage of microfinance is that donor investment is recycled and reused. Direct comparisons show that microfinance can be a more cost-effective poverty-reducing tool than options such as formal rural financial intermediation, targeted food invasions, and rural foundation development projects. Moreover, unlike many other invasions, costs for microfinance tend to diminish with the scale of outreach. Regarding the issue of sustainability, other development tools have the potential to become sustainable to the extent that this is possible in microfinance, where, after initial start-up grants, new inputs are not required for every future client. Adopting a flexible policy for microfinance allows for additional growth and progress while minimising the spread of unlicensed institutions. The regulatory structure should deal with the trade-offs between the depositors' security on the one hand and the stifling of financial improvement, opposition, and costs of regulation on the other hand. Such policies should also consider the sufficiency of internal controls and encourage proper evidence maintenance, including on loan loss recognition. Thus, management inadequacy, loan strength, portfolio at risk, and size are important determinants of MFIs' financial sustainability in Sub-Saharan Africa.

FUTURE RESEARCH DIRECTIONS

The supervision of the microfinance sector appears to be under researched and therefore requires further investigation. Besides, the outcomes of the relationship economic growth and the performance of microfinance institutions appears to be inconclusive. In this regard, future exploring this relationship could enhance our understanding. In view of the fact that the regular financial institutions have a competitive advantage in acquiring a much higher volume of savings from the economy than MFIs, further research on how MFIs can improve their competitive advantage is required in future. Future research on how traditional financial institutions can provide expand their outreach to the poor is also needed as evidence from this chapter show that the official financial sector has difficulties in mobilising funds and providing financial services, especially for the poor.

CONCLUSION

This chapter systematically reviewed the evidence on the performance of microfinance institutions in Sub-Saharan Africa. A conclusion drawn from the review the evidence in this chapter is that microfinance institutions have being providing small direct personal loans to customers like villagers, small entrepreneurs, poor women, and low-income families. Another conclusion drawn from the evidence presented in this chapter is that MFIs appear to operate like traditional banks but operate differently from banks, particularly when they are registered as mutual funds, non-profits, or cooperatives. A major outcome of the analysis of various studies on the activities of microfinance institutions in Africa is that MFIs brought about financial inclusion in various economies by providing financial support to millions of rural families and women of economically marginalised groups. Besides, MFIs have also been found is to provide necessary financial services to poor and low-income families, entrepreneurs, and early-stage businesses who cannot otherwise access these services. Furthermore, evidence from this chapter suggests that the official financial sector has difficulties in mobilising funds and providing financial services, especially for the poor.

In addition to the above, this chapter confirms that a huge number of microfinance institutions provide financial services in such a way that individuals and companies are able to diversify their savings and new businesses can raise capital beyond bank loans. More so the outcome of the analysis conducted in this suggest that microfinance institutions can help to reduce poverty and provide better financing channels for small business start-ups in Africa. Furthermore, the outcome of the analysis carried in this chapter suggests that microfinance institutions have developed a strong interest in mobilising people's deposits, and the supervision of this sector is becoming an important issue. GDP growth was not found to be an important factor in an MFI's wellbeing and financial performance.

Overall, microfinance has been found to help disadvantaged families and entrepreneurs' access affordable financial services, provides funds for income-generating activities, builds wealth through investments, helps them meet their household needs, and protects them from the unexpected risks associated with daily life, including disease. It is designed to provide crucial support for families in cases of death, theft, and natural disasters.

REFERENCES

Abdulai, A., & Tewari, D. D. (2017). Determinants of microfinance outreach in Sub-Saharan Africa: A panel approach. *Acta Commercii*, *17*(1), 1–10.

Adams, A., & Tewari, D. D. (2020). Impact of regulation on microfinance institutions sustainability and outreach in Sub-Saharan Africa. *African Journal of Business and Economic Research*, *15*(3), 11–34. doi:10.31920/1750-4562/2020/v15n3a1

Adams, S. (2009). Foreign direct investment, domestic investment, and economic growth in Sub-Saharan Africa. *Journal of Policy Modeling*, *31*(6), 939–949. doi:10.1016/j.jpolmod.2009.03.003

Agénor, P. R. (2000). *The Economics of Adjustment and Growth*. Academic Press.

Alshebami, A. S., & Khandare, D. M. (2015). The impact of interest rate ceilings on microfinance industry. *International Journal of Social Work*, *2*(2), 10. doi:10.5296/ijsw.v2i2.7953

Asongu, S. A., Uduji, J. I., & Okolo-Obasi, E. N. (2019). Thresholds of external flows for inclusive human development in Sub-Saharan Africa. *International Journal of Community Well-Being*, *2*(3), 213–233. doi:10.100742413-019-00037-7

Bogan, V. L. (2012). Capital structure and sustainability: An empirical study of microfinance institutions. *The Review of Economics and Statistics*, *94*(4), 1045–1058. doi:10.1162/REST_a_00223

Calgagovski, J. (1990). *Microfinance in Africa: Combining the Best Practices of Traditional and Modern Microfinance Approaches towards Poverty Eradication*. The United Nations. Available at: https://www.un.org/esa/africa/microfinanceinafrica.pdf

Chikalipah, S. (2017a). Financial sustainability of microfinance institutions in sub-Saharan Africa: Evidence from GMM estimates. *Enterprise Development & Microfinance*, *28*(3), 182–199. doi:10.3362/1755-1986.16-00023

Chikalipah, S. (2017b). What determines financial inclusion in Sub-Saharan Africa? *African Journal of Economic and Management Studies*, *8*(1), 8–18. doi:10.1108/AJEMS-01-2016-0007

Datar, S. M., Epstein, M. J., & Yuthas, K. (2010). Enamored with scale: scaling with limited impact in the microfinance industry. In P. N. Bloom & E. Skloot (Eds.), *Scaling Social Impact: New Thinking* (pp. 47–64). Palgrave Macmillan. doi:10.1057/9780230113565_4

Diaw, C. T. (2018). Analyst of the determinants of national savings in Senegal. *European International Journal of Science and Technology*, *7*(8), 17–25.

Dichter, T. W. (1996). Questioning the future of NGOs in microfinance. *Journal of International Development*, *8*(2), 259–269. doi:10.1002/(SICI)1099-1328(199603)8:2<259::AID-JID377>3.0.CO;2-7

Doyle, K., & Black, J. (2001). Performance measures for microenterprise in the United States. *Journal of Microfinance/ESR Review*, *3*(1), 4.

Engler, M. (2009). From microcredit to a world without profit? Muhammad Yunus wrestles with moving beyond a society based on greed. *Dissent*, *56*(4), 81–87. doi:10.1353/dss.0.0081

Felsenthal, M. (2010, December 10). *Financial Inclusion on the Rise, But Gaps Remain, Global Findex Database Shows*. World Bank. Available at: https://www.worldbank.org/en/news/press-release/2018/04/19/financial-inclusion-on-the-rise-but-gaps-remain-global-findex-database-shows

Hartarska, V., & Nadolnyak, D. (2007). Do regulated microfinance institutions achieve better sustainability and outreach? Cross-country evidence. *Applied Economics*, *39*(10), 1207–1222. doi:10.1080/00036840500461840

Hermes, N., & Lensink, R. (2007). The empirics of microfinance: What do we know? *Economic Journal (London)*, *117*(517), F1–F10. doi:10.1111/j.1468-0297.2007.02013.x

Hollis, A., & Sweetman, A. (1998). Microcredit: What can we learn from the past? *World Development*, *26*(10), 1875–1891. doi:10.1016/S0305-750X(98)00082-5

Ibrahim, K., & Abdisamad Mohamed, F. (2020). Outreach and performance of microfinance institutions in Sub-Saharan Africa. *International Journal of Sciences, Basic and Applied Research*, *53*(2), 171–185. http://gssrr.org/index.php?journal=JournalOfBasicAndApplied

Lafourcade, A. L., Isern, J., Mwangi, P., & Brown, M. (2005). *Overview of the outreach and financial performance of microfinance institutions in Africa.* Microfinance Information eXchange Available at: http://www.mixmarket.org/medialibrary/mixmarket/Africa_Data_Study.pdf

Ledgerwood, J., & White, V. (2006). *Transforming Microfinance Institutions: Providing Full Financial Services to the Poor.* US World Bank Publications. doi:10.1596/978-0-8213-6615-8

Marson, M., & Savin, I. (2015). Ensuring sustainable access to drinking water in Sub Saharan Africa: Conflict between financial and social objectives. *World Development, 76,* 26–39. doi:10.1016/j.worlddev.2015.06.002

Matin, I., Hulme, D., & Rutherford, S. (2002). Finance for the poor: From microcredit to microfinancial services. *Journal of International Development, 14*(2), 273–294. doi:10.1002/jid.874

Misati, R. N., & Nyamongo, E. M. (2012). Financial liberalisation, financial fragility and economic growth in Sub-Saharan Africa. *Journal of Financial Stability, 8*(3), 150–160. doi:10.1016/j.jfs.2011.02.001

Moyo, J., Nandwa, B., Council, D. E., Oduor, J., & Simpasa, A. (2014). Financial sector reforms, competition and banking system stability in Sub-Saharan Africa. *New Perspectives, 14*(1), 1–47.

Musanganya, I., Nyinawumuntu, C., & Nyirahagenimana, P. (2017). The impact of microfinance banks in rural areas of Sub-Saharan Africa. *International Journal of Research – GRANTHAALAYAH, 5*(9), 80–90. doi:10.29121/granthaalayah.v5.i9.2017.2201

Ndambiri, H. K., Ritho, C., Ng'ang'a, S. I., Kubowon, P. C., Mairura, F. C., Nyangweso, P. M., Muiruri, E. M., & Cherotwo, F. H. (2012). Determinants of economic growths in Sub-Saharan Africa: A panel data approach. *International Journal of Economics and Management Sciences, 2*(2), 18–24.

Neumann, A. (2012, July 24). Microfinance as a Tool to Alleviate Poverty. *Forbes.* Available at: https://www.forbes.com/sites/dell/2012/07/24/microfinance-as-a-tool-to-alleviate-poverty/

Olaosebikan, O., & Adams, M. (2014). Prospects for micro-insurance in promoting micro-credit in sub-Sahara Africa. *Qualitative Research in Financial Markets, 6*(3), 232–257. doi:10.1108/QRFM-09-2012-0028

Oluwaseyi, M. H. (2016). *The Impact of Foreign Capital Inflows on Economic Growth in Selected West African countries* (Doctoral dissertation). Universiti Utara Malaysia.

Pronyk, P. M., Hargreaves, J. R., & Morduch, J. (2007). Microfinance programs and better health: Prospects for sub-Saharan Africa. *JAMA Network Open, 298*(16), 1925–1927. PMID:17954543

Quayes, S. (2012). Depth of outreach and financial sustainability of microfinance institutions. *Applied Economics, 44*(26), 3421–3433. doi:10.1080/00036846.2011.577016

Rhyne, E. (2009). *Microfinance for Bankers and Investors*. US McGraw-Hill Professional Publishing.

Rosenberg R. Gonzalez A. Narain S. (2009, February). *The new moneylenders: are the poor being exploited by high microcredit interest rates?* CGAP Occasional Paper, no. 15, 1–25. https://ssrn.com/abstract=1400291

Saba, H. A. (2021). *Influence of Microfinance Bank Services on the Performance of Micro and Small Enterprises* (Doctoral dissertation). Kwara State University, Nigeria.

Sekabira, H. (2013). Capital structure and its role on performance of microfinance institutions: The Ugandan case. *Sustainable Agriculture Research, 2*(3), 86–100. doi:10.5539ar.v2n3p86

Singh, J., & Yadav, P. (2012). Microfinance as a tool for financial inclusion & reduction of poverty. *Journal of Business Management & Social Sciences Research, 1*(1), 1–12.

Ssewamala, F. M., Sperber, E., Zimmerman, J. M., & Karimli, L. (2010). The potential of asset-based development strategies for poverty alleviation in Sub-Saharan Africa. *International Journal of Social Welfare, 19*(4), 433–443. doi:10.1111/j.1468-2397.2010.00738.x

Suma, D. F. (2007). *The External Debt Crisis and Its Impact on Economic Growth and Investment in Sub-Saharan Africa: A Regional Econometric Approach of ECOWAS Countries* (Doctoral dissertation). WU Vienna University of Economics and Business.

Tehulu, T. A. (2013). Determinants of financial sustainability of microfinance institutions in East Africa. *European Journal of Business and Management, 5*(17), 152–158.

Van Rooyen, C., Stewart, R., & De Wet, T. (2012). The impact of microfinance in sub-Saharan Africa: A systematic review of the evidence. *World Development*, *40*(11), 2249–2262. doi:10.1016/j.worlddev.2012.03.012

Walter, J. R., & Courtois, R. (2009). *The effect of interest on reserves on monetary policy.* Federal Reserve Bank of Richmond Economic Brief EB09-12 (December).

Yahie, A. M. (2000). *Poverty Reduction in Sub-Saharan Africa: Is There a Role for the Private Sector?* African Development Bank.

Yunus, M. (2008). Creating a World without Poverty: Social Business and the Future of Capitalism. Academic Press.

Zikaripa. (2005, April 12). *Micro Finance and Rural Tourism – The Moroccan experience.* PlaNet Finance. Available at: https://www.e-unwto.org/doi/epdf/10.18111/unwtorcmasia.2005.1.v42x00m53127x723

Chapter 9
SME Financing:
Understanding the Barriers and Potentials for Entrepreneurs – Developing and Under-Developed World Perspectives

Emmanuel E. Oghosanine
University of Sunderland, London, UK

ABSTRACT

Small and medium-scale enterprises around the world go through several challenges in a bid to achieve success. Many studies argue SMEs face challenges in different areas; some are critical for success whilst other are not. One of the critical challenges put forward by several studies is finding appropriate funding. Academics have described funds as the blood of every business and a key element that prescribes the supply of entrepreneurship. The challenge of funding remains a problem around the world both in developing and underdeveloped environments. The chapter provides insight into the funding issues faced by SMEs and provides practiced ways in which businesses in developing and underdeveloped environments can address the issue of funding.

INTRODUCTION

One of the main challenges for small and medium scale businesses is finding appropriate resources in operational and expansion activities. In many instances, one of such resource challenges is money. There is ample evidence that money is a critical element for small and medium business success. However, the challenge

DOI: 10.4018/978-1-7998-7499-7.ch009

of finding money to fund small and medium business operations remain. More so, funding SME operations challenge may vary from one environment to another. For instance, finding challenges in developing countries defer from that in developed countries. In this chapter, learners will appreciate the finding challenges of SMEs around the world and would learn practical ways of funding small and medium business operation in an ever-changing environment. The chapter also considers the concept of who an entrepreneur is exploring the concept from a range of theoretical and practice perspective. The objective of this chapter is to introduce the reading audience into different ways of funding small and medium business operations either as a start-up or an established business.

BACKGROUND

Many small business researchers, economics, and entrepreneurship are yet to agree on a definition of entrepreneurship (Brockhaus & Horwitz, 1986; Gartner, 1988). The number of activities that influence the absence of a unified purpose includes establishing a business (Gartner, 1988), risk-taking and identifying opportunities, and managing the factors of production (Schumpeter, 1934; Kirzner, 1973). However, the variation in how scholars understand entrepreneurship is because the concept can address several socio-economic issues while application methods vary. Interestingly, the variation in definition and approach is influenced by various disciplines contributing to the idea from their viewpoints (Story & Green, 2010). Scholars like Story and Green (2010) proposed that fields like economics define entrepreneurship from choice and information processing, while organizational theories see the concepts from rational thinking (Baker and Nelson, 2005).

Notwithstanding this, both economics and corporate views identify a common position based on the range of activities that describe entrepreneurship (Phillips & Tracey, 2007; Shane & Venkataraman, 2000; Venkataraman, 1997). To better understand the concept of entrepreneurship, some definitions that have been useful in addressing Small and Medium Enterprises (SMEs) worldwide are considered. According to Stevenson and Jarillo (1990), entrepreneurs pursue opportunities with resources within their control. Also, Bygrave (1991) describes this concept as a function that creates a business or organization by identifying opportunities. Moreover, Shane and Venkataraman (2000) have defined entrepreneurship as a process driven by chance. In the same vein, professional groups, or bodies like the Global Entrepreneurship Monitor (GEM) believe it is the process of establishing a new business or company (Reynolds et al., 2005). In addition, recent studies have defined entrepreneurship as the formation or creation of Business (Klyver et al., 2008; Reynolds, 2009). These definitions support a position that entrepreneurship cannot be viewed from a narrow perspective given its role in economies (Battilana and Leca, 2008). Hence, it cannot be defined only from opportunity, as other factors like necessity determine the concept. However, irrespective of whether entrepreneurship is opportunity-driven or necessity-driven, it is essential to understand that the formation or creation is central (Battilana et al., 2009; Phillips & Tracey, 2007). Moreover, several elements apply to forming a business, which this study considers by exploring theories. This study defines entrepreneurship as those factors that influence individuals to start up a business and the process that allows for identifying opportunities (ECE, 2005; Battilana et al., 2009). In addition, entrepreneurship combines and mobilizes other resources to meet chance or the forces of market demand (Schumpeter, 1934).

WHO IS AN ENTREPRENEUR?

According to Story (2005), describing an entrepreneur has long been an issue, and the term's meaning has evolved. It is revealed that the most significant drivers of entrepreneur and entrepreneurship research derive from economics, psychology, and sociology (Frese & Gielink, 2014). Most economists describe an entrepreneur as an individual who engages in risky ventures driven by profit or social contribution (Nicolaou et al., 2008; Sarasvathy & Venkataraman, 2011). Other economists understand entrepreneurs as people who identify demands in a market environment and satisfy such needs through a supply (Mitchell et al., 2007; Shane, 2000). According to Viaggi et al. (1883–1950), anyone who can drive innovation and improvement that creates change in the direction of need is an entrepreneur. Viaggi et al., position on the subject identify the entrepreneur as a creative destructive agent, as the individual carries out activities that bring about new ways of doing things (McMullen & Shepherd, 2006).

On the other hand, business, and management experts like Drucker (1909–2005) see the entrepreneur as an individual who anticipates opportunity by searching and responding to opportunity by changing its forms. An example is a change in communication equipment such as from typewriter to computer. Today, economic, Business and management experts agree that entrepreneurship is a crucial element for achieving economic development and creating employment opportunities in societies (McMullen & Shepherd, 2006; Baron, 2007; Drakopoulou & Anderson, 2007). In the view of Alvarez (2008), there may not be a clear and definite description of who an entrepreneur is. This is in light of several elements describing the entrepreneur, ranging from gender, age, skills trait, background, experiences and education, amongst others (Gartner, 2008; see also Gartner, 2010). Researchers, however, have suggested that entrepreneurs share or exhibit the same characteristics or attributes:

they are creative, self-confident, determined, flexible, dedicated, to mention a few (Aldrich, 2005; Gartner, 2008).

According to Story (2005), governments have leveraged SME entrepreneurship as the bedrock for economic development in developing countries. These countries have achieved significant job creation, poverty reduction, and GDP growth (Ramoglou, 2009, 2008). Hence, governments around the world are paying attention to entrepreneurship as a strategic tool for economic development. In the view of Uwem and Ndem (2012), an entrepreneur is an individual with the capacity of converting challenges to opportunities. This position is from the standpoint that entrepreneurs are not intimidated by challenges as they are creative and innovative.

Moreover, they are quick in identifying business or investment opportunities. Shane (2003) supports this position by saying an entrepreneur can manage scarce resources when an opportunity is identified and bears the risk through several methods (Koppl & Minniti, 2003). According to Soyibo (2006), the idea of an entrepreneur is wrongly assumed in many quarters. This is in the light that some authorities mistake the entrepreneur by taking that one as an individual responsible for making decisions. To this end, managers and business executives are called entrepreneurs by some people simply because they make decisions (Steyaert, 2007). Arguments by Soyibo (2006) further highlight that if an individual does not have the responsibility for making decisions that affect the long-term position of the Business or has absolute control of the business decision, they are not an entrepreneur. Nwafor (2007) took the argument further: carrying out certain business activities does not necessarily make an individual an entrepreneur. These scholars justified this view based on a crucial entrepreneurship activity: establishing a business or doing Business (see, for example, Baron, 2004; Mitchell et al., 2007). This allows for a better understanding of who an entrepreneur is, as it goes beyond making a profit on products or services, securing contracts for execution, or buying and selling, amongst others. Rather the entrepreneur must have the ability to create, developing something that adds value (Stevenson & Jarillo, 1990; see also Krueger, 2003; Shane & Venkataraman, 2000).

Other studies believe that those who can take risks in line with the effective management of the factors of production that led to the production of goods and services, which add value, are entrepreneurs. In addition, people who can support investment opportunities irrespective of their environment and establish a business are entrepreneurs (Gartner et al., 2003: Baum et al., 2007). The position of these authors has one common thing: the identification of opportunities and the effective management of resources, irrespective of the environment, describes the entrepreneur (Nicolaou & Shane, 2009). Furthermore, it is essential to establish that entrepreneurs have certain traits, even as Fisher and Koch (2008) identified. The position of these scholars indicates that entrepreneurs have a mindset that seeks to identify opportunities, manage resources, and engage in risky activities, amongst other traits

(Sarasvathy & Venkataraman, 2011). Considering these arguments, it is essential to understand whether the Nigerian business environment has entrepreneurs who can effectively identify opportunities and manage resources. This position is critical, as there has to be a significant supply of entrepreneurs in the Nigerian economy if the SME sector would drive economic growth and development. Some scholars argue that the collection of entrepreneurs in any economy is dependent on the level of enterprise culture reflected in the country (Baron, 2007; Drakopoulou & Anderson, 2007; McMullen & Shepherd, 2006). Hence, this study chooses to understand the lived experience of Nigerian entrepreneurs by exploring altitude and culture.

THE ECONOMIC PERSPECTIVE

Microeconomics has described the entrepreneur in different ways, which has influenced the way the subject of entrepreneurship is viewed. According to Lanino (2011), an entrepreneur is a person who is willing and able to turn ideas into gainful innovation. This definition describes entrepreneurs as innovators who bring about economic growth and development. Hence, entrepreneurs are suggested as change agents from the financial perspective, emphasizing the individual as the drive innovation and growth. Entrepreneurs create activities that are believed to be responsible for firm creation and play a vital role in economic development (Baumol & Strom, 2007). This position is influenced by Schumpeter's creative destruction theory (Schumpeter, 1942). This view suggests that the role of the entrepreneur in an economy is to identify opportunities and exploit them to create economic development (Schumpeter, 1942). In effect, the entrepreneur is the individual whose thoughts and motivation lead to actions that support new businesses or organizations (Bird & Schjoedt, 2009). However, the economic perspective has been criticized for not establishing the reality of entrepreneurship. This is because the individual, either a manager or owner, takes advantage of opportunities by exploiting them through their resource ability. The entrepreneur focuses on individual innovation that leads to the creation of firms, painting a narrow picture of the subject (Baumol, 1968).

THE PSYCHOLOGICAL PERSPECTIVE

The psychological perspective of the entrepreneur emphasizes that who an entrepreneur is can be understood from the individual's mindset. According to Atkinson (1957), an entrepreneur can be understood from the individual's behaviour, focusing on factors or features that identify entrepreneurs from non-entrepreneurs. Studies adopting the psychology perspective make people discuss how psychology affects business creation and success (Frese & Gielink, 2014). Individual personality features and mental attributes are significant subjects because venture creation and entrepreneurial success depend on psychological factors (Frese & Rauch, 2000). Shane and Venkataraman (2000) suggest that an individual's personality and behaviour are crucial to identifying and pursuing an opportunity, making the entrepreneur. They further argue that the entrepreneur's mind is essential in creating innovations and firms, which has become a subject of debate in contemporary entrepreneurship.

TRAIT THEORY AND BEHAVIORAL PERSPECTIVE

Trait theory and behavioral perspective describe the entrepreneur by their behaviors, resulting in new firms or businesses. According to Gartner (1989), trait theory approaches the concept of the entrepreneur from the view that they have a set of inherent characteristics. Drucker (1985) argues that their behaviour can describe entrepreneurs as individuals who search and exploit opportunities. Further argument by Drucker highlighted that an entrepreneur should respond to opportunities for economic exploitation, which is the main element that describes the entrepreneur. On the other hand, McClelland (1961) believes the entrepreneur desires high achievement, making them a risk-taker and energetic. This position gave birth to the study on traits in entrepreneurship with a focus on the individual's personality. Trait theory identifies individuals with seven unique personality traits as entrepreneurs; these personality traits include being a risk-taker, having a high need for achievement and internal locus of control, which is why they become entrepreneurs (Collins et al., 2004). Although trait theory has become popular in the field of entrepreneurship, it has come under intense criticism.

These criticisms led to other perspectives, advocating for how individual entrepreneurs can be identified through their minds (Delgado-Garcia et al., 2012). Notably, there have been debates about whether one's personality traits impact one's entrepreneurial mind (Gartner, 1989). It was suggested by Gartner (1989) that the study of entrepreneurship from a trait position fails to identify what entrepreneurship is about. Therefore, Gartner (1989) suggested that entrepreneurship should be considered a set behavioral position instead of inherent traits. This debate has seen many studies dismissing the personality approach, given its mixed results in facts and figures (Carsrud & Brannback, 2011). An opposing argument puts forward those entrepreneurs need knowledge and expertise in Business and a set of values, abilities, and behaviors that could influence their personality traits (Delgado-Garcia et al., 2012). A study carried out by Delgado-Garcia et al. (2012) established that individual personality features are a significant determinant for becoming an entrepreneur and being successful in a business venture. Another study identified personality as a critical element that influences entrepreneurial decisions and processes (Caliendo et al., 2011). According to Zeffane (2013), trait theory suggests that entrepreneurs can be known from possessing specific personality characteristics, and this would determine their entrepreneurial potential:

> [...] the idea that looking at behaviors rather than traits is a better way to study entrepreneurship seems unfounded, because behaviors are the external manifestation of personality traits. Whether the focus should be on behaviors or features, it is clear that specific characteristics affect entrepreneurial behaviour and success. (Zeffane, 2013, p.76)

Concepts like locus of control (Rotter, 1966) and risk attitudes (Brockhaus, 1982) have found some grounding in their effect on the individual's decision to become and stay self-employed. Other influential scholars have emphasized the influence of personality traits on entrepreneurial choices and behaviour. Personality traits have an important place in the literature regarding our understanding of what makes an entrepreneur (Carsrud & Brannback, 2011). For these reasons, it is fair to believe that we can better understand the entrepreneurial mind by studying an individual's values, beliefs, and behaviors.

THE HISTORY OF ENTREPRENEURSHIP UNDERSTANDING

The concept of entrepreneurship and who is an entrepreneur has evolved. In the 18th century, scholars like Richard Cantillon described the entrepreneur as self-employment irrespective of Business or sector (Amtoin, 2003). This definition was based on the fact that high uncertainty was associated with self-employment. Also, Williams and Napier (2004) argued that self-employed people face a significant degree of risk as they engage in business ventures with no guarantee of profit or success. Approaching the 19th century, some scholars took a different position on the concept of entrepreneur. Notably, three economists –Jean Baptiste Say, John Stuart Mill and Alfred Marshall – argued that their actions and specific skills should identify entrepreneurs. Mill advanced the argument and added that the entrepreneur should have management skills indicating the person should manage a business venture considering associated business risk (Williams & Napier, 2004). Towards the end of the 19th century, Alfred Marshall combined Say's and Mill's understanding of the subject to include the four primary factors of Land, Labor, Capital and Organization necessary for production. He argues that all aspects of production are essential for a successful venture but organizing is the most important for achieving success. Marshall put forward that an entrepreneur should be able to set up a business and manage it.

In the 20th century, the definition extended to include the concept of innovation, which Schumpeter predominantly advocates. Schumpeter (1951) argues an entrepreneur starts a new thing, not necessarily someone who invents something new. He considers an entrepreneur from the position of a function as opposed to a physical individual. Gartner (1989) supports Schumpeter's view that an entrepreneur is not a fixed state of existence. Still, entrepreneurship is a role undertaken by individuals with an idea to create a new business. This position, however, has implications for what defines the entrepreneur. Some studies consider Schumpeter's view as representing the entrepreneur as an individual who creates a business or starts a new venture.

The 21st century presents several views on the concept of entrepreneurship and who an entrepreneur is. It is essential to understand that entrepreneurship is still evolving, and as such, making a list of all known definitions is not the purpose of this study. However, the 21st century provides thought on the subject from known academic authors. Acs and Audretsch (2005), drawing from the early definition of Kirzner (1973), identify two key positions: first, the concept of alertness to opportunities and, secondly, leveraging opportunities through innovative actions. To this end, entrepreneurs are alert to opportunities, and they can innovate or act. From this definition, what entrepreneurs do represent who they are and identify opportunities for their subjective alertness. Bjerke (2007) suggests it is impossible to identify an entrepreneur by a specific or single characteristic, and scholars should be cautious about using a single element to describe the entrepreneur. Bjerke (2007), therefore, sees an entrepreneur as someone who creates new user value. Some other current definitions of the subject include but are not limited to the following.

KNOWLEDGE AND CHALLENGES OF FUNDING SMALL AND MEDIUM-SCALE ENTERPRISE

Access to Finance

Those intending to be entrepreneurs face several barriers concerning starting a business. GEM (2012) reports that in Nigeria, several obstacles to starting a company exist. However, there is one common and major one: lack of access to finance. The report suggests that most intending entrepreneurs cannot start a business and is a primary reason for business discontinuance in Nigeria. The Nigerian business environment does not offer enough platforms for SMEs to access finance domestically. Thus, commercial banks remain the key and almost the only source for SME business financing in the formal sector.

Several financial reforms in Nigeria aim to get SMEs and those intending to be entrepreneurs to access business funds. Some of the reforms include the NERFUND Facility, Small and Medium Scale Enterprise Guarantee Scheme, and the Bank of Industry. Whilst these schemes are meant to encourage the creation and sustenance of small businesses, the challenge is that it is not widely available or accessible. The report suggests that accessing funds through these schemes proves challenging, especially for ordinary businesspeople. Interestingly, these schemes have been accused of being politically influenced, meaning they could only be accessed by a select group of people or by some corrupt means.

Small and Medium Business Finance

Entrepreneurship finance suggests obtaining adequate funds for business start-up and growth is one of the critical challenges small and medium businesses face. Finance is why potential entrepreneurs drop viable business ideas and existing businesses shut down on this account. With the perceived importance of entrepreneurship and its role in economies, policymakers strive to provide solutions to funding issues for entrepreneurs, which is evident across countries worldwide. For instance, the USA provided SMEs with over 200,000 loans at an administrative cost of $1000 per loan in the fiscal year 2007 in a bid to manage the funding issue (SBA, 2008). At the European Union Commission, small and medium business finance assistance is a top priority, with member states charged with advancing risk capital financing for entrepreneurs (OECD, 2004). This has become important because Access to funds or credit in the external market hinders quality entrepreneurs with viable ideas from accessing markets and engaging growth. Several studies have focused on understanding financial hindrances for entrepreneurs concerning its effect on business start-up and growth. Perhaps it is not out of place to say funding limits the supply of entrepreneurs and limits growth potential for businesses. However, some studies argue that entrepreneurs can finance viable ideas through external and internal means. This study discusses some of the external and internal financing options available to entrepreneurs (IMF, 2012).

Self-Funding/Bootstrapping

Entrepreneurs finance viable ideas through self-funding or bootstrapping. This concept is described as using personal funds, which could be savings, personal cash or credit, to invest in a business idea. This model of entrepreneurial financing is famous for several reasons. First, some individuals adopt this method in a bid to lower their risk. They would rather lose their own money as opposed to being in debt to an external source. Another reason is that an individual would like to own a 100 per cent stake of the Business, given the different implications. There are strategic elements of business-like decision-making and what to do with the profit, amongst others.

Nevertheless, some studies argue that self-fund is sometimes because individuals cannot secure the needed resources externally. This could be because of several factors, such as a lack of interest in the company by potential investors. Another is because the entrepreneur may lack the network or social connections to access private capital (Kraemer-Eis et al., 2010). Furthermore, there are other risks associated with self-funding, which have implications for the individual and the Business. Self-funding could result in bankruptcy where the individual runs out of funds and cannot carry out daily business activities.

Family, Friends and Colleagues

One of the long-standing traditions and arguably the second most popular form for entrepreneurial or small business financing is drawing on a network of closely related individuals. Daniels et al. (2016) suggest about 50 per cent of entrepreneurs' fund business ideas through their close relatives. This option is more like bootstrapping and has several benefits, especially if individuals cannot access private capital. Entrepreneurs may access funds from close relatives through interest-free credit, and sometimes the interest is paid. When interest is born, it is usually low compared to a financial house or private capital firm (Haselmann and Wachtel, 2016). While this is a crucial aspect of funding small and medium businesses, Helmer (2014) argues that if close relatives invest in a business and have a stake, the Business may have many challenges, especially decision-making and profit-sharing. However, Zwilling (2016) argues the benefits of funding a company through close relatives outweigh the disadvantages. This is because the individual could leverage the network of their close relations to get a potential investor or may not be under any pressure to return the loan. This form of funding is flexible and allows the entrepreneur to concentrate on the critical aspects of the Business.

Finance Houses

One popular way of financing business ideas for small and medium businesses is through external sources like financial houses through different bank systems. Banks and other financial houses play essential roles in financing small and medium enterprises. The importance of banks and other finance houses ranges from offering significant capital to providing facilities to grow or support an expansion idea. In addition, banks generally do not demand ownership or a stake in a small business but provide a loan facility at an interest rate. However, some entrepreneurs would not mind a stake in their company because of the benefit it could offer. Some of these benefits include a steady supply of funds, network, business advice, and support. The provision of finance could be through different schemes like essential business loans and overdraft facilities; the need for financial houses is more so that a business can actualize a viable idea, drive growth, and achieve the entrepreneur's dream quickly. Access to funds allows the entrepreneur to leverage creativity and innovation.

Nevertheless, accessing bank loans has become a challenge for many entrepreneurs. Sometimes the thought of preparing for a loan interview could seem outdated to today's entrepreneur, which could be the slightest challenge. One of the significant challenges associated with bank financing is the issue of documentation. This has to do with providing banks with relevant information about the individual's creditworthiness, integrity, collateral details and information on what the loan would be used for. Applying for loan facilities could be time-consuming as some entrepreneurs could apply to different banks, which takes time. An entrepreneur or small Business approaches a bank on an average of three times for a loan, which may or may not is approved (ICC, 2012). The second challenge is the flexibility of paying back the loan, which has implications for the Business. If the company fails to meet its payment obligation, it risks certain decisions like a seizure. The banking challenges related to providing finance for the entrepreneur vary from one country's financial system to another. Some countries, especially those in developed environments, may have favourable banking and economic systems than those in developing settings. While these challenges exist, funding a business through banks is very modern, but the entrepreneur understands the banking system. The entrepreneur should understand the different types of banks or financial houses to know how they can benefit. In short, banks play a crucial role in financing small and medium businesses and have several advantages and disadvantages. However, the systems within which they operate define what practices obtain.

Accelerators

This is a recent concept in the entrepreneurial finance ecosystem. It suggests a speed-up in the start-up process within a short time, usually six months. An accelerator is a programme that seeks a network of venture capitalists and investors in supporting start-ups. The accelerator program is carried out through a "Demo Day" where individuals or entrepreneurs pitch their business ideas to secure start-up or growth funds. The entrepreneur is then expected to offer a business percentage to potential investors, usually between six per cent and 10 per cent (Bernthal, 2016). The accelerator program is popular in countries with advanced entrepreneurship understanding. The USA, for instance, has over 700 accelerator programs with well-known names like Y-Combinatory and Techstars, founded in 2005 and 2006, respectively (IMF, 2012).

The accelerator program provides the entrepreneur with funds for the Business and workspace, housing, and mentorship to their accepted entrepreneurs.

Birdsall et al. (2013) found several benefits for entrepreneurs on an accelerator program, such as quick financing and high acquisition. Moreover, the entrepreneur could leverage the network of opportunities associated with the program. According to Adomdza (2016), accelerator graduates receive funding quicker than other entrepreneurs financed by angel investors and are more likely to acquire. However, some drawbacks exist with accelerator programs: first, the program's reputation is gaining much popularity. This could be because of several reasons, but a known cause is difficult to access. An example of this is that only 1.5 per cent of applicants have Access to the US accelerator program (Andruss, 2013).

Angel Investors

The small and medium business sector in certain countries takes advantage of angel investors in financing SMEs. This concept is described as wealthy or high net-worth individuals who identify potential entrepreneurs for investing in their idea. Usually, they demand equity of about 15 per cent in the new company (Bradley et al., 2011). Sometimes angel investors are confused with venture capitalists; however, the difference is that angel investors do not work on behalf of any individual or group for investing. Angel investors aim to invest in businesses they believe in and industries and areas with knowledge and network. These individuals has some features, including mentoring the entrepreneur, being socially responsible, and interested in that field or space. One important fact about them is that they fund the Business from the start and throughout its growth stage. This is what most funding options do not do, like venture capitalists. Thus, an angel investor plays a significant role as a necessary intermediate between entrepreneurs and the formal finance sector (Cohen & Feld, 2011). Countries such as the US have leveraged angel investors in supporting entrepreneurs from the start-up stage through growth. In 2015 angel investors in the US funded about 71,110 ventures (Cohen & Feld, 2011). However, some studies argue that while angel investors' role is critical for funding entrepreneurs, it is difficult to know the number of businesses funded through angel investors (Cohen & Feld, 2011). They also suggest that this kind of funding model requires a structure to be effective in society.

Peer-to-Peer Lending

Another funding or finance option available to entrepreneurs is peer-to-peer (P2P) lending. This concept is relatively new in the finance industry; however, the model works through an online platform where entrepreneurs can get funds from a peer.

The idea behind this model is a twin. First, there must be a platform that allows entrepreneurs to connect with a good number of investors in a short time, usually in minutes. Second, the platform can offer small loans, but the entrepreneur must satisfy the requirements if they need a loan. The loan process involves applying where the applicant's credit score is used to determine if the loan would be granted. Countries with P2P platforms have dozens of companies ready to offer credit for interest. One of the importance of this model is that it helps entrepreneurs looking for small loans with a relatively low interest rate. In the US, the maximum loan offered to a business is $35 000.

However, there are drawbacks to this funding model. It is not practiced in many places; even in America, many states do not allow it. The second is that the interest rate could be high, depending on the lender. The average interest rate on a P2P platform is seven per cent monthly on an excellent creditor, and a low-quality applicant could be charged as much as 30 per cent (Zeng, 2017). Given the interest rate, entrepreneurs would have to consider their options before engaging because it could enormously impact their Business. Bajpai (2019) argues that P2P is not an SME funding option because individuals primarily use it to underwrite consumer debt instead of funding a new idea. Thus, the viability of P2P as a financing model for small and medium businesses is still a subject of debate.

Crowdfunding

This concept is considered the most recent in the finance ecosystem. Crowdfunding is done by advertising a project or business idea to a network of potential global investors, who would require a bit of non-monetary compensation for the investor. An entrepreneur could use crowdfunding for a project, idea, product or service, which could be of profit or non-profit intention. This model presents the entrepreneur with several advantages ranging from flexible payment to free advertising and publicity. Within this model's broad concept, some sub-models exist that depend on the online platform used. Today, Kick starter and Indiegogo are the two biggest platforms for entrepreneurial financing. They advertise projects or ideas through videos, detailed descriptions of what the product is about, and the amount required. Crowdfunding employs two strategies, which are the all-or-nothing strategy and the keep-what-you-get strategy. The first deals with pursuing the project if the funding goal is met, and if the funds raised is not enough, the monies are returned to investors. The latter strategy is employed by keeping whatever is presented irrespective of whether the goal is met or not (Harrison, 2013). The second model is prevalent, and entrepreneurs take advantage of it. Another model is subscription-based and available to entrepreneurs who create content. Entrepreneurs use this model by requesting a subscription fee from individuals interested in their content. One of the famous sites that have leveraged this model is Patreon, which was founded in 2013. Kaltenbeck (2011) argue that crowdfunding has several benefits, which allows for interaction between customers and entrepreneurs, thereby creating future repeat business. In addition, this model is used by entrepreneurs to evaluate the viability of their idea, establishing what the market thinks about it.

ROLE OF GOVERNMENT FINANCIAL POLICIES IN ENTREPRENEURSHIP

The concept of government is a formal structured system with an essential role in developing a state and its market efficiency. Some studies argue two factors directly affect or influence an individual in consideration of starting a business. These factors are said to be important because they determine the success or failure of the company. The government policies and regulations and procurement programs that the government uses to support entrepreneurship are the elements in question. Audretsch et al. (2006) explain that policymakers lead entrepreneurship because they are responsible for designing and implementing policies, programs, and regulations, which allows for a positive environment in which ventures thrive. Thus, the creation of favourable policies is a crucial function or responsibility of government.

The role of new and small businesses in contributing to employment generation and economic development has been examined considering policy determinants across jurisdictions (Audretsch& Keilbach, 2004; Audretsch et al., 2006). Countries worldwide now see the need to foster policies and programs that allow for the establishment and growth of small businesses (e.g., OECD, 1998). Over the years, different studies have tried in understanding the role of policy as it affects the supply of new and small businesses. These studies consider policies concerning business loans and empowerment (see European Commission, 2006b). Likewise, government policies and programs or incentives attract entrepreneurs or potential business owners to foster entrepreneurship development (Shane, 2009). Scholars argue policies and programs give the impression that individuals would be interested in entrepreneurship. However, many studies have questioned the effectiveness of policies and programs in attracting individuals to entrepreneurship.

Furthermore, while the usually recycled incentive policies are repeatedly questioned regarding their effectiveness, these motivation programs may encourage rent-seeking behaviour leading to unintentional, willful consequences. Hoffmann (2007) suggested that entrepreneurial individuals/firms might choose to dedicate their energies to productive activities in wealth creation through lobbying and corruption. Motivated by such rent-seeking reasons, entrepreneurs and firms operating in an environment of enthusiastically accessible and prevalent motivations might be encouraged to lobby and bribe for tax breaks and other subsidies that may boost their profits (Perren & Jennings, 2005). The debate for policies, programs and incentives that encourage entrepreneurs or new businesses has merit and demerits. However, its application and effect vary from one country to another. Nevertheless, evidence suggests government policies and programs impact the supply of entrepreneurs and new businesses in developed and developing environments.

Evidence From the Developed World

Talks on small and medium Businesses have taken center stage amongst policymakers in the USA, given the perceived impact on economic development and job creation. This was not the case over two decades, but in the last ten years, Congress and government across different levels have paid attention to the subject of small and medium businesses. Milestone laws like the Sarbanes-Oxley Act, the Dodd-Frank Wall Street Reform, the Consumer Protection Act, and the Patient Protection and Affordable Care Act (2010) have shown that the government is now supporting small businesses more than ever before, identifying that government has a role to play in fostering entrepreneurship development. Like many developed countries, the US has tried to stimulate business creation through tax incentives and create an environment where medium- and long-term assessments of government policies and programs can be reviewed. The USA, for example, has created avenues for the review of specific policies relating to small and medium businesses: an example of such policies is the new regulation of taxes in the US. Several western nations now see the need to create policies that positively affect small and medium businesses. The United Kingdom's Department of Business, Innovation and Skills announced the elimination of 3000 rules or regulations impacting small firms in 2015 (see: www.gov.uk/bis). According to the then business secretary, in these challenging times, businesses need to focus all their energies on creating jobs and growth, not being tied up in unnecessary red tape. Until a more stable environment built upon policies that engender private sector growth and investment is visible to the job-creating cadre, we can expect sub-par economic growth and missed opportunities.

Evidence From Developing World

Indonesia is one developing country with significant evidence of the role of government policy and its impact on small and medium businesses. A considerable value is placed on SMEs because SMEs have been identified to support creating jobs. These businesses also generate foreign currency as they engage in international trade. They are also relevant in supporting low-income groups by producing cheap domestic goods (Bosman & Schutjens, 2008). Given the role of SMEs in the country, the government, through several routes, provides an enabling environment for their operation. One such effort is the SME cluster, commonly referred to as the accumulation of small and medium businesses with functions in a sub-sector and the exact location.

Clustering is an economic concept, which is described by the United Nations Industrial Development (UNIDO) as "a cluster is a local agglomeration of enterprises producing and selling a range of related or complementary products within a particular industrial sector or subsector" (Holmes & Lee, 2009). Examples of clusters are knitting, dyeing, or printing firms operating within a geographical location. The Indonesian government encourages and supports businesses through SME clustering development policy by providing technical, management and training aid for businesses within sub-sectors. Its traditional approach is where producers, suppliers, buyers, and other stakeholders advance and deepen associations with commonly favorable effects. The government supports businesses with large machinery and raw materials to ease and manage substantial financial investments. They also use local universities and research institutions to provide relevant training and support for businesses. The funding issues of entrepreneurs are addressed through local banks providing loans when needed. The participation of educational and financial institutions is a means of implementing government policies. The cluster policy program has benefited the nation in several ways, from job creation to increasing the nation's GDP and, by extension, improved living standards. It is essential to understand that the role played by the Indonesian government could not have been played by local businesses. This is because there are elements of massive financial involvement like investing in machinery and paying universities and other institutions for strategic business support and advice.

SOLUTIONS AND RECOMMENDATIONS

The concept of the entrepreneur is still developing. However, it is essential to understand that many definitions are consistent across a few elements describing the entrepreneur from the 18th century until today. These elements include the ability for entrepreneurship to evolve, the concept of risk and uncertainty, managerial competence and identifying opportunities. The factors identified describes the entrepreneur across different cultures and environments of the world. Having established who an entrepreneur is, the other question is how people with small and medium scale businesses fund their operations. The answer to this question varies from one environment of Business to another given social, economic factors. For enterprises in developed environments of the world, there are several financing options available. Enterprise in the developing world could have a different narrative.

Nevertheless, small, and medium business financing provides serval options such as crowdfunding, venture capitalist, peer to peer lending, angles investors and others. Business, therefore, should check their environment of operations to identify relevant funding or financing options before establishing that accessing funds is a challenge or barrier to growth and sustainability. Perhaps a country may have opportunities for financing small and medium businesses, which may not be a global practice. Nevertheless, government and banks could consider a number of options in supporting small and medium businesses.

Non-Performing Loans (NPL) and a Perceived Limited Flexibility is Making Some Banks Reluctant to Lend to SMEs

Banks should be the number one lending option for small and medium businesses. However, this is not the case as many high street banks doubt the credibility of SMEs to pay back loans. The experience of many banks with SMEs is SMEs not being able to pay back loans within the agreed period. A situation that is referred to as non-performing loans. In practice SMEs are major risk for banks as such when SMEs make loan request the banks direct them to other financial institution with lower liquidity thereby transferring the risk. Some of the reasons why commercial or high street banks deny SMEs loans includes the ability to repay back the loan, poor credit history and lack of business prospect. Therefore, for banks to support SMEs financially a different system could be developed to assess SMEs performance, prospect, and ability to repay. This is important because in many instances, commercial and high street banks have used the same criteria and system used for large businesses for SMEs. The argument is that the system would not be fair, and it would have several implications which include supporting the economy through employment generation.

Lack of Credit Information is a Factor That Contributes to the Constraints Faced by SMEs for Funding

Providing credit facility depends significantly on access to information and this is a major challenge for small and medium businesses. Many banks use credit reports and rating systems in assessing the credibility of the borrower to access credit facility. This approach has proved to be effective in providing credit to businesses. However, many small and medium business with viable ideas fail to access funds from banks because the credit scores or report does not demonstrate the capacity to borrow. Whilst using credit reports and scores to access SMEs capacity to borrower. It is important for banks to understand that that report may not reflect the business position. More so, there are factors that could be responsible for poor information on the part of SMEs. Such factors may include un-update data of the business at the time of the scoring. On another hand, the business may have been accessed based on previous information. There is a need for banks to consider an approach where small businesses can be accessed based on their offering and current circumstance.

SMEs Require a One Stop Shop

Several factors contribute to how a business can access credit and some of those factors range from information to knowledge of banking and financial products and platforms for accessing credit. The government and banks and provide a one stop shop where small and medium businesses can find information, seek understanding of credit facility and access credit platforms. In practice many banks would have credit advisors who have responsibility for helping the business understand credit options. However, in many instances, such options are limited to a single platform which can only provide information related to its own product. Going forward SMEs should be able should from several options and platforms using the support of government institutions and banks.

A More Focused Organisation Dedicated to Help SME Develop Their Business Capacity is Needed

Some countries in developed environments of the world have dedicated systems and organisations set up to provide information, advice, grants and other support to SMEs. Many small and medium businesses have benefited from this structure as it has become the backbone for start-ups and SMEs. However, some organisations set up for the purpose of supporting SMEs fail because they are underfunded and are unable to provide the funds required for operations. In other instances, the organisation lacks relevant information and understanding on how to support SMEs. The case for developing and under-developed environments of the world is different as there are hardly organisations set-up for supporting SMEs. Governments around the world must understand the role SMEs play in the social economic development of a country. As such there is a need for clear cut support for SMEs through dedicated platforms, relevant policies, platforms, systems, processes, and availability of funds.

FUTURE RESEARCH DIRECTIONS

Many studies have argued access to finance is a major challenge for small and medium businesses (Anduress, 2013). These studies more so, establish that financial challenge of SMEs have significant social economic implication. Nevertheless, more studies call for the review of this position in relation to understanding the link between supporting SMEs financially and economic growth and development. The question therefore is would the promotion of SME financing result in significant economic objective in a country. For instance, would the supporting SMEs financial improve unemployment in a country or result to the creation of innovative products and services (Bajpai, 2019)?

Nevertheless, it could be challenged to establish the above-described position because supporting SMEs is relative in comparison to external economic fluctuations, trends, and pattern. Some studies advocate that the significance of SMEs support in relation to wider economy aggregates remain unknown. In any case there are debates that seek to understand whether small or medium businesses contribute more to economic development and to what extent.

On another hand, there is a need to understand the role of policy in providing relevant support for small and medium businesses. Some studies suggest economic policies should be streamlined to the different business structure as opposed to having same policy for all. The question here is should small businesses have a different policy from medium businesses especially as it relates to providing financial support. Are the current policies used in supporting SMEs good enough to understand the challenges and prospect for businesses? Considering policies supporting small and medium business at different levels indicate the need for further investigation (Carsrud, A., & Brannback, 2011).

CONCLUSION

The chapter has considered the concept of entrepreneurs and the elements that can be used to describe who an entrepreneur is. It provides relevant understanding of the entrepreneur using specific elements of behaviour, psychology, and economy. More so, it provides a picture of the concept of Entrepreneurship exploring developing and under-developed environmental circumstance. The chapter further considered the challenge of funding small and medium businesses with evidence across developing and under-developed nations. Furthermore, the chapter discussed the relevant funding options available for business. Some of the funding options provided may be new for businesses developing environments of the world. Nevertheless, the chapter establishes that businesses could be funded through a range of options which are common and practicable across different environments of the world.

REFERENCES

Aldrich, H. E. (2005). Entrepreneurship. In N. J. Smelser & R. Swedberg (Eds.), *The Handbook of Economic Sociology* (pp. 451–477). Princeton University Press.

Andruss, P. (2013). *What to look for in an accelerator program*. Entrepreneur. https://www.entrepreneur.com/article/225242

Atkinson, S. W. (1957). Motivational determinants of risk-taking behavior. *Psychological Review, 64*(6, Pt.1), 359–372. doi:10.1037/h0043445 PMID:13505972

Audretsch, D. B., & Keilbach, M. (2004). Entrepreneurship and regional growth: An evolutionary interpretation. *Journal of Evolutionary Economics, 14*(5), 605–616. doi:10.100700191-004-0228-6

Audretsch, D. B., Keilbach, M., & Lehmann, E. (2005). *The knowledge spillover theory of entrepreneurship and technological diffusion. University entrepreneurship and technology transfer*. Emerald London.

Audretsch, D. B., Keilbach, M. C., & Lehmann, E. E. (2006). *Entrepreneurship and Economic Growth*. Oxford University Press. doi:10.1093/acprof:oso/9780195183511.001.0001

Bajpai, P. (2019). *The Rise of Peer-to-Peer (2019) Lending*. https://www.nasdaq.com/article/the-rise-of-peertopeer-p2p-lending-cm685513

Baker, T., & Nelson, R. E. (2005). Creating Something from Nothing: Resource Construction through Entrepreneurial Bricolage. *Administrative Science Quarterly, 50*(3), 329–366. doi:10.2189/asqu.2005.50.3.329

Baron, R. (2007). Entrepreneurship: A process perspective. In J.R. Baum, M. Frese, & R. Baron (Eds.), The psychology of entrepreneurship (pp. 19-40). Academic Press.

Baron, R. A. (2004). The cognitive perspective: A valuable tool for analyzing entrepreneurship's basic «Why» Questions. *Journal of Business Venturing, 19*(2), 221–239. doi:10.1016/S0883-9026(03)00008-9

Baumol, W. (1968). Entrepreneurship in economic theory. *The American Economic Review, 56*, 64–71.

Baumol, W. J., Litan, R. E., & Schramm, C. J. (2007). *Good capitalism, bad capitalism, and the economics of growth and prosperity*. Yale University Press. doi:10.2139srn.985843

Bird, B. J., & Schjoedt, L. (2009). Entrepreneurial behavior: Its nature, scope, recent research, and agenda for future research. In A. L. Carsrud & M. Brännback (Eds.), *Understanding the entrepreneurial mind, international studies in entrepreneurship* (pp. 327–358). Springer Science & Business Media. doi:10.1007/978-1-4419-0443-0_15

Birdsall, M., Jones, C., Lee, C., Somerset, C., & Takaki, S. (2013). *Business Accelerators - The Evolution of a Rapidly Growing Industry*. Academic Press.

Bjerke, B. (2007). *Understanding Entrepreneurship*. Edward Elgar.

Bosma, N., & Schutjens, V. (2008). Mapping entrepreneurial activity and entrepreneurial attitudes in European regions. *International Journal of Entrepreneurship and Small Business*.

Bradley, S. W., Aldrich, H., Shepherd, D. A., & Wiklund, J. (2011). Resources, environmental change, and survival: Asymmetric paths of young independent and subsidiary organizations. *Strategic Management Journal, 32*(5), 486–509. doi:10.1002mj.887

Brockhaus, R. H. Sr, & Horwitz, P. S. (1986). The psychology of the entrepreneur. In D. L. Sexton & R. W. Smilor (Eds.), *The Art and Science of Entrepreneurship* (pp. 25–48). Ballinger.

Bygrave, W. D., & Hofer, C. W. (1991). Theorizing about entrepreneurship. *Entrepreneurship Theory and Practice*, (Winter), 12–22.

Caliendo, M., Fossen, F., & Kritikos, A. (2011). *Personality Characteristics and the Decision to Become and Stay Self-Employed*. https://ftp.iza.org/dp5566.pdf

Carsrud, A., & Brannback, M. (2011). Entrepreneurial Motivations: What Do We Still Need to Know? *Journal of Small Business Management, 49*(1), 9–26. doi:10.1111/j.1540-627X.2010.00312.x

Cohen, D., & Feld, B. (2011). Do More Faster: TechStars Lessons to Accelerate Your Startup. John Wiley and Sons.

Collins, C. J., Hanges, P., & Locke, E. A. (2004). The relationship of need for achievement to entrepreneurship: A meta-analysis. *Human Performance, 17*, 95–117. doi:10.1207/S15327043HUP1701_5

Delgado-Garcia, J. B., Rodriguez-Escudero, A. I., & Martin-Cruz, N. (2012). Influence of affective traits on entrepreneur's goals and satisfaction. *Journal of Small Business Management, 50*(3), 408–428. doi:10.1111/j.1540-627X.2012.00359.x

Deo, S. (2005). *Challenges for small business entrepreneurs: A study in the Waikato region of New Zealand.* Available at: http://www.sbaer.uca.edu/research/icsb/2005/056.pdf

Drakopoulou Dodd, S., & Anderson, A. R. (2007). Mumpsimus and my thing of the individualistic entrepreneur. *International Small Business Journal, 25*(4), 341–360. doi:10.1177/0266242607078561

Drucker, P. (1985). *Innovation and entrepreneurship.* Harper & Row.

European Commission, Eurostat. (2005). *Business Demography in Europe–results from 1997 to 2002, Statistics in focus 36/2005.* Author.

European Commission. (2006b). Report on the implementation of the Entrepreneurship Action Plan. European Commission – DG Enterprise and Industry.

Fisher, J. L., & Koch, J. V. (2008). Born, not made: The entrepreneurial personality Journal of Psychology. *Rev., 47,* 777–780.

Frese, M., & Gielink, M. M. (2014). The Psychology of Entrepreneurship. *Annual Review of Organizational Psychology and Organizational Behavior, 1*(1), 413–438. doi:10.1146/annurev-orgpsych-031413-091326

Gartner, W. (2008). *Entrepreneurship hop Entrepreneurship Theory and Practice Advances in entrepreneurship, firm emergence, and growth* (Vol. 7). JAI Press.

Gartner, W. B. (1988). Who is an entrepreneur? Is the wrong question. *American Journal of Small Business, 12*(4), 11–32. doi:10.1177/104225878801200401

Gartner, W. B. (1989). Some suggestions for research on entrepreneurial traits and characteristics. *Entrepreneurship Theory and Practice, 14*(1), 27–38. doi:10.1177/104225878901400103

Gartner, W. B., Carter, N. M., & Hills, G. E. (2003). The language of opportunity. In C. Steyaert & D. Hjorth (Eds.), *New Movements in Entrepreneurship* (pp. 103–124). Edward Elgar. doi:10.4337/9781781951200.00017

Gartner, W. B., Carter, N. M., & Reynolds, P. D. (2010). Entrepreneurial behavior: Firm organizing processes. In Z. Acs & D. Audretsch (Eds.), *International handbook series on entrepreneurship* (Vol. 5, pp. 99–127). Springer. doi:10.1007/978-1-4419-1191-9_5

Harrison, R. (2013). Crowdfunding and the revitalization of the early stage risk capital market: Catalyst or chimera? *Venture Capital, 15*(4), 283–287. doi:10.1080/13691066.2013.852331

Haselmann, R., & Wachtel, P. (2010). Institutions and Bank Behavior: Legal Environment, Legal Perception, and the Composition of Bank Lending. *Journal of Money, Credit and Banking, 42*(5), 965–984. doi:10.1111/j.1538-4616.2010.00316.x

Helmer, J. (2011). *A snapshot on crowdfunding.* Working papers firms and regions, No. R2/2011, Fraunhofer Institute for System's and Innovation Research ISI, Karlsruhe.

Hoffmann, A. (2007). A rough guide to entrepreneurship policy. In D. B. Audretsch, I. Grilo, & A. R. Thurik (Eds.), *Handbook or Research on Entrepreneurship Policy* (pp. 140–171). Edward Elgar. doi:10.4337/9781847206794.00012

Holmes, T., & Lee, S. (2009). *Economies of density versus natural advantage: crop choice on the back forty.* Working Paper.

ICC. (2012). *Rethinking Trade and Finance, ICC Global Survey on Trade Finance 2012.* International Chamber of Commerce.

IMF. (2012b). Global Financial Stability Report October 2012. International Monetary Fund.

Kaltenbeck, J. (2011). *Crowd funding and Social Payments.* Open Educational Resources.

KirznerI. M. (1973). *Competition and Entrepreneurship.* Chicago: The University of Chicago Press. https://ssrn.com/abstract=1496174

Klyver, K., Hindle, K., & Meyer, D. (2008). Influence of social network structure on entrepreneurship participation – a study of 20 national cultures. *The International Entrepreneurship and Management Journal, 4*(3), 331–347. doi:10.100711365-007-0053-0

Koppl, R., & Minniti, M. (2003). Market processes and entrepreneurial studies. In Z. Acs & D. Audretsch (Eds.), *Handbook of Entrepreneurship Research* (pp. 81–102). Kluwer Press International.

Kraemer-Eis, H., Schaber, M., & Tappi, A. (2010). *SME loan securitization. An important tool to support European SME lending.* Working Paper 2010/007, EIF Research & Market Analysis, European Investment Fund.

Krueger, N. (2003). Thinking entrepreneurially: Entrepreneurial cognition. In Z. Acs (Ed.), *International handbook of entrepreneurship.* Kluwer.

McClelland, D. C. (1961). *The achieving society.* The Free Press. doi:10.1037/14359-000

McMullen, J. S., & Shepherd, D. A. (2006). Entrepreneurial action and the role of uncertainty in the theory of the entrepreneur. *Academy of Management Review, 31*(1), 132–152. doi:10.5465/amr.2006.19379628

Mitchell, R. K., Busenitz, L., Bird, B., Gaglio, C. M., McMullen, J. S., Morse, E. A., & Smith, J. B. (2007). The central question in entrepreneurial cognition research 2007. *Entrepreneurship Theory and Practice, 31*(1), 1–27. doi:10.1111/j.1540-6520.2007.00161.x

Nicolaou, N., & Shane, S. (2009). Can genetic factors influence the likelihood of engaging in entrepreneurial activity? *Journal of Business Venturing, 24*(1), 1–22. doi:.jbusvent.2007.11.003 doi:10.1016/j

Nicolaou, N., Shane, S., Cherkas, L., Hunkin, J., & Spector, T. (2008). Is the tendency to engage in entrepreneurship genetic? *Management Science, 54*(1), 167–179. doi:10.1287/mnsc.1070.0761

Nwafor, P. Z. (2007). *Practical Approach to Entrepreneurship: Small and Medium Scale Enterprises (SMEs)*. Retrieved from: www.scirp.org/journal/PaperInformation. aspx?PaperID = 8063

OECD. (2004). *SME Statistics: Towards a More Systematic Statistical Measurement of SME Behaviour*. Background Report for the 2nd OECD Conference of Ministers Responsible for Small and Medium Enterprises (SMEs).

Perren, L., & Jennings, P. J. (2005). Government discourses on entrepreneurship: Issues of legitimization, subjugation, and power. *Entrepreneurship Theory and Practice, 29*(2), 173–184. doi:10.1111/j.1540-6520.2005.00075.x

Phillips, N., & Tracey, P. (2007). Opportunity recognition, entrepreneurial capabilities and bricolage: Connecting institutional theory and entrepreneurship. *Strategic Organization, 5*(3), 313–320. doi:10.1177/1476127007079956

Ramoglou, S. (2008). The question we ought to ask: 'Who is the non-entrepreneur?'. *Proceedings of the Academy of Management Review, 41*(3), 410–434. doi:10.5465/amr.2014.0281

Ramoglou, S. (2009). *In the shadow of entrepreneurs: Taking seriously the 'others' of entrepreneurship*. Paper presented at the 25th EGOS Colloquium 2010.

Reynolds, P., Bosma, N., Autio, E., Hunt, S., De Bono, N., Servais, I., Lopez-Garcia, P., & Nancy, C. (2005). Global entrepreneurship monitor: Data collection design and implementation 1998-2003. *Small Business Economics, 24*(3), 205–231. doi:10.100711187-005-1980-1

Reynolds, P. D. (2009). Screening item effects in estimating the prevalence of nascent entrepreneurs. *Small Business Economics*, *33*(2), 151–163. doi:10.100711187-008-9112-3

Rotter, J. B. (1966). Generalized Expectancies for Internal versus External Control of Reinforcement. *Psychological Monographs*, *80*(1), 1–2. doi:10.1037/h0092976 PMID:5340840

Sarasvathy, S. D., & Venkataraman, S. (2011). Entrepreneurship as Method: Open Questions for an Entrepreneurial Future. *Entrepreneurship Theory and Practice*, *35*(1), 113–135. Advance online publication. doi:10.1111/j.1540-6520.2010.00425.x

SBA. (2008). *Looking Ahead: Opportunities and Challenges for Entrepreneurship and Small Business Owners*. https://www.sba.gov/sites/default/files/rs332tot.pdf

Schumpeter, J. A. (1934). *The theory of economic development: an inquiry into profits, capital, credit, interest, and the business cycle*. Harvard Economic Studies.

Schumpeter, J. A. (1968). *Ensayos*. Oikos-Tau. (Original work published 1951)

Shane, S. (2000). *Prior knowledge and the discovery of entrepreneurial opportunities*. Academic Press.

Shane, S. (2003). *A General Theory of Entrepreneurship: The Individual–Opportunity Nexus*. Elgar. doi:10.4337/9781781007990

Shane, S. (2009). Why encouraging more people to become entrepreneurs is bad public policy? *Small Business Economics*, *33*(2), 141–149. doi:10.100711187-009-9215-5

Shane, S., & Venkataraman, S. (2000). The promise of entrepreneurship as a field of research. *Acad. Manga. Rev.*, *25*(1), 217–226. doi:10.5465/amr.2000.2791611

Shaver, K.G. (1987). *Principles of social psychology*. doi:10.1177/104225879201600204

Soyibo, A. (2006). The concept of entrepreneurship. *Journal of Business Organization. Development*, •••, 15.

Stevenson, H. H., & Jarillo, J. C. (1990). A paradigm of entrepreneurship: Entrepreneurial management. *Strategic Management Journal*, *11*, 17–27.

Storey, D & Greene F (2010). *Small business and entrepreneurship*. doi:10.1787/eco_surveys-srb-2002-5-en

Story, D. J. (2005). Entrepreneurship, Small and Medium Sized Enterprises and Public Policies. In Z. Y. Acs & D. B. Audretsch (Eds.), *Handwork of Entrepreneurship Research* (pp. 473–513). Springer. doi:10.1007/0-387-24519-7_18

ADDITIONAL READING

Timmons, J. A., & Spinelli, S. (2007). *New Venture Creation, Entrepreneurship for the 21. Century* (7th ed.). McGraw Hill.

Venkataraman, S. (1997). The distinctive domain of entrepreneurship research: An editor's perspective. In J. Katz & R. Brockhaus (Eds.), *Advances in entrepreneurship, firm emergence, and growth* (Vol. 3, pp. 119–138). JAI Press.

Zeffane, R. (2013). Need For Achievement, Personality and Entrepreneurial Potential: A Study of Young Adults in the United Arab Emirates. *Journal of Enterprising Culture*, *21*(1), 75–105. doi:10.1142/S0218495813500040

KEY TERMS AND DEFINITIONS

Developed Country: A developed country—also called an industrialized country—has a mature and sophisticated economy, usually measured by gross domestic product (GDP) and/or average income per resident. Developed countries have advanced technological infrastructure and have diverse industrial and service sectors.

Economy: The state of a country or region in terms of the production and consumption of goods and services and the supply of money.

Entrepreneur: An entrepreneur is an individual who creates a new business, bearing most of the risks and enjoying most of the rewards.

Financial Houses: A company concerned primarily with providing money, e.g., for hire-purchase transactions.

Government: The government of a country is the group of people who are responsible for governing it.

Loan: A thing that is borrowed, especially a sum of money that is expected to be paid back with interest.

Small And Medium-Size Enterprise: SME is generally a small or medium-sized enterprise with fewer than 250 employees. While the SME meaning defined by the EU is also business with fewer than 250 employees, and a turnover of less than €50 million, or a balance sheet total of less than €43 million. Within this umbrella there are three different categories: medium-sized, small, and micro-businesses. These categories are defined by turnover and number of employees.

Under-Developed Country: An underdeveloped country is a country characterized by widespread chronic poverty and less economic development than other nations. ... These countries have very low per capita income, and many residents live in very poor conditions, including lacking access to education and health care.

Chapter 10
Service Failure, Recovery, and Sustainable Development:
Towards Justice in the Extractive Industry of Nigeria

Anthony Nduwe Kalagbor
University of Cumbria, London, UK

ABSTRACT

Extant literature on corporate social responsibility (CSR) and marketing shows that CSR plays an important role when a service fails; thus, application of recovery strategy becomes crucial for sustainable development. CSR creates greater performance expectations amongst stakeholders as well as helps to legitimise organisational activities when a service fails. This study maintains that CSR is crucially important not only in legitimising organisational actions, but in ensuring that stakeholders' loyalty, trust, and justice are assured. This CSR, service failure, and recovery nexus is more needed in the controversial extractive industry in Nigeria, which has a history of illegitimacy, irresponsible corporate responsibility, lack of accountability, and failure of justice, which have triggered and sustained corporate-stakeholder conflict. This landscape has negative impact on sustainable development, peace, and justice in the Niger Delta region of Nigeria, where oil is extracted.

INTRODUCTION

Nigeria is one of the West African countries with official population of about 200 million. Nigeria is endowed with huge natural resources, which make it one of the greatest and fifth oil producing countries in the world. However, this is not the case, as one of Nigeria problems in harnessing its natural resources for development, economic prosperity, and sustainable development has been the part played by multinational oil corporations (MNC's) including Shell, TotalFinaElf, Agip, ExxonMobile, and Chevron who have dominated in the industry since oil was discovered in commercial quantities in 1933 (Amao, 2008). More than 90% of the nations GDP come from oil & gas; the multinational corporations serving as extracting industry have been blamed for Nigeria's perennial situation ranging from developmental problems, political conflict, violence, and a corporate stakeholder conundrum. The stakeholders' perceptions of MNC's in Nigeria are that they are not accountable, transparent, and responsible in their practices. (Idemudia, 2009) has noted that MNC's are not living up to their promise in terms of CSR for sustainable development. Fryna, (2005) described this situation as the false developmental promise of corporate social responsibility by the multinational oil companies in Nigeria.

This chapter objective therefore, is to gain a deeper understanding of how stakeholders' in Nigeria's Niger Delta perceive of MNC's CSR practices in the wake of service failure associated with oil exploration in Nigeria. It is hoped that this exploration will unpick how CSR can be utilised in order to repair trust, build confidence in communities and engender loyalty, trust and satisfaction. In terms of service failure, CSR can be a useful development strategy to trigger recovery for sustainable business (Siu, et al., 2013; Grawal, et al., 2008; Thomassen, et al., 2019; Kolk & Tulder, 2010).

BACKGROUND

For service practitioners, academics, and policymakers (La & Choi, 2018) within the field of service recovery strategies, service failure is characterised by inevitability. Service failure can be defined as service performance, which fails to meet the expectations of stakeholders' (Varela-Neira, et al., (2010). While service recovery, can be defined as the actions and steps taken by a service provider as a response to service failure (Fatma, et al., 2016). It also entails systematic business and operational procedures and strategies that are appropriately designed and implemented within an organisation in order to recognise stakeholders' who have issues. The aim is to address these issues to the stakeholders' satisfaction so as to achieve stakeholders' retention (La & Choi, 2018). On the other hand, corporate social responsibility (CSR), according to (Carrorl, 2016; Bowen, 1953) is about the responsibility of a company that makes it a socially responsible organisation beyond what is prescribed by law. However, (Desjardins, 2000) states that sustainable development is sustainability discourse, which began with the reconsideration that economic development on a global level cannot be separated from issues that borders on ecological stability, social justice and equity, hence the role business can play in sustaining the world without jeopardising the wellbeing of people and the environment now and in the future (Barbier, 1987).

PROBLEMATIZING THE NIGERIAN CONTEXT

As well documented (Frynas, 2015, 2005), the presence of oil and gas multinational corporations (MNCs) including Chevron, ExxonMobil, Agip, TotalFinaElf, and Shell BP – the *big five* – have contributed to the destruction and pollution of the environment and related phenomena in the Niger delta region, which produces oil in Nigeria. MNCs have also been accused of engaging in unsustainable business, which is the bane of service failure that requires recovery strategies for sustainable development (Fatma et al., 2016; Ite, 2004). This situation is fundamental to lack of sustainable development in the Niger Delta as observed by researchers (Obi, 2010). CSR entails responsibilities of organisations that are not legally binding; however, when companies engage in CSR irresponsibly it engenders legitimacy problem (Lii, Ding & Lin, 2018), justice issues (Cho et al., 2017), unfairness (Du & Feng, 2010; Visser, 2013), and reputational quagmire (Carroll, 1991) as well as contributes to unsustainable development (Lii et al., 2018; Zwan & Bhamra, 2003). Sustainable development takes into consideration process of achieving human development objectives but sustaining the capability of the natural systems to continue to deliver natural capital and biodiversity upon which the economy and society at large depend (Brundtland Report, 1987).

Preceding from the above, sustainable development discourse came to the fore on the heels of recalibrating and refocusing economic growth dialectics including environmental and social benefits that can be gained when organisations including MNCs (in Nigeria) and social institutions confront social issues for social justice, fairness, equity, community development and poverty alleviation (World Commission on Environment and Development [WCED], 1987). Sustainable development discourse was birthed by the epochal publication of *Our Common Future*, which is also considered as the Brundtland Report by WCED (Crowther & Aras, 2008; WCED, 1987). Similarly, at the 2005 World Summit, which was held in New York at the backdrop of the United Nations' 2000 Millennium Summit, a precursor to the Millennium Development Goals (MDGs), sustainable development concept was given a central place to confront one of humanity's greatest challenges in the coming century (Elkington, 1997).

Understanding Service

This section highlights the conceptual underpinning of this study. Specifically, it will bring to attention the differences between services and goods, as these phenomena are often conflated (Parry, et al., 2011). Thus, there are a range of differences between goods and services; the former is tangible, while the latter is intangible (Parry et al., 2011). Essentially goods are product or objects that are manufactured, transported, stored, marketed, and sold to customers and/or consumers (Gadrey, 2000). On the other hand, services entail outputs of individuals, which can be individualistic or collective performance or action by a specific individual (Breivik, 1995). Contemporarily, all products purchased or sold involve service. For instance, professional activities including postal service, sales and purchasing have elements of service. Additionally, some goods rely on service-based activities for them to have value in use as well as marketing edge over rivals in the same market (Palmer, 2014). It is to this end that it is often problematic to differentiate goods from services. However, the main disparity between goods and services is tangibility (Parry et al., 2011). Therefore, while goods are tangible by their nature and design; services are intangible.

Following from the above, services can be defined as performances, deeds, processes, and procedures that are quite different to goods that are perishable and tangible. They are indeed quite different from goods in terms of inseparability, variability, and intangibility (Kotler, 2003). Lovelock & Wright (2002) observe that the intangible nature of service makes it difficult to define. However, it is basically defined as an intangible entity that is exchanged between at least two parties, with no party essentially owing a material product or object given such exchange undertaken (Kotler, 2003). Writers (Solomon & Stuart, 2006; Holloway & Beatty, 2003; Fisk, Brown & Bitner, 1993) have noted that services differ from goods in a range of ways. Nevertheless, there are five main ways that services differ from goods, and these are:

- Perishability
- Inseparability
- Intangibility
- Ownership
- Heterogeneity

In terms of intangibility, this implies that services are not physical objects in contrast with goods. Services are not palpable and cannot be seen or felt before purchase (Kotler, 2003). As argued by Bateson (1979) intangibility is the most crucial feature of service. It is this characteristic that makes services different from goods. Some scholars (Bielen & Sempels, 2003) have criticised this characteristic of service, arguing that there could be some aspects of tangibility in services, including for example surgery in healthcare; and food and drinks consumed on airplanes. For instance, Gummesson (2000) maintains that there is some form of tangibility in some services including in healthcare.

In terms of services, inseparability can be defined as the lack of feasibility in separating a service from its provider (Palmer, 2011; Kotler & Armstrong, 2010). It is further argued by Palmer (2011) that services and their providers are inseparable when production and consumption is indissoluble. In terms of heterogeneity, Bateson (1995) argues that there is no standardisation of service. It is relative even when provided by a specific provider. Thus, each provider offers a unique service, which cannot be exactly repeated even by the particular provider. Thus, heterogeneity is the standardisation of the quality of service as well as standards from the perspective of the customer. In view of the subjective nature of service, there is no consistency in terms of a *perfect level* of service, as services are viewed differently by customers (Lashley, 1988). In addition, service cannot be stored, sold, and returned or resold (Palmer, 2014, 2011), which makes it imperishable. Goods naturally have a longer life span and are non-perishable in most instances. For example, a car manufacturer like Mercedes can carry forward stocks not sold in a season to another season. In contrast, this is not the same with service, as it cannot be transferred from one season to another. Fifth, the inability/failure to own a service is associated with intangibility and perishability (Kotler, 1982). When goods are sold, the purchaser lawfully and rightfully owns the goods; this contrasts with services that cannot be owned. Consequently, the absence of ownership emphasises the finite nature of services regarding purchasers/customers (Lovestock & Gummesson, 2004).

The Rise of Services Marketing Literature

Services are becoming crucial to almost everything we do, and therefore there has been a paradigm shift from a manufacturing-based economy to a service-based economy (Drucker, 1993). Marketing theorists have argued that services are different from goods and should be studied carefully to see how national economies can grow as well as achieve a competitive advantage based on service (Daniel et al., 2015). Three stages have been identified and developed by scholars including the *crawling out phase* (pre-1980); the *scurrying about phase* (1980-1985); and the *walking erect phase* (1986 to present). Research undertaken in these phases takes into consideration phenomena like customer satisfaction (Olivia & MacMillan, 1992; Bitner, 1990), service quality (Parasuranan, et al., 2003; Bolton & Drew, 1991), and service delivery (Kotler, 2003; Butler & Collins, 2001). Table 1 offers details of the differences between manufacturing and service economies.

Table 1. Comparing manufacturing and service economies

Aspects	Manufacturing economy	Service economy
Tangibility of production inputs	Tangible: Raw materials	Intangible: Knowledge and skills
Tangibility of production outputs	Tangible: Products produced can be touched	Intangible: Services have no physical presence and cannot be touched
Variability of production process	Standardised: Goods produced are expected to be standardised; Small allowance for deviations	Heterogeneous: Service involves interaction between the service provider and recipient; Changing situations and personalisation of service result in heterogeneity
Production and consumption process	Separable: Production and consumption processes are separated	Inseparable: Production and consumption are simultaneous
Organisational structure	Centralised: Decisions are made by authorities high in organisational hierarchy Formalised	Decentralised: Localised decision-making is encouraged
Organisational value	Capital assets	Human assets
Assumptions of workers	Machine-like	Autonomous
Expected roles of workers	Operators of machines	Innovators
Desirable attributes of workers	Semi-skilled: Controllable Predictable	Highly skilled and professional: Creative, Motivated, Possess competencies and knowledge

Source: Modified from Daniel et al., 1993, p. 206-207

Service Failures

Fundamental to the consideration of the delivery of service and its quality is service failure and recovery (Armistead, et al., 1995; Bitner et al., 1994). Service failures are unavoidable and can occur in both the process and outcome of a service offering/delivery (Siu et al., 2013). This entails instances when a service fails to live up to the billings of its promise (Armistead et al., 1995) and when the process through which service is delivered is faulty (Lewis & McCaan, 2004). It can also occur where stakeholders' expectations are not met (Bitner et al, 1990). Service failure can be defined as service performance that fails in meeting the expectations of a customer or stakeholder (Varela-Neira et al., 2010; Bell, 2003; Hess, et al., 2003). Service failure:

- Is a situation in which a customer or stakeholder perception of service fails to equate to his/her expectation (Bitner et al,1990).

- Is a condition where a business provider (or business) fails to meet the customer's or stakeholders' expectations about its product? It occurs when the customer or stakeholder finds service to be improper (Armistead et al., 1995).
- Is a situation in which customers or stakeholders' view of the services received fails to meet their expectations (Lewis & McCaan, 2004).

Central to the above definitional perspectives are two main categories of service failure encounters which are *process-oriented failure* and *outcome-oriented failure* (Hess et al., 2003; Bitner et al, 1990). Whilst outcome failure denotes what stakeholders', customers or purchasers receive from services rendered; the process-oriented dimension takes into consideration the way the providers of a service handle service failure while recovering service that has failed (Armistead et al., 1995).

Service Failure Typologies

Service failures have been classified by Bitner et al. (1990) in relation to employee actions/behaviour when failures occur in relation to: requests, core services, and unexpected employee actions. Other studies have included another typology, which is the *problematic customer or stakeholder* (Bitner, et al., 1994). Research by Hoffman et al., (1995) includes policy failures, which is at the heart of MNCs' activities in Nigeria. Furthermore, Johnston (1995) categorised the sources of service failure as organisational culture or the *customer or stakeholder group*. Additionally, Armistead et al. (1995) developed three more classifications: *customer error, service provider error and related organisational error*. The various consequences of service failure include:

- A decrease in employee commitment, performance, and morale (Bitner et al., 1994);
- Negative word-of-mouth (Siu et al., 2013; Mattila, 2001);
- Dissatisfaction (Thomassen et al., 2019);
- Customer or stakeholder defection (Lewis & McCaan, 2004; Hess et al., 2003);
- Loss of return on investment (ROI) and revenue as well as increased cost (Johnston, 1994; Bitner et al., 1990); and
- Decreases in customer or stakeholder confidence.

In extending the above, Meuter, et al., (2000) further identified four more categories of service failure as indicated below:

- Poor design of service (for example if a customer finds it hard to interact with a webpage).
- Process failure (e.g., goods that were ordered fail to reach the purchaser/customer).
- Technical failures (for instance if a website is not working temporarily).
- Customer or stakeholder-oriented failures (for example in instances where a login does fail to work, or a customer forgets or loses their password).

Service Failure in the Oil and Gas Industry

There have been a range of catastrophic incidents and/or accidents in the petroleum (oil and gas) industry globally in countries such as Kuwait, Venezuela, the United States of America, the United Kingdom, and Nigeria, to name a few (Vaaland & Heide, 2008). Most of these catastrophic accidents were largely due to material failures in which workers were killed, in addition to the ecological and environmental damages and crises. For example, in 1993, a natural gas pipeline in Venezuela exploded triggering a catastrophe, which led to the deaths of at least 50 people. Similarly, in Nigeria there have been cases of oil pipeline explosions causing deaths, devastation, and damage in various communities in the Niger Delta (Omodanisi et al., 2014). A range of other factors can be responsible for such disastrous failures including improper manufacturing, the poor design of products and engineering, oil spillages, inappropriate pipe joinery, and/or corrosion, and low-grade raw materials in the pipe production, which can cause incidents. Omodanisi et al. (2014, p. 69) added that *oil spillages are known to have displaced farmsteads and destroyed farmlands, ancestral homes, lives, and properties. They have caused ecological instability in the Niger Delta region in Nigeria.*

In general, failure occurs in the petroleum industry when a system of operation no longer conforms to its design intent (Makhlouf & Aliofkhazraei, 2015). Service failure may include decreased component stiffness, leakages, an increased rate of corrosive decay, inappropriate refining extraction processes and increased operating and maintenance costs, amongst others. Failures may occur outside the remit of service, and can happen during development, the assembly of products, production, or transportation. Forms of failure can include fractures, mechanical malfunctions, and/or unexpected behaviour resulting in customer or stakeholder dissatisfaction (Lewis & McCann, 2004). Service failures and safety incidents have been experienced in the petroleum industry for many decades (Lindgreen & Swaen, 2010) without warning and with unpredictable amounts of consequential damage to safety, health, business reputations, and the environment (Lindgreen, et al., 2012). This makes the oil and gas industry one of the most controversial industries (Lindgreen and Swaen, 2010). Therefore, an effective failure analysis process and set of guidelines should be established and implemented to prevent the recurrence of service failures in the petroleum industry.

Disastrous failures including the Deepwater Horizon oil spill in 2010 have precipitated amplified attention towards the lack of CSR in the sector, which has undermined trust, satisfaction, and confidence in communities in Nigeria's Niger Delta (Eweje, 2007). Some of the issues raised by stakeholders when failure occurs are a lack of transparency, accountability, and responsibility on the part of oil companies, which elicit wider stakeholder criticism of operations (Idemudia, 2009). Indeed, in the Nigerian situation, service failure is common knowledge, as seen in the unremittingly corporate-stakeholder conundrum in the petroleum sector and its associated crisis in the region (Ite, 2004). This situation has been identified as *the oil curse*, a form of *resource curse* (Auty, 1993) and a *paradox of plenty* thesis (Karl, 1997), which entails the presence of oil wealth that brings more harm than good. This paradox entails that the Nigerian government, civil societies, nongovernmental organizations (NGOs), and the people will continually seek the means to control oil and gas production in the region to minimize the risk of harm and to offer redress should service failure occurs.

Consequently, the oil and gas industry has faced a myriad of criticism for decades, which has prompted various guidelines, regulations and principles aimed at curbing companies' excesses in oil production and refining (McWilliams & Siegel, 2001). Nevertheless, public pressure on firms to be socially responsible and environmentally friendly in their operation to improve social performance is more ubiquitous now following corporate failure globally (Lindgreen et al., 2012). MNCs in developing nations, where legal, political, and social infrastructure is lacking, face considerable pressure to fill governance gaps (Frynas, 2009; Ite, 2004) through investing in social sustainable development (Hamann & Kapelus, 2004).

Thus, socially responsible behaviour and understanding the triggers of a failure are vital to drive well-informed business choices about service recovery strategies as well as for mitigating future failures. A failure analysis can reveal deficiencies in the oil and gas production and transportation as well as in system design to avoid future failures.

Service Recovery

According to Miller, et al., (2000) service recovery can be described as activities involving those *actions designed to resolve problems, alter negative attitudes of dissatisfied stakeholders' or customers and to ultimately retain these customers* (p. 38). It also takes into consideration situations in which a service failure happens, but no complaints are lodged by the stakeholder or customer (Lewis & McCaan, 2004, p. 7). As such, it is the actions and efforts made by a service provider that have consequences for service failure (Krishna et al., 2011). These actions also involve operational strategies that are suitably designed and implemented to recognise stakeholders' or customers who have complaints or issues. Such strategies seek to address these complaints to attain stakeholder or customer loyalty and retention (La & Choi, 2018; Miller et al., 2000).

Characteristically, when a service failure occurs, a stakeholder or customer will expect a form of compensation (Choi & La, 2013; Grewal et al., 2008) for inconvenience caused, including an acknowledgement of the failure by the organisation. Such failure can be mitigated using discounts, refunds, apologies or a combination of some of these (Hess et al., 2003). Extant literature suggests that when an organisation fails to satisfy a stakeholder or customer this can lead to brand hate (Carroll & Ahuvia, 2006), stakeholder or customer defection (Lewis & McCann, 2004; Keaveney, 1995), loss of returns on investment (Harris & Reynolds, 2003), reductions in stakeholder or customer loyalty (Lewis & McCaan, 2004,) and total avoidance of a product, or service dissatisfaction (Grewal et al., 2008). In the long run, the success of a firm is linked to a successful recovery experience (La & Choi, 2018; Weun et al., 2004; Krishna et al., 2011).

Strategies for Service Recovery

The available literature reveals that service failure and recovery strategies are part of a five-fold process including the occurrence of failure (Gustafsson, 2008; Keaveney, 1995); the provision of service recovery (Lewis & McCaan, 2004); the generation of recovery expectations (Weun et al., 2004); recovery evaluation (Kuo & Wu, 2012; Wirtz & Mattila, 2004); and the involvement of stakeholders' or customers in post-recovery actions (Kim et al., 2009). Nevertheless, effective management and recovery methods can be instrumental in strengthening relationships with stakeholders (such as communities or customers), which can enhance *recovery satisfaction* (Choi & Lai, 2013, p. 224) and this can remove the service recovery paradox, rather than build brand loyalty, relationships, and trust (Kim et al., 2009; Keaveney, 1995). One of the strategies for effective, sustained competitive advantage following service failure and recovery effort is CSR (Okazakia et al., 2020).

Successful recovery strategies have significant advantages for the organisation, particularly those in the petroleum industry. They include the following:

- Building of stakeholders' trust, loyalty, and satisfaction.
- Cordial corporate-stakeholder relationship.
- Enhancement of stakeholders' perceptions of ethical organization.
- Positive word-of-mouth.
- Sustainable competitive edge.

- Return on investment (ROI) (Fatma et al., 2016; Gustafsson, 2008).

Nevertheless, the degree of success relies on the following:

- The speed of corporate response and intervention.
- The nature and type of failure.
- The type and nature of service (Lewis & McCann, 2004).

Stakeholder Trust, Loyalty, and Satisfaction in Service Recovery

After a service failure occurs, managing the recovery process is crucial given its importance to recovery satisfaction (Bitner et al., 1990). This situation can be aggravated when an *expectation-disconfirmation* situation occurs, following Oliver's (1989) framework. Stakeholders' are frequently more dissatisfied by a firm's inability to properly recover from service failure than by the service failure itself (Siu et al., 2013; Keaveney, 1995). As noted by Bitner et al. (1994, 90) failed recovery efforts are acknowledged as a main cause of why stakeholders' or customers switch to other service providers. Dissatisfaction owing to inadequate and unsuitable responses to an instance of service failure is considered a *double deviation* (Bitner et al., 1990) and can lead to stakeholder or customer defection (Parasuranan et al., 2003; Lewis & McCaan, 2004) and decreased re-patronage intentions (Bolton & Drew, 1991). Consequently, dissatisfaction is likely to have a negative effect on perceived CSR (Okazakia et al., 2020; Fatma & Rahman, 2016). Consistent with this notion, Lewis & McCaan (2004) have found that a poor recovery strategy could lead to a loss of confidence in stakeholders' or customers triggering switch or displeasure and complaints.

Furthermore, service recovery is fundamental to stakeholder or customer trust, satisfaction, loyalty, and justice (Siu et al., 2013). Given that service recovery experience offers stakeholders' or customers an opportunity to re-evaluate a service provider based on assessment of a service provided, customer satisfaction during recovery encounters will have an impact on the perceptions of CSR (Fatma & Rahman, 2016). Satisfaction during recovery can lead, not only to increased customer loyalty and the spread of positive word-of-mouth but also to more positive views of CSR (Siu et al., 2013). For example, a stakeholder or customer, who has experienced service failure, may encounter intimidating and deceitful behaviour by an organisation that has provided such service. The organisation might be unwilling to address a concern in an effective and timely manner. Such a stakeholder or customer is likely to be dissatisfied with the service recovery procedure and would most likely develop negative perceptions of the organisation's CSR. In supporting this contention, Tax,

Brown, and Chandrashekaran's (1998) concluded that positive prior service encounters reduce and/or buffer the negative effects of poor complaint handling on stakeholder or customer trust and loyalty. Similarly, other empirical works have emphasised that organisations that have a history of good reputation and high-quality performance delivery, are usually protected in instances of service failure as stakeholders' or customers spread positive word-of-mouth (Hess et al., 2003; Tax et al., 1998). In contrast, research has underlined that customer relationships can intensify negative customer responses during service failure encounters (see Thomassen et al., 2019; Coulter & Coulter, 2002). For instance, Goodman et al. (1995) found that customer dissatisfaction with service leads to dissatisfaction with the organisation amongst highly involved customers.

Trust in a service delivery encounter relates to perceptions of the service provider's honesty, integrity, ethicality and confidentiality (Siu et al., 2013). In a survey undertaken by CEOs at the Business Roundtable Institute for Corporate Ethics (2004) it was indicated that one of top issues in business ethics is associated with the need to regain public trust. In line with this insight, Svensson & Wood (2004) offered a conceptual approach for business ethics and trust, arguing that corporate ethics impact customer trust (Tax et al., 1998). Accordingly, Kim, Kim & Kim (2009) maintain that adherence to ethical standards offers the basis for trust and helps organisations to build strong reputational capital. This facilitates the delivery of quality services. Gwinner et al., (1998) and Morgan & Hunt (1994) argue that customer purchase intentions wane when the behaviour of a service provider is perceived as dishonest or unethical (Gwinner et al., 1998). They further specify that the psychological advantage of trust and belief is more important than the social benefits of the firm-customer nexus. Additionally, Gundlach & Murphy (1993) contend that applying ethical codes helps an organisation to build sustainable relationships with stakeholders' or customers. Given that consumers become even more sensitive to ethical issues after service failure, a connection between customer loyalty and perceptions is also expected after service failure and recovery. Consequently, this study maintains that perceived CSR will have a positive effect on both external and internal stakeholders' loyalty after service failure and recovery. See figure 1 for stakeholders' wheel.

Figure 1. The stakeholder wheel
Source: The Author, 2021: Redrawn from Freeman et al, 2007

CSR and Service Recovery Linkage

CSR and ethics are related and can be used interchangeably in certain contexts (Christensen, et al., 2007). Amongst a myriad of perspectives on the disparities between business ethics and CSR, the most widely supported approach proposes that CSR has many dimensions, and one of these is business ethics (Christensen, et al., 2007). More precisely, it is proposed that CSR is a broad notion comprising of four dimensions (Carroll, 1991): philanthropic, ethical, legal, and economic. To investigate the advantages of CSR as a marketing instrument, Salmones, et al., (2005) examined the elements and structure of the phenomenon of social responsibility. Salmones, et al. (2005) noted that there are three dimensions to the concept including philanthropic, economic, and ethical-legal responsibilities.

The mainstream research has focused essentially on the philanthropic dimension that is related to cause-related marketing (Berger & Kanetkar, 1995), while downplaying research on other elements. Nonetheless, as compared to the philanthropic dimension, the ethical-legal dimension will be quite relevant to this thesis. As argued by Salmones, et al. (2005) the ethical-legal considerations are more closely associated with corporate ethics within the context of service failure and recovery; hence, they make clear that there are explicit circumstances in which the organisation's ethical standing and image is at stake (Salmones et al., 2005). Earlier research confirms that CSR affects consumer product and service responses either directly or indirectly (Brown & Dacin, 1997). Additionally, there are a range of other relationship between CSR and service recovery including stakeholder or customer-company identification (Salmones et al., 2005), customer attitudes toward a product (Klein & Dawar, 2004), and positive stakeholder or consumer views of CSR in relation to favourable evaluations and attitudes toward companies (Choi & La, 2013). Nevertheless, the effect of stakeholder or customer satisfaction, trust and loyalty following CSR for sustainable development has not been explored in the Nigerian context. This is the mainstay of this study. Currently firms are often deemed unethical in their activities because there is sometimes little or no integration of CSR into marketing strategies when services fail, which is central to recovery (Choi & La, 2013) and organisational justice (Kuo & Wu, 2012) for sustainable development. Failure to apply appropriate service recovery strategies can lead to a plethora of issues highlighted above including brand aversion, organisational failure, poor organisational image, decreased ROI and a lack of sustainable business (KPMG, 2017; Hamann & Kapelus, 2004; WBCSD, 1992).

Figure 2. CSR Pyramid
Source: Carroll, 1991

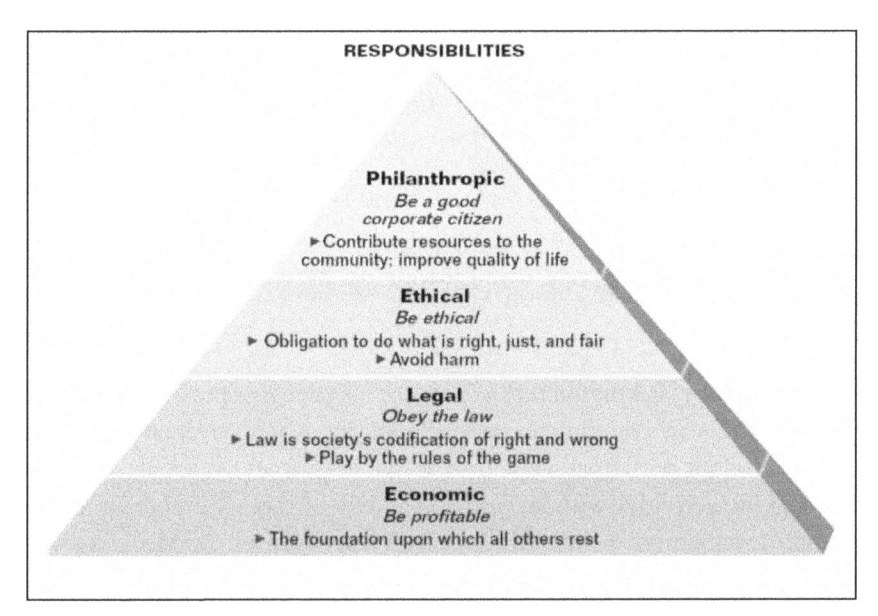

Untangling Sustainable Development Discourse

Sustainable development as a construct or concept is essential to the objective of various organisations, businesses, institutions, and comparable construct aimed at tackling underdevelopment globally (Filho & Brandli, 2018; Elkington, 1997). Within the remit of this chapter's conceptualisation and philosophy, sustainable development entails a democratised and inclusive process that produces and pursues a vision of the community respecting as well as making prudent use of its resources –natural, human, cultural, social and others – for conflict-free and peaceful relationship (Hemmati, 2002). Additionally, as variously argued (see Visser, 2013; Desjardins, 2000) sustainable development came to the fore out of the recognition that economic development particularly on a global level cannot be divorced from fundamental issues such as social justice and ecological stability (Desjardins, 2000). This process elucidates that doing business should not put at risk the wellbeing of the environment and the people now and in the future (Visser, 2013; Crowther & Aras; Bebbington, 1999).

Figure 3. Sustainability triad
Source: The Author, 2021

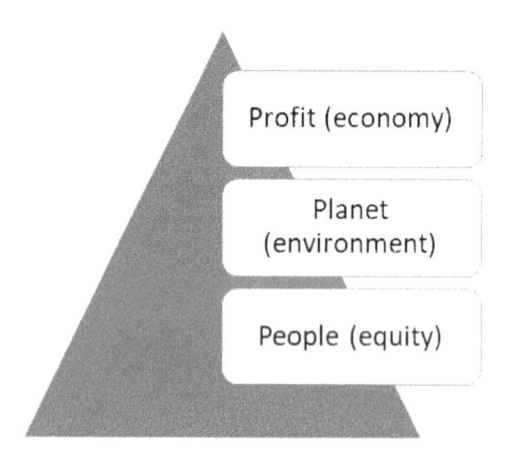

As remarked by Elkington (1997), these challenges present businesses – specifically MNCs in Nigeria's extractive industry – with a dilemma regarding about how to adopt participatory and sustainable business practices and engage in profit-making activities without prioritising any of these variables to deal with sustainable development goals (SDGs) challenges (Jensen & Meckling, 1976). Indeed, the Brundtland Report emphasised three key dimensions of sustainable development such as social equity, economic growth, and environmental protection (Crowther & Aras, 2008; Elkington, 1997). The three interconnected *pillars* (Basiago 1999) notion of sustainable development parallel Elkington's (1997) three pillars of sustainability (Triple bottom line) as seen in Figure 3: profit (economy), people (equity) and planet (environment) are given. Elkington (1997) further noted that such inclusive, democratic, and inclusive business model will advance the rhetoric of win-win approach (Williams & Preston, 2018) for both MNCs and wider society (Sharma & Ruud, 2003).

Sustainable Development Logic

Thus, sustainable development logic (sustainability triad) is central to the tenets of SDGs as seen in Figure 4. Figure 4 highlights the 17 SDGs and their descriptions.

Figure 4. The 17 SDGs and explanations
Source: The Author, 2021

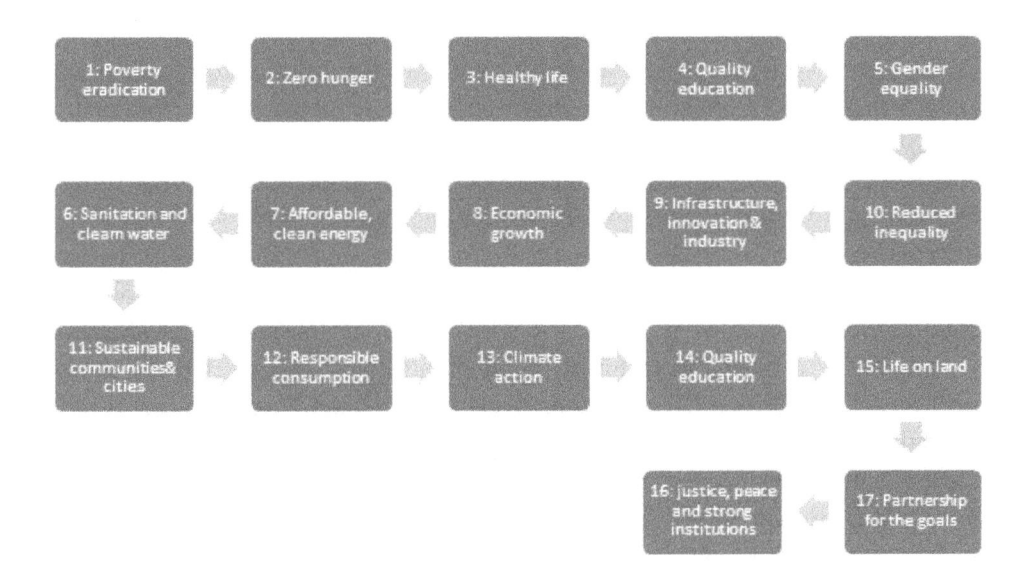

Though SDGs construct has attracted considerable inquiry in the policy circuit, academic discourse and research enterprise including the business-society interface, sustainability, business development, and business management, however, how they affect MNCs' operations is under-researched (Crowther & Aras, 2008). This is the mainstay of this chapter. It has further been contended that MNCs in Nigeria are still far from engaging in sustainable practice and development (Visser, 2013) as well as ensuring that the tenets of sustainable development are achieved (Crowther & Aras, 2008). As Idemudia (2010) argues, these goals are not yet realised given the ascendancy of profit maximisation at the detriment of sustaining their relationship with stakeholders and incidence of this practice on the environment and people in developing countries like Nigeria (Obi, 2010).

CSR, Service Recovery and Sustainable Development

The precursor to sustainable development is sustainability discourse, which began with the reconsideration that economic development on a global level cannot be separated from issues bordering on ecological stability, social justice and equity. CSR is about ensuring that business operations do not harm the chances of future generations to live (Hamann & Kapelus, 2004; WBCSD, 1992). Desjardins (2000) also noted that sustainable development arrived in the wake of reconceptualising the role business can play in sustaining the world without jeopardising the wellbeing of people and the environment now and in the future (Kolk & Tulder, 2010; Barbier, 1987).

Additionally, sustainable development discourse occurred in the wake of rethinking economic growth and the environmental and social benefits derivable when businesses address social and environmental concerns such as using business strategy and justice theory to fight poverty, social exclusion, inequality, and environmental devastation for a more sustainable world (Visser, 2013; Zwan & Bhamra, 2003). This rationality resonates with what Zwan & Bhamra (2003, p. 341) refer to as *eco-efficient services* in services marketing for sustainable development. It also has parallels with sustainability marketing, which takes into consideration building and fostering sustainable relationships with varied organisational stakeholders including customers and communities. Sustainability marketing, which is also called green marketing, ecological marketing, responsible marketing and environmental marketing shares the long-term supposition of relationship marketing, in contrast with the conventional short-term transaction-based orientation of modern marketing (Ginsberg & Bloom, 2004). The paradigm shift to sustainability marketing partly includes the incorporation of environmental and social principles into conventional marketing literature and conceptualisation.

The idea of MNCs in Nigeria working ethically through, for example their marketing services resonates with social justice, equity and responsible business and investing (Fatma & Rahman, 2016). Consequently, this process entails their incorporation into the rethinking of marketing principles and values including instances that require service recovery. An effective definition of service recovery, thus, should incorporate transformative efforts that create value for society, the individual and the environment in terms of environmental restoration and improvement in the

Niger Delta following service failure. To this end, the notion of service recovery, which is allied to green marketing, is very different from a marketing approach, which is based on mitigating societal harm. As noted by Polonsky (2011) mankind, marketing and the natural environment are interdependent.

Within a business model, ethical service recovery runs parallel to societal marketing thought, and it advocates the understanding that satisfying stakeholders' or customers is not enough, and organisations should take into consideration the environmental and social interests of stakeholders in general. Such a service marketing philosophy arose from societal marketing (Handelman, & Stephen, 1999). It is a part of CSR (Kotler, Keller, Koshy, & Jha, 2009). It is to this end that Kotler et al. (2009) recommend that organisations should analyse changing stakeholders' or consumers attitudes while identifying the role which they can play in protecting society and the environment to ensure society's wellbeing.

Justice Theory and Service Failure and Recovery Strategies

Little or less research has been undertaken to interrogate the impact of perceived CSR activities and strategies in the context of recovery satisfaction, trust and loyalty for sustainable development following service failure (Bolton & Mattila, 2015). However, the present research seeks to examine the extent to which stakeholders' perceptions and judgments of socially responsible practices amongst MNCs can bring about a change in stakeholders' perceptions following service failure. The study leveraged on *justice theory* from the perspective of interactional justice to gauge whether stakeholders are involved in the recovery strategies employed by MNCs and to determine if these strategies are effective in delivering fairness, justice, and legitimacy for more sustainable business (Gustafsson, 2008).

By adopting the justice approach in this book chapter, the paper intends to demonstrate that justice theory can potentially lead to a better and more nuanced understanding of corporate-stakeholder conflict in Nigeria following service failure (Fatma et al., 2016). In addition, this approach will potentially contribute to the available literature on service failure and recovery as well as to ideas about CSR, which is still at its incipient stage in developing countries (Idemudia, 2010). Organisational justice theory considers perceptions and opinions of fairness in organisational operations by categorising stakeholders' feelings and views about how they are treated as well as others within a given organisation (Palmer, 2014; Greenberg, 1987; Brown, 1986; Adams, 1965; Homans, 1961). Guided by the assumption that issues and phenomena associated with justice are relevant in conflict situation (Tax et al., 1998), service marketing scholarship proposes the significance and relevance of justice as a conceptual/theoretical lens for studying and elucidating stakeholder-firm nexus (Siu et al., 2013; Goodwin & Ross; 1992; Tax et al., 1998).

As noted by Siu et al (2013) three justice approaches are central to justice theory including distributive (perceptions about outcomes in relation to decisions), interactional (fairness in relation to personal treatment and how it is communicated) and procedural justice (perception of fairness and process) (Siu et al., 2013; Gustafsson, 2008; Greenberg, 1987). For instance, in relation to online recovery context, distributive justice entails whether failed stakeholders' or customers received tangible compensation such as money, discounts, coupons and free upgrades and refunds (Kuo & Wu, 2012), which are aspects of the recovery action (Gelbrich & Roschk, 2011). Examples of procedural justice include the speed at which an organisation remedies or recovers a failed service as well as communicates with stakeholders or customers (Sparks & McColl-Kennedy, 2001). Finally, examples of interactional justice take into consideration the way and way service failure by an organisation is handled or how such failure is communicated to the stakeholder or customer by a service provider (Son & Kim, 2008). For example, Rio-Lanza, et al., (2009) notes the interface between *fairness or perceived justice*, emotions and satisfaction of the service recovery *process* (Gustafsson (2008, p. 1221). They conclude that all the three justice dimensions affect satisfaction in relation to recovery process. It is based on these justice perspectives that the present study derived much of its theoretical/conceptual framing.

SOLUTIONS AND RECOMMENDATIONS

Revealed literatures have shown that service recovery is fundamental to stakeholders' trust, satisfaction, loyalty, and justice (Gustafsson, 2008; Lewis & McCaan, 2004). The MNC's in Nigeria oil & gas industry should acknowledge that successful recovery strategies have significant advantages for the organisations especially in the petroleum industry hence there is need to build on and gain stakeholders' trust, loyalty and satisfaction; cordial corporate-stakeholders' relationship; sustainable competitive edge; return on investment (ROI); positive word-of-mouth; and enhancement of stakeholders' perceptions of ethical organisation (Weun, et al., 2004; Kim, et al., 2009). However, the outlined success can be attained based on the speed of corporation response and intervention; the nature and type of failure; and the type and nature of service. Nevertheless, MNC's in Nigerian should tend to integrate CSR into their marketing strategies; use sustainable development to tackle underdevelopment in Nigeria; adapt participatory and sustainable business practices and engage in profit making activities without prioritising any of these variables to deal with sustainable development goals challenges including: social equality; economic growth; and environmental protection. A proper implementation of the researcher recommendations will see the MNCs in Nigeria oil & gas industry regain public trust and minimise stakeholders' conflicts in the region.

FUTURE RESEARCH DIRECTIONS

This research was done within Nigeria context, and further research could be done within Africa context or even globally. The research theoretically used qualitative method that relied on words and theory development. Further research can apply quantitative method that test theory and aligns with figures and numbers. In addition, this research applied interactional justice, and further research can apply either distributive justice or procedural justice or even both to examine the relationship between CSR, service failure, and recovery strategies for sustainable business.

This contention has implications for justice theory and corporate sustainability and places the thrust of this study within the remit of CSR, justice, and sustainable development (Thomassen et al., 2019; KPMG, 2017).

Although service failure and recovery is at a nascent stage, to date there is little or no known research in Nigeria that has examined the relationship between CSR, service failures and recovery strategies for sustainable business. This is the mainstay of the current and further research (Fatma et al., 2016).

CONCLUSION

This study demonstrates how service recovery can be utilised in the process of service failure and gain sustainable development in the Nigeria context. The study illustrates how the presence of oil and gas multinational corporations (MNCs) has contributed to the destruction and pollution of the environment and related phenomena in the Niger delta region, which produces oil in Nigeria. It highlighted on the major differences between services and goods and the rise of service marketing in literature in consideration to the identified three stages which includes crawling out, scurrying about, and walking erect phases. It also identified service failures and the two main categories of service failures such as process-oriented failure and outcome-oriented failure. Service failure typologies and service failure in the oil and gas industry were further identified. Service recovery approach, strategies for service recovery as a five-fold process, and CSR as a recovery strategy were explained, including a discussion of why organisations engage in CSR. CSR as a marketing instrument and its four dimensions of elements of social responsibility including philanthropic, ethical, legal and economic and the linkage between CSR and service recovery were explored. The perceptions and responses of stakeholders following service failure and stakeholder approaches to stakeholder theory and stakeholder trust, loyalty and satisfaction were also considered. The study presented three justice approaches such as distribution, interaction and procedural justice and leveraged from the perspective of interactional justice to gauge whether stakeholders are involved in the recovery strategies employed by MNCs and to determine if these strategies are effective in delivering fairness, justice, and legitimacy for more sustainable business.

The process of untangling sustainable development discourse elucidates that in doing business, the wellbeing of the environment and the people now and in the future should not be put at risk. The study further advocates that organisation should address social and environmental concerns by way of using business strategy to fight poverty, social exclusion, inequality, and environmental devastation for a more sustainable world. An effective definition of service recovery, therefore, should incorporate transformative efforts that create value for society, the individual and the environment in terms of environmental restoration and improvement in the Niger delta following service failure. This study, therefore, maintained that, by operationalising the tenets of ethical service recovery in times of service failure, such actions have the potential to contribute to social prosperity, economic growth, and environmental protection as well as social justice and equity.

REFERENCES

Adams, J. S. (1965). Inequity in Social Exchange. In Advances in experimental social psychology. New York: Academic Press.

Amao, O. (2008). Corporate Social Responsibility. Multinational Corporations and the Law in Nigeria: Controlling Multinationals in Host States. *Journal of African Law*, 52(1), 89–113.

Armistead, C. G., Clark, G., & Stanley, P. (1995). Managing Service Recovery, Cranfield School of Management. Cranfield.

Auty, R. (1993). *Sustaining development in mineral economies*. Routledge.

Barbier, E. B. (1987). The Concept of Sustainable Economic Development. *Environmental Conservation*, 14(2), 101–110.

Basiago, A. D. (1999). Economic, social, and environmental sustainability in development theory and urban planning practice. *Sustainability Science 123 Environmentalist*, 19(1), 145–161.

Bateson, F. A. (1995). SERVQUAL: Review, critique, research agenda. *European Journal of Marketing*, 30(1), 8–32.

Bebbington, A. (1999). *Capitals and capabilities*. International Institute for Environment and Development.

Berger, I. E., & Kanetkar, V. (1995). Increasing Environmental Sensitivity via Workplace Experiments. *Journal of Public Policy & Marketing, 14*(2), 205–215.

Berry, L. L. (1995). Relationship marketing of services – growing interest emerging perspectives. *Journal of the Academy of Marketing Science, 23*(4), 236–245.

Bielen, F., & Sempels, C. (2003). *The dimensionality of the concept of intangibility: A critical analysis.* IAG Working Papers, 2003/100, 2078.1/5427.

Bitner, M. J. (1990). Evaluating service encounters: The effects of physical surroundings and employee responses. *Journal of Marketing, 54*(2), 69–82.

Bitner, M. J., Booms, B. H., & Mohr, L. A. (1994). Critical service encounters: The employees' viewpoint. *Journal of Marketing, 58*(4), 95–105.

Bitner, M. J., Booms, B. H., & Tetreault, M. S. (1990). The service encounter: Diagnosing favourable and unfavourable incidents. *Journal of Marketing, 54*(1), 77–84.

Bolton, L. E., & Mattila, A. S. (2015). How does corporate social responsibility affect customer response to service failure in buyer/seller relationships? *Journal of Retailing, 91*(1), 140-153.

Bolton, R. N., & Drew, J. H. (1991). A multi-stage model of customers' assessments of service quality and value. *The Journal of Consumer Research, 17*(4), 375–384.

Bowen, H. R. (1953). *Social Responsibilities of the Businessman*. Harper & Row.

Breivik, H. (1995). Benefits, risks and economics of post-operative pain management programmes. *Bailliere's Clinical Anaesthesiology, 9*(3), 403–422.

Brown, R. (1986). *Social psychology* (2nd ed.). The Free Press.

Brown, T. J., & Dacin, P. A. (1997). The company and the product: Corporate associations and consumer product responses. *Journal of Marketing, 61*(1), 68–84.

Brundtland, G. (1987). Our Common Future-Call for Action. *Environmental Conservation, 14*(04), 291.

Butler, P., & Collins, N. (2001). Payment on delivery - Recognising constituency service as political marketing. *European Journal of Marketing, 35*(9/10), 1026–1037.

Carroll, A. B. (1991). The pyramid of corporate social responsibility: Towards the moral management of organisational stakeholders. *Business Horizons, 34*(4), 39–48.

Carroll, A. B., & Ahuvia, A. C. (2006). Some antecedents and outcomes of brand love. *Marketing Letters*, *17*, 79–89.

Cho, S.-B., Jang, Y. M., & Kim, W. G. (2017). The Moderating Role of Severity of Service Failure in the Relationship among Regret/Disappointment, Dissatisfaction, and Behavioural Intention. *Journal of Quality Assurance in Hospitality & Tourism*, *18*(1), 69–85.

Choi, B. & La, S. (2013). The impact of corporate social responsibility (CSR) and customer trust on the restoration of loyalty after service failure and recovery. *Journal of Services Marketing*, *27*(3), 223-233.

Christensen, L. J., Peirce, E., Hartman, L. P., Hoffman, W. M., & Carrier, J. (2007). Ethics, CSR, and sustainability education in the financial times top 50 global business schools: Baseline data and future research directions. *Journal of Business Ethics*, *73*(4), 347–368.

Coulter, K. S., & Coulter, R. A. (2002). Determinants of trust in a service provider: The moderating role of length of relationship. *Journal of Services Marketing*, *16*(1), 35–50.

Crowther, D., & Aras, G. (2008). *The Future of Corporate Governance. Electronic Journal, A Prognosis.*

Daniel, T. L. S., Po, P. Y. C., & Hildie, L. (2015). Manufacturing Economy vs. Service Economy: Implications for Service Leadership. *International Journal on Disability and Human Development: IJDHD*, *14*(3), 205–215.

Desjardins, D. (2000). *Gales guide to genealogical & historical research*. Gale Group.

Drucker, P. F. (1993). *Concept of the corporation*. Transaction Publishers.

Du, J., Fan, X., & Feng, T. (2010). An experimental investigation of the role of face in service failure and recovery encounters. *Journal of Consumer Marketing*, *27*(7), 584–593.

Elkington, J. (1997). *Cannibals with forks: The triple bottom line of 21st century business*. Capstone Publishing Ltd.

Eweje, G. (2007). Multinational oil companies' CSR initiatives in Nigeria. *Managerial Law*, *49*(5/6), 218–235.

Fatma, M., Khan, I., & Rahman, Z. (2016). The effect of CSR on consumer behavioural responses after service failure and recovery. *European Business Review*, *28*(5), 583–599.

Filho, W. L., & Brandli, L. (2018). Engaging Stakeholders for Sustainable Development. In *Engaging Stakeholders in Education for Sustainable Development at University level* (pp. 335–342). Springer.

Fisk, R., Brown, S., & Bitner, M. (1993). Tracking the evolution of the services marketing literature. *Journal of Retailing*, *69*(1), 61–103.

Freeman, E. R., Harrison, J. S., & Wicks, A. C. (2007). Managing for stakeholders: survival, reputation, and success. Yale University Press.

Frynas, J. G. (2005). The false promise of corporate social responsibility: Evidence form multinational oil companies. *International Affairs*, *81*(3), 581–598.

Frynas, J. G. (2009). *Beyond corporate social responsibility*. Oxford University Press. doi:10.1017/CBO9780511581540

Frynas, J. G., & Stephens, S. (2015). Political Corporate Social Responsibility: Reviewing Theories and Setting New Agendas. *International Journal of Management Reviews*, *17*(4), 483–509.

Gadrey, J. (2000). The characterization of goods and services: An alternative approach. *Review of Income and Wealth*, *46*(3), 369–387.

Gelbrich, K., & Roschk, H. (2011). A Meta-Analysis of Organizational Complaint Handling and Customer Responses. *Journal of Service Research*, *14*(1), 24–43.

Ginsberg, J. M., & Bloom, P. N. (2004). Choosing the Right Green Marking Strategy. *MIT Sloan Management Review*, *46*(1), 79–84.

Goodman, P., Fichman, M., Lerch, F., & Snyder, P. (1995). Customer-Firm Relationships: Involvement, and Customer Satisfaction. *Academy of Management Journal*, *38*(5), 1310–1324.

Goodwin, C., & Ross, I. (1992). Consumer responses to service failures: Influence of procedural and interactional fairness perceptions. *Journal of Business Research*, *25*(2), 149–163.

Greenberg, J. (1987). A taxonomy of organizational justice theories. *Academy of Management Review*, *12*(1), 9–22.

Grewal, D., Roggeveen, A. L., & Tsiros, M. (2008). The effect of compensation on repurchases intentions in service recovery. *Journal of Retailing*, *84*(4).

Gummesson, E. (2000). *Qualitative Methods in Management Research*. Sag Publications.

Gundlach, G. T., & Murphy, P. E. (1993). Ethical and Legal: Foundations of Relational Marketing Exchanges. *Journal of Marketing, 57*(4), 35–46.

Gustafsson, A. (2008). Customer satisfaction with service recovery. *Journal of Business Research, 62*, 1220–1222.

Gwinner, K. P., Gremler, D. D., & Bitner, M. J. (1998). Relational Benefits in Service Industries: The Customer's Perspective. *Journal of the Academy of Marketing Science, 26*(2), 101–114.

Hamann, R., & Kapelus, P. (2004). Corporate Social Responsibility in Mining in Southern Africa: Fair accountability or just green wash? *Development, 47*(3), 85–92.

Handelman, J., & Arnold, S. (1999). The role of marketing actions with a social dimension: Appeals to the institutional environment. *Journal of Marketing, 63*(3), 33–48.

Harris, L. C., & Reynolds, K. L. (2003). The consequences of dysfunctional customer behaviour. *Journal of Service Research, 6*(2), 144–161.

Hemmati, M. (2002). *Multi-Stakeholder Processes for Governance and Sustainability. Beyond Deadlock and Conflict*. Routlege.

Hess, R. L. Jr, Ganesan, S., & Klein, N. M. (2003). Service failure and recovery: The impact of relationship factors on customer satisfaction. *Journal of the Academy of Marketing Science, 31*(2), 127–145.

Hoffman, K. D., Kelley, S. W., & Rotalsky, H. M. (1995). Tracking service failure and employee recovery efforts. *Journal of Services Marketing, 9*(2), 49–61.

Holloway, B. B., & Beatty, Sh. E. (2003). Service failure in on-line retailing: A recovery opportunity. *Journal of Service Research, 6*(1), 92–105.

Homans, G. C. (1961). *Social behaviour: Its elementary forms*. Routledge and Kegan Paul.

Idemudia, U. (2009). Oil extraction and poverty reduction in the Niger Delta: A critical examination of partnership initiatives. *Journal of Business Ethics, 90*, 91–116.

Idemudia, U. (2010). Rethinking the role of corporate social responsibility in the Nigerian oil conflict: The limits of CSR. *Journal of International Development, 22*(7), 833–845.

Ite, U. E. (2004). Multinationals and corporate social responsibility in developing countries: A case study of Nigeria. *Corporate Social Responsibility and Environmental Management, 11*(1), 1–11.

Jensen, M. C., & Meckling, W. H. (1976). Theory of Firm: Managerial Behaviour, Agency Costs and Ownership Structure. *Journal of Financial Economics*, *3*(4), 305–360.

Johnston, R. (1995). Service failure and recovery: Impact, attributes and process. In T. A. Swartz, D. E. Bowen, & S. W. Brown (Eds.), *Advances in Services Marketing and Management*. JAI Press.

Karl, T. (1997). *The Paradox of Plenty: Oil booms and petro-states*. California University Press. doi:10.1525/9780520918696

Keaveney, S. M. (1995). Customer switching behaviour in service industries: An exploratory study. *Journal of Marketing*, *59*(2), 71–82.

Kelly, S. W., & Davis, M. A. (1994). Antecedents to customer expectations for service recovery. *Journal of the Academy of Marketing Science*, *22*(1), 52–61.

Kim, T., Kim, W. G., & Kim, H. (2009). The effects of perceived justice on recovery satisfaction, trust, word-of-mouth and revisit intention in upscale hotels. *Tourism Management*, *30*, 51–62.

Klein, J., & Dawar, N. (2004). Corporate social responsibility and consumers' attributions and brand evaluations in a product–harm crisis. *International Journal of Research in Marketing*, *21*(3), 203–217.

Kolk, A., & Van Tulder, R. (2010). International business: Corporate social responsibility and sustainable development. *International Business Review*, *19*(2), 119–125.

Kotler, P. (1982). *Marketing for non-profit organisations*. Prentice Hall.

Kotler, P. (2003). *Marketing Management*. Prentice Hall.

Kotler, P., & Armstrong, G. M. (2010). *Principles of Marketing*. Prentice Hall.

Kotler, P., & Keller, K. L. (2009). *A Framework for Marketing Management* (4th ed.). Pearson Education Inc.

Kotler, P., Keller, K. L., & Koshy, M. J. (2009). Marketing Management: A South Asian Perspective (13th ed.). Pearson Prentice Hall.

KPMG. (2017). *KPMG survey of corporate social responsibility reporting*. http.www. home.kpmg

Krishna, A., Dangayach, G. S., & Jain, R. (2011). A conceptual framework for the Service Recovery Paradox. *The Marketing Review*, *11*(1), 41–56.

Kuo, Y.-F., & Wu, C.-M. (2012). Satisfaction and post-purchase intentions with service recovery of online shopping websites: Perspectives on perceived justice and emotions. *International Journal of Information Management, 32,* 127–138.

La, S., & Choi, B. (2019). Perceived justice and CSR after service recovery. *Journal of Services Marketing, 32*(2), 206–219.

Lashley, C. (1988). Matching the management of human resources to service operations. *International Journal of Contemporary Hospitality Management, 10*(1), 24–33.

Lewis, B. R., & McCann, S. (2004). Service failure and recovery in retail banking: The customers' perspective. *International Journal of Bank Marketing, 19*(1), 37–47.

Lii, Y.-S., Ding, M.-C., & Lin, C.-H. (2018). Fair or Unfair: The Moderating Effect of Sustainable CSR Practices on Anticipatory Justice Following Service Failure Recovery. *Sustainability, 10*(12), 1–21.

Lindgreen, A., Maon, F., Reast, J., & Yani-De-Soriano, M. (2012). Guest Editorial: Corporate Social Responsibility in Controversial Industry Sectors. *Journal of Business Ethics, 110*(4), 393–395.

Lindgreen, A., & Swaen, V. (2010). Corporate social responsibility. *International Journal of Management Reviews, 12*(1), 1–7.

Lovelock, C., & Gummesson, E. (2004). Whither Services Marketing? *Journal of Service Research, 7*(1), 20–41.

Lovelock, C. H., & Wright, L. (2002). *Principles of Service Marketing and Management*. Prentice Hall.

Makhlouf, A. S. H., & Aliofkhazraei, M. (2015). *Handbook of materials failure analysis with case studies from the chemicals, concrete and power industries.* Butterworth-Heinemann.

Mattila, A. S. (2001). The effectiveness of service recovery in a multi-industry setting. *Journal of Services Marketing, 15*(7), 583–596.

McWilliams, A., & Siegel, D. (2001). Corporate social responsibility: A theory of the firm perspective. *Academy of Management Review, 26*(1), 117–127.

Meuter, M. L., Ostrom, A. L., Roundtree, R. I., & Bitner, M. J. (2000). Self-service technologies: Understanding customer satisfaction with technology-based service encounters. *Journal of Marketing, 64*(3), 50–64.

Miller, J. L., Craighead, C. W., & Karwan, K. R. (2000). Service recovery: A framework and empirical investigation. *Journal of Operations Management, 18*(4), 387–400.

Morgan, R., & Hunt, S. D. (1994). The commitment: Trust theory of relationship marketing. *Journal of Marketing, 58*(7), 20–38.

Obi, C. (2010). The petroleum industry: A paradox or (SP) oil of development. *Journal of Contemporary African Studies, 28*(4), 443–457.

Okazakia, S., Plangger, K., West, D., & Menendez, H. D. (2020). (in press). Exploring digital corporate social responsibility communications on Twitter. *Journal of Business Research*.

Oliva, T. A., Oliver, R. L., & MacMillan, I. C. (1992). A catastrophe model for developing service satisfaction strategies. *Journal of Marketing, 56*(3), 83–95.

Oliver, R. L. (1989). Processing of the satisfaction response in consumption: A suggested framework and research propositions. *Journal of Consumer Satisfaction, Dissatisfaction and Complaint Behaviour, 2*, 1-16.

Omodanisi, E., Eludoyin, A., & Salami, A. (2014). A multi-perspective view of the effects of a pipeline explosion in Nigeria. *International Journal of Disaster Risk Reduction, 7*, 68–77.

Palmer, A. (2014). Principles of services marketing (7th ed.). McGrawHill Education.

Palmer, J. (2011). How to predict monitoring issues. *World Pumps, 2011*(5), 38–39.

Parasuraman, A., Zeithaml, V., & Berry, L. L. (1993). Research note: More on improving service quality measurement. *Journal of Retailing, 69*(1), 140–147.

Parry, G., Newnes, L., & Huang, X. (2011). Goods, Products and Services. In B. Hefley & W. Murphy (Eds.), *Service design and delivery*. Springer.

Polonsky, M. J. (2011). Transformative Green Marketing: Impediments and Opportunities. *The Journal of Business*.

Rio-Lanza, A. B. D., Vazquez-Casielles, R., & Diaz-Martin, A. M. (2009). Satisfaction with service recovery: Perceived justice and emotional responses. *Journal of Business Research, 62*(8), 775–781.

Salmones, M. G., Crespo, A. H., & Del Bosque, I. R. (2005). Influence of corporate social responsibility on loyalty and valuation of services. *Journal of Business Ethics, 61*(4), 369–385.

Sharma, S., & Ruud, A. (2003). On the Path to Sustainability: Integrating Social Dimensions into the Research and Practice of Environmental Management. *Business Strategy and the Environment, 12*(1), 205–214.

Siu, N. Y., Zhang, T. J., & Yau, C. J. (2013). The roles of justice and customer satisfaction in customer retention: A lesson from service recovery. *Journal of Business Ethics, 114*(4), 75–686.

Solomon, M., & Stuart, E. (2006). *Marketing: Real People, Real Choices*. Pearson.

Son, J. Y., & Kim, S. (2008). Users' information privacy- protective responses: A Taxonomy and Nomological model. *Management Information Systems Quarterly, 32*(3), 503.

Sparks, B. A., & McColl-Kennedy, J. R. (2001). Justice strategy options for increased customer satisfaction in a services recovery setting. *Journal of Business Research, 54*(3), 209–218.

Svensson, G., & Wood, G. (2004). Corporate ethics and trust in intra-corporate relationships: An in-depth and longitudinal case description. *Employee Relations, 26*(3), 320–336.

Tax, S. S., Brown, S. W., & Chandrashekaran, M. (1998). Customer evaluations of service complaint experiences: Implications for relationship marketing. *Journal of Marketing, 62*(2), 60–76.

Thomassen, J. P., Leliveld, M., Ahaus, K., & Van-De Walle, S. (2019). Developing and implementing a service charter for an integrated regional stroke service: An exploratory case study. *BMC Health Services Research, 14*(141), 2–11.

Vaaland, T., & Heide, M. (2008). Managing corporate social responsibility: Lessons from the oil industry. *Corporate Communications, 13*(2), 212–225.

Varela-Neira, C., Vasques-Cassielles, R., & Iglesias, V. (2010). Explaining customer satisfaction with complain handling. *International Journal of Bank Marketing, 29*(2), 88–112.

Visser, W. (2013). *The age of responsibility: CSR 2.0 and the new DNA of business*. Wile.

Weun, S., Beatty, S. E., & Jones, M. A. (2004). The impact of service failure severity on service recovery evaluations and post-recovery relationships. *Journal of Services Marketing, 18*(2), 133–146.

Williams, S., & Preston, D. (2018). Working with values: An alternative approach to win-win. *International Journal of Corporate Strategy and Social Responsibility*, *1*(4), 302–319.

Wirtz, J., & Matilla, A. S. (2004). Consumer responses to compensation: Speed of recovery and apology after a service failure. *International Journal of Service Industry Management*, *15*(2), 150–166.

World Business Council for Sustainable Development. (1992). *Corporate Social Responsibility*. Author.

World Commission on Environment and Development. (1987). *Our common future*. Oxford University Press.

Zwan, F., & Bhamra, T. (2003). Services marketing: Taking up the sustainable development challenge. *Journal of Services Marketing*, *17*(4), 341–356.

Chapter 11
The Shortfalls of the Nigerian Oil and Gas Industry Content Act 2010 in Achieving Sustainable Development

Manuchim Lawrence Adele
Canterbury Christ Church University, UK

ABSTRACT

This chapter examines the impact that the concept of "sustainable development" in the Nigerian oil and gas industry has had and is likely to have upon the development of energy, resources, and economic growth in the future of Nigeria upon the focus and scope of energy, resource, and environmental law practice associated with that development. The chapter will adopt the definition of sustainable development as articulated in the Brundtland Report by the World Commission on Environment and Development. It will examine the legal status of Sections 10 and 12 of the Nigerian Oil Industry Content Development Act 2010 and its implication on international trade and sustainable development. The chapter argues that Sections 10 and 12 of the Nigerian Oil and Gas Industry Content Act 2010 do not reflect the meaning and intention of the Brundtland's definition of sustainable development, which evinces normative values, values of equity, and justice for all.

INTRODUCTION

There are substantial challenges to sustainable development in Nigeria. Following several decades of emphasis on Nigeria's economic growth, there is now a growing

DOI: 10.4018/978-1-7998-7499-7.ch011

concern in Nigeria that development is not just a higher growth of national income, but rather there is a shift which sees economic successes as a means of achieving basic human needs and development, particularly those related to collective and individual wellbeing. This chapter seeks to unravel these challenges by examining them and proposing appropriate measures that can work towards resolving them as far as possible. This chapter argues that section 10 and 12 of the Nigerian Oil and Gas Industry Content Act 2010 does not reflect the meaning and intention of the Brundtland's definition of sustainable development which evinces normative values, values of equity and justice for all.

This Chapter is a positivist examination of the Nigerian Oil and Gas Industry content laws that is purely qualitative in its method. Thus, the paper examines the current law by examining the history of the legislation, the current shape of the law and its current limitation. The argument will be explored in five sections on this paper. Section 1. will introduce this chapter by adopting the definition of sustainable development as articulated in the Brundtland Report by the World Commission on Environment and Development; Section 2 is the background to this study; While Sustainable Development: Impacts on Oil and Gas Development will be discussed in section 3; The Examination of Section 10 and 12 of the Nigerian Oil and Gas Industry Content Development Act 2010 and Its Implication on the International Trade and Sustainable Development will be discussed in section 4; Section 5 will be Solutions-Recommendations; section 6 will be future research directions; and the concluding section is 7. This chapter adopts the Brundtland definition of sustainable development as noted in the report by World Commission on Environment and Development.

BRUNDTLAND DEFINITION OF SUSTAINABLE DEVELOPMENT

According to the Brundtland Report by the World Commission on Environment and Development, sustainable development is the "development that meets the needs of the present without compromising the ability of future generations to meet their own needs" (WCED, 1987). The Brundtland Report highlights the major socio-political changes that sustainable development implies (Baker et al., 1997). These include poverty elimination, equality in global resource distribution, population control, appropriate technology, lifestyle changes, and effective democratization through increased citizen's participation. Susan Baker, (2006) further argues that sustainable development as espoused in the Brundtland Report is promoted as an agent of social change through three interfaces: the social, the economic, and the ecological. Baker opines that sustainable development is an "on-going" process with "desirable characteristics" that changes over time depending on the locational, historical, political, and cultural contexts, and it would be more appropriate to conceive sustainable development as a concept to "promote" rather than to achieve (Ibid).

Notwithstanding, the three-pillar model of sustainable development has been faulted Dawe and Ryan (Dawe & Kell Ryan, 2003). It has been argued that placing the environment in the same pedestal with economic and social concern is faulty logic as the environment founds the basis for any economic or social wellbeing achieved by man. It is asserted, quite forcefully, that environment is the "floor upon which the stool of sustainable development must stand (Ibid)''. Since the environment sustains the economic and social wellbeing of man, it stands to reason that the environment cannot be a stool in the pillar of sustainable development, rather it must be considered exogenous and at a more significant level than either the economy or social well-being of humanity (Ibid).

Bridging the gap in the scheme which focuses on the way and manner the needs of the poor will be fulfilled and curtailing the wants of the rich is the focus of the Brundtland Report (Susan Baker, 2006). One could argue that it is now an acceptable realisation that the high consumption rate of the industrialized world can no longer be sustained by the earth's ecosystem and therefore it is high time reduction be brought to the rapacious consumption in the global North to allow for even utilisation of ecological provisions for every person on earth particularly those in the global South where the higher percentage of the world's poor reside. Thus, (Nayar, 1994) argues that sustainable development remains an inequitable conceptual schema between the advanced country of the North and the developing ones in the South and that the starting point for sustainable development is the reduction in the consumption and polluting capacity of the advanced countries which has damaged much of their environment and that of the developing countries where they source for resources. Therefore, the political dynamics of sustainable development is "anti-poor, anti-south and thereby anti-ecological (Ibid).

The Brundtland's definition of sustainable development evinces normative values: values of equity and justice. Intergenerational equity that ensures that the needs of all, specifically the poor, are met; that poverty is eradicated in the developing world; that access to energy does not distinguish the rich from the poor and that impractical renewable energy source is not forced on the poor countries (Njiro, 2002). However, sustainable development is said to have a contested meaning being a "notoriously slippery and elusive concept (Williams & Millington, 2004)''. The definitional diversity is often competing and frequently opposing (Baker et al, 1997).

BACKGROUND

The desire for a sound economic development of nations, particularly countries of the South, is no doubt an enduring aspiration of all nations but environmental concerns, pollution, environmental degradation, carbon emission, climate change with the possible eventual in-hospitability of the earth for humanity, had informed the concept of sustainable development (Akinsulore, 2021). The focus of this paper is the Niger Delta region of Nigeria, which is the major theatre of (several decades of) oil and gas exploration in the country, with over 35 billion barrels of proven crude oil reserve and an even larger deposit of natural gas (Okonkwo and Etemire, 2017). It is well established that this region has had a tragic history of massive environmental pollution (damaging land, forests, and rivers etc.), majorly caused by recurring oil spills and continuous gas flaring from the activities of multinational oil companies that commonly fail to take steps to adequately remedy this harm (Worika, 2001) It is also noted that pollution from the oil and gas industry has severely compromised the health of those in the region, especially communities in the oil producing areas, like the Ogoni land (Manuchim, 2021). It has also negatively affected their social, cultural, and economic wellbeing, considering that their major occupation includes farming, fishing, and hunting (UNDP, 2006,). Despite the billions of dollars that have been generated over the years from the industry, the region continues to suffer a lack of basic amenities (Boele, et al, 2001).

Some authors and commentators argue that all these have happened with the complicity of the Nigerian government, which holds a major stake in the industry through the Nigerian National Petroleum Corporation's (NNPC) contractual arrangements, especially the Joint Venture Arrangements (JVA) and Production Sharing Contracts (PSCs) with multinational oil companies (Konne, 2014). Nonetheless, the Nigerian economy depends heavily on its oil industry, with petroleum resources accounting for about 80 per cent of Nigeria's revenue and 95 per cent of its export earnings (UNEP Report, 2011). Consequently, the government has over the years demonstrated its reluctance to properly hold the industry accountable for its human and environmental impacts; this is so considering its own involvement, as not just a regulator, through the Department of Petroleum Resources (DPR) (Etemire & Lucky Worika, 2018), but a commercial player in the industry, as well as the fear that such action may affect the economic fortunes derived from the industry for both the nation and the multinational oil companies that have invested massive resources in money and expertise (ibid). Jay Martin and Ann McNaughton argues that:

The shadows of environmental degradation, poverty, and lack of economic opportunity lie across the regions of the world that are fertile ground for ethnic conflicts, hatred, and violence. The private sector has a more important role than ever before to develop products and practices and to support policies that protect and restore the environment, that eradicate poverty, and that create a fair and transparent society. The challenge of the future is to choose a course that satisfies the market requirements for growth, maintains the natural balance that sustains our economies, and meets the needs and rights of global communities awakening to new dreams of health, prosperity, and peace. (Martin & MacNaughton, 2004)

Furthermore, a sharply rising worldwide demand for carbon-based energy, along with (Ibid) rapidly declining oil and gas reserves in the United States and Europe, and a keen interest in developing nations to develop their natural resources in order to fund high priority social and economic development projects, are combining to lead multinational oil and gas companies to increase exploration and development activities in areas such as the Middle East, Eastern Europe, Africa, and South America that still have substantial remaining oil and gas reserves (Ibid). All stakeholders in the global petroleum industry-including oil and gas companies-recognize that increasing concerns about economic, environmental, and social consequences of carbon-based energy solutions may eventually lead to a declining demand for petroleum products and a greater use of alternative sources of energy (Ibid).Consequently, one could argue that in the next two decades oil and gas companies will need not only to maintain, but also to expand their hydrocarbon reserve bases in order to meet the rapidly growing demand for hydrocarbons in both developed and lesser developed countries. Considering this, oil, and gas developers in Nigeria, particularly in the Niger-Delta region must engage in careful prior assessment of policies, projects, and technologies to establish long-term effectiveness in environmental protection and social impact standards (Manuchim, 2021). Additionally, host governments must understand legitimate industry concerns and set key economic terms in a manner that encourages private companies to anticipate reasonable rates of return (Martin & McNaughton, 2004).

SUSTAINABLE DEVELOPMENT: IMPACTS ON OIL AND GAS DEVELOPMENT

Anyone could ask the question, what does sustainable development mean in practical terms to legal practitioners who provide legal counsel to oil and gas companies and regulatory authorities in Nigeria? To develop and retain key advisory roles to clients confronting challenges that present legal issues, legal practitioners to oil-producing nations, oil and gas companies, and their service company contractors must comprehend the critical global trends transforming client business models (MacNaughton & Stephens, 2003). These trends include greater transparency in government and corporate budgeting processes, implementation of good governance practices, promotion of integrity and ethics, greater care for ecological and social environments, and strict enforcement of anti-corruption measures. Oil and gas companies that have established sustainable development standards, policies, and procedures also expect their service contractors to do the same (World Business Council of Sustainable Development, 2004). Companies and governments must establish environmental and social management systems that include awareness and compliance standards; effective policies and procedures; and efficient implementation and enforcement mechanisms. Energy and resource lawyers must be able to help their clients create innovative solutions that fit the shifting twenty-first century paradigm; otherwise, clients inevitably will look to other professional services providers for solutions (Gary et al, 2001).

Notwithstanding, research has shown that, globally, poor and minority communities, like those in the Niger Delta region of Nigeria, are disproportionately exposed to environmental hazards and burdens (Camacho, 1998). Oil exploration and exploitation activities, as earlier noted, have resulted in massive air, water, and land pollution in many communities in the Niger Delta region, way beyond the environmental impact of the oil and gas industry in the rest of the country. For example, recent research has shown that infant mortality rate in the many Niger Delta communities with oil spill sites is about a 100% higher, (76 deaths per 1000 births) than the national average (38 deaths per 1000 births), because of the pollution from oil spills (Bruederlea & Hodle, 2019). This unfair distribution of the industry's environmental burden has been occasioned mostly by the severe inadequacy of the environmental protection regulatory framework applicable to the industry (Worika et al, 2019). In support, the UNEP Report notes that the environmental laws applicable to the industry cannot sufficiently guarantee the prevention of environmental harms and the restoration of degraded environment in affected communities, due to their general weakness and poor enforcement by government regulators (UNEP Report, 2017- 2019).

In addition to this, section 6(3) of the National Oil Spill Detection and Response Agency (Establishment) (NOSDRA) Act stipulates a (roughly $2,500) *fine for failure by a polluting oil company to clean up oil spill sites. Considering the financial size of oil companies, that fine is too low to motivate oil firms to commit time and material resource to improving their operations with the aim of preventing environmental harm that may emanate therefrom (Amnesty International)*. Additionally, Oil Pipelines Act (Cap 07 Laws of the Federation of Nigeria) which appears to facilitate rather than prevent environment harm. (Section 5) of the Act grants those licensed to install oil pipelines and ancillary facilities, the right to conduct environmentally harmful activities on land covered by their permits in the process of executing their rights, without any corresponding obligation to restore the damaged environment after the permitted activity is concluded.

Furthermore, there is the 2018 revised Environmental Guidelines and Standards for the Petroleum Industry in Nigeria (EGASPIN, 1991, revised 2002, 2016, 2018), an important regulatory instrument in the oil and gas industry, which outlines environmental standards that must be complied with by oil operators, to prevent, minimise, and control pollution from the oil industry. However, some authors argue that while the EGASPIN 'seeks to adopt best practice, using methods and guidelines that are consistent with international standards', contrary to international best practice in the field, it contains several gaps that limit its overall efficiency and capacity to prevent pollution and ensure remediation of damaged ecosystems (Olawuyi & Tubodenyefa, 2018). For instance, in some part of the world, including the emerging markets in Asia, Africa, South America, and Eastern Europe, petroleum and other resource companies obtain their legal license to operate from sovereign governments that typically hold title to all the natural resources (including but not limited to oil and gas) within their borders. While the philosophy that underlies sovereign ownership of natural resources may be stewardship of common resources for the common good, development of these natural resources in practice too often benefits only an elite few. For this reason, increasingly sophisticated-and interconnected---civil society stakeholders such as indigenous communities, multilateral institutions, and global non-governmental organizations (NGOs) are attempting to block or disrupt natural resource development projects that they believe are proceeding in ways that are inimical to the common good (DJSI Media Governance News, 2003).

EXAMINATION OF SECTION 10 AND 12 OF THE NIGERIAN OIL AND GAS INDUSTRY CONTENT DEVELOPMENT ACT 2010 AND ITS IMPLICATION ON INTERNATIONAL TRADE AND SUSTAINABLE DEVELOPMENT

Despite the huge oil reserves in Nigeria and the unlimited potentials that come with it, Nigeria continues to be plagued by unemployment and low capacity in the oil and gas industry (Aladejare, 2010). The Federal Executive Council of Nigeria have pointed out repeatedly that the problem can be rectified by having a local content enactment to ensure greater participation by Nigerians (ibid). The whole idea was to create jobs and build capacity in the industry. The Nigerian Oil and Gas Industry Content Development Act 2010 was signed into law in the year 2010. *The Act requires that preference and priority should be given to Nigerians and Nigerian products (Section 10 and 12).* This move has stirred up questions on whether the provisions of the Act violate the non-discrimination principles under the GATT regime (Aladejare, 2015). This section examines section 10 and 12 of the

Nigerian Oil and Gas Industry Content Development Act 2010, and the implication on International Trade.

The Act was established to integrate local participation and representation in oil and gas investments and activities in the Nigerian oil and gas industry (Oil and Gas Industry Content Development Act 2010). It entrenched a regulatory framework for the participation of Nigerians, Nigerian companies and Nigerian products in project investments and activities (Aladejare, 2015 pp. 132). One mandatory requirement of the Act is that operators are to submit a Nigerian Content Plan when bidding for any permit or licence and before embarking on any project (Section 7 of the Oil and Gas Industry Content Development Act, 2010). It is only after this plan has been certified to follow the Act that a 'Certificate of Authorization' will be issued (Section 8 of the Oil and Gas Industry Content Development Act, 2010). The Nigerian Content Plan should be drawn in such a way as to ensure that:

First consideration shall be given to services provided from within Nigeria and goods manufactured in Nigeria; and Nigerians shall be given first consideration for training and employment in the work programme for which the plan was submitted. (Ibid)

The implication of the Nigerian content plan in section 10 is that where there are domestic products and equipment to be used, they should be given priority over and above 'like' products and equipment that have been imported. For instance, for operators not to make mistake against section 10 (1)(a), they must grant a less-favourable treatment to 'like' imported products in their operations in this regard (Section 10 (1)(a) of the Oil and Gas Industry Content Development Act, 2010). One could argue that this section faltered in its inability to develop a set of concepts, criteria and policies that are coherent or consistent both externally and internally. In addition to this, section 12 goes on to impose another obligation on the operators and their contractors (Section 12 of the Oil and Gas Industry Content Development Act, 2010). It provides as follows:

Subject to section 7 of this Act, the Nigerian Content Plan submitted to the board by an operator shall contain a detailed plan, satisfactory to the board, setting out how the operators and their contractors will give first consideration to Nigerian goods and services, including specific examples showing how first consideration is considered and assessed by the operator in its evaluation of bids for goods and services required by the project. (Ibid)

It could be argued that the government's objective for local content policy initiative is quite noble but not consistent with the World Trade Organisation (WTO) non-discriminatory principle. The non-discriminatory principle is cardinal in laws and policies of the World Trade Organisation (Aladejare, 2015, pp.147). Yet, under this provision, operators are not just compelled to apply the provisions of the Act, they are also required to hold their contractors to the same standard and give a convincing explanation on how the Nigerian content plan has been implemented. Whatever procurement is to be made must be in conformity with this provision. With emphasis on '...first consideration to Nigerian goods', like imported goods which have passed all the border measures at the port of entry will invariably be placed at a competitive disadvantage (Aladejare, 2015, pp.133). One of the key problems with these sections is that it does not secure or attract foreign investment and does not promote economic development. It is narrowing choice and opportunity for the vulnerable. Additionally, foreign investment treatment standards applicable under international investment law are implicated in the application and administration of Nigeria's Local Content Law (Okpe, 2015, pp.255).

In the quest to achieve the objective of economic development through the exercise of legislative sovereignty, many developing countries pass legislation or take measures that conflict with the substantive rights of foreign investors in the host State (Okpe, 2015, pp.258). Often, such measures or legislation may be held to be expropriation of the proprietary rights of the foreign investor in the host State as manifested in section 10 and 12 of the Nigerian Oil and Gas Industry Content Development Act 2010.

Nonetheless, some authors and commentators argue that since the coming into force of the Local Content Act in Nigeria, it has been reported that because of the preferential treatment given to Nigerian indigenous companies particularly in the Oil and Gas Industry, the Local Content Act has been successful in achieving its objectives (Okpe, 2015, pp.294) Amanze-Nwachukwu, reporting on the implementation of the Local Content Act, observed that since it was signed into law, there has been an increase in the participation of indigenous companies in the Oil and Gas Industry of Nigeria with the result that indigenous contractors are now able to compete with their foreign counterparts (Ibid). Yet, on 17 March 2021, the federal government of Nigeria approved $1.5bn for the rehabilitation of Port Harcourt Refinery oil in the Niger-Delta region with Italian contractor Tecnimont (Iruoma, 2021).

SOLUTION AND RECOMMENDATION

There are recent developments in the literature whereby commentators have identified that the Nigerian Oil and Gas Content Act 2010 which is now functional cannot address trade policy by focussing solely on domestic products because it is not compatible with the principles of the World Trade Organization's Non-discriminatory clause. There have been alternatives key policy proposals to address this. One of the key policy alternatives is to indirectly regulate where and how IOCs procure materials to be used in the Nigerian oil and gas industry through contractual provisions (Aladejare, 2015). In addition to this, contractual alternatives to legislation provide more practical and indirect alternative that must be explored. For instance, the Nigerian 1993 Model Production Sharing Contract allows the NNPC to hold Oil Mining Lease (OML) in Nigeria while the International Oil Companies (IOCs) work as contractors in a joint venture-like arrangement. There is however a clause in the contract that stipulates inter alia, how, and where the contractor should obtain materials to be used in its operations. This stipulation mandates the contractor to make procurements locally where such is available, and it meets industry standards. Furthermore, the contractor is required to submit its work plan and budget to the joint venture management committee for approval periodically.

No doubt, at the fundamental trade policy level, non-discrimination is indeed a desirable policy in "levelling the playing field", an important aspiration of the WTO (Mosoti, 2003). Other than such broad or universal policy support for non-discrimination, one may also look at it from the perspective of a foreign investor and say that it is positive to the extent that it allows the rational allocation and re-allocation of Foreign Direct Investment (FDI) capital to be channelled into a particular high-return host country (Ibid).

The proposal in this chapter is to address the inconsistencies of discrimination in the Nigeria Oil and Gas Industry Content Act 2010. This work suggests that to a great extent, appropriate constitutional and legislative amendments supported by clarification of roles for the multi-national corporations will support reduction of challenges arising in the Nigerian Oil and Gas Industry. According to Odoleye (2013), the constitutions of Nigeria and some legislations since independence were either a product of a colonial or a military parting gift to Nigerians and needs to be reviewed. This is because, between theory and reality, there is conflict as to whether what is in existence is rule by law or rule of law, because of the clear departure from the legalism of the strict adherence to law or good governance as advocated by the leaders (Snowiss, 1990).

FUTURE RESEARCH DIRECTION

Some writers and commentators have criticised the Nigerian Oil and Gas industry Content Act 2010 from the lens of attempting to deal with trade policy solely on domestic products (Okpe, 2015). Nonetheless, a vigorous local content policy is undoubtedly desirable for sustainable development and growth of the Nigerian oil and gas sector. Thus, efforts made by Nigerian authorities towards actualising this objective are highly commendable. Given the huge investments made in the

Nigerian oil and gas sector annually and the boundless prospects and potentials of the sector to create jobs and stimulate the Nigerian economy, the decision to enact a local content law becomes even more logical. However, key provisions of the Act conspicuously conflict with Nigeria's obligations under international trade regime to proscribe discriminatory trade policies and to remove local barriers to foreign participation in trade. The chapter aims to start the conversation about this change. This is something scholars, legal practitioners, and further commentators could continue to examine and critique so that proposed meaningful suggestions from those new debates could be used for future research.

CONCLUSION

Many countries in the world have developed environmental regulatory and enforcement frameworks based largely on the U.S. environmental law framework. Nevertheless, economic development is a major policy objective of the governments of developing countries that are rich in natural resources. Nigeria has promoted, through legislation, the concept of Nigerian content through domestic capacity building and preferential participation as a policy in its Oil and Gas Industry("OGI") to achieve the objective of economic development. This vibrant local content policy which is undoubtedly desirable for sustainable development and growth of the Nigerian oil and gas sector is not compatible with the World Trade Organisation non-discriminatory principle which Nigeria is also a signatory to. Section 10 and 12 of the Nigerian Oil and Gas Industry Content Act 2010 does not reflect the meaning and intention of the Brundtland's definition of sustainable development which evinces normative values: values of equity and justice for all. It is not consistent with the World Trade Organisation (WTO) non-discriminatory principle. The non-discriminatory principle is cardinal in laws and policies of the World Trade Organisation (Aladejare, 2015) Thus, there could be far reaching and negative economic implications on the local economy, where the objective of economic development through the promotion of local content in the Oil and Gas Industry is achieved with a mechanism that is conflicted with the substantive and procedural rights of foreign investors in the context of international investment law and investment treaty arbitration. The need to employ a balanced approach in Nigeria's international investment regime should further be reinforced by its commitment to constantly observe obligations it has assumed in connection with specific foreign investments in its territory that includes the Oil and Gas Industry.

CONFLICT OF INTEREST

The author declares no conflict of interest regarding the publication of this chapter.

REFERENCES

Akinsulore, A., & Akinsulore, O.M. (2021). Sustainable Development and the Exploitation of Bitumen in Nigeria: Assessing the Environmental Laws. Faultline's Beijing Law Review, 113.

Aladejare. A. A (2015). Legal Status of Sections 10 and 12 of the Nigerian Oil Gas Industry Content Development Act (2010) under the GATT Regime' (2015). *Journal of Sustainable Development Law & Policy, 5*, 129-147.

Amnesty International Nigeria. (2012). *Joint Memorandum on Petroleum Industry Bill March 2012.* Author.

Baker, S. (2006). *Sustainable Development Abingdon-on-Thames: Routledge.* Taylor and Francis Group. doi:10.4324/9780203495933

Baker, Kousis, Richardson, & Young. (1997). *The Politics of Sustainable Development: Theory, Policy and Practice within the European Union.* Routledge.

Bruederlea & Hodle. (2019). Effect of oil spills on infant mortality in Nigeria. *Proceedings of the National Academy of Sciences, 116(12), 1-5.*

Camacho, D. (1998). *Environmental Injustices, Political Struggles: Race.* Class, and the Environment Duke University Press.

Cap 07 Laws of the Federation of Nigeria, 2004

Dawe, N. K., & Ryan, K. L. (2003). The Faulty Three-Legged-Stool Model of Sustainable Development. *Conservation Biology, 17*(5), 1458–1460. doi:10.1046/j.1523-1739.2003.02471.x

Etemire & Worika. (2018). Environmental Ethics and the Nigerian Oil and Gas Industry: Rumpus and Resolution. *U Botswana Law Journal, 26,* 58.

Iruoma, K. (2021). *Energy & Resources.* African Business.

MacNaughton. (2004). Sustainable Development: Impacts of Current Trends on Oil and Gas Development. *Journal of Land Resources & Environmental Law, 24,* 259.

MacNaughton, A. L. (2001). Multidisciplinary Trends in an Evolving Marketplace: Practicing with Other Professions. In Multidisciplinary practice: Staying Competitive and Adapting to change. Academic Press.

MacNaughton A.L & Stephens J (2003). Improving Infrastructure Project Results in Sensitive Areas, U.S. and Abroad. In *Aba Section on Environment, Energy & Resources, 11th Annual Fall Meeting*, 6-7.

Manuchim, A. (2021). The short fall of the Nigerian Oil and Gas Act 2010 in Achieving sustainable. *Development*, 5.

Mosoti, V. (2003). Non-discrimination and its dimensions in possible WTO framework agreement on investment reflections on the scope and policy space for the development of poor economies. *Journal of World Investment*, 4(6), 1011–1046. doi:10.1163/221190003X00057

Nayar, K. R. (1994). Politics of Sustainable Development. *Economic and Political Weekly*, 29, 1328.

Njiro, E. (2002). Introduction to Sustainable Development and Oxymoron? *Empowering Women for Gender Equity*, (52), 3–7.

Odeleye, D. O. (2013). The Doctrine of Natural Justice under Civil and Military Administrations in Nigeria. *Journal of Policy & Law*, 6(2), 234. doi:10.5539/jpl.v6n2p231

Okonkwo, T., & Etemire, U. (2017). "Oil Injustice" in Nigeria's Niger Delta Region: A Call for Responsive Governance. *Journal of Environmental Protection*, 8(1), 42–43. doi:10.4236/jep.2017.81005

Okpe, F.O. (2015). Economic Development and the Utility of Local Content Legislation in the Oil and Gas Industry: Conflicts and Effects of Nigeria's Local Content Act in the Context of International Investment Law. *Pac McGeorge Global Business & Development Law Journal*, 28, 255-294.

Olawuyi, D. S., & Tubodenyefa, Z. (2018). Review of the Environmental Guidelines and Standards for the Petroleum Industry in Nigeria (EGASPIN). OGEES Institute.

Section 10(1)(a) *of the Nigerian Oil and Gas Industry Content Development Act 2010*

Section 12 of *the Nigerian Oil and Gas Industry Content Development Act 2010*

Section 6(2) *of the Act only encourages caution, calling on the holder of a permit under section 5 of the Act to 'take all reasonable steps to avoid unnecessary damage...' Emphasis added*

Section 7 *of the Nigerian Oil and Gas Industry Content Development Act 2010*

Section 8 *of the Nigerian Oil and Gas Industry Content Development Act 2010*

Section 8 *of the Nigerian Oil and Gas Industry Content Development Act 2010*

Snowiss, S. (1990). *Judicial Review and the Law of Constitution.* Yale University Press.

The World Commission on Environment and Development. (1987). *Our Common Future.* Author.

United Nations Development Program Niger Delta Human Development Report. (2006). *(UN Development Program Publication, Nigeria.* United Nations Environmental Programme.

Williams, C., & Millington, A. (2004). The Diverse and Contested Meaning of Sustainable Development. *The Geographical Journal, 170*(2), 99–104. doi:10.1111/j.0016-7398.2004.00111.x

Worika, L., Etemire, U., & Tamuno, P. S. (2019). *Oil Politics and the Application of Environmental Laws to the Pollution of the Niger Delta: Current Challenges and Prospects. Oil, Gas and Energy Law Journal, 17*(1).

KEY TERMS AND DEFINITIONS

Consideration: Additional things of value to be provided under the terms of a contract. Something such as an act, a forbearance, or a return promise bargained for and received by a promisor from a promise; that which motivates a person to do something, especially, to engage in a legal act. Consideration, or a substitute such a as promissory estoppel, is necessary for an agreement to be enforceable.

Contractors: Persons or firms that undertakes a contract to provide materials or labour to perform a service or do a job. A party to a contract. A contractor who has the knowledge, skills, experience, and available equipment to do the work that he or she is employed to do without creating an unreasonable risk of injury to others and who has the personal characteristics necessary to carry out the work.

Goods and Services: Tangible or moveable personal property other than money. Things that have value, whether tangible or not the importance of social goods varies from society to society. All things including specially manufactured goods which are moveable at time of identification to the contract for other than money in which is to be paid. Investment securities and things in action.

Local Content: Is the value that an extraction project brings to the local, regional, or national economy beyond the resource revenues. The fastest growing of these measures are local content requirements (LCRs), which are policies imposed by governments that require firms to use domestically manufactured goods or domestically supplied services to operate in an economy.

Non-Discriminatory: Not making an unfair or prejudicial distinction between different categories of people or things. This means that individuals or groups of individuals which are in comparable situations should not be treated less favourably simply because of a particular characteristic, such as their sex, racial or ethnic origin, religion or belief, disability, age, or sexual orientation.

Oil and Gas Industry: Oil and gas industry is the sector of industry focused on exploration, data acquisition, development, drilling, production, gathering, refining, distribution, and transportation of hydrocarbons and includes but is not limited to major resource holders, national oil companies, multinational oil companies, drilling, etc.

Operative: Being in or having force or effect; especially, designating the part of a legal instrument that gives effect to the transaction involved. Having principal relevance; essential to the meaning of the whole operative word of the statute or legislation.

Procurement: The act of getting or obtaining something. Procurer is one who induces or prevails upon another to do something.

Standard: A level of quality or attainment. A model accepted as correct by custom, consent, or authority. A criterion for measuring acceptability, quality, or accuracy. A legal standard that is based on contract and perceptions external to a particular person.

Chapter 12
The Relationship Between Developmental Social Work, Poverty Alleviation, and Sustainable Development in Nigeria:
Issues, Challenges, and Opportunities

Chigozie Ugwoji
Canterbury Christ Church University, UK

ABSTRACT

This chapter explores the nexus between developmental social work (DSW) and sustainable development in Nigeria with the specific aim of outlining the issues, challenges, and opportunities involved therein as they affect Nigeria's social development and social work. Social work, which promotes the advancement of social wellbeing, social change, empowerment, and liberation of the vulnerable groups, is an integral concept of DSW. DSW maps out a new direction for social work practice, offering processes to address the causes of societal dysfunction and socioeconomic challenges faced by the people. This approach could be used to tackle Nigeria's social issues and poverty. This chapter argues that there is overlap for DSW to promote and contribute to the realisation of sustainable development, the literary and documentary sources, and the review thereof shows that there is a relationship between DSW and sustainable development as both are geared towards promoting the welfare of the people.

DOI: 10.4018/978-1-7998-7499-7.ch012

INTRODUCTION

The Nigerian government has made commitments to sustainable development through various government policies, such as the National Vision 20:2020, Transformation Agenda, and the NEEDS I and II (National Planning Commission [NPC], 2009), which focuses on the economic, social, and environmental dimensions of development. These policies are aimed at poverty alleviation (by improving the national standard of living) and wealth creation (by supporting investors). The policy also aims to protect and conserve natural resources and to ensure people's life and property are secured (Muleya, 2020). These goals are in line with the goals of the United Nations (UN) 2030 developmental sustainability agenda, which calls upon its member nations to, for example, protect the planet, guarantee the wellbeing of their people, and end world poverty. Thus, sustainable development is seen as a standard for attaining sustainability, poverty alleviation, and social development in all spheres of life.

Professional social workers have the necessary skills and knowledge required for enabling and empowering development practice and processes, resulting in the upholding of human rights, social justice, and protection of people's welfare. Apart from acquiring skills to support social development, The White Paper on Welfare (1997) asserts that through a developmental approach/social development, social workers are required to contribute towards poverty alleviation, thereby enabling the active involvement of the people in their own development. This encourages a partnership, with social workers working together with the people in welfare and social development processes (Gray, 2002). The key emphasis of the social development approach, as outlined in the White Paper on Welfare (1997), is the need to harmonise social and economic policies with meeting the needs of the people. This in line with the UN World Summit's Declaration of Social Development (1995), followed by Patel's research in South Africa (1992) and Midgley's theory of developmental welfare (Midgley, 1995). The policy takes a social investment approach and asserts that social investment in human capabilities is critical for economic development, as it improves people's wellbeing (Patel and Hochfeld, 2012). In addition, the policy recognises the significance of economic intervention at both macro- and micro-levels as a means of strengthening people to achieve economic justice and as a means of social development. In this regard, the objective of this chapter is to explore the nexus between developmental social work (DSW) and sustainable development in Nigeria with the specific aim of outlining the issues, challenges, and opportunities involved therein as they affect Nigeria's social development and social work.

BACKGROUND

Understanding Social Development

'Development' includes political, physical, social, economic, and environmental development. It entails changes for a more inclusive and equitable society as well as the creation of economic and social conditions that alleviate poverty and social exclusion. Thus, the crux of development is that it enables individual to maximise their potential. Accordingly, Midgley (2001) argues that social development first emerged as an approach to social welfare in the 1950s with the aim of eradicating global poverty. The social developmental approach seeks to link social and economic policies and promote social welfare (also known as 'social development').

The concept of social development is discussed in detail by scholars of sociology, social work, and social policy (Midgley, 2014). Social development has emerged as a multidisciplinary and distinct field of practice and academic enquiry, which is practised across all regions – both at international and national levels – that supports people's social and material improvement and their wellbeing (Midgley, 1995, 1997; Hokenstad and Midgley, 1997). In the social work field, social development is practised within the context of international and national (local, state) social work (Elliott and Mayadas, 1996). The concept of social development lacks precise definition and covers a wide range of issues. Midgley (2014) defined social development as a multifaceted development process, which aims to promote social change and people's welfare. Gray (2002) used the term in both descriptive and prescriptive ways (Gray, 2002). In the former sense, social development refers to a measurement of the quality of life (Sirolli, 1999) of the people in any given society (using this meaning, it is obvious that third-world countries, specifically African nations, are less developed than first-world countries – in Europe, the USA, and Canada). The latter refers to the type of quality-of-life people ought to live and enjoy in a developed society. This quality of life basically refers to the attainment of and access to basic social amenities of life, e.g., good healthcare, housing, education, and potable water.

Thus, given that third world (less developed) countries require more social development than their first-world counterparts, a policy paradigm was developed to draw attention to the connection between economic and social development (Midgley, 2014; Gray, 2002) as well as to explain how needs of the people ought to be maintained. Arguably, in developed countries, attention is geared more towards economic development than social development, and the goals of caring and promoting the social needs of the people are considered secondary to economic development. However, in less developed countries, reports of social development only document what governments and non-governmental agencies have done to eradicate and alleviate poverty in the society. Yet, the actual countries remain poor and underdeveloped (Gray, 2002).

Social development promotes a sustainable society, with the empowerment of marginalised groups, the eradication of poverty, and improvement of people's social and economic positions. It takes a multisectoral approach that requires all sectors of the society to work together (Gray, 2002). This means bringing different sectors together, requiring them to work cooperatively in addressing socio-political and socioeconomic problems – for better outcomes for the people. For example, social workers work with primary healthcare workers, police departments, and education and housing departments among others to achieve this aim. Sanders (1982) conceptualised social development practice in social work as meaning a movement, practice, and policy perspective for strategic intervention aiming to reduce social ills faced by the people.

Thus, DSW is seen as the application of principles, values, theories, and approaches to social work, informed by social development (Van Breda, 2018; Midgley and Conley, 2010). This means that social development is a critical approach that supports DSW as a practice model for making a significant contribution towards reducing inequality and poverty as well as promoting the general welfare of the people. This is in line with prior research (Plagerson et al., 2019; Lombard and Twikirize, 2014) that argued that DSW could affect sustainability and bring about positive changes in resolving social ills for people's general wellbeing. This is the essence of this chapter. It can be argued that there is a connection between DSW and sustainable development as they are both geared towards promoting people's welfare and economic development, which places people at the centre of social planning.

Understanding Developmental Social Work (DSW)

DSW (also known as the Social Development Approach to Social Work [SDASW]) is gaining a global recognition in the social work profession. In western countries, DSW can be traced as far back as the profession's early social work, when the founding fathers (established settlement houses that mobilised local people to improve their neighbourhoods) and the advocates of the governmental social welfare intervention group offered an alternative to the casework model, which challenged the individualised casework approach (Midgely and Conley, 2013). In Africa, it gained considerable attention following the adoption of the White Paper for Social Welfare in South Africa in 1994 and the Copenhagen Declaration the year after (Amadasun, 2019; Hochfeld et al., 2014; Lombard, 2008; Selipsky, Mupedziswa and Chitereka, 2009; UN, 1995, 2005). DSW integrates social developmental theory and practice as a panacea for solving people's social and economic problems (Manyama, 2018; Mabeyo et al., 2014; Patel and Hochfeld, 2012; Midgley and Conley, 2010; Patel,

2005; Gray, 2002 and 1998; Estes, 1997). The intense level of poverty in some parts of the world, specifically in Africa, and the widespread issues bordering on social development continue to shape global discourse on DSW. Arguably, the social work profession cannot be separated from the dynamics of development (Patel and Hochfeld, 2012). This means that DSW affirms the social work profession's commitment to the eradication of poverty, duty to address discrimination and inequalities and ability of people to access resources and social services, which aims at meeting people's needs.

DSW is defined as a planned and organised way of achieving social change, aimed at promoting the wellbeing of the populace within the context of a multisectoral developmental process (Midgley, 2013). According to Patel (2005), it is a way of achieving social work processes, social development, and economic justice – by enabling and strengthening communities as well as improving people's livelihoods (Manyama, 2018). In this context, DSW involves working collaboratively with individuals and groups to achieve social change, which is designed to promote people's social and economic wellbeing. This means that the main goal of DSW is to make sure that people are supported to achieve their full potential, guided by a quest for increased social justice; economic and political stability; peace; and meeting basic human needs. Additionally, Gray et al. (2017) argue that DSW considers welfare as an investment in human capital rather than a drain on limited resources, and it involves a commitment to eradicate poverty, inequality, and social injustice. DSW comprises non-remedial forms of intervention. This is done by engaging in community development as a major means of intervention strategy, contribution to reconstruction, and development of any given society for people's welfare.

Developmental Social Work in Africa: Contextualising Nigeria

Taylor and Roberts (1985) argue that DSW in developed countries (such as in Europe and the USA) started around 20th century as a community welfare centre, with the establishment of settlement houses and neighbourhood centres that cater for the social welfare of the people. According to Midgley (1985), DSW is rooted in Africa and was widely applied in order to alleviate poverty and other social and economic problems before the advent of the modern welfare system (Mwansa, 2012). In Nigeria, this general idea of creating a better environment for all has its origins in the country's pre-colonial period and social structure, which includes clans, kingdoms, family lineages, and other entities that enabled a communal, collaborative, and concerted community support and efforts in times of social and economic problems (Amadasun, 2019; Patel and Hochfeld; 2012; Lombard 2015; Green, 2008). As observed by Mbah et al. (2017), the social dynamics of traditional Nigerian society could be described as a web of blood relationships and relationships established by marriage, enabling everyone in society to see each other as a family member and help each other meet their social and economic needs. Accordingly, MacPherson and Midgley (1987) argue that African countries have informal yet well-established structural values and cultures (which emerged from the pre-colonial era) based on meeting people's social needs. Additionally, the Christian missionary period formed the second era of social work and social welfare (Okoye, 2019; Mbah, et al, 2017; Irele, 2011). The spread of the missionary started from Lagos colonies and spread to the various regions such as the Western, Eastern and Northern regions. These missionaries who began social work (welfare) activities in Nigeria were the Roman Catholic Church(RCC) and the Salvation Army, they based their social work assumption on the teachings of Christ, including charity, community service, and supporting/helping the destitute, among others (Okoye, 2019).

Consequently, changes in DSW by applying the social case work method are influenced by globalisation and colonialism by the West. As a result, these changes create a vacuum in the provision of social welfare services (Spitzer and Twikirize, 2014). This is because the services provided by practitioners are not in line with the developmental nature of African or Nigerian society and culture. To this end, researchers (Wairire, 2014; Kalinganire and Rutikanga, 2014) have highlighted the decline of the developmental approach in social work practice. They argue that social work's emphasis on remedial solutions has become so dominant that many of its developmental activities (including advocacy, human capital development, social reforms, social activism, community development programmes, and community organisation), which were initially linked with the social work profession, are no longer called 'social work' (Mayama, 2018; Patel and Rochfeld, 2012).

Against this background, Spitzer and Twikirize (2014) question the validity of African social work practice relying heavily on the Western model in its remedial approach to Africa's and Nigeria's problems (Chitereka, 2005), specifically social and economic problems, such as unemployment, poverty, homelessness, illiteracy, child labour, and diseases, among others (Mupedziswa, 2005). Extant literature on this phenomenon (Gray et al., 2008; Ose-Hwedie and Rankhopo, 2008) focus on the remedial orientation of social work in eradicating and/or preventing the rise of these social problems in African and Nigerian society. It is to this end that Leterrier (2000) asserts that social work in Africa is different to social work in the West. The approach warrants the prioritisation of a developmental approach to social work practice. As highlighted by Selipsky et al (2009), DSW is a strategy designed to foster sustainable economy that places people and human rights at the centre of social planning, with the consequence of promoting the wellbeing of the people. Similarly, Gray and Lombard (2008) assert that DSW practice has broad goals of working simultaneously on many connected issues (alleviation of poverty, injustice, discrimination, inequalities, and other social problems), while using a range of seamless strategies for attaining present social and economic needs without compromising the future that is occasioned through sustainable development.

The growing rate of poverty, gross injustice, discrimination, and among others are exponentially high, with poverty being the highest. The global poverty rate stands at 9.2% (or 689 million people) surviving on just $1.90 or less per day. This high rate of poverty is experienced mostly in third-world countries, especially Africa – and Nigeria has a poverty rate of 40.1% (World Bank, 2020). Addressing this challenge (poverty) and widening both social and economic opportunities within the nations and local communities can be achieved through sustainable development. Addressing poverty is also in line with the UN 2030 Agenda for Sustainable Development, which outlined 17 goals for the sustainable development for all countries by 2030 — with poverty alleviation topping the list. Sustainable development is seen as a developmental pathway for transforming nations' social change without making the impoverished worse off. Sustainable development meets people and communities present needs without compromising the future.

DEVELOPMENTAL SOCIAL WORK (DSW) AND SUSTAINABLE DEVELOPMENT

Sustainable Development (SD): Definitions and Clarifications

Sustainable development first became a priority against the backdrop of a rethink in economic growth as well as in the environmental and social benefits accruable when business and social institutions deal with social issues like social justice, equity, community development and poverty alleviation (World Commission on Environment and Development [WCED], 1987; Barbier, 1987). Sustainable development is a global discourse that started over 30 decades ago. The publication *'Our Common Future'*, also known as *'The Brundtland Report'*, introduced the concept of sustainable development discourse and how it could be achieved (WCED 1987; Crowther and Aras, 2008). This was followed by the 2005 World Summit, held in New York City following the UN 2000 Millennium Summit, which, in some respects, was the harbinger of the Millennium Development Goals (MDGs). Sustainable development issues are critical, as they define and address viable schemes to combating economic, social, and environmental problems faced by the society.

Purvis et al. (2018) highlight that the concept of sustainable development appears in many academic discourses and debates. Sustainable development has been defined in different ways (Gladwin et al., 1995). It is seen 'as a desired future or better world' (Gladwin et al., 1995, p. 876); from the prism of vision expression; as a value change (Bebbington et al., 2014); as a part of the social transformation process (Visser, 2013); as moral development (Gray et al., 1996); and as social and environmental reconfiguration (Bebbington and Larrinaga, 2014). More so, like social work, sustainable development integrates different concepts, issues, terms, as well as sustainability, development, and capacity building including other related phenomena, which are generally used interchangeably (Ihlen and Roper, 2011). The concepts, goals, movements, and aspirations involved in sustainable development are central to the objectives of numerous sustainable societies, businesses, and national institutions (Purvis et al., 2018; Emeseh, 2009). Thus, 'The Brundtland Commission' offered a classic definition of the concept: '[sustainable development is] development that meets the needs of the present without compromising the ability of future generations to meet their own needs' (WCED, 1987, p. 16). This definition expresses the importance of fairness and continuity of practice. For the purpose in this chapter, sustainable development is seen as a collaborative effort to pursue societal goals by making good use of its resources – human, social, environmental, natural, and others – for collegial existence (Filho and Brandli, 2018). The overall goal of sustainable development is the long-term sustainability of resources, which is enabled due to the utilisation and acknowledgement of economic, environmental, and social concerns.

As argued by Desjardins (2000), sustainable development has been recognised on a global level, and economic development is considered inseparable from issues such as ecological stability and social justice. Thus, 'The new worldview emerging as an alternative to the reigning paradigm of economic growth and free markets holds that long-term sustainability is the criterion for successful economic and social development' (Desjardins, 2000, pp. 10–11). This means that business operations should not jeopardise the wellbeing of the people and their environment – now and in the future (Bebbington et al, 2014). This view is in line with Visser's (2013) contention that sustainable development aims to ensure that people achieve a high level of economic prosperity and stability – now and in the future.

Nevertheless, some researchers such as Chichilinisky (2004) and Parris and Kates (2003) have argued that the concept of sustainable development is ambiguous as it could mean different thing to different people. For example, Greenpeace has described the concept as a form of 'deceptive jargon' of anti-environmentalism (Hayward et al., 2000, p. 45). Notwithstanding the criticism, vital to its conceptualisation are development, protection of the environment and social participation (Purvis et al., 2018). However, the idea of sustainable development is being adopted to tackle wide range of developmental challenges faced the populace (Crowther & Aras, 2008). Another ambiguity of the concept is that it is based on 'what it specifically seeks to achieve' and 'how it is measured'; for instance, making use of the indicators such as Environmental Sustainability Index, the Global Reporting Initiative, and the Wellbeing Index (Parris and Kates, 2003). Consequently, in the social work profession, the social and economic dimensions of sustainable development (i.e., social justice, economic growth, and development) are vital elements in fighting underdevelopment, unemployment, poverty, inequality, and social problems. This is undeniably the basic concept of social work, which continues to value the principles of social justice, gearing efforts towards a better and equitable society, which is a fundamental strategy and process of promoting countries' sustainable development.

Subsequently, in Africa, the debate of sustainable development has been taken more seriously since the publication of *'Our Common Interest'* (Commission for Africa, 2005). In 2010, a follow-up report, *'Still Our Common Interest'*, was prepared with the goal of expediting efforts by African leaders by converting economic opportunities in Africa into meeting the social needs of the people, advancing national development, protecting the environment, and promoting sustainable development. Additionally, the issues with socioeconomic development in Africa have been shaped by the MDGs, which have since been replaced by the Sustainable Development Goals (SDGs-are the blueprint to achieve a better and more sustainable future for all), which support the disadvantaged and society at large and aim to help them experience equal and equitable opportunities while maintaining a healthy lifestyle, devoid of hunger and diseases – towards greater survival prospects for all (UN, 2017). The SDGs extended the work started by the MDGs that drove the global campaign from 2000 to 2015 that aimed to alleviate poverty in all spheres of life. While the MDGs apply to developing countries, the SDGs apply to United Nations member states. Furthermore, SDGs are more ambitious and comprehensive in orientation than the MDGs (KPMG, 2017).

Thus, given their influential power, it is expected that Multinational Corporations (MNCs) can play an important role in realising the principles and ideals of the SDGs, which lay out the processes for eradicating poverty; promoting social justice and equality; and more. The Business Initiative 2030 Agenda is intended to create business opportunities, requiring both the responsible private sectors and MNCs to demonstrate their central role in promoting sustainable development and human prosperity. These goals can be achieved by investing responsibly, which can help raise living standards through job creation; skills and technological development; and appropriate distribution of wealth. It is also important to improve the financial and technical capacity necessary to achieve the SDGs. A responsible business practice should integrate economic, social, and environmental concerns within its core business operations to support SDGs. In this vein, UN (2017) found that 82% of blue-chip companies showed commitment and devotion to SDGs in their 2016 annual reports, with good health, climate action, and reduced inequalities ranking among their top priorities. *'The Brundtland Report'*, also called *'Our Common Future'* (WCED, 1987) heralded the concept of the sustainable development path.

The Brundtland Report identified seven main strategies for sustainable development, including:

- Reviving growth;
- Meeting essential human needs;
- Changing the quality of growth;
- Ensuring a sustainable level of population;
- Conserving and enhancing the resource base;
- Merging environment and economics in decision-making; and
- Reorienting technology and managing risk.

Crowther and Aras (2008) assert that *'The Brundtland Report'* makes legal and institutional endorsements for a process of change, to deal with global issues. Businesses depend on human and natural resources, which should be preserved for generational use (World Business Council for Sustainable Development [WBCSD], 1992). In this context, businesses (at micro and macro levels) should address societal problems, such as social, environmental, developmental, and economic issues. In Pan et al.'s (2018) study, the researchers found that micro- and macro-level problems are different but seem somewhat related. Management teams are thereby enabled to strategise their business operations with meeting the SDGs in mind (Filho and Brandli, 2018). As opined by Elkington (1997), businesses are faced with challenges (how to deal with the challenges) and dilemmas about how to implement sustainable and inclusive business practices while also maximising profit (Jensen, 2009). Elkington (1997) further argued that a sustainable and inclusive business model would advance a win-win approach (Williams and Preston, 2018) for all business organisations.

Furthermore, it has also been argued that when businesses foster sustainable and inclusive stakeholder relationships, it challenges businesses and society to understand the three dimensions of sustainability in an integrated way (social equity, environmental protection, and economic growth) (Sharma and Ruud, 2003). This has been acknowledged as the most significant characteristic of sustainable development (Purvis et al., 2018; Crowther et al., 2019; Crowther and Aras, 2008). A combination of the three dimensions of sustainable development can have mutually reinforcing outcomes for sustainable development (United Nation Environment Programme [UNEP], 2015). Also, Basiago (1995) contends that the beginning of sustainable development is based on a combination of the three 'pillars', which is 'the dominant interpretation within the literature' (Purvis et al., 2018, p. 1). These three pillars are in line with Elkington's (1997) three dimensions of sustainability: people (equity), profit (economy), and planet (environment). Figure 1 shows a diagram of these three pillars.

Figure 1. Sustainability Triad
Source: Ugwoji (2021)

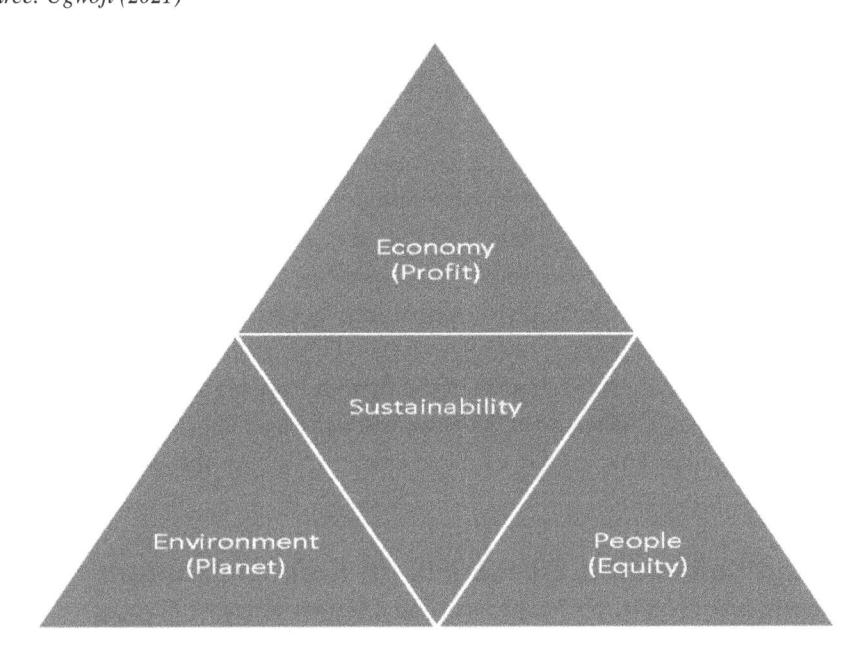

Economy (Profit)

Sustainability

Environment (Planet)

People (Equity)

Economic sustainability (a system that satisfies consumption levels both now and, in the future,) is based on growth, development, efficiency, and productivity, and it aims to expand its development frontiers with monetary capital. The hallmark benefits of economic sustainability are unlimited resources and the belief that the growth will 'trickle down' to the poor people and nations (Kahn, 1995). Environmental sustainability involves ecosystem integrity, biodiversity, and a capacity for natural resources to be made as a 'source of economic inputs and as a sink for wastes' (Kahn, 1995). Social sustainability considers the importance of meeting human needs (Filho and Brandli, 2018) and comprises of empowerment, accessibility, equity, institutional stability, and participation that aims to sustain environment through economic growth and poverty eradication. Kahn (1995) argues that economic, social, and environmental sustainability must be 'integrated' and 'interlinked', and it is only when they are coordinated in a comprehensive way that positive synergies are fostered, and that development and sustainability is encouraged; leading to a sustainable environment that promotes the wellbeing of the populace. Furthermore, sustainable development encourages businesses to be responsible and focus on short- and long-term environmental, social, and economic performance. Additionally, sustainable development stresses the importance of the three pillars in the context of long-term wellbeing and sustainability (Crowther et al., 2019), calling on businesses to tackle and address the identified issues in their environment beyond their main objectives (Belal, 2008).

Hence, the focus of *The Brundtland Report* is that corporate business dealings, at present and their impact in the future, are considered a 'glib assumption' (Crowther and Aras, 2008, p. 43). This means that the sustainable development debate is vital and that organisations can demonstrate sustainability by their continued existence. Thus, the rationale for sustainable development is that businesses should pay particular attention to how the development of their products and services affect the environment and society as well as how they interact with external stakeholders. This relationship with the environment is a valuable activity undertaken by businesses that goes beyond legal requirements (Banerjee, 2008). Thus, given that Nigeria and other developing countries are at the bottom of the pyramid, scholars (see Ashiomanedu, 2008) have emphasised how social development can be used for sustainability and developmental gains. This is part of the rhetoric of 'filling the governance gap', when the government retreats (Palazzo and Scherer, 2011).

Achieving Sustainable Development: From Millennium Development Goals to Sustainable Development Goals

The General Assembly of the UN urged the government on its 27th special session in 2002 to commit to and promote specific time-bound goals (MDGs to SDGs), strategies, and actions to support social justice, equity, global partnership, empowerment, healthy living, environmental sustainability, reduction of child mortality, and alleviation of poverty, among others. These commitments underscore the MDGs (Lomazzi et al., 2018), which superseded the international development goals, which were created to reduce poverty and set specific targets. Table 1 shows the MDGs.

Table 1. The Eight Millennium Development Goals

MDG1: Eradicating extreme hunger and poverty
MDG2: Achieving a universal primary education
MDG3: Promoting gender equality and empowering women
MDG4: Reducing child mortality
MDG5: Improving maternal health
MDG6: Combatting HIV/AIDS, malaria, and other diseases
MDG7: Ensuring environmental sustainability
MDG8: Developing a global partnership for development

Source: Ugwoji (2021)

The eight MDGs were created to address global development challenges, specifically socioeconomic issues that have shaped the direction of global development (Schutt, 2015). The MDGs ushered in the adoption and official launch of the 2030 Agenda for Sustainable Development by the General Assembly of the UN in 2017 (Jackson, 2018), which welcomes countries and business organisations to work collaboratively towards the realisation of the SDGs. The SDGs cover a wide range of issues, including the traditional MDGs as well as new goals (energy, infrastructure, and others), and a broad set of 17 Sustainable Development Goals (SDGs) and 169 targets (to tackle poverty and climate change as well as fight social and economic injustices) set key objectives in terms of the environment, society, and economy (Kolk et al., 2017), which serve as the overall framework to guide global and national development action that are mapped to be achieved by 2030. Individual country states, businesses, including international and local solidarity movements are responsible for achieving and sustaining SDGs, which are widely accepted and approved of by all the nation states (Lomazzi et al., 2018; UN, 2017). Figure 2 highlights the 17 SDGs and their explanations.

Figure 2. The 17 Sustainable Development Goals
Source: Ugwoji (2021)

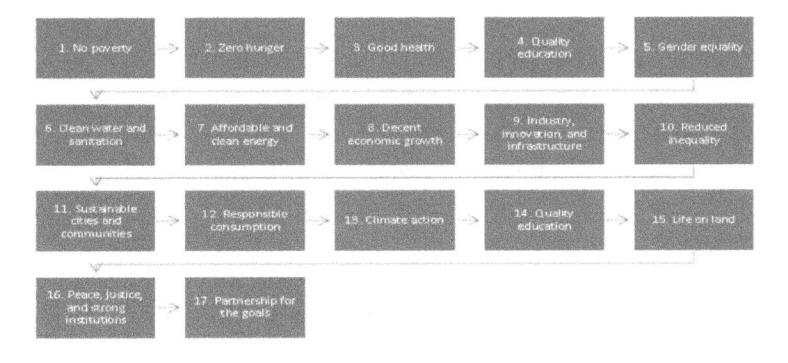

Despite that the SDGs have sparked a growing discourse and reactions among policymakers, academics, and practitioners, as well as its relation to the connections between business and society, stakeholder engagement, and business management, however, how they affect the business of MNCs is largely under-researched and vague (Kolk et al., 2017). In addition, Crowther and Aras (2008) postulate that MNCs are still far from enabling the realisation of the SDGs. This is because of their interest in profit maximisation at the expense of sustaining a viable relationship with shareholders has had a great impact on society, especially people in developing countries (Idemudia, 2010). Another problem raised concerning the lack of realisation of the SDGs is that of the systemic deficiencies in the initiatives at the design and implementation levels. Societies see MNC leaders as being primarily responsible for achieving and promoting SDGs and sustainable development. Thus, MNCs will not aim to achieve the SDGs alone; rather, a collaborative effort with nongovernmental organisations, intergovernmental organisations, and stakeholders are vital for dealing with, achieving, and sustaining the SDGs (Kolk et al., 2017).

In addition, Imoh-Ita and Amadi (2016) argue that the effects of the asymmetrical structure of the international capitalist system; social and natural capital deterioration; economic underdevelopment; an under-representation of poverty; and bad governance in African societies (especially in Nigeria) have all contributed to the non-realisation of the SDGs (Hickel, 2016). According to Blowfield and Murray (2011), the commercial approach to sustainable development implies fair distribution across the world's population in relation to quality of life (WBCSD, 1992). As they further noted, this must be realised by businesses without hindering the ability of future generations to meet their own needs in the context of economic efficiency, economic justice, social justice, and investment. Achieving this goal is central to tackling poverty, climate change issues, and social inequality that are rife in developing countries, especially in developing countries – particularly Nigeria.

In contrast, the world view of oil MNCs is shaped by neo-liberalism and the pure market logic driven by profitability and the assumption that everyone would benefit from oil exploration activities (Jenkins, 2004). Oil MNCs therefore see government as largely responsible for community development and the redistribution of the wealth generated from oil exploration. This clash in world views and expectations between communities and oil MNCs invariably fosters the violation of the psychological contract 7 that exists between local communities and oil MNCs from the perspective of the communities.

The Nexus Between Developmental Social Work (DSW) and Sustainable Development (SD)

Research has found that approaches to social development have a longstanding history in social work practice, which address human and social development issues with respect to sustainability policies and programmes (Mohan, 2007). An analysis of the current socio-ecological crisis suggests that issues of sustainable development are of direct concern for DSW and are relevant to promote (Peeters, 2011). The mission of social work with the agenda of sustainable development – The Brundtland Report – is a good starting point, of sustainable development towards maintaining, sustaining and meeting people's needs (WCED, 1987). DSW, on the other hand, is a context-based profession that uses a multidimensional developmental process that is concerned with the ways in which people are supported in their environment. Addressing social and economic problems against the backdrop of case work in view of promoting social change and eliminating the barriers, inequities, injustices, and poverty that exist in society, development social work is utilised, which promotes wellbeing of the people (Mingle, 2013). This means utilising the support system and social networks that enable people to lead meaningful lives at home, in the community, and in society at large. In this context, Jayasooria (2016) asserts that the SDGs, ideals, principles, and values of social work intersect to a considerable extent. The SDGs concerning equality; human dignity; self-reliance; good health and wellbeing; and empowerment are also among the core values and principles of DSW, which align very closely with the acceptable definition of social work established by the International Association of Schools of Social Work (IASSW) and the International Federation of Social Workers (IFSW). "Social work is a practice-based profession 'that promotes social change and development, social cohesion, and the empowerment and liberation of people. Principles of social justice, human rights, collective responsibility are central to social work'' (IASSW and IFSW, 2014).

This definition prioritises social development as crucial in promoting people's wellbeing. Accordingly, IASSW and IFSW report call on social development practitioners and social workers to be at the centre in tackling social hardship (this is one of the agendas of social sustainability) that reduces people's wellbeing and general progress in life. Sustainable development is in sync with the above definition as it maintains a positive process of social change with the aim of meeting the needs of the people, which takes account of people's needs and development (Baker, 2006). Furthermore, social justice is an essential component in the definition of social work, which stands for the creation of a sustainable society. Sustainability similarly expresses reconciliation of social justice, ecological integrity, and people's wellbeing. Sustainable development is a concept, a goal, and a strategy that involves collaborative working to achieve sustainability for all. Working together (multiagency) is another concept in social work that enables quicker response in satisfying people's needs, improving their wellbeing, and improving their future.

Furthermore, the global agenda and mission for social development and social work provide opportunities for social workers to implement the agenda of DSW in relation to attaining social development goals. One such opportunity is to work with a concerted effort to challenge structural issues and social injustices in the society that would enable people to defend their rights. It can be argued here that there is a normative concurrence between DSW and sustainable development in terms of attending to people's wellbeing, human rights, participation, and equality, which possibly give rise for each to reinforce another (Peeters, 2011). The DSW profession is strongly founded on human rights values and its interventions to scrutinise violations of human rights. As well as integrating relevant personal and political considerations into social work interventions and policy development (by adopting critical reflective practice). DSW ensures accountability with respect to the actions of developmental social workers and reasons for which such actions were taken. Consequently, social development and the global agenda for social work strengthens the legitimacy of the relationship between DSW practice and interventions in order to attain social SDGs.

In addition, Lombard (2015) stresses how crucial it is for developmental social workers to jointly utilise micro-, mezzo-, and macro-level practice in a systematic manner in the realisation of economic and social development and to serve as an optimal means of accomplishing SDGs in a manner that promotes sustainable social development. In Coates's (2005) ecological model of sustainability, environment is considered a dynamic outcome that begin from interactions between all elements in society. These elements can be grouped into systems and observing interactions among various systems provides an easy approach to understanding the changing environment. The perspective that systems comprise individuals, groups, and communities support social work theory. Thus, ecological approaches to sustainability mirror social work processes for restoring, rehabilitating, and maintaining people's systems to a satisfactory level of functioning.

DSW and Poverty Alleviation: Towards the Realisation of the Ideals of Sustainable Development

There is a growing recognition of the crucial role of social work in fostering social development. This role is important in situations of persistent poverty, which affects people's capabilities, functioning, and wellbeing, and this results in a vicious cycle of poverty (Twikirize et al., 2013). The basic meaning of poverty is the failure of an individual to acquire the essentials of life, such as food, healthcare, clothing, shelter, and education. Poverty is seen as a major problem of global environmental dysfunction as stated in the influential Brundtland Commission that captures widely held beliefs. This is because poverty has a crippling effect on the functioning and wellbeing of individuals and society. Researchers have argued that human poverty goes beyond the lack of necessities of life, including issues of powerlessness, low self-dignity, exclusion, and absence of the necessary basic capabilities for an acceptable level of functioning in society (UNDP, 1997). Misturelli and Heffernan (2010) define poverty as a 'lack of control over economic, social, and political needs.

However, one can argue here that not being able to meet any need could not necessarily be a feature of poverty (for instance, a lack of affection from someone cannot be categorised as 'poverty'). This is because not all human needs require access to material resources. Therefore, an inability to meet a wide category of needs is thus a feature of poverty experienced in any society. On the other hand, if there is access to resources and, for no reason, people choose not to utilise such opportunities to meet their needs in terms of participation, then that is not considered as poverty – it is a product of an 'enforced lack of necessities' (Goulden and D'Arcy, 2014). Other scholars have defined poverty as a lack or deprivation of basic human rights, which essentially include democracy, equal opportunities, justice, participation, subsistence, and protection (Doyal and Gough, 1991). Thus, poverty is a structural imbalance that manifests in all spheres of human life, which relates to vulnerability, powerlessness, social exclusion, deprivation, isolation, and marginalisation (Omotola, 2008). Accordingly, Jensen (2009) classified poverty into six types to explain the dimensions of the concept. Table 2 highlights the classifications of poverty and their explanations.

Table 2. Six Classifications of Poverty

Situational poverty	This is commonly triggered by crisis, and it is usually a temporary situation. Problems that trigger situational poverty include pandemics (e.g., COVID-19, HIV/AIDS, Malaria), severe health problems, environmental/ecological disasters (e.g., earthquakes, tsunamis), relationship breakdown, and others.
Urban poverty	This is a set of economic and social difficulties that are found in industrialised cities, which are caused by overcrowding, noise, and pollution; lack of sanitation and waste disposal facilities; and poor ventilation.
Rural poverty	This is poverty in rural areas, including factors of rural society, rural economy, and political systems and governance. People experiencing rural poverty have less access to public services, education, job opportunities, support for disabilities, and access to healthcare than others.
Relative poverty	This refers to people's standard of living compared to economic standards of other people living within the same surroundings.
Generational poverty	This is defined as people having been born into poverty for at least two generations. People with this type of poverty are not usually equipped with the material and emotional tools to better their living conditions.
Absolute poverty	This is the most common type of poverty, especially in developing countries, which entails a scarcity of the necessities of life, such as food, potable water, shelter, and clothing. People who are experiencing absolute poverty only focus on meeting day-to-day needs.

Source: Adapted from Jensen, 2009

The above classifications give different perspectives on the incidences or effects of poverty experienced by society. Sachs (2005) asserts that Africa's poverty is reflected in the interactions between domestic policies, history, geopolitics, and geography, which left the society trapped in poverty. This poverty trap has been worsened by the recent COVID-19 pandemic and HIV/AIDS, which have had a devastating effect on all levels of society. In Nigeria, widespread and severe poverty is a big challenge and reality. Nigeria seems to experience most of the characteristics of poverty described above, which involves a lack of food, clothes, education, and other basic amenities. Ucha (2010) argues that there are several causes of poverty in Nigeria, including unemployment, corruption, non-diversification of the economy, income inequality, and poor education system. For instance, few of these will be explained:

1. **Unemployment:** Unemployment among youths is one of the major factors contributing to poverty in Nigerian economic system (Ede, Ndubisi, and Nwankwo, 2013). It results to a decrease in the production and less consumption of goods and services by the people and as such the cost of living becomes high whilst the standard of living drops. Unemployment also, increases the crime rate and violence in Nigeria including kidnapping for ransom, internet fraud, armed robbery, and other forms of fraudulent activities. Thus, unemployment and its associated crime issues in Nigeria, can be dealt with by providing enabling environment, development of entrepreneurial skills and initiatives and re-prioritization of agrarian economy to facilitate employability of people (Anyadike, Emeh, and Ukah, 2012).

2. **Corruption:** The abuse of entrusted power for personal gain, include bribery, misappropriation, embezzlement, and money laundering by public officials is quite prevalent in Nigerian system (Okpara, 2007). This manifest in political, institutional, and other public offices. Corruption destabilizes the political, social, economic growth and educational system of a nation, by creating negative national image and loss of much needed revenue. For instance, the revenues generated in oil, trade and commerce are not distributed to the needs of the people and the state. They are diverted to private pockets, leaving the rest of the people to wallow in abject poverty. Similarly, Institutional leaders demand bribe to offer students admission into the universities. It is estimated that corruption amounts to 20% of the gross domestic product of Nigeria, and the transparency international's (TI) corrupt perception index (CPI) ranked Nigeria at the bottom (CBN, 2006). In order to combat corruption in the system the anti-corruption must be guided by legislative framework for transparent and accountable government and comprehensive strategy that is systematic, consistent, focus, comprehensive, non-selective and non-partisan (Igbuzor, 2008).

Additionally, the effects of poverty pose risks factors that adversely affect individuals and society at large in a variety of ways. Some of the effects of poverty include:

- Powerlessness of the victims
- Cognitive lags

Developmental Social Work, Poverty Alleviation, and Sustainable Development

- Acute and chronic stressors
- Marginalisation
- Social and emotional challenges
- Conflict and violence
- Poor health and safety issues
- Lack of participation in the political process
- Unemployment and economic challenges
- Civil unrest

These causes and their effects are associated with and reinforces each other (Peeters, 2011). The poverty status explains the need for social workers to intensify efforts by means of a community approach to confront the menacing consequences of poverty that take hold of individuals or society. Social workers have legal duties, powers, and training to intervene and rectify social injustice, inequality, financial exclusion, and risk, among other duties. They engage with issues of poverty eradication as this is consistent with social workers' professional values (British Association of Social Workers [BSAW], 2010).

Additionally, the connection between social work and poverty appears to have been influenced by the longstanding philosophy and practice of social work, which started with the Charity Organisation Society (COS). COS, which served as an offshoot of social work, was founded in 1869 to support the concept of self-help and reduce government intervention mechanisms in order to deal with the effects of poverty in society. This means the history and origins of social work are crucial for understanding the training, attitudes, and actions of social workers today in relation to poverty issues. In the 1970s, the British Association of Social Workers (BASW) worked in partnership with the Child Poverty Action Group to increase awareness of and campaign for social policies to tackle poverty.

Social workers engage with and mobilise collective action within poor communities, working collaboratively with other agencies and multidisciplinary teams to campaign against government financial cuts. They argue that these measures cause harm to children, adults, and families and link this problem with other problems, such as the rising numbers of children in the care system, substance addiction, homelessness, and mental illness (BSAW, 2010). Social workers engage in anti-poverty campaigns, which entail maximising opportunities for the development of asset-based welfare schemes in local communities (Gregory and Drakeford, 2008). They work collaboratively with other agencies for collective opposition and intervention in political decisions to cut funding, services, and financial benefits for vulnerable people (Webb and Bywaters, 2019), causing social exclusion and thereby disempowering people from involvement in issues affecting them. It can be argued here that respecting the right to self-determination and empowerment as processes aim to enable people to take control over their lives by 'distributing power at all levels and working towards establishing free and fair (egalitarian) social relations (Dominelli, 2006). This means that people experiencing poverty can be empowered to overcome personal challenges through a shift away from the excesses of capitalism and necessary support to meet their needs.

Therefore, DSW plays a major role in poverty alleviation in terms of the realisation of the ideals of sustainable development. Poverty alleviation is necessary for sustainable development, which is geared towards meeting people's present needs and the future, as well as promotes systems/ society's transformations. It is due to the realisation of the urgent need for poverty alleviation that major international agencies carved out specific programmes, such as the MDGs and SDGs, to help reduce the level of poverty in the world and foster sustainable development. Similarly, in Nigeria, numerous attempts at poverty reduction have been put in place, notably Operation Feed the Nation in 1976 and the National Poverty Eradication Programme in 2001. Poverty alleviation strategies and implemented policies have been able to curtail the negative impacts of poverty on sustainable development to some extent in Nigeria (Inam, 2015; Ucha, 2010). Therefore, this chapter argues that there is a relationship between DSW, poverty alleviation, and sustainable development, all with the goal of maintaining a sustainable environment for all.

SOLUTIONS AND RECOMMENDATIONS

This chapter has made effort to extend the frontiers of sustainable development discourse as well as DSW, which needs broadening for a better understanding of socio-economic and developmental challenges within the context of developing countries like Nigeria. Research in the domain of social work, development studies and sustainable development has called for widening empirical research and theoretical perspectives to shed light on how developmental issues are inextricably linked to DSW and practice, which is crucially important in reframing the contours and approaches that would help achieve the Sustainable Developmental Goals (SDGs). Developmental social workers are required to develop innovative strategy within a multisectoral approach to address social, economic problems, and socio-ecological crisis in a manner that promotes sustainable social development.

FUTURE RESEARCH DIRECTIONS

Although this chapter has deepened insights on the above argumentation, however, scholarship can be extended that would employ triangulation of theoretical/conceptual lenes as well as comparative studies for more nuanced understanding of these phenomena. Additionally, studies could be furthered to help widen the ballpark of DSW through data-driven approach and/or a multidisciplinary approach to ensure a better understanding of how to tackle poverty and related issues in the developing countries.

CONCLUSION

In conclusion, the chapter has looked at the concepts and perspective of social development and DSW in Africa and Nigeria as a reference point. It has explored in-depth the meaning of sustainable development and DSW as well as clarified issues around the relationship between sustainable development and DSW. Furthermore, this chapter has highlighted the nexus between DSW and SD, and the argumentation here is premised on the assumption that SD has a direct a correlation with DSW, which is relevant in promoting social justice and equity for social change that would contribute immensely to creation of sustainable society and ecological integrity, as well as meeting the SDGs, which is vital for global wholesomeness, poverty alleviation and overall development on the globe beyond the purview of Africa. This chapter has also provided an understanding of poverty alleviation in fostering social development, by engaging in anti-poverty campaigns for the development of asset-based welfare scheme including promoting social justice and fairness within the local communities. As has been delineated in the foregoing sections, most societies, including Nigeria, are confronted with varying degrees of socioeconomic, political, and environmental problems, and interrogating the synergy between development social work and sustainable development could contribute to the realisation of humanity's quest for a better world that is just, fair, and sustainable.

REFERENCES

Amadasun, S. (2019). Mainstreaming a developmental approach to social work education and practice in Africa? Perspectives of Nigerian BSW students. *Social Work Education*, *6*(2), 196–207. doi:10.25128/2520-6230.19.2.8

Anyadike, N., Emeh, I. E. J., & Ukah, F. I. (2012). Entrepreneurship development and employment generation in Nigeria: Problems and prospects. *Universal Journal of Education and General Studies*, *1*(4), 88-102.

Ashiomanedu, J. (2008). Poverty and Sustainable Development in the Niger Delta Region of Nigeria. *Journal of Sustainable Development in Africa*, *10*(3), 155–171.

Banerjee, S. B. (2008). Corporate social responsibility: The good, the bad and the ugly. *Critical Sociology, 34*(1), 51–79. doi:10.1177/0896920507084623

Barbier, E. B. (1987). The concept of sustainable economic development. *Environmental Conservation, 14*(2), 101–110. doi:10.1017/S0376892900011449

Bazeley, P., & Jackson, K. (2013). *Qualitative data analysis with NVivo* (2nd ed.). Sage.

Bebbington, J., Unerman, J., & O'Dwyer, B. (2014). *Sustainability accounting and accountability*. Routledge.

Belal, A. R. (2008). *Corporate social responsibility reporting in developing countries: The case of Bangladesh*. Ashgate.

British Association of Social Workers. (2010). *Poverty Eradication and the Role of Social Workers*. Author.

Business for 2030. (n.d.). *Business for 2030*. Available at http://www.businessfor2030.org

Chichilinisky, G. (1994). North–South trade and the global environment. *The American Economic Review, 84*(4), 851–874.

Chitereka, C. (2005). The impact of HIV/AIDS on development and the role of social workers: The case of Lesotho. In G. Jacques & G. N. Lesetedi (Eds.), *The new partnership for Africa's development: Debates, opportunities, and challenges* (pp. 384–398). Africa Institute of South Africa.

Commission for Africa. (2005). *Our common interest: report of the commission for Africa*. Penguin.

Crowther, D., & Aras, G. (2008). *Corporate social responsibility*. Ventus Publishing.

Desjardins, J. R. (2000). *Business, ethics, and the environment*. Pearson.

Dominelli, L. (2006). News and Views...from IASSW. *International Social Work, 49*(4), 543–546. doi:10.1177/0020872806065486

Doyal, L., & Gough, I. (1991). *A Theory of Human Need*. Macmillan. doi:10.1007/978-1-349-21500-3

Ede, C. E., Ndubisi, E. C., & Nwankwo, C. A. (2013). Tackling unemployment through private sector. *International Journal of Innovation Research in Management, 2*(2), 41–52.

Elkington, J. (1997). *Cannibals with Forks: The triple bottom line of 21st century business*. Earthscan.

Elliott, & Mayadas. (1996). Integrating clinical practice and social development. *The Journal of Applied Social Sciences*, *21*, 61–68.

Emeseh, E. (2009). Social responsibility in practice in the oil-producing Niger Delta: Assessing corporations and government actions. *Journal of Sustainable Development in Africa*, *11*(2), 113–125.

Estes, R. J. (1997). Social work, social development and community welfare centres in international perspective. *International Social Work*, *40*(1), 43–55. doi:10.1177/002087289704000104

Filho, L., & Brandli, L. (Eds.). (2016). *Engaging stakeholders in education for sustainable development at university level*. Springer. doi:10.1007/978-3-319-26734-0

Gladwin, T. N., Kennelly, J. J., & Krause, T.-S. (1995). Shifting paradigms for sustainable development: Implications for management theory and research. *Academy of Management Review*, *20*(4), 874–907. doi:10.2307/258959

Goulden, C., & D'Arcy, C. (2014). *A definition of poverty – Anti-poverty strategies for the UK*. Available at https://www.jrf.org.uk/file/45780/download?token=zjlY4i-Jandfiletype=full-report

Gray, M. (2002). Developmental social work: A 'Strengths' praxis for social development. *Social Development Issues*, *24*(1), 4–14.

Gray, M., Mupedziswa, R., & Mugumbate, J. (2017). The expansion of developmental social work in Southern and East Africa: Opportunities and challenges for social work field programmes. *International Social Work*, *61*(6), 1–14.

Gray, R., Owen, D., & Adams, C. (1996). *Accounting and accountability : changes and challenges incorporate social and environmental reporting*. Prentice Hall.

Gregory, L., & Drakeford, M. (2008). Anti-Poverty Practice and the Changing World of Credit Unions: New Tools for Social Workers. *Journalism Practice*, *20*(3), 141–150.

Hayward, S., Fowler, E., & Steadman, L. (2000). *Environmental Quality 2000: Assessing Michigan and America at the 30th Anniversary of Earth Day*. Mackinac Center for Public Policy and the Pacific Research Institute for Public Policy.

Hokenstad, M. C., & Midgley, J. (Eds.). (1997). *Issues in International Social Work: Global Challenges for a New Century*. NASW Press.

Idemudia, U. (2010). Rethinking the role of corporate social responsibility in the Nigerian oil conflict: The limits of CSR. *Journal of International Development*, *22*(7), 833–845. doi:10.1002/jid.1644

Igbuzor, O. (2008). *Strategies for winning the anticorruption war in Nigeria*. Available at https://nigeria.actionaid.org/sites/nigeria/files/winning_anti-corruption_war_in_nigeria1.pdf

Ihlen, O & Roper, J. (2011). Corporate Reports on Sustainability and Sustainable Development: 'We Have Arrived'. *Sustainable Development Journal*, *22*(1), 1-11.

Inam, U. S. (2015). Poverty Alleviation Strategies in Nigeria: A Call for An Inclusive Growth. *Journal of Poverty. Investment and Development*, *15*, 110–118.

Irele, A.O. (2011). The Evolution of Social Welfare and Social Work in Nigeria. *A Journal of Contemporary Research, 8*(3), 238-252.

Jackson, E. A. (2018). Contested terrain of sustainable development paradigm in sierra Leone. *Management of Sustainable Development*, *10*(1), 5–11. doi:10.2478/msd-2018-0001

Jayasooria, D. (2016). Sustainable development goals and social work: Opportunities and challenges for social work practice in Malaysia. *Journal of Human Rights and Social Work*, *1*(1), 19–29. doi:10.100741134-016-0007-y

Jensen, E. (2009). *Teaching with poverty in mind: What being poor does to kids' brains and what schools can do about it*. ASCD.

Kahn, M. A. (1995). Sustainable development: The key concepts, issues and implications. Keynote paper given at the international sustainable development research conference, 27–29 March 1995, Manchester, UK. *Sustainable Development*, *3*(2), 63–69. doi:10.1002d.3460030203

Kolk, A., Kourula, A., & Pisani, N. (2017). Multinational enterprises and the Sustainable Development Goals: What do we know and how to proceed? *Journal of transnational Corporations*, *24*(3), 9-32.

KPMG. (2017). *KPMG survey of corporate social responsibility reporting*. Available at http.www. home.kpmg

Lomazzi, M., Borisch, B., & Laaser, U. (2018). The millennium development goals: Experiences, achievements and what's next. *Global Health Action*, *7*(1), 23695. doi:10.3402/gha.v7.23695 PMID:24560268

Lombard, A. (2008). The implementation of the White Paper for Social Welfare: a ten-year review. *Challenges and Innovation in Developmental Social Welfare, 20*(2), 154–173.

Lombard, A. (2015). Global agenda for social work and social development: A path towards sustainable social work. *Social Work Journal, 50*(2), 481–498. doi:10.15270/51-4-462

Lombard, A., & Twikirize, J. M. (2014). Promoting social and economic equality: Social workers' contribution to social justice and social development in South Africa and Uganda. *International Social Work, 57*(4), 313–325. doi:10.1177/0020872814525813

Mbah, F., Ebue, M., & Ugwu, C. (2017). History of Social work in Nigeria. In Social work in Nigeria: Book of readings (pp. 1–14). Nsukka: University of Nigeria Press Ltd.

Midgley, J. (1995). *Social Development: The Developmental Perspective in Social Welfare.* Sage.

Midgley, J. (1997). *Social Welfare in Global Context.* Sage. doi:10.4135/9781483327945

Misturelli, F., & Heffernan, C. (2010). The concept of poverty: A synchronic perspective. *Progress in Development Studies, 10*(1), 35–58. doi:10.1177/146499340901000103

Mohan, B. (2007). *Fallacies of development: Crises of human and social development.* Atlantic Publishers.

Muleya, E. (2020). Developmental social work and the sustainable development goals in South Africa: Opportunities and challenges. *The International Journal of Community and Social Development, 2*(4), 470–486. doi:10.1177/2516602620975226

Mupedziswa, R. (2005). Challenges and prospects of social work services in Africa. In J. C. Akeibunor & E. E. Anugwom (Eds.), The social sciences and socio-economic transformation in Africa (pp. 271-317). Nsukka: Great AP Express Publishing.

National Planning Commission. (2009). Economic Transformation Blueprint. *Nigeria Vision, 20.*

Ogujiuba, K., & Ehigiamusoe, K. U. (2013). The challenges and implications of sustainable development in Africa: Policy options for Nigeria. *Journal of Economic Cooperation and Development, 34*(4), 77–111.

Omotola, J. S. (2008). Combating Poverty for Sustainable Human Development in Nigeria: The Continuing Struggle. *Journal of Poverty, 12*(4), 496–517. doi:10.1080/10875540802352621

Opara, I. (2007). Nigerian Anti-Corruption Initiatives. *Journal of International Business and Law*, 6(1), 63–94.

Osei-Hwedie, K., & Rankopo, M. (2008). Developing culturally relevant social work education in Africa: The Case of Botswana. In M. Gray, J. Coates, & M. Y. Bird (Eds.), *Indigenous social work around the world* (pp. 203–219). Ashgate.

Palazzo, A. G., & Scherer, G. (2011). The New Political Role of Business in a Globalized World–A Paradigm Shift in CSR and its Implications for the Firm, Governance, and Democracy. *Journal of Management Studies*, 48(4), 899–931. doi:10.1111/j.1467-6486.2010.00950.x

Pan, X., Chen, X., & Ning, L. (2018). The roles of macro and micro institutions in corporate social responsibility (CSR): Evidence from listed firms in China. *Management Decision*, 56(5), 955–971. doi:10.1108/MD-05-2017-0530

Parris, T. M., & Kates, R. W. (2003). Characterising and measuring sustainable development. *Annual Review of Environment and Resources*, 28(13), 113–128.

Patel, L., & Hochfeld, T. (2012). Developmental social work in South Africa: Translating policy into practice. *International Social Work*, 56(5), 1–15.

Peeters, J. (2011). The place of social work in sustainable development: Towards ecosocial practice. *International Journal of Social Welfare*, 21(3), 287–298. doi:10.1111/j.1468-2397.2011.00856.x

Plagerson, S., Patel, L., Hochfeld, T., & Ulriksen, M. S. (2019). Social policy in South Africa: Navigating the route to social development. *Journal of World Development*, 113, 1–9. doi:10.1016/j.worlddev.2018.08.019

Purvis, B., Mao, Y., & Robinson, D. (2018). Three pillars of sustainability: In search of conceptual origins. *Sustainability Science*, 14(3), 681–695. doi:10.100711625-018-0627-5

Report, B. (1987). (*Our common future*). Oxford University Press.

Sachs, J. (2005). *The End of Poverty: Economic Possibilities for our Time*. The Penguin Press.

Selipsky, L., Mupedziswa, R., & Chitereka, C. (2009). *Developmental Social Work Education in Southern and East Africa*. University of Johannesburg.

Sharma, S., & Ruud, A. (2003). On the Path to Sustainability: Integrating Social Dimensions into the Research and Practice of Environmental Management. *Business Strategy and the Environment*, 12(4), 205–214. doi:10.1002/bse.366

Spitzer, H., & Twikirize, J. M. (2014). A vision for social work in East Africa. In H. Spitzer, J.M. Twikirize, & G.G. Wairire (Eds.), Professional Social Work in East Africa. Kampala: Fountain Publishers.

Twikirize, J. M., Asingwire, N., Omona, J., Rosalind, L., & Kafuko, A. (2013). *The Role of Social Work in Poverty Reduction and the Realisation of Millennium Development Goals in Uganda*. Fountain Publishers.

Ucha, C. (2010). Poverty in Nigeria: Some dimensions and contributing factors. *Global Majority E-Journal*, *1*(1), 46–56.

United Nations Development Project. (1997). *Human Development Report: Human Development to Eradicate Poverty*. Oxford University Press.

United Nations Environment Programme (UNEP). (2015). *Integrating the three dimensions of sustainable development*. Available at https://sustainabledevelopment.un.org/content/documents/3782unep2.pdf

United Nations (UN). (2017). *Sustainable development goals report 2017*. Available at http.www.un.org

Van Breda, A. (2018). Developmental social case work: A process model. *International Social Work*, *61*(1), 66–78. doi:10.1177/0020872815603786

Visser, W. (2013). *The age of responsibility: CSR 2.0 and the New DNA of Business*. Wiley.

Wairire, G. G. (2014). 'The state of social work education and practice in Kenya. In *Our Common Future. World Commission on Environment and Development*. Oxford University Press.

Webb, C., & Bywaters, P. (2018). Austerity, rationing and inequity: Trends in children's & young peoples' services expenditure in England between 2010 and 2015. *Local Government Studies*, *44*(3), 391–415. doi:10.1080/03003930.2018.1430028

World Bank. (1986). *Environmental Aspects of Bank Work. The World Bank Operations Manual Statements, OMS 2.36*. World Bank.

World Business Council for Sustainable Development (WBCSD). (2012). *Corporate Social Responsibility*. Author.

World Commission on Environment and Development (WCED). (1987). *Our Common Future*. Oxford University Press.

Compilation of References

Abate, G. T., Borzaga, C., & Getnet, K. (2014). Financial Sustainability and Outreach of MFIs in Ethiopia: Does Ownership Form Matter? In Microfinance Institutions (pp. 244-270). Palgrave Macmillan.

Abdul Rahman, R. K., Siwar, C., Ismail, A. G., Bahrom, H., & Khalid, M. M. (2013). Zakah and microfinance. *International Proceedings of Economics Development and Research*, *61*(3), 10–13. 10.7763

Abdul Razak, H. (2019). Zakah and waqf as instrument of Islamic wealth in poverty alleviation and redistribution: Case of Malaysia. *Malaysia International Journal of Sociology and Social Policy*, *40*(3/4), 249–266. doi:10.1108/IJSSP-11-2018-0208

Abdulai, A., & Tewari, D. D. (2017). Determinants of microfinance outreach in Sub-Saharan Africa: A panel approach. *Acta Commercii*, *17*(1), 1–10.

Abe, M., Troilo, M. & Batsaikhan, O. (2015). Financing small and medium enterprises in Asia and the Pacific. *Journal of Entrepreneurship and Public Policy, 4*(1), 2-32.

Abu Dawud, S. (2008). *Sunan Abi Dawud*. Dar Al- Kotob Al- Ilmiyah.

Adams, J. S. (1965). Inequity in Social Exchange. In Advances in experimental social psychology. New York: Academic Press.

Adams, A., & Tewari, D. D. (2020). Impact of regulation on microfinance institutions sustainability and outreach in Sub-Saharan Africa. *African Journal of Business and Economic Research*, *15*(3), 11–34. doi:10.31920/1750-4562/2020/v15n3a1

Adams, S. (2009). Foreign direct investment, domestic investment, and economic growth in Sub-Saharan Africa. *Journal of Policy Modeling*, *31*(6), 939–949. doi:10.1016/j.jpolmod.2009.03.003

Adawiah, E. R. (2019). Successful Models of Social Finance Initiatives: Lessons from Amanah Ikhtiar Malaysia (AIM). In S. Kassim, A. H. Othman, & R. Haron (Eds.), *Handbook of Research on Islamic Social Finance and Economic Recovery After a Global Health Crisis*. IGI Global.

Addae-Korankye, A. (2012). Microfinance: A tool for poverty reduction in developing countries. *The Journal of Business and Retail Management Research*, *7*(1), 138–149.

Compilation of References

Addae-Korankye, A., & Abada, A. (2017). Microfinance and women empowerment in Madina in Accra, Ghana. *Asian Economic and Financial Review*, *7*(3), 222–230. doi:10.18488/journal.aefr/2017.7.3/102.3.222.231

Addai, B. (2017). Women empowerment through microfinance: Empirical evidence from Ghana. *Journal of Finance and Accounting, 5*(1), 1-11.

Adegbite, S. A. (2007). Evaluation of the impact of entrepreneurial characteristics on the performance of small scale manufacturing industries in Nigeria. *Journal of Asia Entrepreneurship and Sustainability*, *3*(1), 1.

Adjei, J., Arun, T., & Hossain, F. (2009). Asset building and poverty reduction in Ghana: The case of microfinance. *Savings and Development, 33*(3), 265-291. Retrieved July 30, 2021, from https://www.jstor.org/stable/41406497

Adjei, J. K., Arun, T., & Hossain, F. (2009). *The role of microfinance in asset-building and poverty reduction: The case of Sinapi Aba Trust of Ghana*. Brooks World Poverty Institute, University of Manchester.

Adom, K., & Asare-Yeboa, I. T. (2016). An evaluation of human capital theory and female entrepreneurship in sub-Sahara Africa: Some evidence from Ghana. *International Journal of Gender and Entrepreneurship*, *8*(4), 402–423. doi:10.1108/IJGE-12-2015-0048

Adu, J. K., Anarfi, B. O., & Poku, K. (2014). The Role of Microfinance on Poverty Reduction: A Case Study of Adansi Rural Bank in Ashanti Region, Ghana. *Social and Basic Sciences Research Review*, *2*(3), 96–109.

Afazeli, H., Jafari, A., Rafiee, S., & Nosrati, M. (2014). An investigation of biogas production potential from livestock and slaughterhouse wastes. *Renewable & Sustainable Energy Reviews*, *34*, 380–386. doi:10.1016/j.rser.2014.03.016

African 2030. (2021). *Africa 2030: SDGs within Social Boundaries Leaving No One Behind Outlook.* https://sdgcafrica.org/wp-content/uploads/2021/07/20210721_Full_Report_Final_Web_En.pdf

Agbola, F. W., Acupan, A., & Mahmood, A. (2017). Does microfinance reduce poverty? New evidence from Northeastern Mindanao, the Philippines. *Journal of Rural Studies*, *50*, 159–171. doi:10.1016/j.jrurstud.2016.11.005

Agénor, P. R. (2000). *The Economics of Adjustment and Growth*. Academic Press.

Aggarwal, S., Klapper, L. F., & Singer, D. (2012). *Financing businesses in Africa: The role of microfinance*. World Bank Policy Research Working Paper, (5975).

Ahl, H., & Nelson, T. (2015). How policy positions women entrepreneurs: A comparative analysis of state discourse in Sweden and the United States. *Journal of Business Venturing*, *30*(2), 273–291. doi:10.1016/j.jbusvent.2014.08.002

Ahmad, N., & Hoffmann, A. N. (2008). A framework for addressing and measuring entrepreneurship. *OECD Statistics Working Paper*, *2*, 2–36.

Ahmed, H. (2015). *Zakah, Macroeconomic Policies, and Poverty Alleviation: Lessons from Simulations on Bangladesh.* https://ibtra.com/pdf/journal/v4_n2_article4.pdf

Ahmed, S. (2009). Microfinance institutions in Bangladesh: Achievements and challenges. *Managerial Finance*, *35*(12), 999–1010. doi:10.1108/03074350911000052

Aidoo, F., Adjei, D. M., Akoto, B., Attakora, M., & Carl, C. (2012). *The Role of Microfinance Institutions on the Economic Development of Ghana* (Doctoral dissertation).

Ajuna, A., Ntale, J., & Ngui, T. (2018). Impact of training on the performance of women entrepreneurs in Kenya: Case of Meru Town. *International Academic Journal of Innovation, Leadership and Entrepreneurship*, *2*(2), 93–112.

Akanfewon, P. A., & Kere, O. D. (2016). The Role of Microfinance in the Growth and Development of Small and Medium Scale Businesses in the Builsa Districts of Upper East Region, Ghana. *ADRRI Journal (Multidisciplinary)*, *25*(10), 1–24.

Akinboade, O. A. (2015). Determinants of SMEs growth and performance in Cameroon's central and littoral provinces' manufacturing and retail sectors. *African Journal of Economic and Management Studies*, *6*(2), 183–196. doi:10.1108/AJEMS-03-2013-0033

Akingunola, R., Olowofela, E., & Yunusa, L. (2018). Impact of Microfinance Banks on Micro and Small Enterprises in Ogun State, Nigeria. *Binus Business Review*, *9*(2), 163–169. doi:10.21512/bbr.v9i2.4253

Akinsulore, A., & Akinsulore, O.M. (2021). Sustainable Development and the Exploitation of Bitumen in Nigeria: Assessing the Environmental Laws. Faultline's Beijing Law Review, 113.

Akinyemi, F. O., Alarape, A. A., & Erinfolami, T. P. (2017). The impact of socio-demographic factors on performance of small and medium enterprises in Lagos State, Nigeria. *IFE Research Publications in Geography*, *15*, 107–115.

Al Mamun, A., Malarvizhi, C. A., Abdul Wahab, S. & Mazumder, M. N. H. (2011). Investigating the effect of microcredit on microenterprise income in Peninsular Malaysia. *European Journal of Economics, Finance and Administrative Sciences,* 122-132.

Al Mamun, A., Abdul Wahab, S., & Malarvizhi, C. (2010). Impact of Amanah Ikhtiar Malaysia's microcredit schemes on microenterprise assets in Malaysia. *International Research Journal of Finance and Economics*, *60*, 144–154. doi:10.2139srn.1946089

Al Mamun, A., Adaikalam, J., & Mazumder, M. N. H. (2012). Examining the effect of Amanah Ikhtiar Malaysia's microcredit program on microenterprise assets in rural Malaysia. *Asian Social Science*, *8*(4), 272–280. doi:10.5539/ass.v8n4p272

Aladejare. A. A (2015). Legal Status of Sections 10 and 12 of the Nigerian Oil Gas Industry Content Development Act (2010) under the GATT Regime' (2015). *Journal of Sustainable Development Law & Policy, 5*, 129-147.

Aldrich, H. (1999). *Organisations Evolving.* Sage Publications.

Compilation of References

Aldrich, H. E. (2005). Entrepreneurship. In N. J. Smelser & R. Swedberg (Eds.), *The Handbook of Economic Sociology* (pp. 451–477). Princeton University Press.

Al-Gamal, M. (2020). Shart Tamleek al-Zakah wa 'Atharuhu fi Kayfiyat Tawzi'iha. *Dirasat: Ulum al-Shariah waAlqanun, 47*(3), 30-42. https://journals.ju.edu.jo/DirasatLaw/article/download/104603/11635

Al-Hamamre, Z., Saidan, M., Hararah, M., Rawajfeh, K., Alkhasawneh, H. E., & Al-Shannag, M. (2017). Wastes and biomass materials as sustainable-renewable energy resources for Jordan. *Renewable & Sustainable Energy Reviews, 67*, 295–314. doi:10.1016/j.rser.2016.09.035

Alhassan, Y., & Nwagbara, U. (2021). Institutions, Corruption and Microfinance Viability in Developing Countries: The Case of Ghana and Nigeria. *Economic Insights - Trends and Challenges, 10*(73), 61–70. doi:10.51865/EITC.2021.02.06

Ali, M., Saeed, G., Zeb, A., & Jan, F. (2016). Microcredit & its Significance in Sustainable Development and Poverty Alleviation: Evidence from Asia, Africa, Latin America and Europe. Dialogue, 11(3).

Alimukhamedova, N. & Hanousek, J. (2015). *What Do We Know about Microfinance at Macro Glance?* Academic Press.

Al-Qaradaghi, A. (2014). القرض غادي وعدي الحكومات الإسلامية إلخراج زكاة اورث واخُمس النفط لإنهاء الفقر. https://arabic.cnn.com/middleeast/2014/07/17/ali-qaradahji-islamic-finance

Alshebami, A. S., & Khandare, D. M. (2015). The impact of interest rate ceilings on microfinance industry. *International Journal of Social Work, 2*(2), 10. doi:10.5296/ijsw.v2i2.7953

Alvarez, S. & Busenitz, L. (2001). The entrepreneurship of resource based theory. *Journal of Management, 27*, 755-775.

Alvi, E., & Senbeta, A. (2012). Does foreign aid reduce poverty? *Journal of International Development, 24*(8), 955–976. doi:10.1002/jid.1790

Amadasun, S. (2019). Mainstreaming a developmental approach to social work education and practice in Africa? Perspectives of Nigerian BSW students. *Social Work Education, 6*(2), 196–207. doi:10.25128/2520-6230.19.2.8

Amao, O. (2008). Corporate Social Responsibility. Multinational Corporations and the Law in Nigeria: Controlling Multinationals in Host States. *Journal of African Law, 52*(1), 89–113.

Amin, M. F. B., & Uddin, S. J. (2018). Microfinance-economic growth nexus: A case study on Grameen bank in Bangladesh. *International Journal of Islamic Economics and Finance, 1*(1). Advance online publication. doi:10.18196/ijief.112

Amnesty International Nigeria. (2012). *Joint Memorandum on Petroleum Industry Bill March 2012.* Author.

Amoa-Awua, W. K., Ngunjiri, P., Anlobe, J., Kpodo, K., Halm, M., Hayford, A. E., & Jakobsen, M. (2007). The effect of applying GMP and HACCP to traditional food processing at a semi-commercial kenkey production plant in Ghana. *Food Control*, *18*(11), 1449–1457. doi:10.1016/j.foodcont.2006.10.009

Amodu, Aondoseer, & Audu. (2015). Effects of gender and cultural beliefs on women entrepreneurs in Nigeria. *Journal of African Business*, *12*(2), 64–83.

Anane, G. K., Cobbinah, P. B., & Manu, J. K. (2013). Sustainability of small and medium scale enterprises in rural Ghana: The role of microfinance institutions. *Asian Economic and Financial Review*, *3*(8), 1003–1017.

Anane, G. K., Cobbinah, P. B., & Manu, J. K. (2013). Sustainability of Small and Medium Scale Enterprises in Rural Ghana: The Role of Microfinance Institutions. *Asian Economic and Financial Review*, *3*(8), 1003–1017.

Ananth, S., & Öncü, T. (2013). Challenges to Financial Inclusion in India: The Case of Andhra Pradesh. *Economic and Political Weekly*, *48*(7), 77-83. Retrieved July 30, 2021, from https://www.jstor.org/stable/23391312

Andruss, P. (2013). *What to look for in an accelerator program*. Entrepreneur. https://www.entrepreneur.com/article/225242

Antoncic, B. (2009). The entrepreneur's general personality traits and technological developments. *World Academy of Science, Engineering and Technology*, *53*, 236–241.

Anyadike, N., Emeh, I. E. J., & Ukah, F. I. (2012). Entrepreneurship development and employment generation in Nigeria: Problems and prospects. *Universal Journal of Education and General Studies*, *1*(4), 88-102.

APEC. (2005). *The Need and Availability of Micro Finance Service for the Micro Enterprise: Bringing multi-level Good Practices into Local Context*. https://www.sica.int/documentos/the-need-and-availability-of-micro-finance-service-for-micro-enterprise-bringing-multi-level-good-practices-into-local-context_1_86513.html

Appah, E., John, M. S., & Wisdom, S. (2012). An analysis of microfinance and poverty reduction in Bayelsa State of Nigeria. *Kuwait Chapter of the Arabian Journal of Business and Management Review*, *1*(7), 38–58.

Aras, G., & Crowther, D. (2008). Governance and sustainability: An investigation into the relationship between corporate governance and corporate sustainability. *Management Decision*, *46*(3), 433–448. doi:10.1108/00251740810863870

Aras, G., & Crowther, D. (2016). *A Handbook of Corporate Governance and Social Responsibility*. Routledge. doi:10.4324/9781315564791

Arenius, P., & Minniti, M. (2005). Perceptual variables and nascent entrepreneurship. *Small Business Economics*, *24*(3), 233–247. doi:10.100711187-005-1984-x

Compilation of References

Armistead, C. G., Clark, G., & Stanley, P. (1995). Managing Service Recovery, Cranfield School of Management. Cranfield.

Arnold, K. J. (2012). *Microfinance for microenterprises? Investigating the usefulness of microfinance services for microenterprises in Bolivia.* Simon Fraser University.

Arora, M., & Singh, S. (2018). Microfinance, Women Empowerment, and Transformational Leadership: A Study of Himachal Pradesh. *International Journal on Leadership*, *6*(2), 23.

Arora, R. U. (2012). Gender inequality, economic development, and globalization: A state level analysis of India. *Journal of Developing Areas*, *46*(1), 147–164. doi:10.1353/jda.2012.0019

Arregle, J. L., Batjargal, B., Hitt, M. A., Webb, J. W., Miller, T., & Tsui, A. S. (2015). Family ties in entrepreneurs' social networks and new venture growth. *Entrepreneurship Theory and Practice*, *39*(2), 313–344. doi:10.1111/etap.12044

Arsalan, S., & Ali, S. (2020). Key determinants of SMEs' export performance. *Journal of Business and Industrial Marketing*, *35*(4), 635–654.

Aruna, M., & Jyothirmayi, M. R. (2011). The role of microfinance in women empowerment: A study on the SHG bank linkage program in Hyderabad (Andhra Pradesh). *Indian Journal of Commerce & Management Studies ISSN*, *2229*, 5674.

Ashcroft, M. O. (2008). Microfinance in Africa–The challenges, realities and success stories. *Microbanking Bulletin*, *17*, 5–11.

Asher, S. N. (2014). Improving the well-being of the women through microfinance: Evidence from Swabi District. *Putaj Humanities & Social Sciences*, *21*(1), 57–65.

Ashiomanedu, J. (2008). Poverty and Sustainable Development in the Niger Delta Region of Nigeria. *Journal of Sustainable Development in Africa*, *10*(3), 155–171.

Asnaf, M. A. I. S. (2015). *Bersama kami membantu Asnaf*. Lembaga Zakah Selangor.

Asongu, S. A., Uduji, J. I., & Okolo-Obasi, E. N. (2019). Thresholds of external flows for inclusive human development in Sub-Saharan Africa. *International Journal of Community Well-Being*, *2*(3), 213–233. doi:10.100742413-019-00037-7

As-Sallabi, A. (2015). *Umar Bin 'Abd- 'Aziz*. Dar Ibn Katheer.

Atkinson, S. W. (1957). Motivational determinants of risk-taking behavior. *Psychological Review*, *64*(6, Pt.1), 359–372. doi:10.1037/h0043445 PMID:13505972

Atmadja, A. S., Sharma, P., & Su, J. J. (2018). Microfinance and microenterprise performance in Indonesia: An extended and updated survey. *International Journal of Social Economics*, *45*(6), 957–972. doi:10.1108/IJSE-02-2017-0031

Atmadja, A. S., Su, J. J., & Sharma, P. (2016). Examining the impact of microfinance on microenterprise performance (implications for women-owned microenterprises in Indonesia. *International Journal of Social Economics*, *43*(10), 962–981. doi:10.1108/IJSE-08-2014-0158

Attanasio, O., Augsburg, B., De Haas, R., Fitzsimons, E., & Harmgart, H. (2013). Group lending or individual lending? Evidence from a randomized field experiment in rural Mongolia. *American Economic Journal: Applied Economics*.

Attanasio, O., Augsburg, B., De Haas, R., Fitzsimons, E., & Harmgart, H. (2015). The impacts of microfinance: Evidence from joint-liability lending in Mongolia. *American Economic Journal. Applied Economics*, 7(1), 90–122. doi:10.1257/app.20130489

Audretsch, D. B., & Keilbach, M. (2004). Entrepreneurship and regional growth: An evolutionary interpretation. *Journal of Evolutionary Economics*, 14(5), 605–616. doi:10.100700191-004-0228-6

Audretsch, D. B., Keilbach, M. C., & Lehmann, E. E. (2006). *Entrepreneurship and Economic Growth*. Oxford University Press. doi:10.1093/acprof:oso/9780195183511.001.0001

Audretsch, D. B., Keilbach, M., & Lehmann, E. (2005). *The knowledge spillover theory of entrepreneurship and technological diffusion. University entrepreneurship and technology transfer*. Emerald London.

Augsburg, B., De Haas, R., Harmgart, H. & Meghir, C. (2013). Microfinance and Poverty Alleviation. *American Economic Journal: Applied Economics*.

Auty, R. (1993). *Sustaining development in mineral economies*. Routledge.

Avolio, B. (2017). Why women enter into entrepreneurship? An emerging conceptual framework based on the Peruvian case. *Journal of Women's Entrepreneurship and Education*, (3-4), 43–63.

Awojobi, O. N. (2014). Empowering women through micro-finance: Evidence from Nigeria. *Australian Journal of Business and Management Research*, 4(1), 17–26. doi:10.52283/NSWRCA.AJBMR.20140401A03

Awudjah, I. E. (2019). *Microfinance and Women Empowerment in Ghana* (Doctoral dissertation). University of Ghana.

Ayodele, A. E., & Arogundade, K. (2014). The impact of microfinance on economic growth in Nigeria. *Journal of Emerging Trends in Economics and Management Science*, 5(5), 397–405.

Babajide, A. (2011). Impact analysis of microfinance in Nigeria. *International Journal of Economics and Finance*, 3(4).

Babajide, A. A. (2012). Effects of microfinance on micro and small enterprises (MSEs) growth in Nigeria. *Asian Economic and Financial Review*, 2(3), 463–477.

Badan Pusat Statistik (BPS). (2016). *Gini Ratio Maret 2016*. BPS Official News. https://bali.bps.go.id/

Bagwell, S. (2008). Transnational family networks and ethnic minority business development: The case of Vietnamese nail-shops in the UK. *International Journal of Entrepreneurial Behaviour & Research*, 14(6), 377–394. doi:10.1108/13552550810910960

Compilation of References

Bajpai, P. (2019). *The Rise of Peer-to-Peer (2019) Lending.* https://www.nasdaq.com/article/the-rise-of-peertopeer-p2p-lending-cm685513

Baker, Kousis, Richardson, & Young. (1997). *The Politics of Sustainable Development: Theory, Policy and Practice within the European Union.* Routledge.

Baker, S. (2006). *Sustainable Development Abingdon-on-Thames: Routledge.* Taylor and Francis Group. doi:10.4324/9780203495933

Baker, T., & Nelson, R. E. (2005). Creating Something from Nothing: Resource Construction through Entrepreneurial Bricolage. *Administrative Science Quarterly, 50*(3), 329–366. doi:10.2189/asqu.2005.50.3.329

Bakhtiari, S. (2006). Microfinance and poverty reduction: some international evidence. *International Business & Economics Research Journal, 5*(12).

Bakhtiari, S. (2011). Microfinance and poverty reduction: some international evidence. International Business and Economics Research Journal, 5(12).

Balwi, M. A., & Halim, A. H. A. (2008). Mobilising zakah dalam pewujudan usahawan Asnaf: Satu tinjauan. Shariah Journal, 16, 567-584.

Banerjee, S. B. (2008). Corporate social responsibility: The good, the bad and the ugly. *Critical Sociology, 34*(1), 51–79. doi:10.1177/0896920507084623

Bangoura, L. (2012). Microfinance as an Approach to Development in Low Income Countries. *Bangladesh Development Studies, 35*(4), 87–111. Retrieved July 30, 2021, from https://www.jstor.org/stable/41968844

Baporikar, N. (2018b). Entrepreneurship Development and Project Management (Text & Cases). Himalaya Publishing House.

Baporikar, N. (2015). Societal Influence on the Cognitive Aspects of Entrepreneurship. *International Journal of Civic Engagement and Social Change, 2*(4), 1–15. doi:10.4018/ijcesc.2015100101

Baporikar, N. (2016). *Handbook of Research on Entrepreneurship in the Contemporary Knowledge-Based Global Economy.* IGI Global. doi:10.4018/978-1-4666-8798-1

Baporikar, N. (2017). Cluster Approach for Entrepreneurship Development in India. *International Journal of Asian Business and Information Management, 8*(2), 46–61. doi:10.4018/IJABIM.2017040104

Baporikar, N. (2018a). *Knowledge Integration Strategies for Entrepreneurship and Sustainability.* IGI Global. doi:10.4018/978-1-5225-5115-7

Baporikar, N. (2019). Influence of Business Competitiveness on SMEs Performance. *International Journal of Productivity Management and Assessment Technologies, 7*(2), 1–25. doi:10.4018/IJPMAT.2019070101

Baporikar, N. (2020a). *Handbook of Research on Entrepreneurship Development and Opportunities in Circular Economy*. IGI Global. doi:10.4018/978-1-7998-5116-5

Baporikar, N. (2020b). Learning Link in Organizational Tacit Knowledge Creation and Dissemination. *International Journal of Sociotechnology and Knowledge Development*, *12*(4), 70–88. doi:10.4018/IJSKD.2020100105

Baporikar, N. (2021). Fintech Challenges and Outlook in India. In Y. A. Albastaki, A. Razzaque, & A. M. Sarea (Eds.), *Innovative Strategies for Implementing FinTech in Banking* (pp. 136–153). IGI Global. doi:10.4018/978-1-7998-3257-7.ch008

Baporikar, N., & Akino, S. (2020). Financial Literacy Imperative for Success of Women Entrepreneurship. *International Journal of Innovation in the Digital Economy*, *11*(3), 1–21. doi:10.4018/IJIDE.2020070101

Baporikar, N., & Shikokola, S. (2020). Information Technology Adoption Dynamics for SMEs in the Manufacturing Sector of Namibia. *International Journal of ICT Research in Africa and the Middle East*, *9*(2), 60–77. doi:10.4018/IJICTRAME.2020070104

Barazandeh, M., Parvizian, K., Alizadeh, M. & Khosravi, S. (2015). Investigating the effect of entrepreneurial competencies on business performance among early stage entrepreneurs Global Entrepreneurship Monitor (GEM 2010 survey data). *Journal of Global Entrepreneurship Research, 5*(1), 18.

Barbier, E. B. (1987). The Concept of Sustainable Economic Development. *Environmental Conservation*, *14*(2), 101–110.

Barbier, E. B. (1987). The concept of sustainable economic development. *Environmental Conservation*, *14*(2), 101–110. doi:10.1017/S0376892900011449

Baron, R. (2007). Entrepreneurship: A process perspective. In J.R. Baum, M. Frese, & R. Baron (Eds.), The psychology of entrepreneurship (pp. 19-40). Academic Press.

Baron, R. A. (2004). The cognitive perspective: A valuable tool for analyzing entrepreneurship's basic «Why» Questions. *Journal of Business Venturing*, *19*(2), 221–239. doi:10.1016/S0883-9026(03)00008-9

Basiago, A. D. (1999). Economic, social, and environmental sustainability in development theory and urban planning practice. *Sustainability Science 123 Environmentalist*, *19*(1), 145–161.

Bastian, B. L., Sidani, Y. M., & El Amine, Y. (2018). Women entrepreneurship in the Middle East and North Africa: A review of knowledge areas and research gaps. *Gender in Management*, *33*(1), 14–29. doi:10.1108/GM-07-2016-0141

Basu, P., & Srivastava, P. (2005). Exploring Possibilities: Microfinance and Rural Credit Access for the Poor in India. *Economic and Political Weekly*, *40*(17), 1747–1756. https://www.jstor.org/stable/4416534

Bateman, M. (Ed.). (2011). *Confronting Microfinance: Undermining Sustainable Development*. Kumarian Press.

Bateman, M. (2012). The role of microfinance in contemporary rural development finance policy and practice: Imposing neoliberalism as best practice. *Journal of Agrarian Change*, *12*(4), 587–600.

Bateman, M. (2017). Local economic development and microcredit. In *The Essential Guide to Critical Development Studies* (pp. 235–248). Routledge. doi:10.4324/9781315612867-19

Bateson, F. A. (1995). SERVQUAL: Review, critique, research agenda. *European Journal of Marketing*, *30*(1), 8–32.

Battilana, J., & Dorado, S. (2010). Building sustainable hybrid organizations: The case of commercial microfinance organizations. *Academy of Management Journal*, *53*(6), 1419–1440. doi:10.5465/amj.2010.57318391

Baumol, W. (1968). Entrepreneurship in economic theory. *The American Economic Review*, *56*, 64–71.

Baumol, W. J., Litan, R. E., & Schramm, C. J. (2007). *Good capitalism, bad capitalism, and the economics of growth and prosperity*. Yale University Press. doi:10.2139srn.985843

Bayulgen, O. (2008). Muhammad Yunus, Grameen Bank and the Nobel Peace Prize: What political science can contribute to and learn from the study of microcredit. *International Studies Review*, *10*(3), 525–547. doi:10.1111/j.1468-2486.2008.00803.x

Bazeley, P., & Jackson, K. (2013). *Qualitative data analysis with NVivo* (2nd ed.). Sage.

Bebbington, A. (1999). *Capitals and capabilities*. International Institute for Environment and Development.

Bebbington, J., & Unerman, J. (2018). Achieving the United Nations Sustainable Development Goals: An enabling role for accounting research. *Accounting, Auditing & Accountability Journal*, *31*(1), 2–24. doi:10.1108/AAAJ-05-2017-2929

Bebbington, J., Unerman, J., & O'Dwyer, B. (2014). *Sustainability accounting and accountability*. Routledge.

Becker, G. S. 1975. Human Capital. Chicago, IL: Chicago University Press.

Belal, A. R. (2008). *Corporate social responsibility reporting in developing countries: The case of Bangladesh*. Ashgate.

Berger, I. E., & Kanetkar, V. (1995). Increasing Environmental Sensitivity via Workplace Experiments. *Journal of Public Policy & Marketing*, *14*(2), 205–215.

Berhane, G., & Gardebroek, C. (2011). Does microfinance reduce rural poverty? Evidence based on household panel data from northern Ethiopia. *American Journal of Agricultural Economics*, *93*(1), 43–55. doi:10.1093/ajae/aaq126

Berry, L. L. (1995). Relationship marketing of services – growing interest emerging perspectives. *Journal of the Academy of Marketing Science*, *23*(4), 236–245.

Bhattacharya, S. C., Thomas, J. M., & Salam, P. A. (1997). Greenhouse gas emissions and the mitigation potential of using animal wastes in Asia. *Energy*, *22*(11), 1079–1085. doi:10.1016/S0360-5442(97)00039-X

Bielen, F., & Sempels, C. (2003). *The dimensionality of the concept of intangibility: A critical analysis*. IAG Working Papers, 2003/100, 2078.1/5427.

Bird, B. J., & Schjoedt, L. (2009). Entrepreneurial behavior: Its nature, scope, recent research, and agenda for future research. In A. L. Carsrud & M. Brännback (Eds.), *Understanding the entrepreneurial mind, international studies in entrepreneurship* (pp. 327–358). Springer Science & Business Media. doi:10.1007/978-1-4419-0443-0_15

Birdsall, M., Jones, C., Lee, C., Somerset, C., & Takaki, S. (2013). *Business Accelerators - The Evolution of a Rapidly Growing Industry*. Academic Press.

Bitner, M. J. (1990). Evaluating service encounters: The effects of physical surroundings and employee responses. *Journal of Marketing*, *54*(2), 69–82.

Bitner, M. J., Booms, B. H., & Mohr, L. A. (1994). Critical service encounters: The employees' viewpoint. *Journal of Marketing*, *58*(4), 95–105.

Bitner, M. J., Booms, B. H., & Tetreault, M. S. (1990). The service encounter: Diagnosing favourable and unfavourable incidents. *Journal of Marketing*, *54*(1), 77–84.

Bjerke, B. (2007). *Understanding Entrepreneurship*. Edward Elgar.

Blumberg, R. L. (2005). Women's Economic Empowerment as the Magic Potion of Development? *100th Annual Meeting of the American Sociological Association*, Philadelphia, PA.

Boateng, G. O., Boateng, A. A., & Bampoe, H. S. (2015). Microfinance and poverty reduction in Ghana: Evidence from policy beneficiaries. *Review of Business & Finance Studies*, *6*(1), 99–108.

Bogan, V. L. (2012). Capital structure and sustainability: An empirical study of microfinance institutions. *The Review of Economics and Statistics*, *94*(4), 1045–1058. doi:10.1162/REST_a_00223

Bolton, L. E., & Mattila, A. S. (2015). How does corporate social responsibility affect customer response to service failure in buyer/seller relationships? *Journal of Retailing*, *91*(1), 140-153.

Bolton, R. N., & Drew, J. H. (1991). A multi-stage model of customers' assessments of service quality and value. *The Journal of Consumer Research*, *17*(4), 375–384.

Bondinuba, F. K., Stephens, M., Jones, C., & Buckley, R. (2020). The motivations of microfinance institutions to enter the housing market in a developing country. *International Journal of Housing Policy*, *20*(4), 534–554. doi:10.1080/19491247.2020.1721411

Compilation of References

Bosma, N., & Schutjens, V. (2008). Mapping entrepreneurial activity and entrepreneurial attitudes in European regions. *International Journal of Entrepreneurship and Small Business*.

Bowen, H. R. (1953). *Social Responsibilities of the Businessman*. Harper & Row.

Bradley, S. W., Aldrich, H., Shepherd, D. A., & Wiklund, J. (2011). Resources, environmental change, and survival: Asymmetric paths of young independent and subsidiary organizations. *Strategic Management Journal*, *32*(5), 486–509. doi:10.1002mj.887

Brana, S. (2013). Microcredit: An answer to the gender problem in funding? *Small Business Economics*, *40*(1), 87–100. doi:10.100711187-011-9346-3

Branisa, B., Klasen, S., & Ziegler, M. (2013). Gender inequality in social institutions and gendered development outcomes. *World Development*, *45*, 252–268. doi:10.1016/j.worlddev.2012.12.003

Brau, J. C., Cardell, S. N., & Woodworth, W. P. (2015). Does microfinance fill the funding gap for microentrepreneurs? A conceptual analysis of entrepreneurship seeding in impoverished nations. *International Business Research*, *8*(5), 30. doi:10.5539/ibr.v8n5p30

Breivik, H. (1995). Benefits, risks and economics of post-operative pain management programmes. *Bailliere's Clinical Anaesthesiology*, *9*(3), 403–422.

British Association of Social Workers. (2010). *Poverty Eradication and the Role of Social Workers*. Author.

Brockhaus, R. H. Sr, & Horwitz, P. S. (1986). The psychology of the entrepreneur. In D. L. Sexton & R. W. Smilor (Eds.), *The Art and Science of Entrepreneurship* (pp. 25–48). Ballinger.

Brown, A., & Swersky, A. (2012). *The First Billion, A forecast of social investment demand*. The Boston Consulting Group and Big Society Capital. http://impactstrategist.com/wp-content/uploads/2015/12/First-Billion-forecast-demand.pdf

Brown, R. (1986). *Social psychology* (2nd ed.). The Free Press.

Brown, T. J., & Dacin, P. A. (1997). The company and the product: Corporate associations and consumer product responses. *Journal of Marketing*, *61*(1), 68–84.

Bruederlea & Hodle. (2019). Effect of oil spills on infant mortality in Nigeria. *Proceedings of the National Academy of Sciences, 116(12), 1-5.*

Bruhn, M., & Love, I. (2014). The real impact of improved access to finance: Evidence from Mexico. *The Journal of Finance*, *69*(3), 1347–1376. doi:10.1111/jofi.12091

Brundtland, G. (1987). Our Common Future-Call for Action. *Environmental Conservation*, *14*(04), 291.

Buana, G. K. (2018). *Innovative financing for SDGs: Mobilizing ummah's potential to leave no one behind*. https://www.asia-pacific.undp.org/content/rbap/en/home/blog/2018/innovative-financing-for-sdgs.html

Bukhari, M. (1422H). *Al-Jami' al-ṣaḥiḥ al-mukhtaṣar min umur rasuli Llah wasunanihi waayyamihi* (Ṣaḥiḥ al-Bukhari) Dar Tawq al- Najah, 14(22), 1331.

Bulanova, O., Isaksen, E. J., & Kolvereid, L. (2016). Growth aspirations among women entrepreneurs in high growth firms. *Baltic Journal of Management*, *11*(2), 187–206. doi:10.1108/BJM-11-2014-0204

Bullough, A., De Luque, M. S., Abdelzaher, D., & Heim, W. (2015). Developing women leaders through entrepreneurship education and training. *The Academy of Management Perspectives*, *29*(2), 250–270. doi:10.5465/amp.2012.0169

Burns, P. (2016). *Entrepreneurship and small business*. Palgrave Macmillan Limited. Available at: https://uws-primo.hosted.exlibrisgroup.com/

Business for 2030. (n.d.). *Business for 2030*. Available at http://www.businessfor2030.org

Butler, P., & Collins, N. (2001). Payment on delivery - Recognising constituency service as political marketing. *European Journal of Marketing*, *35*(9/10), 1026–1037.

Bygrave, W. D., & Hofer, C. W. (1991). Theorizing about entrepreneurship. *Entrepreneurship Theory and Practice*, (Winter), 12–22.

Cabrera, E. M., & Mauricio, D. (2017). Factors affecting the success of women's entrepreneurship: A review of literature. *International Journal of Gender and Entrepreneurship*, *9*(1), 31–65. doi:10.1108/IJGE-01-2016-0001

Calgagovski, J. (1990). *Microfinance in Africa: Combining the Best Practices of Traditional and Modern Microfinance Approaches towards Poverty Eradication*. The United Nations. Available at: https://www.un.org/esa/africa/microfinanceinafrica.pdf

Caliendo, M., Fossen, F., & Kritikos, A. (2011). *Personality Characteristics and the Decision to Become and Stay Self-Employed*. https://ftp.iza.org/dp5566.pdf

Camacho, D. (1998). *Environmental Injustices, Political Struggles: Race*. Class, and the Environment Duke University Press.

Cap 07 Laws of the Federation of Nigeria, 2004

Carroll, A. B. (1991). The pyramid of corporate social responsibility: Towards the moral management of organisational stakeholders. *Business Horizons*, *34*(4), 39–48.

Carroll, A. B., & Ahuvia, A. C. (2006). Some antecedents and outcomes of brand love. *Marketing Letters*, *17*, 79–89.

Carsrud, A., & Brannback, M. (2011). Entrepreneurial Motivations: What Do We Still Need to Know? *Journal of Small Business Management*, *49*(1), 9–26. doi:10.1111/j.1540-627X.2010.00312.x

Chakraborty, S., Thompson, J. C., & Yehoue, E. B. (2016). The culture of entrepreneurship. *Journal of Economic Theory*, *163*, 288–317.

Compilation of References

Chasserio, S., Pailot, P., & Poroli, C. (2014). When entrepreneurial identity meets multiple social identities: Interplays and identity work of women entrepreneurs. *International Journal of Entrepreneurial Behaviour & Research, 20*(2), 128–154. doi:10.1108/IJEBR-11-2011-0157

Chen, J., Chang, A. Y., & Bruton, G. D. (2017). Microfinance: Where are we today and where should the research go in the future? *International Small Business Journal, 35*(7), 793–802. doi:10.1177/0266242617717380

Cheraghali, A. R. (2011). *Factors affecting the development of entrepreneurship in agricultural cooperatives* (Master's thesis). Entrepreneurship Department, Tehran University.

Cheston, S., & Kuhn, L. (2002). Empowering women through microfinance. *Draft. Opportunity International, 64*, 1–64.

Chichilinisky, G. (1994). North–South trade and the global environment. *The American Economic Review, 84*(4), 851–874.

Chikalipah, S. (2017a). Financial sustainability of microfinance institutions in sub-Saharan Africa: Evidence from GMM estimates. *Enterprise Development & Microfinance, 28*(3), 182–199. doi:10.3362/1755-1986.16-00023

Chikalipah, S. (2017b). What determines financial inclusion in Sub-Saharan Africa? *African Journal of Economic and Management Studies, 8*(1), 8–18. doi:10.1108/AJEMS-01-2016-0007

Chinomona, E., & Maziriri, E. T. (2015). Women in action: Challenges facing women entrepreneurs in the Gauteng Province of South Africa. *The International Business & Economics Research Journal (Online), 14*(6), 835. doi:10.19030/iber.v14i6.9487

Chirwa, E. W. (2008). Effects of gender on the performance of micro and small enterprises in Malawi. *Development Southern Africa, 25*(3), 347–362. doi:10.1080/03768350802212139

Chitereka, C. (2005). The impact of HIV/AIDS on development and the role of social workers: The case of Lesotho. In G. Jacques & G. N. Lesetedi (Eds.), *The new partnership for Africa's development: Debates, opportunities, and challenges* (pp. 384–398). Africa Institute of South Africa.

Chliova, M., Brinckmann, J., & Rosenbusch, N. (2015). Is microcredit a blessing for the poor? A meta-analysis examining development outcomes and contextual considerations. *Journal of Business Venturing, 30*(3), 467–487. doi:10.1016/j.jbusvent.2014.10.003

Choi, B. & La, S. (2013). The impact of corporate social responsibility (CSR) and customer trust on the restoration of loyalty after service failure and recovery. *Journal of Services Marketing, 27*(3), 223-233.

Cho, S.-B., Jang, Y. M., & Kim, W. G. (2017). The Moderating Role of Severity of Service Failure in the Relationship among Regret/Disappointment, Dissatisfaction, and Behavioural Intention. *Journal of Quality Assurance in Hospitality & Tourism, 18*(1), 69–85.

Chowdhury, A. (2009). *Microfinance as a poverty reduction tool-a critical assessment.* United Nations, Department of Economic and Social Affairs (DESA) working paper.

Chowdhury, M. S., Alam, Z., & Arif, M. I. (2013). Success factors of entrepreneurs of small and medium sized enterprises: Evidence from Bangladesh. *Business and Economic Review*, *3*(2), 38. doi:10.5296/ber.v3i2.4127

Christensen, L. J., Peirce, E., Hartman, L. P., Hoffman, W. M., & Carrier, J. (2007). Ethics, CSR, and sustainability education in the financial times top 50 global business schools: Baseline data and future research directions. *Journal of Business Ethics*, *73*(4), 347–368.

Churchill, S. A. (2020). Impact of Microfinance on Poverty and Microenterprises. In *Moving from the Millennium to the Sustainable Development Goals*. Palgrave Macmillan. doi:10.1007/978-981-15-1556-9_14

Cizakca, M. (2011). *The Waqf, its Contribution and Basic Operational Structure.* http://www.iqra.org.my/slide/Iqra%20Waqf%20101.pptx

Clausen, T. H. (2006). Who identifies and exploits entrepreneurial opportunities? Centre for Technology, Innovation, and Culture, University of Oslo.

Coduras, A., Saiz-Alvarez, J. M., & Ruiz, J. (2016). Measuring readiness for entrepreneurship: An information tool proposal. *J Inn Knowledge*, *1*(2), 99–108. doi:10.1016/j.jik.2016.02.003

Cohen, D., & Feld, B. (2011). Do More Faster: TechStars Lessons to Accelerate Your Startup. John Wiley and Sons.

Collins, C. J., Hanges, P., & Locke, E. A. (2004). The relationship of need for achievement to entrepreneurship: A meta-analysis. *Human Performance*, *17*, 95–117. doi:10.1207/S15327043HUP1701_5

Commission for Africa. (2005). *Our common interest: report of the commission for Africa.* Penguin.

Cooper, J. N. (2012). *The impact of microfinance services on the growth of small and medium enterprises in Kenya* (Doctoral dissertation). University of Nairobi.

Copestake, J. (2007). Mainstreaming microfinance: Social performance management or mission drift? *World Development*, *35*(10), 1721–1738. doi:10.1016/j.worlddev.2007.06.004

Coulter, K. S., & Coulter, R. A. (2002). Determinants of trust in a service provider: The moderating role of length of relationship. *Journal of Services Marketing*, *16*(1), 35–50.

Crépon, B., Devoto, F., Duflo, E., & Parienté, W. (2011). *Impact of microcredit in rural areas of Morocco: Evidence from a Randomized Evaluation.* MIT Working Paper.

Crépon, B., Devoto, F., Duflo, E., & Pariente, W. (2014). Estimating the impact of microcredit on those who take it up: Evidence from a randomized experiment in Morocco. National Bureau of Economic Research. doi:10.3386/w20144

Compilation of References

Crépon, B., Devoto, F., Duflo, E., & Parienté, W. (2015). Estimating the impact of microcredit on those who take it up: Evidence from a randomized experiment in Morocco. *American Economic Journal. Applied Economics*, *7*(1), 123–150. doi:10.1257/app.20130535

Creswell, J. W. (2013). *Research design: Qualitative, quantitative, and mixed methods approaches*. SAGE Publications Ltd.

Creswell, J. W. (2015). *A concise introduction to mixed methods research*. SAGE Publications Ltd.

Creswell, J. W., & Poth, C. N. (2017). *Qualitative inquiry and research design: Choosing among five approaches*. SAGE Publications Ltd.

Crisp, R. (2016). *Community-led approaches to reducing poverty in neighbourhoods: A review of evidence and practice*. Sheffield University: Centre for Regional Economic and Social Research.

Crowther, D., & Aras, G. (2008). *Corporate social responsibility*. Ventus Publishing.

Crowther, D., & Aras, G. (2008). *The Future of Corporate Governance. Electronic Journal, A Prognosis*.

Cull, R., Demirgüç-Kunt, A., & Morduch, J. (2014). Banks and microbanks. *Journal of Financial Services Research*, *46*(1), 1–53. doi:10.100710693-013-0177-z

D'espallier, B., Guérin, I., & Mersland, R. (2011). Women and repayment in microfinance: A global analysis. *World Development*, *39*(5), 758–772. doi:10.1016/j.worlddev.2010.10.008

Dalborg, C., von Friedrichs, Y., & Wincent, J. (2015). Risk perception matters: Why women's passion may not lead to a business start-up. *International Journal of Gender and Entrepreneurship*, *7*(1), 87–104. doi:10.1108/IJGE-01-2013-0001

Daniel, T. L. S., Po, P. Y. C., & Hildie, L. (2015). Manufacturing Economy vs. Service Economy: Implications for Service Leadership. *International Journal on Disability and Human Development: IJDHD*, *14*(3), 205–215.

Dankelman, I., & Davidson, J. (2013). *Women and the environment in the third world: alliance for the future*. Routledge. doi:10.4324/9781315066219

Datar, S. M., Epstein, M. J., & Yuthas, K. (2010). Enamored with scale: scaling with limited impact in the microfinance industry. In P. N. Bloom & E. Skloot (Eds.), *Scaling Social Impact: New Thinking* (pp. 47–64). Palgrave Macmillan. doi:10.1057/9780230113565_4

David, A. (2017). Amanah Ikhtiar willing to give more loans to women entrepreneurs. *New Straits Time*. https://www.nst.com.my/news/nation/2017/10/297067/amanah-ikhtiar-willing-give-more-loans-women-entrepreneurs

Davidsson, P., Low, M., & Wright, M. (2001). Editors' introduction: Low and Macmillan ten years on–achievements and future directions for entrepreneurship research. *Entrepreneurship Theory and Practice*, *25*(4), 5–16. doi:10.1177/104225870102500401

Dawe, N. K., & Ryan, K. L. (2003). The Faulty Three-Legged-Stool Model of Sustainable Development. *Conservation Biology*, *17*(5), 1458–1460. doi:10.1046/j.1523-1739.2003.02471.x

Delgado-Garcia, J. B., Rodriguez-Escudero, A. I., & Martin-Cruz, N. (2012). Influence of affective traits on entrepreneur's goals and satisfaction. *Journal of Small Business Management*, *50*(3), 408–428. doi:10.1111/j.1540-627X.2012.00359.x

Deo, S. (2005). *Challenges for small business entrepreneurs: A study in the Waikato region of New Zealand.* Available at: http://www.sbaer.uca.edu/research/icsb/2005/056.pdf

Desjardins, D. (2000). *Gales guide to genealogical & historical research.* Gale Group.

Desjardins, J. R. (2000). *Business, ethics, and the environment.* Pearson.

Devaraja, T. S. (2011). *Microfinance in India-A tool for poverty reduction. University of Mysore.* University Grants Commission of India.

Devine, R. A., & Kiggundu, M. N. (2016). Entrepreneurship in Africa: Identifying the frontier of impactful research. *Africa Journal of Management*, *2*(3), 349–380. doi:10.1080/23322373.2016.1206802

De-Vita, L., Mari, M., & Poggesi, S. (2014). Women entrepreneurs in and from developing countries: Evidences from the literature. *European Management Journal*, *32*(3), 451–460. doi:10.1016/j.emj.2013.07.009

Diaw, C. T. (2018). Analyst of the determinants of national savings in Senegal. *European International Journal of Science and Technology*, *7*(8), 17–25.

Dichter, T. W. (1996). Questioning the future of NGOs in microfinance. *Journal of International Development*, *8*(2), 259–269. doi:10.1002/(SICI)1099-1328(199603)8:2<259::AID-JID377>3.0.CO;2-7

Dineen, K., & Le, Q. V. (2015). The impact of an integrated microcredit program on the empowerment of women and gender equality in rural Vietnam. *Journal of Developing Areas*, *49*(1), 23–38. doi:10.1353/jda.2015.0028

Din, N. M., Rosdi, M. S. M., Ismail, M., Muhammad, M. Z., & Mukhtar, D. (2019). Contributions of Asnaf Entrepreneurs in Zakah of Business: A Revisiting Based on Turning over Model. *International Journal of Academic Research in Business & Social Sciences*, *9*(9), 744–752.

Dominelli, L. (2006). News and Views...from IASSW. *International Social Work*, *49*(4), 543–546. doi:10.1177/0020872806065486

Donou-Adonsou, F., & Sylwester, K. (2017). Growth effect of banks and microfinance: Evidence from developing countries. *The Quarterly Review of Economics and Finance*, *64*, 44–56. doi:10.1016/j.qref.2016.11.001

Donthu, N. (2020). Effects of Covid-19 on businesses and research. *Elsevier Public Health Journal, 117*, 284-289. Available at https://www.ncbi.nlm.nih.gov/pmc/articles/PMC7280091/ doi:10.1016/j.jbusres.2020.06.008

Doumbia. D. & Lauridsen, M. (2019). *Closing the SDG Financing Gap—Trends and Data.* Note 73.

Dowla, A., & Alamgir, D. (2003). From microcredit to microfinance: Evolution of savings products by MFIs in Bangladesh. *Journal of International Development, 15*(8), 969–988. doi:10.1002/jid.1032

Doyal, L., & Gough, I. (1991). *A Theory of Human Need.* Macmillan. doi:10.1007/978-1-349-21500-3

Doyle, K., & Black, J. (2001). Performance measures for microenterprise in the United States. *Journal of Microfinance/ESR Review, 3*(1), 4.

Drakopoulou Dodd, S., & Anderson, A. R. (2007). Mumpsimus and my thing of the individualistic entrepreneur. *International Small Business Journal, 25*(4), 341–360. doi:10.1177/0266242607078561

Drucker, P. (1985). *Innovation and entrepreneurship.* Harper & Row.

Drucker, P. F. (1993). *Concept of the corporation.* Transaction Publishers.

Du, J., Fan, X., & Feng, T. (2010). An experimental investigation of the role of face in service failure and recovery encounters. *Journal of Consumer Marketing, 27*(7), 584–593.

Dunn, E., & Arbuckle, J. G. (2012). *Microcredit and microenterprise performance: impact evidence from Peru.* Small Enterprise Development.

Duong, H. A., & Nghiem, H. S. (2014). Effects of microfinance on poverty reduction in Vietnam: A pseudo-panel data analysis. *Journal of Accounting, Finance and Economics, 4*(2), 58–67.

Duru, I. U., Yusuf, A., & Kwazu, V. C. (2017). Role of microfinance banks credit in the development of small and medium enterprises in Lokoja, Kogi State, Nigeria. *Asian Journal of Economics, Business and Accounting,* 1-9.

Dutta, A., & Banerjee, S. (2018). Does microfinance impede sustainable entrepreneurial initiatives among women borrowers? Evidence from rural Bangladesh. *Journal of Rural Studies, 60*, 70–81. doi:10.1016/j.jrurstud.2018.03.007

Ebomuche, N. C., Ihugba, O. A., & Bankong, B. (2014). The impact of Nigeria microfinance banks on poverty reduction: Imo State experience. *International Letters of Social and Humanistic Sciences,* (05), 92–113.

Ede, C. E., Ndubisi, E. C., & Nwankwo, C. A. (2013). Tackling unemployment through private sector. *International Journal of Innovation Research in Management, 2*(2), 41–52.

Egyir, I. S. (2014). *Microfinance, Women and Local Economic Development in Ghana.* University of Ghana Readers.

Elhadary, Y. A. E. & Samat, N. (2012). Political economy and urban poverty in the developing countries: Lessons learned from Sudan and Malaysia. *Journal of Geography and Geology, 4*(1), 212 -223.

Elkington, J. (1997). *Cannibals with forks: The triple bottom line of 21st century business.* Capstone Publishing Ltd.

Elkington, J. (1997). *Cannibals with Forks: The triple bottom line of 21st century business.* Earthscan.

Elliott, & Mayadas. (1996). Integrating clinical practice and social development. *The Journal of Applied Social Sciences, 21,* 61–68.

Ellis, V., & Bosworth, G. (2015). Supporting rural entrepreneurship in the UK microbrewery sector. *British Food Journal, 117*(11), 2724–2738. doi:10.1108/BFJ-12-2014-0412

Emeseh, E. (2009). Social responsibility in practice in the oil-producing Niger Delta: Assessing corporations and government actions. *Journal of Sustainable Development in Africa, 11*(2), 113–125.

Engler, M. (2009). From microcredit to a world without profit? Muhammad Yunus wrestles with moving beyond a society based on greed. *Dissent, 56*(4), 81–87. doi:10.1353/dss.0.0081

Estes, R. J. (1997). Social work, social development and community welfare centres in international perspective. *International Social Work, 40*(1), 43–55. doi:10.1177/002087289704000104

Etemire & Worika. (2018). Environmental Ethics and the Nigerian Oil and Gas Industry: Rumpus and Resolution. *U Botswana Law Journal, 26,* 58.

Etzensperger, C. (2014). *Microfinance market outlook 2014: no "sudden stop": demand for microfinance soars.* ResponsAbility.

European Commission, Eurostat. (2005). *Business Demography in Europe–results from 1997 to 2002, Statistics in focus 36/2005.* Author.

European Commission. (2006b). Report on the implementation of the Entrepreneurship Action Plan. European Commission – DG Enterprise and Industry.

European Commission. (2020). *Microfinance in the European Union: Market analysis and recommendations for delivery options in 2021-2027.* https://ec.europa.eu/social/BlobServlet?docId=23029&langId=en

Eweje, G. (2007). Multinational oil companies' CSR initiatives in Nigeria. *Managerial Law, 49*(5/6), 218–235.

Fadahunsi, A. (2012). The growth of small businesses: Towards a research agenda. *American Journal of Economics and Business Administration, 4*(1), 105–115. doi:10.3844/ajebasp.2012.105.115

Fant, E. K. (2011). *Fighting poverty with micro-credit. Experiences from Micro-Finance and Small-Loan Center (MASLOC) in Savelugu/Nanton District of Northern Ghana.* Academic Press.

Compilation of References

Farrelly, D. (1996). *The book of bamboo: A comprehensive guide to this remarkable plant, its uses, and its history*. Thames and Hudson Ltd.

Fatma, M., Khan, I., & Rahman, Z. (2016). The effect of CSR on consumer behavioural responses after service failure and recovery. *European Business Review, 28*(5), 583–599.

Felsenthal, M. (2010, December 10). *Financial Inclusion on the Rise, But Gaps Remain, Global Findex Database Shows*. World Bank. Available at: https://www.worldbank.org/en/news/press-release/2018/04/19/financial-inclusion-on-the-rise-but-gaps-remain-global-findex-database-shows

Ferdousi, F. (2015). Impact of microfinance on sustainable entrepreneurship development. *Development Studies Research, 2*(1), 51–63. doi:10.1080/21665095.2015.1058718

Filho, L., & Brandli, L. (Eds.). (2016). *Engaging stakeholders in education for sustainable development at university level*. Springer. doi:10.1007/978-3-319-26734-0

Filho, W. L., & Brandli, L. (2018). Engaging Stakeholders for Sustainable Development. In *Engaging Stakeholders in Education for Sustainable Development at University level* (pp. 335–342). Springer.

Fisher, J. L., & Koch, J. V. (2008). Born, not made: The entrepreneurial personality Journal of Psychology. *Rev., 47*, 777–780.

Fisk, R., Brown, S., & Bitner, M. (1993). Tracking the evolution of the services marketing literature. *Journal of Retailing, 69*(1), 61–103.

Fossgard, K., & Fredman, P. (2019). Dimensions in the nature-based tourism experience scape: An explorative analysis. *Journal of Outdoor Recreation and Tourism, 28*.

Fox, M. (2010). *Micro capital Brief: Malaysian Microfinance Institution (MFI), Amanah Ikhtiar Malaysia (AIM), Claims "World's Highest" Microcredit Repayment Rate of 99.2 Percent*. http://www.microcapital.org/microcapital-brief-malaysian-microfinance-institution-mfi-amanah-ikhtiar-m

Freeman, E. R., Harrison, J. S., & Wicks, A. C. (2007). Managing for stakeholders: survival, reputation, and success. Yale University Press.

Frese, M., & Gielink, M. M. (2014). The Psychology of Entrepreneurship. *Annual Review of Organizational Psychology and Organizational Behavior, 1*(1), 413–438. doi:10.1146/annurev-orgpsych-031413-091326

Frynas, J. G. (2005). The false promise of corporate social responsibility: Evidence form multinational oil companies. *International Affairs, 81*(3), 581–598.

Frynas, J. G. (2009). *Beyond corporate social responsibility*. Oxford University Press. doi:10.1017/CBO9780511581540

Frynas, J. G., & Stephens, S. (2015). Political Corporate Social Responsibility: Reviewing Theories and Setting New Agendas. *International Journal of Management Reviews*, *17*(4), 483–509.

Gadrey, J. (2000). The characterization of goods and services: An alternative approach. *Review of Income and Wealth*, *46*(3), 369–387.

Ganle, J. K., Afriyie, K., & Segbefia, A. Y. (2015). Microcredit: Empowerment and disempowerment of rural women in Ghana. *World Development*, *66*, 335–345. doi:10.1016/j.worlddev.2014.08.027

Garcia, A., Lensink, R., & Voors, M. (2020). Does microcredit increase aspirational hope? Evidence from a group lending scheme in Sierra Leone. *World Development*, *128*, 108861. doi:10.1016/j.worlddev.2019.104861

García-Pérez, I., Fernández-Izquierdo, M. A., & Muñoz-Torres, M. J. (2020). Microfinance Institutions Fostering Sustainable Development by Region. *Sustainability*, *12*(7), 1–23. doi:10.3390u12072682

García-Pérez, I., Muñoz-Torres, M. J., & Fernández-Izquierdo, M. A. (2018). Microfinance institutions fostering sustainable development. *Sustainable Development*, *26*(6), 606–619. doi:10.1002d.1731

Gartner, W. (2008). *Entrepreneurship hop Entrepreneurship Theory and Practice Advances in entrepreneurship, firm emergence, and growth* (Vol. 7). JAI Press.

Gartner, W. B. (1988). Who is an entrepreneur? Is the wrong question. *American Journal of Small Business*, *12*(4), 11–32. doi:10.1177/104225878801200401

Gartner, W. B. (1989). Some suggestions for research on entrepreneurial traits and characteristics. *Entrepreneurship Theory and Practice*, *14*(1), 27–38. doi:10.1177/104225878901400103

Gartner, W. B., Carter, N. M., & Hills, G. E. (2003). The language of opportunity. In C. Steyaert & D. Hjorth (Eds.), *New Movements in Entrepreneurship* (pp. 103–124). Edward Elgar. doi:10.4337/9781781951200.00017

Gartner, W. B., Carter, N. M., & Reynolds, P. D. (2010). Entrepreneurial behavior: Firm organizing processes. In Z. Acs & D. Audretsch (Eds.), *International handbook series on entrepreneurship* (Vol. 5, pp. 99–127). Springer. doi:10.1007/978-1-4419-1191-9_5

Gartner, W. B., & Shane, S. A. (1995). Measuring entrepreneurship over time. *Journal of Business Venturing*, *10*(4), 283–301. doi:10.1016/0883-9026(94)00037-U

Geetha, C., Savarimuthu, A., & Majid, A. (2017). Assessing Financial Returns on Microloans from Socioeconomic, Social and Environment Impact: A Case in Kota Kinabalu. *Malaysian Journal of Business and Economics.*, *4*(2), 7–29.

Gelbrich, K., & Roschk, H. (2011). A Meta-Analysis of Organizational Complaint Handling and Customer Responses. *Journal of Service Research*, *14*(1), 24–43.

Compilation of References

Ghosh, J. (2013). Microfinance and the challenge of financial inclusion for development. *Cambridge Journal of Economics*, *37*(6), 1203–1219. doi:10.1093/cje/bet042

Gielnik, M. M., Zacher, H., & Frese, M. (2012). Focus on opportunities as a mediator of the relationship between business owners' age and venture growth. *Journal of Business Venturing*, *27*(1), 127–142. doi:10.1016/j.jbusvent.2010.05.002

Gill, A., & Biger, N. (2012). Barriers to small business growth in Canada. *Journal of Small Business and Enterprise Development*, *19*(4), 656–668. doi:10.1108/14626001211277451

Ginsberg, J. M., & Bloom, P. N. (2004). Choosing the Right Green Marking Strategy. *MIT Sloan Management Review*, *46*(1), 79–84.

Gladwin, T. N., Kennelly, J. J., & Krause, T.-S. (1995). Shifting paradigms for sustainable development: Implications for management theory and research. *Academy of Management Review*, *20*(4), 874–907. doi:10.2307/258959

Gloukoviezoff, G. (2016). *Evaluating the impact of European microfinance*. The Foundations. (No. 2016/33). EIF Working Paper.

Goldberg, M., & Ramanathan, C. S. (2008). *Micro insurance matters in Latin America*. Academic Press.

Goodman, P., Fichman, M., Lerch, F., & Snyder, P. (1995). Customer-Firm Relationships: Involvement, and Customer Satisfaction. *Academy of Management Journal*, *38*(5), 1310–1324.

Goodwin, C., & Ross, I. (1992). Consumer responses to service failures: Influence of procedural and interactional fairness perceptions. *Journal of Business Research*, *25*(2), 149–163.

Gough, K. V., & Langevang, T. (Eds.). (2016). *Young entrepreneurs in sub-Saharan Africa*. Routledge. doi:10.4324/9781315730257

Goulden, C., & D'Arcy, C. (2014). *A definition of poverty – Anti-poverty strategies for the UK*. Available at https://www.jrf.org.uk/file/45780/download?token=zjlY4i-J andfiletype=full-report

Gray, M. (2002). Developmental social work: A 'Strengths' praxis for social development. *Social Development Issues*, *24*(1), 4–14.

Gray, M., Mupedziswa, R., & Mugumbate, J. (2017). The expansion of developmental social work in Southern and East Africa: Opportunities and challenges for social work field programmes. *International Social Work*, *61*(6), 1–14.

Gray, R., Owen, D., & Adams, C. (1996). *Accounting and accountability : changes and challenges incorporate social and environmental reporting*. Prentice Hall.

Green, J., & Thorogood, N. (2010). Qualitative Methods for Health Research (3rd ed.). London: Observational Methods, SAGE Publications Ltd.

Greenberg, J. (1987). A taxonomy of organizational justice theories. *Academy of Management Review*, *12*(1), 9–22.

Gregory, L., & Drakeford, M. (2008). Anti-Poverty Practice and the Changing World of Credit Unions: New Tools for Social Workers. *Journalism Practice*, *20*(3), 141–150.

Gretta, S. A. A. B. (2017). Financial inclusion and growth. *The Business & Management Review*, *8*(4), 434.

Grewal, D., Roggeveen, A. L., & Tsiros, M. (2008). The effect of compensation on repurchases intentions in service recovery. *Journal of Retailing*, *84*(4).

Griffin, D. J. (2012). *Loan methodology, gender, environment and the formation of capital by Mexican microfinance institutions* (Doctoral dissertation). Instituto Technologico De Estudios Superiores De Monterrey.

Gueyie, J. P., Manos, R. & Yaron, J. (2013). *Microfinance in developing countries: issues, policies and performance evaluation.* Palgrave Macmillan.

Gummesson, E. (2000). *Qualitative Methods in Management Research*. Sag Publications.

Gundlach, G. T., & Murphy, P. E. (1993). Ethical and Legal: Foundations of Relational Marketing Exchanges. *Journal of Marketing*, *57*(4), 35–46.

Gustafsson, A. (2008). Customer satisfaction with service recovery. *Journal of Business Research*, *62*, 1220–1222.

Gwinner, K. P., Gremler, D. D., & Bitner, M. J. (1998). Relational Benefits in Service Industries: The Customer's Perspective. *Journal of the Academy of Marketing Science*, *26*(2), 101–114.

Hagenaars, A. J. (2014). The perception of poverty. Elsevier.

Haile, H. B., Bock, B., & Folmer, H. (2012, August). Microfinance and female empowerment: Do institutions matter? *Women's Studies International Forum*, *35*(4), 256–265. doi:10.1016/j.wsif.2012.04.001

Hamann, R., & Kapelus, P. (2004). Corporate Social Responsibility in Mining in Southern Africa: Fair accountability or just green wash? *Development*, *47*(3), 85–92.

Hameed, W. U., Hussin, T., Azeem, M., Arif, M., & Basheer, M. F. (2017). Combination of microcredit and micro-training with mediating role of formal education: A micro-enterprise success formula. *Journal of Business and Social Review in Emerging Economies*, *3*(2), 285–291. doi:10.26710/jbsee.v3i2.191

Handelman, J., & Arnold, S. (1999). The role of marketing actions with a social dimension: Appeals to the institutional environment. *Journal of Marketing*, *63*(3), 33–48.

Hansen, D. J., Lumpkin, G. T., & Hills, G. E. (2011). A multidimensional examination of a creativity-based opportunity recognition model. *International Journal of Entrepreneurial Behaviour & Research*, *17*(5), 515–533. doi:10.1108/13552551111158835

Haque, T., Siwar, C., Bhuiyan, A. B., & Joarder, M. H. (2019). Contributions of Amanah ikhtiar Malaysia (AIM) in microfinance to economic empowerment (EE) of women borrowers in Malaysia. *Economia e Sociologia*, *12*(4), 241–256. doi:10.14254/2071-789X.2019/12-4/15

Harij, K., & Hebb, T. (2010). Investing for Impact: Issues and Opportunities for Social Finance in Canada. In *ANSER Conference*. Carleton Centre for Community Innovation.

Harper, M. (2012). Microfinance interest rates and client returns. *Journal of Agrarian Change*, *12*(4), 564–574. doi:10.1111/j.1471-0366.2012.00374.x

Harris, L. C., & Reynolds, K. L. (2003). The consequences of dysfunctional customer behaviour. *Journal of Service Research*, *6*(2), 144–161.

Harrison, R. (2013). Crowdfunding and the revitalization of the early stage risk capital market: Catalyst or chimera? *Venture Capital*, *15*(4), 283–287. doi:10.1080/13691066.2013.852331

Hartarska, V., & Nadolnyak, D. (2007). Do regulated microfinance institutions achieve better sustainability and outreach? Cross-country evidence. *Applied Economics*, *39*(10), 1207–1222. doi:10.1080/00036840500461840

Hartarska, V., & Nadolnyak, D. (2008). An impact analysis of microfinance in Bosnia and Herzegovina. *World Development*, *36*(12), 2605–2619. doi:10.1016/j.worlddev.2008.01.015

Hartarska, V., Nadolnyak, D., & McAdams, T. (2013). Microfinance and microenterprises' financing constraints in Eastern Europe and Central Asia. In *Microfinance in Developing Countries* (pp. 22–35). Palgrave Macmillan. doi:10.1057/9781137301925_2

Haselmann, R., & Wachtel, P. (2010). Institutions and Bank Behavior: Legal Environment, Legal Perception, and the Composition of Bank Lending. *Journal of Money, Credit and Banking*, *42*(5), 965–984. doi:10.1111/j.1538-4616.2010.00316.x

Hatta, Z. A., & Ali, I. (2013). Poverty reduction policies in Malaysia: Trends, strategies and challenges. *Asian Culture and History*, *5*(2), 48–56. doi:10.5539/ach.v5n2p48

Haugh, H. M., & Talwar, A. (2016). Linking social entrepreneurship and social change: The mediating role of empowerment. *Journal of Business Ethics*, *133*(4), 643–658. doi:10.100710551-014-2449-4

Hayton, J., Chandler, G. N., & DeTienne, D. R. (2011). Entrepreneurial opportunity identification and new firm development processes: A comparison of family and non-family new ventures. *International Journal of Entrepreneurship and Innovation Management*, *13*(1), 12–31. doi:10.1504/IJEIM.2011.038445

Hayward, S., Fowler, E., & Steadman, L. (2000). *Environmental Quality 2000: Assessing Michigan and America at the 30th Anniversary of Earth Day*. Mackinac Center for Public Policy and the Pacific Research Institute for Public Policy.

Headd, B., & Kirchoff, B. (2009). The growth, decline and survival of small businesses: An exploratory study of life cycles. *Journal of Small Business Management, 47*(4), 531–550. doi:10.1111/j.1540-627X.2009.00282.x

Helmer, J. (2011). *A snapshot on crowdfunding*. Working papers firms and regions, No. R2/2011, Fraunhofer Institute for System's and Innovation Research ISI, Karlsruhe.

Hemmati, M. (2002). *Multi-Stakeholder Processes for Governance and Sustainability. Beyond Deadlock and Conflict*. Routlege.

Hermes, N., & Hudon, M. (2018). Determinants of the performance of microfinance institutions: A systematic review. *Journal of Economic Surveys, 32*(5), 1483–1513. doi:10.1111/joes.12290

Hermes, N., & Lensink, R. (2007). The empirics of microfinance: What do we know? *Economic Journal (London), 117*(517), F1–F10. doi:10.1111/j.1468-0297.2007.02013.x

Hermes, N., & Lensink, R. (2011). Microfinance: Its impact, outreach, and sustainability. *World Development, 39*(6), 875–881. doi:10.1016/j.worlddev.2009.10.021

Hermes, N., Lensink, R., & Meesters, A. (2011). Outreach and efficiency of microfinance institutions. *World Development, 39*(6), 938–948. doi:10.1016/j.worlddev.2009.10.018

Hess, R. L. Jr, Ganesan, S., & Klein, N. M. (2003). Service failure and recovery: The impact of relationship factors on customer satisfaction. *Journal of the Academy of Marketing Science, 31*(2), 127–145.

Heuer, A. (2017). Women-to-women entrepreneurial energy networks: A pathway to green energy uptake at the base of pyramid. *Sustainable Energy Technologies and Assessments, 22*, 116–123. doi:10.1016/j.seta.2017.02.020

Hilson, G., & Ackah-Baidoo, A. (2010). Can microcredit services alleviate hardship in African Samll-scale mining communities? *World Development, 39*(7), 1191–1203. doi:10.1016/j.worlddev.2010.10.004

Hoff, T. S. (2013). *Female loan clients-a safer bet?: A study of default rates in a microfinance institution* (Master's thesis).

Hoffman, K. D., Kelley, S. W., & Rotalsky, H. M. (1995). Tracking service failure and employee recovery efforts. *Journal of Services Marketing, 9*(2), 49–61.

Hoffmann, A. (2007). A rough guide to entrepreneurship policy. In D. B. Audretsch, I. Grilo, & A. R. Thurik (Eds.), *Handbook or Research on Entrepreneurship Policy* (pp. 140–171). Edward Elgar. doi:10.4337/9781847206794.00012

Hokenstad, M. C., & Midgley, J. (Eds.). (1997). *Issues in International Social Work: Global Challenges for a New Century*. NASW Press.

Holliday, A. (2007). *Doing and Writing Qualitative Research*. SAGE Publication Ltd. doi:10.4135/9781446287958

Hollis, A., & Sweetman, A. (1998). Microcredit: What can we learn from the past? *World Development*, *26*(10), 1875–1891. doi:10.1016/S0305-750X(98)00082-5

Holloway, B. B., & Beatty, Sh. E. (2003). Service failure in on-line retailing: A recovery opportunity. *Journal of Service Research*, *6*(1), 92–105.

Holmes, T., & Lee, S. (2009). *Economies of density versus natural advantage: crop choice on the back forty*. Working Paper.

Holth, L. C. R. (2011). *Commercialization of Microfinance*. Oslo University College: Faculty of Social Science.

Homans, G. C. (1961). *Social behaviour: Its elementary forms*. Routledge and Kegan Paul.

Howson, C. (2013). Adverse Incorporation and Microfinance among Cross-Border Traders in Senegal. *World Development*, *42*, 199–208. doi:10.1016/j.worlddev.2012.06.002

Hudson, S., Krogman, N., & Beckie, M. (2016). Social practices of knowledge mobilization for sustainable food production: Nutrition gardening and fish farming in the kolli hills of India. *Food Security*, *8*(3), 523–533. doi:10.100712571-016-0580-z

Ibn 'Abidin, M. (2011). *Hashiyat ibn 'Abidin: radd al-muhtar 'ala al-Durr al-mukhtar*. Dar al-Ma'rifah.

Ibn Qudaamah, M. (1997). *Al-Mughni*. Dar Alam al-Kutub.

Ibrahim, S. A. (2018). *Effect of Microfinance Banks Activities on Financial Inclusion in Nigeria* (Doctoral dissertation). Kwara State University, Nigeria.

Ibrahim, K., & Abdisamad Mohamed, F. (2020). Outreach and performance of microfinance institutions in Sub-Saharan Africa. *International Journal of Sciences, Basic and Applied Research*, *53*(2), 171–185. http://gssrr.org/index.php?journal=JournalOfBasicAndApplied

Ibrahim, P., & Ghazali, R. (2014). Zakah As an Islamic Micro-Financing Mechanism to Productive Zakah Recipients. *Asian Economic and Financial Review*, *4*(1), 117–125.

ICC. (2012). *Rethinking Trade and Finance, ICC Global Survey on Trade Finance 2012*. International Chamber of Commerce.

Idemudia, U. (2009). Oil extraction and poverty reduction in the Niger Delta: A critical examination of partnership initiatives. *Journal of Business Ethics*, *90*, 91–116.

Idemudia, U. (2010). Rethinking the role of corporate social responsibility in the Nigerian oil conflict: The limits of CSR. *Journal of International Development*, *22*(7), 833–845.

Idrus, S., Pauzi, N. M., & Munir, Z. A. (2014). The effectiveness of training model for women entrepreneurship program. *Procedia: Social and Behavioral Sciences*, *129*, 82–89. doi:10.1016/j.sbspro.2014.03.651

IFC. (2014). *IFC and Microfinance*. The World Bank Group.

Igbuzor, O. (2008). *Strategies for winning the anticorruption war in Nigeria*. Available at https://nigeria.actionaid.org/sites/nigeria/files/winning_anti-corruption_war_in_nigeria1.pdf

Ihlen, O & Roper, J. (2011). Corporate Reports on Sustainability and Sustainable Development: 'We Have Arrived'. *Sustainable Development Journal, 22*(1), 1-11.

Ilavbarhe, K. O., & Izekor, O. B. (2015). The role of microcredit in women empowerment and poverty alleviation in Edo State, Nigeria. *Journal of Agricultural and Crop Research, 3*(6), 80–84.

Imai, K. S., Arun, T., & Annim, S. K. (2010). Microfinance and household poverty reduction: New evidence from India. *World Development, 38*(12), 1760–1774. doi:10.1016/j.worlddev.2010.04.006

Imai, K. S., Gaiha, R., Thapa, G., & Annim, S. K. (2012). Microfinance and poverty—A macro perspective. *World Development, 40*(8), 1675–1689. doi:10.1016/j.worlddev.2012.04.013

IMF. (2012b). Global Financial Stability Report October 2012. International Monetary Fund.

Inam, U. S. (2015). Poverty Alleviation Strategies in Nigeria: A Call for An Inclusive Growth. *Journal of Poverty. Investment and Development, 15*, 110–118.

Indonesia Zakah Outlook. (2019). *Centre of Strategic Studies the National Board of Zakah, Republic of Indonesia (BAZNAS)*. https://www.puskasbaznas.com/publications/outlook/indonesia-zakat-outlook-2019

Inman, K. (2016). *Women's resources in business start-up: A study of black and white women entrepreneurs*. Routledge. Available at: https://uws-primo.hosted.exlibrisgroup.com/

Insights, I. M. (2020). *Malaysia's Selangor State Zakah Board Allots MYR 15 Million Fund to Assist Small Business Vendors*. https://islamicmarkets.com/articles/malaysia-s-selangor-state-zakah-board-allots-myr-15-million-fund

Institute for Business Studies and Research. (2005). *The role of clustering in increasing the competitiveness of small and medium-sized enterprises with a focus on marketing development*. Author.

International Labour Organisation. (2017). *Growing microenterprises: how gender and family can impact outcomes – evidence from Uganda, Issue Brief No 2, March 2017*. Author.

Iqbal, Z., Iqbal, S., & Mushtaq, M. A. (2015). Impact of Microfinance on Poverty Alleviation: The Study of District Bahawal Nagar, Punjab, Pakistan. *Management and Administrative Sciences Review, 4*(3), 487–503.

Ireland, D. R., Hitt, M. A., & Sirmon, D. G. (2003). A model of strategic entrepreneurship: The construct and its dimensions. *Journal of Management, 29*(6), 963–989. doi:10.1016/S0149-2063(03)00086-2

Irele, A.O. (2011). The Evolution of Social Welfare and Social Work in Nigeria. *A Journal of Contemporary Research, 8*(3), 238-252.

Iruoma, K. (2021). *Energy & Resources*. African Business.

Compilation of References

Isaga, N. (2015). Owner-managers' demographic characteristics and the growth of Tanzanian small and medium enterprises. *International Journal of Business and Management*, *10*(5), 168–181. doi:10.5539/ijbm.v10n5p168

Isaia, E. (2005). *Microcredit in Morocco: The Zakoura Foundation's Experience*. University of Turin.

Islamic, S. F. R. (2014). *Islamic Research and Training Institute, Islamic Development Bank, Jeddah*. https://irti.org/product/islamic-social-finance-report-2014/

Islam, M. A., Khan, M. A., Obaidullah, A. Z. M., & Alam, M. S. (2011). Effect of entrepreneur and firm characteristics on the business success of small and medium enterprises (SMEs) in Bangladesh. *International Journal of Business and Management*, *6*(3), 289.

Islam, T. (2012). *Microcredit and poverty alleviation*. Ashgate Publishing, Ltd.

Ismail, I., Husin, N., Rahim, N. A., Kamal, M. H. M., & Mat, R. C. (2016). Entrepreneurial success among single mothers: The role of motivation and passion. *Procedia Economics and Finance*, *37*, 121–128. doi:10.1016/S2212-5671(16)30102-2

ISRA. (2012). Islamic Financial System: principles and Operations. International Shari'ah Research Academy for Islamic Finance (ISRA).

Ite, U. E. (2004). Multinationals and corporate social responsibility in developing countries: A case study of Nigeria. *Corporate Social Responsibility and Environmental Management*, *11*(1), 1–11.

Iversen, J., Jorgensen, R., & Malchow-Moller, N. (2008). Defining and measuring entrepreneurship. *Foundations Trends Entrepreneur*, *4*(1), 1–63. doi:10.1561/0300000020

Jachimowicz, J. (2013). Microfinance: Fortune at or also for the bottom of the pyramid? *Journal of Sustainability*, *1*(1), 13–13.

Jackson, E. A. (2018). Contested terrain of sustainable development paradigm in sierra Leone. *Management of Sustainable Development*, *10*(1), 5–11. doi:10.2478/msd-2018-0001

James, V. (Ed.). (2018). Capacity Building for Sustainable Development. Boston: CABI.

Jang, R. (2013). *Microfinance business models: comparing and contrasting Grameen Bank and Compartamos Banco* (Doctoral dissertation). Massachusetts Institute of Technology.

Javid, A., & Abrar, A. (2015). Microfinance Institutions and Poverty Reduction: A Cross Regional Analysis. *Pakistan Development Review*, *54*(4), 371–387. doi:10.30541/v54i4I-IIpp.371-387

Jawhar. (2020). *Department of Awqaf, Zakah & Hajj (Jawhar)*. = https://www.jawhar.gov.my/en/profil-jabatan/mengenai-jawhar/sejarah-jawhar/

Jayasooria, D. (2016). Sustainable development goals and social work: Opportunities and challenges for social work practice in Malaysia. *Journal of Human Rights and Social Work*, *1*(1), 19–29. doi:10.100741134-016-0007-y

Jensen, E. (2009). *Teaching with poverty in mind: What being poor does to kids' brains and what schools can do about it.* ASCD.

Jensen, M. C., & Meckling, W. H. (1976). Theory of Firm: Managerial Behaviour, Agency Costs and Ownership Structure. *Journal of Financial Economics*, *3*(4), 305–360.

Johnston, R. (1995). Service failure and recovery: Impact, attributes and process. In T. A. Swartz, D. E. Bowen, & S. W. Brown (Eds.), *Advances in Services Marketing and Management*. JAI Press.

Kabasakal, H., Karakaş, F., Maden, C., & Aycan, Z. (2016). 15 Women in management in Turkey. Women in Management Worldwide: Signs of Progress, 2000(2014), 226.

Kabeer, N. (2005). Is microfinance a 'magic bullet' for women's empowerment? Analysis of findings from South Asia. *Economic and Political Weekly*, 4709–4718.

Kachkar, O. (2019). Islamic social finance: Mobilizing Zakah (almsgiving) funds to support refugees' microenterprises pogroms. *International Congress of Islamic Economy, Finance & Ethics*.

Kadri, F. (2011). The Role of Microfinance in Poverty Alleviation: AIM's Experience. The 2nd Working Group on the Development of Islamic Financial Service Industry, Jakarta.

Kahf, M. (2003). The role of waqf in improving the Ummah welfare. In *The International Seminar on Waqf as a Private Legal Body*. Islamic University of North Sumatra.

Kahf, M. (1998). *Financing the Development of Awqaf Property*. The Seminar on Development of Awqaf.

Kahn, M. A. (1995). Sustainable development: The key concepts, issues and implications. Keynote paper given at the international sustainable development research conference, 27–29 March 1995, Manchester, UK. *Sustainable Development*, *3*(2), 63–69. doi:10.1002d.3460030203

Kaladhar, K. (1997). Microfinance in India: Design, Structure and Governance. *Economic and Political Weekly*, *32*(42), 2687–2706. https://www.jstor.org/stable/4405979

Kaleem, A., & Ahmed, S. (2011). The Quran and Poverty Alleviation: A Theoretical Model for Zakah-Based Islamic Microfinance Institutions. *Nonprofit and Voluntary Sector Quarterly*, *39*(3), 409–428. doi:10.1177/0899764009332466

Kaltenbeck, J. (2011). *Crowd funding and Social Payments*. Open Educational Resources.

Kanyare, N., & Mungai, J. (2017). Access to Microcredit Determinants and Financial Performance of Small and Medium Retailing Enterprises in Wajir County, Kenya. *International Journal of Finance*, *2*(6), 103–136. doi:10.47941/ijf.164

Kapur, S. (2021). *A Finance Structure That Matches India's Ambitions For Renewable Energy Sector*. Moneycontrol. Available at: https://www.moneycontrol.com/news/business/companies/a-finance-structure-that-matches-indias-ambitions-for-renewable-energy-sector-5467911.html

Karl, T. (1997). *The Paradox of Plenty: Oil booms and petro-states*. California University Press. doi:10.1525/9780520918696

Compilation of References

Kasali, T. A., Ahmad, S. A., & Lim, H. E. (2015). The role of microfinance in poverty alleviation: Empirical evidence from South-West Nigeria. *Asian Social Science*, *11*(21), 183–192. doi:10.5539/ass.v11n21p183

Kato, M. P., & Kratzer, J. (2013). Empowering women through microfinance: Evidence from Tanzania. *ACRN Journal of Entrepreneurship Perspectives*, *2*(1), 31–59.

Keaveney, S. M. (1995). Customer switching behaviour in service industries: An exploratory study. *Journal of Marketing*, *59*(2), 71–82.

Kelly, S. W., & Davis, M. A. (1994). Antecedents to customer expectations for service recovery. *Journal of the Academy of Marketing Science*, *22*(1), 52–61.

Kessy, S., & Temu, S.S. (2010). *The impact of training on performance of micro and small enterprises served by microfinance institutions in Tanzania*. Academic Press.

Khalaf, L. S., & Saqfalhait, N. I. (2019). The effect of microfinance institutions activities on economic growth in Arab countries. *Academy of Accounting and Financial Studies Journal*, *23*(1), 1–8.

Khalily, B. (2020). Microfinance in Sustainable Development and Economic Growth in Bangladesh. In Bangladesh's Macroeconomic Policy (pp. 419-448). Palgrave Macmillan.

Khalily, B., Mujeri, M., Hasan, M., & Muneer, F. (2017). *Diagnostics of Micro-enterprise (ME) Lending by MFIs in Bangladesh: Opportunities and Challenges*. http://inm.org.bd/wp-content/uploads/2017/07/Policy-Brief_ME_English.pdf

Khandelwal, A. K. (2007). Microfinance development strategy for India. *Economic and Political Weekly*, 1127–1135.

Khandker, S. R. & Samad, H. (2013). *Microfinance growth and poverty reduction in Bangladesh: what does the longitudinal data say?* World Bank Working Paper.

Khandker, S. R. (2012). *Grameen bank lending: does group liability matter?* World Bank Policy Research Working Paper, (6204).

Khandker, S. R., & Samad, H. (2013). *Microfinance growth and poverty reduction in Bangladesh: what does the longitudinal data say?* World Bank Working Paper.

Khandker, S. R. (1998). *Fighting poverty with microcredit: experience in Bangladesh*. Oxford University Press.

Khan, E., & Quaddusm, M. (2014). Examining the influence of business environment on socio-economic performance of informal microenterprises Content analysis and partial least square approach. *The International Journal of Sociology and Social Policy*, *35*(3/4), 273–288. doi:10.1108/IJSSP-02-2014-0016

Khan, H. R. (2011). *Financial Inclusion and Financial stability: are they two sides of the same coin*. Speech at BANCON.

Khan, R. E. A., & Noreen, S. (2012). Microfinance and women empowerment: A case study of District Bahawalpur (Pakistan). *African Journal of Business Management, 6*(12), 4514–4521.

Khan, S. (2015). Impact of sources of finance on the growth of SMEs: Evidence from Pakistan. *Decision, 42*(1), 3–10.

Kim, T., Kim, W. G., & Kim, H. (2009). The effects of perceived justice on recovery satisfaction, trust, word-of-mouth and revisit intention in upscale hotels. *Tourism Management, 30*, 51–62.

Kinde, B. A. (2012). Financial sustainability of microfinance institutions (MFIs) in Ethiopia. *European Journal of Business and Management, 4*(15), 1–10.

KirznerI. M. (1973). *Competition and Entrepreneurship*. Chicago: The University of Chicago Press. https://ssrn.com/abstract=1496174

Klein, J., & Dawar, N. (2004). Corporate social responsibility and consumers' attributions and brand evaluations in a product–harm crisis. *International Journal of Research in Marketing, 21*(3), 203–217.

Klyver, K., Hindle, K., & Meyer, D. (2008). Influence of social network structure on entrepreneurship participation – a study of 20 national cultures. *The International Entrepreneurship and Management Journal, 4*(3), 331–347. doi:10.100711365-007-0053-0

Kodongo, O., & Kendi, L. G. (2013). Individual lending versus group lending: An evaluation with Kenya's microfinance data. *Review of Development Finance, 3*(2), 99–108. doi:10.1016/j.rdf.2013.05.001

Kolk, A., Kourula, A., & Pisani, N. (2017). Multinational enterprises and the Sustainable Development Goals: What do we know and how to proceed? *Journal of transnational Corporations, 24*(3), 9-32.

Kolk, A., Kourula, A., & Pisani, N. (2017). Multinational enterprises and the sustainable development goals: What do we know and how to proceed? *Transnational Corporations, 24*(3), 9–32. doi:10.18356/6f5fab5e-en

Kolk, A., & Van Tulder, R. (2010). International business: Corporate social responsibility and sustainable development. *International Business Review, 19*(2), 119–125.

Kondo, T., Orbeta, A. Jr, Dingcong, C., & Infantado, C. (2008). Impact of microfinance on rural households in the Philippines. *IDS Bulletin, 39*(1), 51–70. doi:10.1111/j.1759-5436.2008.tb00432.x

Koppl, R., & Minniti, M. (2003). Market processes and entrepreneurial studies. In Z. Acs & D. Audretsch (Eds.), *Handbook of Entrepreneurship Research* (pp. 81–102). Kluwer Press International.

Kotler, P., Keller, K. L., & Koshy, M. J. (2009). Marketing Management: A South Asian Perspective (13th ed.). Pearson Prentice Hall.

Kotler, P. (1982). *Marketing for non-profit organisations*. Prentice Hall.

Compilation of References

Kotler, P. (2003). *Marketing Management*. Prentice Hall.

Kotler, P., & Armstrong, G. M. (2010). *Principles of Marketing*. Prentice Hall.

Kotler, P., & Keller, K. L. (2009). *A Framework for Marketing Management* (4th ed.). Pearson Education Inc.

KPMG. (2017). *KPMG survey of corporate social responsibility reporting*. Available at http.www. home.kpmg

KPMG. (2017). *KPMG survey of corporate social responsibility reporting*. http.www. home.kpmg

Kraemer-Eis, H., Schaber, M., & Tappi, A. (2010). *SME loan securitization. An important tool to support European SME lending*. Working Paper 2010/007, EIF Research & Market Analysis, European Investment Fund.

Krishna, A., Dangayach, G. S., & Jain, R. (2011). A conceptual framework for the Service Recovery Paradox. *The Marketing Review*, *11*(1), 41–56.

Kristiansen, S., Furuholt, B., & Wahid, F. (2003). Internet cafe entrepreneurs: Pioneers in information dissemination in Indonesia. *International Journal of Entrepreneurship and Innovation*, *4*(4), 251–263. doi:10.5367/000000003129574315

Kristof, N. D. (2009). The role of microfinance. *New York Times*.

Krueger, N. (2003). Thinking entrepreneurially: Entrepreneurial cognition. In Z. Acs (Ed.), *International handbook of entrepreneurship*. Kluwer.

Kumar, A., Kumar, N., Baredar, P., & Shukla, A. (2015). A review on biomass energy resources, potential, conversion and policy in India. *Renewable & Sustainable Energy Reviews*, *45*, 530–539. doi:10.1016/j.rser.2015.02.007

Kumar, K. N. (2017). Microfinance for entrepreneurial development: Study of women's group enterprise development in India. In *Microfinance for Entrepreneurial Development* (pp. 53–71). Palgrave Macmillan. doi:10.1007/978-3-319-62111-1_3

Kuo, Y.-F., & Wu, C.-M. (2012). Satisfaction and post-purchase intentions with service recovery of online shopping websites: Perspectives on perceived justice and emotions. *International Journal of Information Management*, *32*, 127–138.

Kusters, K., Achdiawan, R., Belcher, B., & Pérez, M. R. (2006). Balancing development and conservation? An assessment of livelihood and environmental outcomes of nontimber forest product trade in Asia, Africa, and Latin America. *Ecology and Society*, *11*(2), art20. doi:10.5751/ES-01796-110220

Lafourcade, A. L., Isern, J., Mwangi, P., & Brown, M. (2005). *Overview of the outreach and financial performance of microfinance institutions in Africa*. Microfinance Information eXchange Available at: http://www.mixmarket.org/medialibrary/mixmarket/Africa_Data_Study.pdf

La, S., & Choi, B. (2019). Perceived justice and CSR after service recovery. *Journal of Services Marketing, 32*(2), 206–219.

Lashley, C. (1988). Matching the management of human resources to service operations. *International Journal of Contemporary Hospitality Management, 10*(1), 24–33.

Ledgerwood, J., & White, V. (2006). Transforming microfinance institutions: providing full financial services to the poor. World Bank Publications. doi:10.1596/978-0-8213-6615-8

Ledgerwood, J., Earne, J., & Nelson, C. (2013). The new microfinance handbook: A financial market system perspective. World Bank Publications. doi:10.1596/978-0-8213-8927-0

Ledgerwood, J. (1998). *Microfinance handbook: An institutional and financial perspective*. World Bank Publications. doi:10.1596/978-0-8213-4306-7

Ledgerwood, J. (1999). *Microfinance handbook: an institutional and financial perspective*. World Bank.

Ledgerwood, J. (2013). *Measuring Financial Inclusion and Assessing Impact. The New Microfinance Handbook: A Financial Market System Perspective*. The World Bank.

Leikem, K. (2012). Microfinance: a tool for Poverty Reduction. *Senior Honors Projects. Paper, 300*.

Lewis, B. R., & McCann, S. (2004). Service failure and recovery in retail banking: The customers' perspective. *International Journal of Bank Marketing, 19*(1), 37–47.

Lewis, J. J., Hollingsworth, J. W., Chartier, R. T., Cooper, E. M., Foster, W. M., Gomes, G. L., Kussin, P. S., MacInnis, J. J., Padhi, B. K., Panigrahi, P., Rodes, C. E., Ryde, I. T., Singha, A. K., Stapleton, H. M., Thornburg, J., Young, C. J., Meyer, J. N., & Pattanayak, S. K. (2017). Biogas stoves reduce firewood use, household air pollution, and hospital visits in Odisha, India. *Environmental Science & Technology, 51*(1), 560–569. doi:10.1021/acs.est.6b02466 PMID:27785914

Leyshon, A., & Thrift, N. (1995). Geographies of Financial Exclusion: Financial Abandonment in Britain and the United States. *Transactions of the Institute of British Geographers, 20*(3), 312–341. doi:10.2307/622654

Lii, Y.-S., Ding, M.-C., & Lin, C.-H. (2018). Fair or Unfair: The Moderating Effect of Sustainable CSR Practices on Anticipatory Justice Following Service Failure Recovery. *Sustainability, 10*(12), 1–21.

Lindgreen, A., Maon, F., Reast, J., & Yani-De-Soriano, M. (2012). Guest Editorial: Corporate Social Responsibility in Controversial Industry Sectors. *Journal of Business Ethics, 110*(4), 393–395.

Lindgreen, A., & Swaen, V. (2010). Corporate social responsibility. *International Journal of Management Reviews, 12*(1), 1–7.

Lloyd-Jones, T., & Rakodi, C. (2014). *Urban livelihoods: A people-centred approach to reducing poverty*. Routledge. doi:10.4324/9781849773805

Compilation of References

Lobovikov, M., Paudel, S., Ball, L., Piazza, M., Guardia, M., Ren, H., ... & Wu, J. (2007). *World bamboo resources: a thematic study prepared in the framework of the global forest resources assessment 2005* (No. 18). Food & Agriculture Org.

Lomazzi, M., Borisch, B., & Laaser, U. (2018). The millennium development goals: Experiences, achievements and what's next. *Global Health Action*, *7*(1), 23695. doi:10.3402/gha.v7.23695 PMID:24560268

Lombard, A. (2008). The implementation of the White Paper for Social Welfare: a ten-year review. *Challenges and Innovation in Developmental Social Welfare*, *20*(2), 154–173.

Lombard, A. (2015). Global agenda for social work and social development: A path towards sustainable social work. *Social Work Journal*, *50*(2), 481–498. doi:10.15270/51-4-462

Lombard, A., & Twikirize, J. M. (2014). Promoting social and economic equality: Social workers' contribution to social justice and social development in South Africa and Uganda. *International Social Work*, *57*(4), 313–325. doi:10.1177/0020872814525813

Louis, P., Seret, A., & Baesens, B. (2013). Financial efficiency and social impact of microfinance institutions using self-organizing maps. *World Development*, *46*, 197–210. doi:10.1016/j.worlddev.2013.02.006

Lovelock, C. H., & Wright, L. (2002). *Principles of Service Marketing and Management*. Prentice Hall.

Lovelock, C., & Gummesson, E. (2004). Whither Services Marketing? *Journal of Service Research*, *7*(1), 20–41.

Lucas, S. (2017). The impact of demographic and social factors on firm performance in Kenya. *Journal of Business and Economic Development*, *2*(4), 255–261.

Luo, J., & Rahman, M. W. (2010). The development perspective of finance and microfinance sector in China: How far Is microfinance regulations? *International Journal of Economics and Finance*, *3*(1).

MacNaughton A.L & Stephens J (2003). Improving Infrastructure Project Results in Sensitive Areas, U.S. and Abroad. In *Aba Section on Environment, Energy & Resources, 11th Annual Fall Meeting*, 6-7.

MacNaughton, A. L. (2001). Multidisciplinary Trends in an Evolving Marketplace: Practicing with Other Professions. In Multidisciplinary practice: Staying Competitive and Adapting to change. Academic Press.

MacNaughton. (2004). Sustainable Development: Impacts of Current Trends on Oil and Gas Development. *Journal of Land Resources & Environmental Law*, *24*, 259.

Mahmood, S., Hussain, J. Z., & Matlay, H. (2014). Optimal microfinance loan size and poverty reduction amongst female entrepreneurs in Pakistan. *Journal of Small Business and Enterprise Development*, *21*(2), 231–249. doi:10.1108/JSBED-03-2014-0043

Makhlouf, A. S. H., & Aliofkhazraei, M. (2015). *Handbook of materials failure analysis with case studies from the chemicals, concrete and power industries.* Butterworth-Heinemann.

Mann, G. (2019). *Does Consumer Microfinance Expand Financial Inclusion in the UK?* Academic Press.

Manos, R., Gueyie, J. P. & Yaron, J. (2013). Dilemmas and Directions in Microfinance Research. *Microfinance in Developing Countries: Issues, Policies and Performance Evaluation.*

Manuchim, A. (2021). The short fall of the Nigerian Oil and Gas Act 2010 in Achieving sustainable. *Development,* 5.

Mari, M., Poggesi, S., & De Vita, L. (2016). Family embeddedness and business performance: Evidences from women-owned firms. *Management Decision,* 54(2), 476–500. doi:10.1108/MD-07-2014-0453

Marina, S., Tatiana, I., & Anna, T. (2019). Motivation of female entrepreneurs: A cross-national study. *Journal of Small Business and Enterprise Development,* 26(5), 684–705. doi:10.1108/JSBED-10-2018-0306

Marini, L., Andrew, J., & Van der Laan, S. (2017). Tools of accountability: Protecting microfinance clients in South Africa? *Accounting, Auditing & Accountability Journal,* 30(6), 1344–1369. doi:10.1108/AAAJ-04-2016-2548

Marson, M., & Savin, I. (2015). Ensuring sustainable access to drinking water in Sub Saharan Africa: Conflict between financial and social objectives. *World Development,* 76, 26–39. doi:10.1016/j.worlddev.2015.06.002

Masakure, O., Henson, S., & Cranfield, J. (2009). erformance of microenterprises in Ghana: A resource-based view. *Journal of Small Business and Enterprise Development,* 16(3), 466–484. doi:10.1108/14626000910977170

Masanga, G. G., & Jera, M. (2017). The Significance of Microfinance to Urban Informal Traders in Zimbabwe. *ADRRI Journal (Multidisciplinary),* 26(3), 44–61.

Masanga, G. G., & Jera, M. (2017). The Significance of Microfinance to Urban Informal Traders in Zimbabwe. *Development and Resources Research Institute Journal, Ghana,* 26(3), 4.

Matin, I., Hulme, D., & Rutherford, S. (2002). Finance for the poor: From microcredit to microfinancial services. *Journal of International Development,* 14(2), 273–294. doi:10.1002/jid.874

Mattila, A. S. (2001). The effectiveness of service recovery in a multi-industry setting. *Journal of Services Marketing,* 15(7), 583–596.

Mayoux, L., & Hartl, M. (2009). *Gender and rural microfinance: Reaching and empowering women.* International Fund for Agricultural Development. IFAD.

Compilation of References

Mazumder, M. S. U. (2015). Role of Microfinance in Sustainable Development in Rural Bangladesh. *Sustainable Development*, *23*(6), 396–413. doi:10.1002d.1599

Mbabazi, N. M. (2018). *The contribution of microfinance institutions to the economic development of women: A case of Uganda Cooperative Savings and Credit Union Limited (UCSCU) in Katabi Town Council* (Doctoral dissertation). Nkumba University.

Mbah, F., Ebue, M., & Ugwu, C. (2017). History of Social work in Nigeria. In Social work in Nigeria: Book of readings (pp. 1–14). Nsukka: University of Nigeria Press Ltd.

Mbugua, M. (2010). *Impact of microfinance services on financial performance of small and micro enterprises in Kenya. Unpublished MBA project.* University of Nairobi.

McClelland, D. C. (1961). *The achieving society*. The Free Press. doi:10.1037/14359-000

McHugh, N., Baker, R., & Donaldson, C. (2019). Microcredit for enterprise in the UK as an 'alternative' economic space. *Geoforum*, *100*, 80–88. doi:10.1016/j.geoforum.2019.02.004

McMullen, J. S., & Shepherd, D. A. (2006). Entrepreneurial action and the role of uncertainty in the theory of the entrepreneur. *Academy of Management Review*, *31*(1), 132–152. doi:10.5465/amr.2006.19379628

McWilliams, A., & Siegel, D. (2001). Corporate social responsibility: A theory of the firm perspective. *Academy of Management Review*, *26*(1), 117–127.

Mekhilef, S., Saidur, R., & Safari, A. (2011). A review on solar energy use in industries. *Renewable & Sustainable Energy Reviews*, *15*(4), 1777–1790. doi:10.1016/j.rser.2010.12.018

Mersland, R., & Strøm, Ø. (Eds.). (2014). *Microfinance institutions: Financial and social performance*. Springer. doi:10.1057/9781137399663

Metcalfe, J. S. (2004). The entrepreneur and the style of modern economics. *Journal of Evolutionary Economics*, *14*(2), 157–175. doi:10.100700191-004-0210-3

Meuter, M. L., Ostrom, A. L., Roundtree, R. I., & Bitner, M. J. (2000). Self-service technologies: Understanding customer satisfaction with technology-based service encounters. *Journal of Marketing*, *64*(3), 50–64.

Mia, M. A., Lee, H. A., Chandran, V. G. R., Rasiah, R., & Rahman, M. (2019). History of microfinance in Bangladesh: A life cycle theory approach. *Business History*, *61*(4), 703–733. doi:10.1080/00076791.2017.1413096

Midgley, J. (1995). *Social Development: The Developmental Perspective in Social Welfare*. Sage.

Midgley, J. (1997). *Social Welfare in Global Context*. Sage. doi:10.4135/9781483327945

Midgley, J. (2008). Microenterprise, global poverty and social development. *International Social Work*, *51*(4), 467–479. doi:10.1177/0020872808090240

Milana, C., & Ashta, A. (2012). Developing microfinance: A survey of the literature. *Strategic Change*, *21*(7-8), 299–330. doi:10.1002/jsc.1911

Miller, J. L., Craighead, C. W., & Karwan, K. R. (2000). Service recovery: A framework and empirical investigation. *Journal of Operations Management*, *18*(4), 387–400.

Minde, G., Magdum, S., & Kalyanraman, V. (2013). Biogas as a sustainable alternative for current energy need of India. *Journal of Sustainable Energy & Environment*, *4*, 121–132.

Misati, R. N., & Nyamongo, E. M. (2012). Financial liberalisation, financial fragility and economic growth in Sub-Saharan Africa. *Journal of Financial Stability*, *8*(3), 150–160. doi:10.1016/j.jfs.2011.02.001

Misturelli, F., & Heffernan, C. (2010). The concept of poverty: A synchronic perspective. *Progress in Development Studies*, *10*(1), 35–58. doi:10.1177/146499340901000103

Mitchell, R. K., Busenitz, L., Bird, B., Gaglio, C. M., McMullen, J. S., Morse, E. A., & Smith, J. B. (2007). The central question in entrepreneurial cognition research 2007. *Entrepreneurship Theory and Practice*, *31*(1), 1–27. doi:10.1111/j.1540-6520.2007.00161.x

Mittal, S., Ahlgren, E. O., & Shukla, P. R. (2019). Future biogas resource potential in India: A bottom-up analysis. *Renewable Energy*, *141*, 379–389. doi:10.1016/j.renene.2019.03.133

Mochona, S. (2006). *Impact of microfinance in Addis Ababa: The case of GASHA microfinance institute* (Doctoral dissertation). University School of Graduate studies, Regional and Local Development Studies.

Modéer, U. (2018). *Unlocking Islamic Social Finance to Help Communities Address Vulnerability and Inequality*. https://www.undp.org/content/undp/en/home/news-centre/speeches/2018/Unlocking_Islamic_Social_Finance_to_Help_Communities_Address_Vulnerability_and_Inequality.html

Mohamed, N., Mastuki, N., Yusuf, S., & Zakaria, M. (2018). Management Control System in Asnaf Entrepreneurship Development Program by Lembaga Zakah Selangor [Sistem Kawalan Dalamanbagi Program Pembangunan Usahawan Asnaf di Lembaga Zakah Selangor]. *JurnalPengurusan*, *53*, 13–22.

Mohamed, Z. O., Che Supian, M. N., & Norziani, D. (2012). The economic performance of the Amanah Ikhtiar Malaysia rural microcredit program: A case study in Kedah. *World Journal of Social Sciences*, *2*(5), 286–302.

Mohan, B. (2007). *Fallacies of development: Crises of human and social development*. Atlantic Publishers.

Monahan, M., Shah, A., & Mattare, M. (2011). The road ahead: Micro enterprise perspectives on success and challenge factors. *Journal of Management Policy and Practice*, *12*(4), 113–125.

Monitor Institute. (2009). *Investing for Social and Environmental Impact, A Design for Catalyzing an Emerging Industry*. http://monitorinstitute.com/what-wethink/#

Compilation of References

Monroy, R., & Huerga, A. (2012). A Study of Four Listed Micro Finance Institutions. *6th International Conference on Industrial Engineering and Industrial Management*, 44-51.

Morduch, J., & Haley, B. (2002). *Analysis of the effects of microfinance on poverty reduction* (Vol. 1014). New York: NYU Wagner working paper.

Morduch, J. (1999). The microfinance promise. *Journal of Economic Literature*, *37*(4), 1569–1614. doi:10.1257/jel.37.4.1569

Morgan, R., & Hunt, S. D. (1994). The commitment: Trust theory of relationship marketing. *Journal of Marketing*, *58*(7), 20–38.

Morris, M. H., Miyasaki, N. N., Watters, C. E., & Coombes, S. M. (2006). The dilemma of growth: Understanding venture size choices of women entrepreneurs. *Journal of Small Business Management*, *44*(2), 221–244. doi:10.1111/j.1540-627X.2006.00165.x

Mosoti, V. (2003). Non-discrimination and its dimensions in possible WTO framework agreement on investment reflections on the scope and policy space for the development of poor economies. *Journal of World Investment*, *4*(6), 1011–1046. doi:10.1163/221190003X00057

Mottaleb, K. A., & Rahut, D. B. (2019). Biogas adoption and elucidating its impacts in India: Implications for policy. *Biomass and Bioenergy*, *123*, 166–174. doi:10.1016/j.biombioe.2019.01.049

Moyo, J., Nandwa, B., Council, D. E., Oduor, J., & Simpasa, A. (2014). Financial sector reforms, competition and banking system stability in Sub-Saharan Africa. *New Perspectives*, *14*(1), 1–47.

Mshenga, P. M., Richardson, R. B., Njehia, B. K., & Birachi, E. A. (2010). The contribution of tourism to micro and small enterprise growth. *Tourism Economics*, *16*(4), 953–964. doi:10.5367/te.2010.0018

Muleya, E. (2020). Developmental social work and the sustainable development goals in South Africa: Opportunities and challenges. *The International Journal of Community and Social Development*, *2*(4), 470–486. doi:10.1177/2516602620975226

Mupedziswa, R. (2005). Challenges and prospects of social work services in Africa. In J. C. Akeibunor & E. E. Anugwom (Eds.), The social sciences and socio-economic transformation in Africa (pp. 271-317). Nsukka: Great AP Express Publishing.

Murad, A. B., & Idewele, I. E. O. (2017). The impact of microfinance institution in economic growth of a country: Nigeria in focus. *International Journal of Development and Management Review*, *12*(1), 1–17.

Musanganya, I., Nyinawumuntu, C., & Nyirahagenimana, P. (2017). The impact of microfinance banks in rural areas of Sub-Saharan Africa. *International Journal of Research – GRANTHAALAYAH*, *5*(9), 80–90. doi:10.29121/granthaalayah.v5.i9.2017.2201

Mustapa, W. N., Mamun, A., & Ibrahim, M. (2018). Development Initiatives, Micro-Enterprise Performance and Sustainability. *International Journal of Financial Studies*, *6*(3), 74. doi:10.3390/ijfs6030074Omar, M. Z., Noor, C. S. M., & Dahalan, N. (2012). The economic performance of the Amanah Ikhtiar Malaysia rural microcredit programme: A case study in Kedah. *WORLD (Oakland, Calif.)*, *2*(5).

Mutaleb, M. Z., Baharanyi, N. R., Tackie, N. O., & Zabawa, R. (2015). An assessment of microlending programs in the Alabama black belt region. *Professional Agricultural Workers Journal*, *2*(2), 1–10.

Muthoni, M. P. (2016). Assessing Borrower's and Business' Factors Causing Microcredit Default in Kenya: A Comparative Analysis of Microfinance Institutions and Financial Intermediaries. *Journal of Education and Practice*, *7*(12), 97–118.

Naeem, A., Khan, S., Ali, M., & Hassan, F. S. (2015). The Impact of Microfinance on Women Micro-Enterprises "A Case Study of District Quetta, Pakistan. *American International Journal of Social Science*, *4*(4), 19–27.

Naeem, A., & Rehman, S. (2016). Gender Based Utilization of Microfinance: An Empirical Evidence from District Quetta, Pakistan. *International Business Research*, *9*(10), 162–168. doi:10.5539/ibr.v9n10p162

Nair, T. S. (2018). Microfinance in India: Approaches, Outcomes, Challenges. Taylor & Francis. doi:10.4324/9781315656250

Naituli, G., Wegulo, F. N., & Kaimenyi, B. (2006). Entrepreneurial characteristics among micro and small-scale women owned enterprises in North and Central Meru districts, Kenya. Gender Inequalities in Kenya, 7-25.

Namrata, G., & Anita, M. (2018). Investigating entrepreneurial success factors of women owned SMEs in UAE. *Management Decision*, *56*(1), 219–232. doi:10.1108/MD-04-2017-0411

Nasir, S. (2013). Microfinance in India: Contemporary issues and challenges. *Middle East Journal of Scientific Research*, *15*(2), 191–199.

National Planning Commission. (2009). Economic Transformation Blueprint. *Nigeria Vision*, 20.

Nawaz, S. (2010). Microfinance and poverty reduction: Evidence from a village study in Bangladesh. *Journal of Asian and African Studies*, *45*(6), 670–683. doi:10.1177/0021909610383812 PMID:21174878

Nayar, K. R. (1994). Politics of Sustainable Development. *Economic and Political Weekly*, *29*, 1328.

Ndambiri, H. K., Ritho, C., Ng'ang'a, S. I., Kubowon, P. C., Mairura, F. C., Nyangweso, P. M., Muiruri, E. M., & Cherotwo, F. H. (2012). Determinants of economic growths in Sub-Saharan Africa: A panel data approach. *International Journal of Economics and Management Sciences*, *2*(2), 18–24.

Nelson, N. (2013). Why has development neglected rural women? A review of the South Asian literature. Elsevier.

Neumann, A. (2012, July 24). Microfinance as a Tool to Alleviate Poverty. *Forbes*. Available at: https://www.forbes.com/sites/dell/2012/07/24/microfinance-as-a-tool-to-alleviate-poverty/

Ngugi, V. W., & Kerongo, F. (2014). Effects of Micro-Financing on Growth of Small and Micro Enterprises in Mombasa County. *International Journal of Scientific and Engineering Research*, 2(4), 2347–3878.

Nicolaou, N., & Shane, S. (2009). Can genetic factors influence the likelihood of engaging in entrepreneurial activity? *Journal of Business Venturing, 24*(1), 1–22. doi:.jbusvent.2007.11.003 doi:10.1016/j

Nicolaou, N., Shane, S., Cherkas, L., Hunkin, J., & Spector, T. (2008). Is the tendency to engage in entrepreneurship genetic? *Management Science, 54*(1), 167–179. doi:10.1287/mnsc.1070.0761

Njiro, E. (2002). Introduction to Sustainable Development and Oxymoron? *Empowering Women for Gender Equity*, (52), 3–7.

Nwafor, P. Z. (2007). *Practical Approach to Entrepreneurship: Small and Medium Scale Enterprises (SMEs)*. Retrieved from: www.scirp.org/journal/PaperInformation.aspx?PaperID = 8063

Nwagbara, U. (2014). *Leading Sustainability in Nigeria: Problems, Processes and Prospects*. Lambert Academic Press.

Nwigwe, C. A., Omonona, B. T., & Okoruwa, V. O. (2012). Microfinance and poverty reduction in Nigeria: A critical assessment. *Australian Journal of Business and Management Research*, 2(4), 33–40. doi:10.52283/NSWRCA.AJBMR.20120204A05

Obebo, F., Wawire, N., & Muniu, J. (2018). Determinants of Participation of Micro and Small Enterprises in Microfinance in Kenya. *Int J Econ Manag Sci, 7*(523), 2. doi:10.4172/2162-6359.1000523

Obi, C. (2010). The petroleum industry: A paradox or (SP) oil of development. *Journal of Contemporary African Studies, 28*(4), 443–457.

Odebiyi, O. C., & Olaoye, O. J. (2012). Small and medium scale aquaculture enterprises (SMES) development in Ogun State, Nigeria: The role of microfinance banks. *Development, 2*(3), 1–6.

Odeleye, D. O. (2013). The Doctrine of Natural Justice under Civil and Military Administrations in Nigeria. *Journal of Policy & Law, 6*(2), 234. doi:10.5539/jpl.v6n2p231

Odell, K. (2010). *Measuring the impact of microfinance*. Grameen Foundation.

Odoom, D., Fosu, K. O., Ankomah, K., & Amofa, M. B. (2019). Exploring the Contributions of Microfinance Institutions to the Ghanaian Economy: A Study at Takoradi. *Journal of Economics and Sustainable Development, 10*(1), 77–90.

OECD. (2004). *SME Statistics: Towards a More Systematic Statistical Measurement of SME Behaviour.* Background Report for the 2nd OECD Conference of Ministers Responsible for Small and Medium Enterprises (SMEs).

Ogujiuba, K., & Ehigiamusoe, K. U. (2013). The challenges and implications of sustainable development in Africa: Policy options for Nigeria. *Journal of Economic Cooperation and Development*, *34*(4), 77–111.

Ojo, S. (2013). *Diaspora entrepreneurship: A study of Nigerian entrepreneurs in London* (PhD thesis). University of East London, UK.

Ojo, S. (2018). Identity, Ethnic Embeddedness, and African Cuisine Break-Out in Britain. *Journal of Foodservice Business Research*, *21*(1), 33–54. doi:10.1080/15378020.2016.1263058

Okazakia, S., Plangger, K., West, D., & Menendez, H. D. (2020). (in press). Exploring digital corporate social responsibility communications on Twitter. *Journal of Business Research*.

Okonkwo, T., & Etemire, U. (2017). "Oil Injustice" in Nigeria's Niger Delta Region: A Call for Responsive Governance. *Journal of Environmental Protection*, *8*(1), 42–43. doi:10.4236/jep.2017.81005

Okpe, F.O. (2015). Economic Development and the Utility of Local Content Legislation in the Oil and Gas Industry: Conflicts and Effects of Nigeria's Local Content Act in the Context of International Investment Law. *Pac McGeorge Global Business & Development Law Journal*, *28*, 255-294.

Olaosebikan, O., & Adams, M. (2014). Prospects for micro-insurance in promoting micro-credit in sub-Sahara Africa. *Qualitative Research in Financial Markets*, *6*(3), 232–257. doi:10.1108/QRFM-09-2012-0028

Olawuyi, D. S., & Tubodenyefa, Z. (2018). Review of the Environmental Guidelines and Standards for the Petroleum Industry in Nigeria (EGASPIN). OGEES Institute.

Oliva, T. A., Oliver, R. L., & MacMillan, I. C. (1992). A catastrophe model for developing service satisfaction strategies. *Journal of Marketing*, *56*(3), 83–95.

Oliver, R. L. (1989). Processing of the satisfaction response in consumption: A suggested framework and research propositions. *Journal of Consumer Satisfaction, Dissatisfaction and Complaint Behaviour*, *2*, 1-16.

Oluwaseyi, M. H. (2016). *The Impact of Foreign Capital Inflows on Economic Growth in Selected West African countries* (Doctoral dissertation). Universiti Utara Malaysia.

Oluyombo, O. O. (2011). The impact of microfinance bank credit on economic development of Nigeria (1992–2006). *International Journal of Development and Management Review*, *6*(1), 139–150.

Omodanisi, E., Eludoyin, A., & Salami, A. (2014). A multi-perspective view of the effects of a pipeline explosion in Nigeria. *International Journal of Disaster Risk Reduction*, *7*, 68–77.

Compilation of References

Omotola, J. S. (2008). Combating Poverty for Sustainable Human Development in Nigeria: The Continuing Struggle. *Journal of Poverty*, *12*(4), 496–517. doi:10.1080/10875540802352621

Opara, I. (2007). Nigerian Anti-Corruption Initiatives. *Journal of International Business and Law*, *6*(1), 63–94.

Osei-Assibey, E., Bokpin, G. A., & Twerefou, D. K. (2012). Microenterprise financing preference: Testing POH within the context of Ghana's rural financial market. *Journal of Economic Studies (Glasgow, Scotland)*, *39*(1), 84–105. doi:10.1108/01443581211192125

Osei-Hwedie, K., & Rankopo, M. (2008). Developing culturally relevant social work education in Africa: The Case of Botswana. In M. Gray, J. Coates, & M. Y. Bird (Eds.), *Indigenous social work around the world* (pp. 203–219). Ashgate.

Oshora, B., Fekete-Farkas, M., & Zeman, Z. (2020). Role Of Microfinance Institutions In Financing Micro And Small Enterprises In Ethiopia. *Copernican Journal of Finance & Accounting*, *9*(3), 115–130. doi:10.12775/CJFA.2020.015

Outsios, G., & Farooqi, S. A. (2017). Gender in sustainable entrepreneurship: Evidence from the UK. *Gender in Management*, *32*(3), 183–202. doi:10.1108/GM-12-2015-0111

Palazzo, A. G., & Scherer, G. (2011). The New Political Role of Business in a Globalized World–A Paradigm Shift in CSR and its Implications for the Firm, Governance, and Democracy. *Journal of Management Studies*, *48*(4), 899–931. doi:10.1111/j.1467-6486.2010.00950.x

Palmer, A. (2014). Principles of services marketing (7th ed.). McGrawHill Education.

Palmer, J. (2011). How to predict monitoring issues. *World Pumps*, *2011*(5), 38–39.

Panda, D. K. (2016). Microfinance Spurs Microenterprise Development: An Exploration of the Latent Processes. *Strategic Change*, *25*(5), 613–623. doi:10.1002/jsc.2084

Pan, X., Chen, X., & Ning, L. (2018). The roles of macro and micro institutions in corporate social responsibility (CSR): Evidence from listed firms in China. *Management Decision*, *56*(5), 955–971. doi:10.1108/MD-05-2017-0530

Pappu, A., Saxena, M., & Asolekar, S. R. (2007). Solid wastes generation in India and their recycling potential in building materials. *Building and Environment*, *42*(6), 2311–2320. doi:10.1016/j.buildenv.2006.04.015

Parasuraman, A., Zeithaml, V., & Berry, L. L. (1993). Research note: More on improving service quality measurement. *Journal of Retailing*, *69*(1), 140–147.

Parker, S. C. (2018). *The economics of entrepreneurship*. Cambridge University Press. doi:10.1017/9781316756706

Parris, T. M., & Kates, R. W. (2003). Characterising and measuring sustainable development. *Annual Review of Environment and Resources*, *28*(13), 113–128.

Parry, G., Newnes, L., & Huang, X. (2011). Goods, Products and Services. In B. Hefley & W. Murphy (Eds.), *Service design and delivery*. Springer.

Patel, L., & Hochfeld, T. (2012). Developmental social work in South Africa: Translating policy into practice. *International Social Work*, *56*(5), 1–15.

Pathak, H. P., & Gyawali, M. (2012). Role of microfinance in employment generation: A case study of Microfinance Program of Paschimanchal Grameen Bikash Bank. *Journal of Nepalese Business Studies*, *7*(1), 31–38. doi:10.3126/jnbs.v7i1.6401

Peeters, J. (2011). The place of social work in sustainable development: Towards ecosocial practice. *International Journal of Social Welfare*, *21*(3), 287–298. doi:10.1111/j.1468-2397.2011.00856.x

Perren, L., & Jennings, P. J. (2005). Government discourses on entrepreneurship: Issues of legitimization, subjugation, and power. *Entrepreneurship Theory and Practice*, *29*(2), 173–184. doi:10.1111/j.1540-6520.2005.00075.x

Phillips, N., & Tracey, P. (2007). Opportunity recognition, entrepreneurial capabilities and bricolage: Connecting institutional theory and entrepreneurship. *Strategic Organization*, *5*(3), 313–320. doi:10.1177/1476127007079956

Plagerson, S., Patel, L., Hochfeld, T., & Ulriksen, M. S. (2019). Social policy in South Africa: Navigating the route to social development. *Journal of World Development*, *113*, 1–9. doi:10.1016/j.worlddev.2018.08.019

Polonsky, M. J. (2011). Transformative Green Marketing: Impediments and Opportunities. *The Journal of Business*.

Poon, J. P., Thai, D. T., & Naybor, D. (2012). Social capital and female entrepreneurship in rural regions: Evidence from Vietnam. *Applied Geography (Sevenoaks, England)*, *35*(1), 308–315. doi:10.1016/j.apgeog.2012.08.002

Porter, M. E., & Kramer, M. R. (2018). Creating shared value. In *Managing Sustainable Business* (pp. 327–350). Springer.

Pronyk, P. M., Hargreaves, J. R., & Morduch, J. (2007). Microfinance programs and better health: Prospects for sub-Saharan Africa. *JAMA Network Open*, *298*(16), 1925–1927. PMID:17954543

Psaltopoulos, D., Stathopoulou, S., & Skuras, D. (2005). The location of markets, perceived entrepreneurial risk, and start-up capital of micro rural firms. *Small Business Economics*, *25*(2), 147–158. doi:10.100711187-003-6456-6

Purvis, B., Mao, Y., & Robinson, D. (2018). Three pillars of sustainability: In search of conceptual origins. *Sustainability Science*, *14*(3), 681–695. doi:10.100711625-018-0627-5

Qardawi, Y. (2009). A comparative study of *Zakah*: Regulations and Philosophy in the light of qur'an and sunnah. *Fiqh Al Zakah*, *I*, 1–309.

Compilation of References

Qin, M., Wachenheim, C. J., Wang, Z., & Zheng, S. (2019). Factors affecting Chinese farmers' microcredit participation. *Agricultural Finance Review*, *79*(1), 48–59. doi:10.1108/AFR-12-2017-0111

Quaye, I., Abrokwah, E., Sarbah, A., & Osei, J. Y. (2014). Bridging the SME financing gap in Ghana: The role of microfinance institutions. *Open Journal of Business and Management*, *2*(04), 339–413. doi:10.4236/ojbm.2014.24040

Quayes, S. (2012). Depth of outreach and financial sustainability of microfinance institutions. *Applied Economics*, *44*(26), 3421–3433. doi:10.1080/00036846.2011.577016

Quibria, M. G. (2012). *Microcredit and Poverty Alleviation: Can microcredit close the deal?* WIDER Working Paper.

Quinones, B., & Remenyi, J. (2014). *Microfinance and poverty alleviation: Case studies from Asia and the Pacific*. Routledge. doi:10.4324/9781315800455

Radhakrishnan, S. (2015). "Low Profile" or Entrepreneurial? Gender, Class, and Cultural Adaptation in the Global Microfinance Industry. *World Development*, *74*, 264–274. doi:10.1016/j.worlddev.2015.05.017

Radipere, S., & Dhliwayo, S. (2014). The role of gender and education on small business performance in the South African small enterprise sector. *Mediterranean Journal of Social Sciences*, *5*(9), 104–110.

Raghunandan, V. (2018). Changing Equations: Empowerment, Entrepreneurship and the Welfare of Women. *Journal of International Women's Studies*, *19*(3), 187–198.

Rahman, A. (2004). Microcredit and poverty reduction: Trade-off between building institutions and reaching the poor. *Livelihood and microfinance. Anthropological and sociological perspectives on savings and debt*, 25-42.

Ramadani, V. (2015). The woman entrepreneur in Albania: An exploratory study on motivation, problems and success factors. *Journal of Balkan & Near Eastern Studies*, *17*(2), 204–221. doi: 10.1080/19448953.2014.997488

Ramoglou, S. (2009). *In the shadow of entrepreneurs: Taking seriously the 'others' of entrepreneurship*. Paper presented at the 25th EGOS Colloquium 2010.

Ramoglou, S. (2008). The question we ought to ask: 'Who is the non-entrepreneur?'. *Proceedings of the Academy of Management Review*, *41*(3), 410–434. doi:10.5465/amr.2014.0281

Ranjani, K. S., & Bapat, V. (2015). Deepening Financial Inclusion beyond account opening: Road ahead for banks. *Business Perspectives and Research*, *3*(1), 52–65. doi:10.1177/2278533714551864

Rao, P. V., Baral, S. S., Dey, R., & Mutnuri, S. (2010). Biogas generation potential by anaerobic digestion for sustainable energy development in India. *Renewable & Sustainable Energy Reviews*, *14*(7), 2086–2094. doi:10.1016/j.rser.2010.03.031

Razimi, M., Romle, A., & Erdris, M. (2016). Zakah Management in Malaysia: A Review. *American-Eurasian Journal of Scientific Research, 11*(6), 453–457.

Rehman, A. (2019). *Islamic finance for social good.* https://www.undp.org/content/undp/en/home/blog/2019/IFN_ANNUAL_GUIDE_2019_Islamic_Social_Finance.html

Rehman, A., & Pickup, F. (2018). *Zakah for the SDGs.* https://www.undp.org/blog/zakah-sdgs

Rehman, A., & Pickup, F. (2018). *Zakah for the SDGs.* https://www.undp.org/content/undp/en/home/blog/2018/zakah-for-the-sdgs.html

Rehman, H., Moazzam, A., & Ansari, N. (2015). Role of Microfinance Institutions in Women Empowerment: A Case Study of Akhuwat, Pakistan. *South Asian Studies, 30*(1), 107.

Rehman, S., & Azam, R. M. (2012). Gender and work-life balance: A phenomenological study of women entrepreneurs in Pakistan. *Journal of Small Business and Enterprise Development, 19*(2), 209–228. doi:10.1108/14626001211223865

Remenyi, J., & Quiñones, B. (2000). *Microfinance and poverty alleviation: Case studies from Asia and the Pacific.* Routledge.

Reynolds, P. D. (2009). Screening item effects in estimating the prevalence of nascent entrepreneurs. *Small Business Economics, 33*(2), 151–163. doi:10.100711187-008-9112-3

Reynolds, P., Bosma, N., Autio, E., Hunt, S., De Bono, N., Servais, I., Lopez-Garcia, P., & Nancy, C. (2005). Global entrepreneurship monitor: Data collection design and implementation 1998-2003. *Small Business Economics, 24*(3), 205–231. doi:10.100711187-005-1980-1

Rhyne, E. (1998). *The yin and yang of microfinance: reaching the poor and sustainability.* Micro Banking Bulletin.

Rhyne, E. (2009). *Microfinance for Bankers and Investors.* US McGraw-Hill Professional Publishing.

Rio-Lanza, A. B. D., Vazquez-Casielles, R., & Diaz-Martin, A. M. (2009). Satisfaction with service recovery: Perceived justice and emotional responses. *Journal of Business Research, 62*(8), 775–781.

Robinson, M. S. (2001). *The microfinance revolution: sustainable finance for the poor* (Vol. 1). World Bank Publications.

Robinson, S., & Finley, J. (2007). Rural women's self-employment: A look at Pennsylvania. *Academy of Entrepreneurship Journal, 13*(2).

Robson, C., & McCartan, K. (2016). *Real world research.* John Wiley & Sons.

Ronoh, E. K., Korir, S., Rotich, J. C., & Onguso, B. (2014). Constraints to the Success of Women Small Scale Entrepreneurs in Kenya. A Case of Microfinance Institution Borrowers in Rongai District of Nakuru County, Kenya. *European Journal of Business and Management, 6*(21), 124–136.

Compilation of References

Roodman, D., & Morduch, J. (2009). *The Impact of Microcredit on the Poor in Bangladesh: Revisiting the Evidence.* Working Paper Number 174. Centre for Global Development.

RosenbergR.GonzalezA.NarainS. (2009, February). *The new moneylenders: are the poor being exploited by high microcredit interest rates?* CGAP Occasional Paper, no. 15, 1–25. https://ssrn.com/abstract=1400291

Rose, R. C., Kumar, N., & Yen, L. L. (2006). The dynamics of entrepreneurs' success factors in influencing venture growth. *Journal of Asia Entrepreneurship and Sustainability, 2*(2), 1–122.

Rotich, I., Lagat, C., & Kogei, J. (2015). Effects of microfinance services on the performance of small and medium enterprises in Kenya. *African Journal of Business Management, 9*(5), 206–211. doi:10.5897/AJBM2014.7519

Rotter, J. B. (1966). Generalized Expectancies for Internal versus External Control of Reinforcement. *Psychological Monographs, 80*(1), 1–2. doi:10.1037/h0092976 PMID:5340840

Rowe-Haynes, M. D. (2017). *Micro-finance and small and medium-sized enterprises: the social, economic and environmental impacts of community development finance institutions in the UK* (Doctoral dissertation). University of Birmingham.

Rozenberg, J., & Fay, M. (2019). *Beyond the Gap How Countries Can Afford the Infrastructure They Need while Protecting the Planet.* https://openknowledge.worldbank.org/handle/10986/31291

Rutherford, S. (2000). The poor and their money. Oxford: Oxford University Press.

Saba, H. A. (2021). *Influence of Microfinance Bank Services on the Performance of Micro and Small Enterprises* (Doctoral dissertation). Kwara State University, Nigeria.

Sabahat, A., Imran, S., & Safina, M. (2015). Socio-Economic Empowerment of Women Through Micro Enterprises: A Case Study of Ajk. *European Scientific Journal, 11*(22).

Sabouri, M. S., Saberiyan, M., & Arayesh, M. B. (2016). The Role of Socio-economic Factors of Micro-credit Funds in Improving Rural Women Entrepreneurship Development. *Journal of Sustainable Development, 9*(5), 187. doi:10.5539/jsd.v9n5p187

Sabri, H., & Hasan, Z. (2006). *Zakah: Instrumen penyumbang pembentuk anusahawan. In Prosiding Seminar Kebangsaan Pengurusan Harta Dalam Islam. Jabatan Syariah.* Universiti Kebangsaan Malaysia.

Sachs, J. (2005). *The End of Poverty: Economic Possibilities for our Time.* The Penguin Press.

Saldana, J. (2016). *The Coding Manual for Qualitative Researchers.* SAGE Publication Ltd.

Salia, P. J. (2014). The effect of microcredit on the household welfare (empirical evidences from women micro-entrepreneurs in Tanzania). *International Journal of Academic Research in Business & Social Sciences, 4*(5), 259. doi:10.6007/IJARBSS/v4-i5/853

Salia, P. J., & Mbwambo, J. S. (2014). Does microcredit make any difference on borrowers' businesses? Evidences from a survey of women owned microenterprises in Tanzania. *International Journal of Social Sciences and Entrepreneurship*, *1*(9), 431–444.

Salia, S., Hussain, J., Tingbani, I., & Kolade, O. (2018). Is women empowerment a zero sum game? Unintended consequences of microfinance for women's empowerment in Ghana. *International Journal of Entrepreneurial Behaviour & Research*, *24*(1), 273–289. doi:10.1108/IJEBR-04-2017-0114

Salmones, M. G., Crespo, A. H., & Del Bosque, I. R. (2005). Influence of corporate social responsibility on loyalty and valuation of services. *Journal of Business Ethics*, *61*(4), 369–385.

Sanyal, P. (2009). From credit to collective action: The role of microfinance in promoting women's social capital and normative influence. *American Sociological Review*, *74*(4), 529–550. doi:10.1177/000312240907400402

Sarasvathy, S. D., & Venkataraman, S. (2011). Entrepreneurship as Method: Open Questions for an Entrepreneurial Future. *Entrepreneurship Theory and Practice*, *35*(1), 113–135. Advance online publication. doi:10.1111/j.1540-6520.2010.00425.x

Sarumathi, S., & Mohan, K. (2011). Role of Microfinance in women's empowerment; an empirical study in Pondicherry region rural SHG's. *Journal of Management and Science*, *1*(1), 1–10.

SBA. (2008). *Looking Ahead: Opportunities and Challenges for Entrepreneurship and Small Business Owners*. https://www.sba.gov/sites/default/files/rs332tot.pdf

Schaper, M. (Ed.). (2016). *Making ecopreneurs: developing sustainable entrepreneurship*. CRC Press. doi:10.4324/9781315593302

Schumpeter, J. A. (1934). *The theory of economic development: an inquiry into profits, capital, credit, interest, and the business cycle*. Harvard Economic Studies.

Schumpeter, J. A. (1968). *Ensayos*. Oikos-Tau. (Original work published 1951)

Scott, D. M., Curci, R., & Mackoy, R. (2012). Hispanic business enterprise success: Ethnic resources, market orientation, or market exchange embeddedness? *Journal of International Business and Cultural Studies*, *6*, 1.

Section 10(1)(a) *of the Nigerian Oil and Gas Industry Content Development Act 2010*

Section 12 of *the Nigerian Oil and Gas Industry Content Development Act 2010*

Section 6(2) *of the Act only encourages caution, calling on the holder of a permit under section 5 of the Act to 'take all reasonable steps to avoid unnecessary damage...' Emphasis added*

Section 7 *of the Nigerian Oil and Gas Industry Content Development Act 2010*

Section 8 *of the Nigerian Oil and Gas Industry Content Development Act 2010*

Sekabira, H. (2013). Capital structure and its role on performance of microfinance institutions: The Ugandan case. *Sustainable Agriculture Research*, *2*(3), 86–100. doi:10.5539ar.v2n3p86

Selipsky, L., Mupedziswa, R., & Chitereka, C. (2009). *Developmental Social Work Education in Southern and East Africa*. University of Johannesburg.

Sethi, D., & Acharya, D. (2018). Financial inclusion and economic growth linkage: Some cross country evidence. *Journal of Financial Economic Policy*, *10*(3), 369–385. doi:10.1108/JFEP-11-2016-0073

Shane, S. (2000). *Prior knowledge and the discovery of entrepreneurial opportunities*. Academic Press.

Shane, S. (2000). Prior knowledge and the discovery of entrepreneurial opportunities. *Organization Science*, *11*(4), 448–469. doi:10.1287/orsc.11.4.448.14602

Shane, S. (2003). *A General Theory of Entrepreneurship: The Individual–Opportunity Nexus*. Elgar. doi:10.4337/9781781007990

Shane, S. (2009). Why encouraging more people to become entrepreneurs is bad public policy? *Small Business Economics*, *33*(2), 141–149. doi:10.100711187-009-9215-5

Shane, S., & Venkataraman, S. (2000). The promise of entrepreneurship as a field of research. *Acad. Manga. Rev.*, *25*(1), 217–226. doi:10.5465/amr.2000.2791611

Sharma, G. L., & Puri, H. (2013). An empirical testing of relationship between microfinance and economic growth in india. *Journal of Indian Research*, *1*(2), 87–94.

Sharma, S., & Ruud, A. (2003). On the Path to Sustainability: Integrating Social Dimensions into the Research and Practice of Environmental Management. *Business Strategy and the Environment*, *12*(1), 205–214.

Shaver, K.G. (1987). *Principles of social psychology*. doi:10.1177/104225879201600204

Sheremenko, G., Escalante, C. L. & Florkowski, W. J. (2017). Financial sustainability and poverty outreach: The case of microfinance institutions in Eastern Europe and Central Asia. *The European Journal of Development Research, 29*(1), 230-245.

Shiyuti, H., & Al-Habshi, S. (2018). An Overview of *Asnaf* Entrepreneurship Program by Lembaga Zakah Selangor. *Malaysia 6 th ASEAN Universities International Conference on Islamic Finance (AICIF)*.

Siddiqui, A. B. (2012). Problems encountered by women entrepreneurs in India. *International Journal of Applied Research & Studies*, *1*(2), 1–11.

Simpson, M., Tuck, N., & Bellamy, S. (2004). Small business success factors: The role of education and training. *Education + Training*, *46*(8), 481–491. doi:10.1108/00400910410569605

Singh, J., & Yadav, P. (2012). Microfinance as a tool for financial inclusion & reduction of poverty. *Journal of Business Management & Social Sciences Research, 1*(1), 1–12.

Siu, N. Y., Zhang, T. J., & Yau, C. J. (2013). The roles of justice and customer satisfaction in customer retention: A lesson from service recovery. *Journal of Business Ethics, 114*(4), 75–686.

Snowiss, S. (1990). *Judicial Review and the Law of Constitution.* Yale University Press.

Solomon, M., & Stuart, E. (2006). *Marketing: Real People, Real Choices.* Pearson.

Song, X., Zhou, G., Jiang, H., Yu, S., Fu, J., Li, W., Wang, W., Ma, Z., & Peng, C. (2011). Carbon sequestration by Chinese bamboo forests and their ecological benefits: Assessment of potential, problems, and future challenges. *Environmental Reviews, 19*(NA), 418–428. doi:10.1139/a11-015

Son, J. Y., & Kim, S. (2008). Users' information privacy- protective responses: A Taxonomy and Nomological model. *Management Information Systems Quarterly, 32*(3), 503.

Soriano, F. I. (2012). Conducting needs assessments: A multidisciplinary approach (Vol. 68). Sage.

Soyibo, A. (2006). The concept of entrepreneurship. *Journal of Business Organization. Development*, •••, 15.

Sparks, B. A., & McColl-Kennedy, J. R. (2001). Justice strategy options for increased customer satisfaction in a services recovery setting. *Journal of Business Research, 54*(3), 209–218.

Spiegel, S. J. (2012). Microfinance services, poverty and artisanal mineworkers in Africa: In search of measures for empowering vulnerable groups. *Journal of International Development, 24*(4), 485–517. doi:10.1002/jid.1781

Spitzer, H., & Twikirize, J. M. (2014). A vision for social work in East Africa. In H. Spitzer, J.M. Twikirize, & G.G. Wairire (Eds.), Professional Social Work in East Africa. Kampala: Fountain Publishers.

Ssewamala, F. M., Sperber, E., Zimmerman, J. M., & Karimli, L. (2010). The potential of asset-based development strategies for poverty alleviation in Sub-Saharan Africa. *International Journal of Social Welfare, 19*(4), 433–443. doi:10.1111/j.1468-2397.2010.00738.x

Stearns, K., & Otero, M. (1990). *The Critical Connection: Governments.* Private Institutions, and the Informal Sector in Latin America.

Steinwand, D. (2013). The Indonesian People's Credit Banks (Bpr). Southeast Asia's Credit Revolution: From Moneylenders to Microfinance, 95-112.

Stevenson, H. H., & Jarillo, J. C. (1990). A paradigm of entrepreneurship: Entrepreneurial management. *Strategic Management Journal, 11*, 17–27.

Storey, D & Greene F (2010). *Small business and entrepreneurship.* doi:10.1787/eco_surveys-srb-2002-5-en

Story, D. J. (2005). Entrepreneurship, Small and Medium Sized Enterprises and Public Policies. In Z. Y. Acs & D. B. Audretsch (Eds.), *Handwork of Entrepreneurship Research* (pp. 473–513). Springer. doi:10.1007/0-387-24519-7_18

Compilation of References

Suleiman, M. S. (2014). Microfinance banks and their impact on small and medium scale industries for economic growth. In *Green technology applications for enterprise and academic innovation* (pp. 48–64). IGI Global. doi:10.4018/978-1-4666-5166-1.ch004

Sulemana, M., Naiim, F. M., & Adjanyo, C. (2019). Role of microfinance in poverty reduction in the Ashaiman Municipality, Ghana. *African Research Review*, *13*(3), 1–14. doi:10.4314/afrrev.v13i3.1

Sultan, Y., & Masih, M. (2016). Does microfinance affect economic growth? Evidence from Bangladesh based on ARDL approach (No. 72123). University Library of Munich, Germany.

Sultana, H. Y., Jamal, M. A., & Najaf, D. E. (2017). Impact of Microfinance on Women Empowerment Through Poverty Alleviation: An Assessment of Socio-Economic Conditions in Chennai City of Tamil Nadu. *Asian Journal for Poverty Studies*, *3*(2).

Suma, D. F. (2007). *The External Debt Crisis and Its Impact on Economic Growth and Investment in Sub-Saharan Africa: A Regional Econometric Approach of ECOWAS Countries* (Doctoral dissertation). WU Vienna University of Economics and Business.

Surendra, K. C., Takara, D., Hashimoto, A. G., & Khanal, S. K. (2014). Biogas as a sustainable energy source for developing countries: Opportunities and challenges. *Renewable & Sustainable Energy Reviews*, *31*, 846–859. doi:10.1016/j.rser.2013.12.015

Susan & Ozkazanc-Pan. (2016). A Gender integrative conceptualization of entrepreneurship. *New England Journal of Entrepreneurship*, *18*(1), 27–40.

Svensson, G., & Wood, G. (2004). Corporate ethics and trust in intra-corporate relationships: An in-depth and longitudinal case description. *Employee Relations*, *26*(3), 320–336.

Swibel, M. (2007). *The 50 top microfinance institutions*. Forbes.com.

Tåg, J., Åstebro, T., & Thompson, P. (2016). Hierarchies and entrepreneurship. *European Economic Review*, *89*, 129–147. doi:10.1016/j.euroecorev.2016.06.007

Taimur, I., & Hamid, S. (2013). Determinants of women empowerment: The role of microfinance in the devastated areas of Pakistan. *The Journal of Business Strategy*, *7*(2), 39–52.

Taiwo, J. N., Agwu, M. E., Adetiloye, K. A., & Afolabi, G. T. (2016). Financing women entrepreneurs and employment generation–a case study of microfinance banks. *European Journal of Soil Science*, *52*(1), 112–141.

Talebi, K. (2007). *Strategic role of small and medium enterprises in national development*. Tehran. University Press.

Tambunan, T. T. (2015). Development of Women Entrepreneurs in Indonesia: Are they being Pushed or Pulled? *Journal of Socio-Economics*, *2*(3), 131–149.

Taneja, S., Pryor, M. G., & Hayek, M. (2016). Leaping innovation barriers to small business longevity. *The Journal of Business Strategy*, *37*(3), 44–51. doi:10.1108/JBS-12-2014-0145

Tanveer, M. A., Akbar, A., Gill, H., & Ahmed, I. (2013). Role of Personal Level Determinants in Entrepreneurial Firm's Success. *Journal of Basic and Applied Scientific Research*, *3*(1), 449–458.

Tax, S. S., Brown, S. W., & Chandrashekaran, M. (1998). Customer evaluations of service complaint experiences: Implications for relationship marketing. *Journal of Marketing*, *62*(2), 60–76.

Tchuigoua, H. T. (2014). Institutional framework and capital structure of microfinance institutions. *Journal of Business Research*, *67*(10), 2185–2197. doi:10.1016/j.jbusres.2014.01.008

Tehulu, T. A. (2013). Determinants of financial sustainability of microfinance institutions in East Africa. *European Journal of Business and Management*, *5*(17), 152–158.

Temitope, A., & Sharma, S. (2019). Entrepreneurial Challenges faced by Nigerian Women entrepreneur in UK. *International Journal of Entrepreneurship Management Innovation and Development*, *3*(2), 57–69.

Terano, R., Mohamed, Z., & Jusri, J. (2015). Effectiveness of microcredit program and determinants of income among small business entrepreneurs in Malaysia. *Journal of Global Entrepreneurship Research*, *5*(22), 22. doi:10.118640497-015-0038-3

Thai-Ha, L. (2021). *Microfinance and Social Development: A Selective Literature Review*. Background Note. https://www.adb.org/sites/default/files/institutional-document/691951/ado2021bn-microfinance-social-development.pdf

Thapa, A. (2015). Determinants of microenterprise performance in Nepal. *Small Business Economics*, *45*(3), 581–594. doi:10.100711187-015-9654-0

The World Commission on Environment and Development. (1987). *Our Common Future*. Author.

Thokchom, A., & Yadava, P. S. (2015). Bamboo and its role in climate change. *Current Science*, *108*(5), 762–763. https://www.jstor.org/stable/24216487

Thomassen, J. P., Leliveld, M., Ahaus, K., & Van-De Walle, S. (2019). Developing and implementing a service charter for an integrated regional stroke service: An exploratory case study. *BMC Health Services Research*, *14*(141), 2–11.

Thurik, R., & Wennekers, S. (2004). Entrepreneurship, small business and economic growth. *Journal of Small Business and Enterprise Development*, *11*(1), 140–149. doi:10.1108/14626000410519173

Townsend, P. (2014). *International Analysis Poverty*. Routledge. doi:10.4324/9781315835099

Tuzun, I. K., & Takay, B. A. (2017). Patterns of female entrepreneurial activities in Turkey. *Gender in Management*, *32*(3), 166–182. doi:10.1108/GM-05-2016-0102

Twikirize, J. M., Asingwire, N., Omona, J., Rosalind, L., & Kafuko, A. (2013). *The Role of Social Work in Poverty Reduction and the Realisation of Millennium Development Goals in Uganda*. Fountain Publishers.

Ucha, C. (2010). Poverty in Nigeria: Some dimensions and contributing factors. *Global Majority E-Journal*, *1*(1), 46–56.

Compilation of References

Udmale, P., Pal, I., Szabo, S., Pramanik, M., & Large, A. (2020). Global food security in the context of COVID-19: A scenario-based exploratory analysis. *Progress in Disaster Science, 7*, 100120. doi:10.1016/j.pdisas.2020.100120 PMID:34173442

Ukwueze, E. R., Asogwa, H. T., David-Wayas, O. M., Emecheta, C., & Nchege, J. E. (2019). How Does Microfinance Empower Women in Nigeria? A Study. In Handbook of Research on Microfinancial Impacts on Women Empowerment, Poverty, and Inequality (pp. 1-22). IGI Global.

UN-DESA. (2020). *Supporting Micro-, Small and Medium-sized Enterprises (MSMEs) to Achieve the Sustainable Development Goals (SDGs) in Cambodia through Streamlining Business Registration Policies.* https://sdgs.un.org/publications/supporting-micro-small-and-medium-sized-enterprises-msmes-achieve-sustainable

UNHCR. (2019). *Refugees: The Most in Need of zakah Funds UNHCR Zakah Program:2019, Launch Report.* https://zakah.unhcr.org/wp-content/uploads/2019/04/UNHCR-Annual-Zakah-Report-2019-En.pdf

UNHCR. (2020). *Consequences of underfunding in 2020.* https://www.unhcr.org/underfunding-2020/wp-content/uploads/sites/107/2020/09/Underfunding-2020-Full-Report.pdf

UNHCR. (2020a). *UNHCR's 2020 Islamic Philanthropy Mid-Year Report Winter Edition.* https://zakah.unhcr.org/wp-content/uploads/2020/11/UNHCR-2020-Mid-Year-Islamic-Philanthropy-Report-English-Compressed.pdf

UNICEF. (2019). *UNICEF and the Islamic Development Bank launch first global Muslim philanthropy fund for children.* https://www.unicef.org/press-releases/unicef-and-islamic-development-bank-launch-first-global-muslim-philanthropy-fund

United Nations (UN). (2017). *Sustainable development goals report 2017.* Available at http.www.un.org

United Nations (UN). (2017). *Sustainable development goals report 2017.* http.www.un.org

United Nations Development Program Niger Delta Human Development Report. (2006). *(UN Development Program Publication, Nigeria.* United Nations Environmental Programme.

United Nations Development Programme (UNDP). (2006). *Beyond scarcity: power, poverty and the global water crisis.* United Nations Development Programme.

United Nations Development Project. (1997). *Human Development Report: Human Development to Eradicate Poverty.* Oxford University Press.

United Nations Environment Programme (UNEP). (2015). *Integrating the three dimensions of sustainable development.* Available at https://sustainabledevelopment.un.org/content/documents/3782unep2.pdf

Vaaland, T., & Heide, M. (2008). Managing corporate social responsibility: Lessons from the oil industry. *Corporate Communications, 13*(2), 212–225.

Van Breda, A. (2018). Developmental social case work: A process model. *International Social Work*, *61*(1), 66–78. doi:10.1177/0020872815603786

Van Den Berg, M., Lensink, R., & Servin, R. (2015). Loan Officers' Gender and Microfinance Repayment Rates. *The Journal of Development Studies*, *51*(9), 1–14. doi:10.1080/00220388.2014.997218

Van Rooyen, C., Stewart, R., & de Wet, T. (2012). The impact of microfinance in sub-Saharan Africa: A systematic review of the evidence. *World Development*, *40*(11), 2249–2262. doi:10.1016/j.worlddev.2012.03.012

Varela-Neira, C., Vasques-Cassielles, R., & Iglesias, V. (2010). Explaining customer satisfaction with complain handling. *International Journal of Bank Marketing*, *29*(2), 88–112.

Vatta, K. (2003). Microfinance and Poverty Alleviation. *Economic and Political Weekly*, *38*(5), 432–433. https://www.jstor.org/stable/4413155

Venkatesh, V., Shaw, J. D., Sykes, T. A., Wamba, S. F., & Macharia, M. (2017). Networks, Technology, and Entrepreneurship: A Field Quasi-experiment among Women in Rural India. *Academy of Management Journal*, *60*(5), 1709–1740. doi:10.5465/amj.2015.0849

Vijay, V. K., Kapoor, R., Trivedi, A., & Vijay, V. (2015). Biogas as clean fuel for cooking and transportation needs in India. In *Advances in Bioprocess Technology* (pp. 257–275). Springer. doi:10.1007/978-3-319-17915-5_14

Vikas, B., & Vijayalakshmi, B. (2017). Microfinance and Women's Empowerment: An Exploratory Demographic Study in Karnataka, India. *South Asian Journal of Management*, *24*(3), 46–61.

Visser, W. (2013). *The age of responsibility: CSR 2.0 and the new DNA of business*. Wile.

Visser, W. (2013). *The age of responsibility: CSR 2.0 and the New DNA of Business*. Wiley.

Wairire, G. G. (2014). 'The state of social work education and practice in Kenya. In *Our Common Future. World Commission on Environment and Development*. Oxford University Press.

Walter, J. R., & Courtois, R. (2009). *The effect of interest on reserves on monetary policy*. Federal Reserve Bank of Richmond Economic Brief EB09-12 (December).

Wang, C. L., & Altinay, L. (2012). Social embeddedness, entrepreneurial orientation and firm growth in ethnic minority small businesses in the UK. *International Small Business Journal*, *30*(1), 3–23. doi:10.1177/0266242610366060

Wang, M. C., & Fang, S. C. (2012). The moderating effect of environmental uncertainty on the relationship between network structures and the innovative performance of a new venture. *Journal of Business and Industrial Marketing*, *27*(4), 311–323. doi:10.1108/08858621211221689

Warnecke, T. (2016). Informal sector entrepreneurship for women in China and India: Building networks, gaining recognition, and obtaining support. *Journal of Small Business and Entrepreneurship*, *28*(6), 479–491. doi:10.1080/08276331.2016.1202092

Compilation of References

Webb, C., & Bywaters, P. (2018). Austerity, rationing and inequity: Trends in children's & young peoples' services expenditure in England between 2010 and 2015. *Local Government Studies*, *44*(3), 391–415. doi:10.1080/03003930.2018.1430028

Weber, O. (2012). *Social Finance and Impact Investing*. Working Paper, University of Waterloo.

We-Fi Secretariat. (2020b). *Women entrepreneurs amidst COVID-19 crisis: balancing family and work. Women Entrepreneurs Finance Initiative.* Women Entrepreneurs Finance Initiative. Available at: https://we-fi.org/women-entrepreneurs-amidst-covid-19-crisis/

Weun, S., Beatty, S. E., & Jones, M. A. (2004). The impact of service failure severity on service recovery evaluations and post-recovery relationships. *Journal of Services Marketing*, *18*(2), 133–146.

Williams, C., & Millington, A. (2004). The Diverse and Contested Meaning of Sustainable Development. *The Geographical Journal*, *170*(2), 99–104. doi:10.1111/j.0016-7398.2004.00111.x

Williams, S., & Preston, D. (2018). Working with values: An alternative approach to win-win. *International Journal of Corporate Strategy and Social Responsibility*, *1*(4), 302–319.

Wilson, J. (2014). *Essentials of Business Research* (2nd ed.). SAGE Publication Ltd.

Wirtz, J., & Matilla, A. S. (2004). Consumer responses to compensation: Speed of recovery and apology after a service failure. *International Journal of Service Industry Management*, *15*(2), 150–166.

Woller, G., Dunford, C., & Woodworth, W. (1999). Where to microfinance? *International Journal of Economic Development*.

Worika, L., Etemire, U., & Tamuno, P. S. (2019). *Oil Politics and the Application of Environmental Laws to the Pollution of the Niger Delta: Current Challenges and Prospects. Oil, Gas and Energy Law Journal*, *17*(1).

World Bank. (1986). *Environmental Aspects of Bank Work. The World Bank Operations Manual Statements, OMS 2.36*. World Bank.

World Bank. (2018). *Poverty and Shared Prosperity 2018: Piecing Together the Poverty Puzzle*. World Bank.

World Bank. (2020). *Supporting Women Throughout the Coronavirus (Covid-19) Emergency Response and Economic Recovery*. Available at: https://openknowledge.worldbank.org/bitstream/handle/10986/33612/Supporting-Women-Throughout-the-CoronavirusCovid-19-Emergency-Response-and-Economic-Recovery.pdf?sequence=5&isAllowed=y

World Business Council for Sustainable Development. (1992). *Corporate Social Responsibility*. Author.

World Commission on Environment and Development (WCED). (1987). *Our Common Future*. Oxford University Press.

World Commission on Environment and Development. (1987). *Our common future.* Oxford University Press.

Wright, G. A. N., & Rippey, P. (2003). *The competitive environment in Uganda: implications for microfinance institutions and their clients.* MicroSave Africa.

Yahie, A. M. (2000). *Poverty Reduction in Sub-Saharan Africa: Is There a Role for the Private Sector?* African Development Bank.

Yin, R. K. (2014). *Case Study Research: Design and Methods* (5th ed.). SAGE Publication Ltd.

Yonis. B. (2012). *Islamic Microfinance System and Poverty Alleviation in Somaliland.* BBA research paper presented to the of Hargeisa.

Yudha, A. T., & Lathifah, N. (2018). Productive Zakah as a Fiscal Element for the Development and Empowerment of Micro Enterprises in East Java Province. *The International Conference of Zakah (ICONZ).* https://www.iconzbaznas.com/submission/index.php/proceedings/article/view/123/68

Yumna, A. (2019). Islamic charity based micro-finance: lessons from Indonesia. *The Third International Conference on Economics Education, Economics, Business and Management, Accounting and Entrepreneurship (PICEEBA 2019).* 10.2991/piceeba-19.2019.18

Yunus, M. (2008). *Creating a World without Poverty: Social Business and the Future of Capitalism.* Academic Press.

Zikaripa. (2005, April 12). *Micro Finance and Rural Tourism – The Moroccan experience.* PlaNet Finance. Available at: https://www.e-unwto.org/doi/epdf/10.18111/unwtorcmasia.2005.1.v42x00m53127x723

Zwan, F., & Bhamra, T. (2003). Services marketing: Taking up the sustainable development challenge. *Journal of Services Marketing, 17*(4), 341–356.

About the Contributors

Marwa Alfares is currently a PhD candidate at Istanbul Sabahattin Zaim University in Islamic Economics and Finance, She holds a Master's degree from the University of Malaya in Kuala Lumpur. She has an excellent background in Islamic law with excellent command of the Arabic and English languages. Marwa is equipped with excellent research skills. Her research interests include Waqf, Zakah, social finance, Green Sukuk, alternative finance, and Credit Guarantee.

Bernard Appiah has expertise across a number of key business topics, including the management of business operations, the use of research methods in business, entrepreneurship, managing human resource and developments in modern business. His area of research is in looking at wealth creation through business and entrepreneurship across cultures. He is particularly interested in how these areas are promoted by agents and agencies in different countries.

Manpreet Arora is an Assistant Professor of Management in the School of Commerce and Management Studies, Central University of Himachal Pradesh Dharamshala, India. With around nineteen years of teaching experience, she has varied interest areas. A Gold medalist at undergraduate and distinction holder at post graduate level, she obtained her Ph.d in International Trade from Himachal Pradesh University, Shimla, India. Her areas of research interest include Accounting and Finance, Strategic Management, Entrepreneurial Leadership, Qualitative Research, Case Study Development, Communication Skills and Microfinance. She has been guiding research at the doctoral level and has worked in the area of Microfinance. As an active seminarian, she has attended more than hundred seminars/ conferences, and has visited several universities and colleges to deliver invited talks on Finance, Strategic Management, Qualitative Research, Business Communication, Interpersonal skills, Entrepreneurship and Skill Development. She is a motivational speaker and conducts workshops on communication and motivation. Having published more than 20 papers in various journals of national and international repute, she has also worked as content developer of MHRD e-PG Pathshala Project. She has written thirty book chapters in national as well as international books/handbooks. She has also published in category journals as well as Scopus and WOS indexed journals. With four edited books in her credit, she is a persistent researcher in the field of Management. She is an active social worker also and is working towards the protecting the rights of women.

Neeta Baporikar is currently Professor (Management) at Harold Pupkewitz Graduate School of Business (HP-GSB), Namibia University of Science and Technology, Namibia. Prior to this, she was Head-Scientific Research, with the Ministry of Higher Education CAS-Salalah, Sultanate of Oman, Professor (Strategic Management and Entrepreneurship) at IIIT Pune and BITS India. With more than a decade of experience in the industry, consultancy, and training, she made a lateral switch to research and academics in 1995. Prof Baporikar holds D.Sc. (Management Studies) USA, Ph.D. in Management, the University of Pune INDIA with MBA (Distinction) and Law (Hons.) degrees. Apart from this, she is an external reviewer, Oman Academic Accreditation Authority, Accredited Management Teacher, Qualified Trainer, FDP from EDII, Doctoral Guide, and Board Member of Academic and Advisory Committee in accredited B-Schools. She has to her credit many conferred doctorates, is a member of the international and editorial advisory board, reviewer for Emerald, IGI, Inderscience, etc., published numerous refereed papers, and authored books in the area of entrepreneurship, strategy, management, and higher education.

Lawrence Jones-Esan is a Lecturer and Associate Programme Manager at the University of Sunderland in London. He is the founder and the CEO of the London Academy Business School in London. He has written books and articles including Managing your boss in a culturally diverse economy Sept 2013, Banks and Small Business Credit Scoring March 2020. He holds a Doctor of Philosophy (PhD) in International Business Management from the International School of Management & St John's University New York (ISM). He is also a holder of a Postgraduate qualification, PgDip in Educational Leadership Management, Master of Education from RMIT University, Australia. He is a Chartered member and a Fellow of professional bodies, including Fellow of Chartered Management Institute (FCMI), Fellow of the Institute of Leadership Management (FinstLM), Fellow of the Chartered Institute of Marketing (FCIM), Fellow of the Higher Education Academy (FHEA), and Fellow of Society for Education and Training (FSET). He is also a Member of the London Chamber of Commerce and Industries, the Canadian Institute of Entrepreneurship (MCIE), the American Management Association (MAMA).

Omar Kachkar is currently an assistant professor at Ibn Haldun University in Istanbul, he holds a PhD in Business Administration (Islamic Finance) from the

International Islamic university Malaysia IIUM, an MA in Islamic Banking, Finance and Management from Loughborough Univerity UK, and a B.A (Islamic Law) from Al-Azhar University (Cairo). He has an Excellent background on Islamic Law, Islamic Economics, Banking & Finance in both academic and industry. Omar is a Registered Shariah Advisor at Securities Commission Malaysia and an Associate of Association of Shariah Advisors In Islamic Finance – ASAS. He has a Long experience lecturing in universities in Damascus, Kuala Lumpur and Turkey. Omar has presented a number of papers in local and international conferences on Islamic microfinance, cash waqf and micro enterprises. He has also published some papers in international journals. Main interests include Islamic finance, Shari'ah Standards, microfinance, micro enterprises and cash waqf.

Francis Kuagbela is the Programme Manager for finance courses at the University of Sunderland in London, teaching on a range of financial subjects including financial management, management accounting and corporate finance. He is a certified chartered accountant with degrees in law and business. He is also a member of the Association of Chartered Certified Accountants (ACCA) and the Chartered Institute of Taxation (CIOT).

Caesar Nurokina is a Lecturer in finance at the University of Sunderland in London.

Samuel Salia has held various academic roles both within the UK and abroad (for over 9 years) before joining De Montfort University as Senior Lecturer in Accounting and Finance in July 2019. He holds PhD in Finance from Birmingham City University, as well as MSc Financial and Legal Management from University of West London. He has also worked as a Management Consultant at the Management Development and Productivity Institute, under the Ghana Ministry of Employment and Labour Relations. He has supervised PhDs in the area of finance.

Swati Singh is an Assistant Professor in the Department of Management, PCJ School of Management, Maharaja Agrasen University, Baddi, Himachal Pradesh. She holds her Ph.D in the area of Microfinance from Central University of Himachal Pradesh. She has presented research papers in many national and international conferences. She also has publications in conference proceedings and indexed journals.

Index

A

Accelerators 217, 227
affect 8, 30, 34, 38, 53, 80, 87, 103, 162, 196-197, 210, 213, 220-221, 249, 252, 255, 267, 279-280, 282, 290-291, 296
Africa 1-2, 4-5, 11, 17, 19, 25, 48, 51, 54, 56-57, 61-62, 67, 69, 71, 81, 84-86, 88-90, 92-98, 100, 104, 118, 120-121, 131, 135, 151, 153, 168, 182-185, 188-206, 253, 258, 268, 270, 280, 282-285, 287, 295, 299-301, 303-305
angel investors 218
assets 1, 4-7, 11-13, 15-16, 18-19, 25, 34, 38, 43-44, 55, 58, 62, 103-104, 107-108, 110-111, 115-116, 119-120, 125, 197-198
attributes 8, 103-104, 106, 111-119, 209, 212, 259

B

Baitul Maal Muamalat Indonesia (BMMI) 127, 148-149, 158
BAZNAS 129, 138-139, 148-149, 155, 158
behavioral perspective 212
bootstrapping 215-216
business 1, 4-5, 7-8, 11-13, 15-16, 18, 20-22, 24-27, 29, 34, 37-40, 42-45, 47-48, 50-53, 56-57, 63, 66, 68, 72-82, 85, 96-100, 103-104, 107-111, 113-117, 119-125, 133, 144-148, 150, 154-158, 160-166, 168-176, 178-187, 189-192, 194, 196, 198-202, 205-228, 230-232, 235-236, 240-242, 245-263, 268-269, 275-276, 285-288, 290-291, 300-301, 304-305
Business Management 24, 56, 76, 79, 122-124, 144, 150, 180, 205, 227, 249, 291
business success 107, 114, 122, 125, 160-162, 166, 169-173, 175-176, 178, 180, 182, 207

C

capital 1, 4-7, 11-13, 15-18, 20, 25, 35, 41, 43-44, 47, 55, 59, 62, 65, 67, 74, 79-80, 103-104, 109-111, 116-117, 119-120, 124-125, 130, 144-147, 150-151, 154, 164, 166, 172-175, 177, 179, 182-183, 189, 193, 195, 197-199, 201-202, 205, 213, 215-216, 228, 231, 236, 245, 273, 283-284, 289, 292
challenges 24, 29, 34, 37, 50, 53, 65, 75, 78, 84, 87-88, 93, 99, 101-102, 120, 128, 130, 150, 156, 162, 173, 178, 180, 182, 184, 187, 195, 198, 207-208, 210, 214-217, 225, 228, 231, 236, 248, 252, 264-265, 268, 273, 277, 279-280, 286, 288, 291, 297-298, 300-303
competence 53, 222
consideration 44, 144, 220, 236, 238-240, 242, 250-253, 271-272, 277
contractors 268-269, 271-273, 277
control group experiment 1-2
costs 27, 33, 37, 43-47, 60, 84, 134, 179, 191, 193, 197-198, 200, 241, 259
Crowd funding 229

Index

D

develop 26-27, 30, 37, 40, 49, 56, 81, 126, 141, 146, 149, 165, 169, 173, 181, 188, 198, 200, 224, 244, 268, 271, 298
developed country 232
development 1-5, 7-12, 14-15, 17-25, 27-31, 35, 37-42, 44-54, 56-58, 61-79, 81-82, 84, 86-95, 98-112, 114-118, 121-125, 128, 133-139, 141, 144, 146, 151-153, 155-159, 161, 165-166, 185-193, 195-197, 199-200, 202-206, 209-211, 220-222, 224-225, 231, 233-236, 241-242, 247-259, 261, 263-294, 296-305
Developmental Social Work 279-280, 282-283, 285, 292, 301, 303-304

E

economic 1-2, 14-15, 20-25, 27-30, 32, 34, 37-40, 44, 46, 49, 51-53, 55-61, 63-74, 76, 78, 80, 84, 87-88, 91, 95, 97-100, 102-103, 120-121, 124, 127-128, 132, 139-141, 146, 149, 151-156, 161-162, 166, 187-189, 191-193, 195-197, 199-206, 209-212, 217, 220-222, 224-226, 231, 233, 235-236, 246, 248-250, 252-254, 264-268, 272, 274, 276, 280-289, 291-294, 296-298, 300, 303-304
economic growth 1, 15, 20, 25, 28, 37-39, 52, 56-57, 61, 63-64, 67, 69-70, 72, 76, 78, 80, 103, 152, 188-189, 193, 195, 201-202, 204-205, 211, 221, 225-226, 236, 249-250, 252, 254, 264, 285-289, 296
economic perspective 211
economy 37, 50, 65, 74, 78, 84, 96, 146, 151, 155, 165, 189, 192, 195, 201, 211, 223, 225, 232, 236, 238, 249, 256, 266-267, 274, 278, 284, 288, 291, 296
empowerment 2, 9, 22, 25, 54-57, 60-62, 64-73, 75-76, 79-81, 85, 99, 125, 129, 133, 149, 154, 157-158, 185-186, 220, 279, 282, 289-290, 293, 297
enterprise 11, 21, 23-24, 27, 38-39, 42-43, 52, 61, 66, 70, 77, 79-80, 108, 122-123, 125, 129, 153, 175, 180, 185, 202, 211, 214-215, 222, 228, 232, 249
entrepreneur 8, 11, 27, 38-39, 43, 52, 103-104, 106-117, 119-120, 122, 149, 164-165, 169-171, 173, 180-181, 186-187, 208-214, 216-219, 222, 225-228, 230, 232
entrepreneurial success factors 160-162, 168-169, 171, 177-178, 180, 182, 186
entrepreneurs 6, 11, 25, 27, 29-30, 38-40, 42-43, 46-49, 59, 61, 68, 77, 79-80, 107-108, 111, 113-115, 118-119, 121-125, 133, 140, 144, 146, 148-150, 154, 157, 160-171, 173-187, 189-190, 192, 194, 196, 199-202, 207-222, 225, 228, 230-231
entrepreneurship 7-8, 19-20, 25, 27-31, 38-42, 46-52, 61, 76, 79, 120-122, 124, 127, 141, 146-147, 156-158, 160-164, 168, 170, 174, 177-178, 182-187, 207-215, 217, 220-222, 225-232, 299
experiment 1-2, 10, 17, 21, 26, 63, 69, 72-73, 112, 119

F

facilitate 37, 68, 103-105, 111-120, 125, 269, 296
family and friends 176
female 6, 22, 60-62, 64, 69, 75, 77, 79, 104, 106-108, 115, 161-162, 174, 177, 183, 185, 187, 194, 196
finance 2-3, 5, 18-21, 23-24, 31-32, 35, 42, 54, 56-57, 59, 66-67, 70-74, 77-78, 85, 90-91, 94-95, 97-100, 104, 120, 122-124, 127, 129-131, 134, 152-153, 155-158, 175, 180, 185, 187, 190, 192, 198-199, 204, 206, 214-219, 224, 229
financial 1-8, 10, 14, 20, 22-25, 29-37, 42-43, 45-46, 48, 50, 53, 55-61, 63-68, 70-71, 74, 76-77, 79, 81, 83-86, 91, 97-102, 105-106, 113, 121-125, 128-132, 134, 139, 145, 147, 150, 152, 154-156, 158-159, 161, 163, 165-166, 172, 175-177, 188-205, 211, 215-217, 220, 222-225, 229, 232, 256, 259, 269, 287, 297
financial houses 216-217, 232

365

G

Gas 93, 99, 235-236, 241-242, 252-253, 264-265, 267-278
Ghana 1-2, 5-11, 15-18, 20, 22-23, 25, 54, 56-57, 64-72, 74, 79-80, 98-99, 103-108, 110-115, 117-118, 123-124, 183
goods and services 57-58, 210, 232, 237, 257, 271, 277, 296
government 1, 15, 30-31, 37-38, 40, 46-48, 68, 82, 84-85, 91, 93-94, 103, 152, 161-162, 166, 171, 173, 175-176, 180-181, 190, 192, 198-199, 220-224, 230, 232, 242, 267, 269, 271-272, 280, 290, 292, 296-297, 301, 305
growth 1-2, 4-10, 15-17, 20-25, 27-28, 32, 36-39, 46, 48, 51-52, 54, 56-57, 59-64, 67, 69-74, 76-78, 80, 84-85, 95, 103-105, 107-115, 117-125, 143, 147, 152, 174, 183-184, 188-189, 193-197, 199-202, 204-205, 210-211, 215, 217-218, 220-221, 223, 225-226, 228, 232, 236, 249-250, 252, 254, 264-265, 268, 273-274, 285-289, 296, 302

I

impact 1-2, 4-7, 9-26, 29, 34, 39, 43, 46-50, 52-53, 55-56, 58-59, 61-64, 66-67, 70, 72-78, 80-81, 84, 104, 106-110, 112-123, 130, 141, 146, 151, 154-156, 158, 166, 172, 174, 182-183, 189, 193, 196, 202-206, 212, 219, 221, 234, 244-245, 251, 256, 258-259, 262, 264, 268-269, 290-291, 300
impede 103-105, 111-121, 125
inclusion 2, 22-25, 55, 58-59, 61, 74, 76, 99, 105-106, 122, 130, 189, 192, 201, 203, 205
India 6, 23-24, 27-28, 50, 59, 61, 63, 72, 75, 78, 80-86, 89-96, 98-102, 104, 108, 113, 117, 125, 187
industry 8, 11, 17, 34, 36, 41, 48, 79, 89, 93, 95, 97, 104, 117-118, 140, 155-156, 196, 199-200, 202-203, 215, 218, 227-228, 234-235, 241-243, 248, 252-253, 260-265, 267-278
interest 9, 30, 43, 57, 59, 66, 75, 86, 105, 133, 140, 144, 146, 174, 179, 181-182, 190-191, 193-194, 196-198, 200-202, 205-206, 216, 219, 231-232, 255, 268, 275, 287, 291, 300
Islamic Social Finance 127, 129-131, 152-153, 155-156, 158

J

JAWHAR 142, 144, 155, 158

K

Knowledge Development 47, 50, 53

L

Lembaga Zakah Selangor (LZS) 159
lending 2-3, 20, 22, 28, 72, 76-77, 81, 83, 97-98, 156, 189, 194, 198, 218, 223, 226, 229
loan 2, 31-33, 43, 45-46, 55, 59-60, 62, 66, 68, 74-75, 77, 81, 112-113, 140, 149, 152, 175, 189-191, 195-198, 200, 215-217, 219, 223, 229, 232
local content 270-274, 276, 278

M

microbusiness 1, 4-18, 25-26, 56-57, 62, 64, 67-70, 81, 103-120, 125
microbusiness development 1, 4, 7-12, 14-15, 17-18, 62, 64, 68-70, 103-112, 114-115, 117-118, 125
microcredit 1, 9-13, 18-26, 54, 56, 58-60, 63, 68, 73-77, 79, 81, 88, 91, 98, 100-101, 120, 122-124, 126, 133, 139, 141, 154, 156-157, 159, 188, 190, 194, 196, 199-200, 203-205
microenterprises 2, 4-7, 16-17, 20-21, 25, 32, 37-38, 42-45, 62, 67, 72, 75, 106-107, 109, 113, 116-118, 123, 127, 129, 137-139, 144, 151-152, 155-156, 159, 198-199
microfinance 1-33, 35-38, 42, 45-46, 48-49, 52-86, 90-93, 96-127, 130, 133, 137-141, 144, 149-159, 183, 188-206

Index

N

Nigeria 5, 20, 22, 50, 54, 56-57, 64, 66-70, 72, 74-76, 78, 80, 106, 108-110, 112, 116, 120-122, 166, 174, 183, 196, 205, 214-215, 234-236, 240-242, 248-254, 256, 258, 261, 264-265, 267-277, 279-280, 283-285, 290, 292, 295-296, 298-299, 302-303, 305

Nigerian women entrepreneurs 160-162, 167-168, 174, 176-183

non-discriminatory 271-272, 274, 278

O

oil 234-236, 241-242, 252-253, 256-259, 261-262, 264-265, 267-278, 292, 296, 302

Oil and Gas Industry 241-242, 253, 264-265, 267, 269-278

operative 278

outcomes 4-6, 15-18, 21, 24, 54, 56-60, 62-64, 66-70, 73, 81, 100, 105-110, 112-114, 116-118, 155, 200, 252, 256, 282, 288

P

personal 8, 11, 41, 103-104, 106, 110-113, 115-116, 118-119, 125, 160, 162, 169-173, 175, 178, 180, 182, 189, 192, 195, 201, 215, 252, 277, 293, 296, 298

personal success factors 162, 169-172, 178

poverty 2, 4, 9, 17, 19-21, 23, 25, 30, 37-38, 43, 45-46, 54-59, 62, 64-88, 95, 98-102, 105-106, 112, 118, 122, 127-130, 135, 139, 141, 146, 148, 152-153, 155-158, 180, 189, 191-196, 198-199, 201-202, 204-206, 210, 233, 236, 250, 254, 258, 265-268, 279-285, 287, 289-305

poverty alleviation 2, 19-20, 25, 43, 55, 58-59, 75-76, 79, 83, 102, 105-106, 128-129, 139, 148, 153, 155-158, 192, 205, 236, 279-280, 285, 294, 298-299, 302

procurement 53, 220, 272, 278

profit 60, 65, 83, 96, 108, 134, 161, 192, 197, 203, 209-210, 213, 216, 219, 249-250, 252, 288, 291

Q

qualitative method 253

R

reduction 17, 21, 23, 38, 45, 55, 57-59, 64-66, 69-75, 77-78, 80, 85, 98-101, 118, 122, 141, 180, 195, 197, 205-206, 210, 258, 261, 266, 273, 290, 298, 305

S

SDGs 89-90, 127-129, 134-135, 138, 152-154, 157, 159, 248-249, 287-288, 290-294, 298-299

Small And Medium-Size Enterprise 232

small loans 26, 56, 61-63, 81, 126, 188-190, 192, 199-200, 219

SME 41, 48, 79, 207-208, 210-211, 214, 219, 222, 224-225, 229-230, 232

SME financing 79, 207, 225

social work 101, 202, 279-287, 292-294, 297-305

standard 12-13, 17, 58, 65, 69, 81-82, 84-85, 93, 95-97, 118, 131, 151, 180, 272, 278, 280, 296

Sub-Saharan Africa 4, 11, 25, 62, 81, 104, 185, 188-206

sustainability 20, 25, 32-33, 43, 50, 52-53, 59-60, 71, 75-77, 79, 82, 85-89, 92-93, 96-98, 102, 120, 124, 127, 130, 152, 156, 188, 191, 193, 195, 197-198, 200, 202-203, 205, 223, 235, 248-250, 253-254, 256, 258, 260, 262, 264, 280, 282, 286, 288-290, 292-294, 300, 302, 304

sustainable 17, 19, 21, 24, 32, 37, 45, 47, 59-60, 72, 76, 78, 82, 85-90, 92-98, 100-102, 118, 121, 134-138, 151, 157, 159, 185-186, 191-192, 196-198, 200, 204-205, 234-236, 242-243, 245, 247-254, 257, 259-260, 263-270, 273-277, 279-280, 282, 284-294, 298-305 sustainable development 17, 19, 21, 76, 78, 82, 86-90, 92-95, 102, 118, 134-138, 151, 157, 159, 186, 191-192, 234-236, 242, 247-254, 257, 259, 263-270, 273-277, 279-280, 282, 285-294, 298-299, 301-305

Sustainable Development Goals 21, 82, 87-90, 92-93, 95, 102, 134, 138, 157, 159, 248, 252, 287, 290-291, 302-303, 305

sustainable practices 60, 82, 85-86, 96, 98, 102

U

UK 1, 23-24, 54, 103, 114, 121, 125, 160-162, 167-169, 174-180, 182-183, 185-188, 207, 221, 234, 264, 279, 301-302

Under-Developed Country 233

V

venture capitalist 223

W

women 2, 4-5, 15-16, 22-25, 37, 45, 50, 54-57, 60-62, 64-76, 78-81, 83-85, 90-91, 98-99, 104, 107-108, 113-114, 117, 121, 123-125, 141, 152, 154, 157, 160-169, 171, 173-187, 189, 191-192, 196, 201, 276

Z

zakah 127-134, 137-139, 141-159

zakah funds 127-129, 133-134, 137-139, 141-143, 148-149, 151-152, 158

Recommended Reference Books

IGI Global's reference books can now be purchased from three unique pricing formats:
Print Only, E-Book Only, or Print + E-Book.
Shipping fees may apply.

www.igi-global.com

The Impact of Fandom in Society and Consumerism
ISBN: 978-1-7998-1048-3
EISBN: 978-1-7998-1049-0
© 2020; 605 pp.
List Price: US$ 285

Social and Organizational Dynamics in the Digital Era
ISBN: 978-1-5225-8933-4
EISBN: 978-1-5225-8934-1
© 2020; 667 pp.
List Price: US$ 295

Managerial Practices and Disruptive Innovation in Asia
ISBN: 978-1-7998-0357-7
EISBN: 978-1-7998-0359-1
© 2020; 451 pp.
List Price: US$ 235

Impact of Risk Perception Theory and Terrorism on Tourism Security
ISBN: 978-1-7998-0070-5
EISBN: 978-1-7998-0071-2
© 2020; 144 pp.
List Price: US$ 175

Breaking Down Language and Cultural Barriers Through Contemporary Global Marketing Strategies
ISBN: 978-1-5225-6980-0
EISBN: 978-1-5225-6981-7
© 2019; 339 pp.
List Price: US$ 235

Organizational Leadership for the Fourth Industrial Revolution
ISBN: 978-1-5225-5390-8
EISBN: 978-1-5225-5391-5
© 2018; 125 pp.
List Price: US$ 165

Do you want to stay current on the latest research trends, product announcements, news, and special offers?
Join IGI Global's mailing list to receive customized recommendations, exclusive discounts, and more.
Sign up at: **www.igi-global.com/newsletters**.

Publisher of Peer-Reviewed, Timely, and Innovative Academic Research

IGI Global
PUBLISHER of TIMELY KNOWLEDGE

www.igi-global.com | Sign up at www.igi-global.com/newsletters | facebook.com/igiglobal | twitter.com/igiglobal

Ensure Quality Research is Introduced to the Academic Community

Become an Evaluator for IGI Global Authored Book Projects

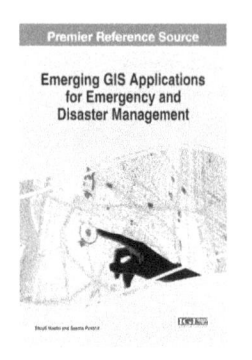

The overall success of an authored book project is dependent on quality and timely manuscript evaluations.

Applications and Inquiries may be sent to:
development@igi-global.com

Applicants must have a doctorate (or equivalent degree) as well as publishing, research, and reviewing experience. Authored Book Evaluators are appointed for one-year terms and are expected to complete at least three evaluations per term. Upon successful completion of this term, evaluators can be considered for an additional term.

If you have a colleague that may be interested in this opportunity, we encourage you to share this information with them.

IGI Global Author Services

Providing a high-quality, affordable, and expeditious service, IGI Global's Author Services enable authors to streamline their publishing process, increase chance of acceptance, and adhere to IGI Global's publication standards.

Benefits of Author Services:

- **Professional Service:** All our editors, designers, and translators are experts in their field with years of experience and professional certifications.
- **Quality Guarantee & Certificate:** Each order is returned with a quality guarantee and certificate of professional completion.
- **Timeliness:** All editorial orders have a guaranteed return timeframe of 3-5 business days and translation orders are guaranteed in 7-10 business days.
- **Affordable Pricing:** IGI Global Author Services are competitively priced compared to other industry service providers.
- **APC Reimbursement:** IGI Global authors publishing Open Access (OA) will be able to deduct the cost of editing and other IGI Global author services from their OA APC publishing fee.

Author Services Offered:

English Language Copy Editing
Professional, native English language copy editors improve your manuscript's grammar, spelling, punctuation, terminology, semantics, consistency, flow, formatting, and more.

Scientific & Scholarly Editing
A Ph.D. level review for qualities such as originality and significance, interest to researchers, level of methodology and analysis, coverage of literature, organization, quality of writing, and strengths and weaknesses.

Figure, Table, Chart & Equation Conversions
Work with IGI Global's graphic designers before submission to enhance and design all figures and charts to IGI Global's specific standards for clarity.

Translation
Providing 70 language options, including Simplified and Traditional Chinese, Spanish, Arabic, German, French, and more.

Hear What the Experts Are Saying About IGI Global's Author Services

"Publishing with IGI Global has been *an amazing experience* for me for sharing my research. The *strong academic production* support ensures quality and timely completion." – Prof. Margaret Niess, Oregon State University, USA

"The service was *very fast, very thorough, and very helpful* in ensuring our chapter meets the criteria and requirements of the book's editors. I was *quite impressed and happy* with your service." – Prof. Tom Brinthaupt, Middle Tennessee State University, USA

Learn More or Get Started Here:

For Questions, Contact IGI Global's Customer Service Team at cust@igi-global.com or 717-533-8845

IGI Global
PUBLISHER of TIMELY KNOWLEDGE
www.igi-global.com

InfoSci®-Books

Celebrating Over 30 Years of Scholarly Knowledge Creation & Dissemination

www.igi-global.com

A Database of Nearly 6,000 Reference Books Containing Over 105,000+ Chapters Focusing on Emerging Research

GAIN ACCESS TO **THOUSANDS** OF REFERENCE BOOKS AT **A FRACTION** OF THEIR INDIVIDUAL LIST **PRICE**.

InfoSci®-Books Database

The **InfoSci®-Books** is a database of nearly 6,000 IGI Global single and multi-volume reference books, handbooks of research, and encyclopedias, encompassing groundbreaking research from prominent experts worldwide that spans over 350+ topics in 11 core subject areas including business, computer science, education, science and engineering, social sciences, and more.

Open Access Fee Waiver (Read & Publish) Initiative

For any library that invests in IGI Global's InfoSci-Books and/or InfoSci-Journals (175+ scholarly journals) databases, IGI Global will match the library's investment with a fund of equal value to go toward **subsidizing the OA article processing charges (APCs) for their students, faculty, and staff** at that institution when their work is submitted and accepted under OA into an IGI Global journal.*

INFOSCI® PLATFORM FEATURES

- Unlimited Simultaneous Access
- No DRM
- No Set-Up or Maintenance Fees
- A Guarantee of No More Than a 5% Annual Increase for Subscriptions
- Full-Text HTML and PDF Viewing Options
- Downloadable MARC Records
- COUNTER 5 Compliant Reports
- Formatted Citations With Ability to Export to RefWorks and EasyBib
- No Embargo of Content (Research is Available Months in Advance of the Print Release)

*The fund will be offered on an annual basis and expire at the end of the subscription period. The fund would renew as the subscription is renewed for each year thereafter. The open access fees will be waived after the student, faculty, or staff's paper has been vetted and accepted into an IGI Global journal and the fund can only be used toward publishing OA in an IGI Global journal. Libraries in developing countries will have the match on their investment doubled.

To Recommend or Request a Free Trial:
www.igi-global.com/infosci-books

eresources@igi-global.com • Toll Free: 1-866-342-6657 ext. 100 • Phone: 717-533-8845 x100

www.igi-global.com

IGI Global
PUBLISHER of TIMELY KNOWLEDGE
www.igi-global.com

Publisher of Peer-Reviewed, Timely, and Innovative Academic Research Since 1988

IGI Global's Transformative Open Access (OA) Model:
How to Turn Your University Library's Database Acquisitions Into a Source of OA Funding

Well in advance of Plan S, IGI Global unveiled their OA Fee Waiver (Read & Publish) Initiative. Under this initiative, librarians who invest in IGI Global's InfoSci-Books and/or InfoSci-Journals databases will be able to subsidize their patrons' OA article processing charges (APCs) when their work is submitted and accepted (after the peer review process) into an IGI Global journal.

How Does it Work?

Step 1: **Library Invests in the InfoSci-Databases:** A library perpetually purchases or subscribes to the InfoSci-Books, InfoSci-Journals, or discipline/subject databases.

Step 2: **IGI Global Matches the Library Investment with OA Subsidies Fund:** IGI Global provides a fund to go towards subsidizing the OA APCs for the library's patrons.

Step 3: **Patron of the Library is Accepted into IGI Global Journal (After Peer Review):** When a patron's paper is accepted into an IGI Global journal, they option to have their paper published under a traditional publishing model or as OA.

Step 4: **IGI Global Will Deduct APC Cost from OA Subsidies Fund:** If the author decides to publish under OA, the OA APC fee will be deducted from the OA subsidies fund.

Step 5: **Author's Work Becomes Freely Available:** The patron's work will be freely available under CC BY copyright license, enabling them to share it freely with the academic community.

Note: This fund will be offered on an annual basis and will renew as the subscription is renewed for each year thereafter. IGI Global will manage the fund and award the APC waivers unless the librarian has a preference as to how the funds should be managed.

Hear From the Experts on This Initiative:

"I'm very happy to have been able to make one of my recent research contributions *freely available* along with having access to the *valuable resources* found within IGI Global's InfoSci-Journals database."

— **Prof. Stuart Palmer**, Deakin University, Australia

"Receiving the support from IGI Global's OA Fee Waiver Initiative *encourages me to continue my research work without any hesitation*."

— **Prof. Wenlong Liu**, College of Economics and Management at Nanjing University of Aeronautics & Astronautics, China

For More Information, Scan the QR Code or Contact:
IGI Global's Digital Resources Team at eresources@igi-global.com.

IGI Global
PUBLISHER of TIMELY KNOWLEDGE

Are You Ready to Publish Your Research?

IGI Global
PUBLISHER of TIMELY KNOWLEDGE

IGI Global offers book authorship and editorship opportunities across 11 subject areas, including business, computer science, education, science and engineering, social sciences, and more!

Benefits of Publishing with IGI Global:

- Free one-on-one editorial and promotional support.
- Expedited publishing timelines that can take your book from start to finish in less than one (1) year.
- Choose from a variety of formats, including: Edited and Authored References, Handbooks of Research, Encyclopedias, and Research Insights.
- Utilize IGI Global's eEditorial Discovery® submission system in support of conducting the submission and double-blind peer review process.
- IGI Global maintains a strict adherence to ethical practices due in part to our full membership with the Committee on Publication Ethics (COPE).
- Indexing potential in prestigious indices such as Scopus®, Web of Science™, PsycINFO®, and ERIC – Education Resources Information Center.
- Ability to connect your ORCID iD to your IGI Global publications.
- Earn honorariums and royalties on your full book publications as well as complimentary copies and exclusive discounts.

Join Your Colleagues from Prestigious Institutions, Including:

Australian National University
Massachusetts Institute of Technology
JOHNS HOPKINS UNIVERSITY
HARVARD UNIVERSITY
TSINGHUA UNIVERSITY
COLUMBIA UNIVERSITY IN THE CITY OF NEW YORK

Learn More at: www.igi-global.com/publish
or by Contacting the Acquisitions Department at: acquisition@igi-global.com

Purchase Individual IGI Global InfoSci-OnDemand Book Chapters and Journal Articles

InfoSci®-OnDemand

Pay-Per-View Articles and Chapters from IGI Global

For More Information, Visit: www.igi-global.com/e-resources/infosci-ondemand

Browse through nearly 150,000+ articles/chapters to find specific research related to their current studies and projects that have been contributed by international researchers from prestigious institutions, including MIT, Harvard University, Columbia University, and many more.

Easily Identify, Acquire, and Utilize Published Peer-Reviewed Findings in Support of Your Current Research:

Accurate and Advanced Search: Utilize the advanced InfoSci-OnDemand search engine to identify research in your area of interest.

Affordably Acquire Research: Provides an affordable alternative to purchasing an entire reference book or scholarly journal.

Fast and Easy One-Click Shopping: Simply utilize the OnDemand "Buy Now" button on the webpage.

Instantly Download/Access Your Content: Receive an immediate link to download your InfoSci-OnDemand content to your personal computer and device.

Access Anywhere, Anytime, and on Any Device: Additionally, receive access to your OnDemand articles and chapters through a personal electronic library.

Benefit from the InfoSci Platform Features: Providing formatted citations, full-text PDF and HTML format, no embargo of content, no DRM, and more.

"It really provides an excellent entry into the research literature of the field. It presents a manageable number of highly relevant sources on topics of interest to a wide range of researchers. The sources are scholarly, but also accessible to 'practitioners'."

- Ms. Lisa Stimatz, MLS, University of North Carolina at Chapel Hill, USA

Interested in Additional Savings and Acquiring Multiple Articles and Chapters Through InfoSci-OnDemand?

Learn More

Subscribe to InfoSci-OnDemand Plus

Ingram Content Group UK Ltd.
Milton Keynes UK
UKHW031929220323
418981UK00007B/275